Poetic Trespass

Poetic Trespass

Writing between HEBREW AND ARABIC in Israel/Palestine

Lital Levy

Princeton University Press / Princeton and Oxford

Published by Princeton University Press, 41 William Street, Princeton, New Jersey 08540
In the United Kingdom: Princeton University Press, 6 Oxford Street, Woodstock, Oxfordshire OX20 1TR

press.princeton.edu

Proofreading and indexing were supported by a subvention grant from Princeton University's University Committee on Research in the Humanities and Social Sciences.

Cover art: Hebrew letters are from *Seder hagada shel pesaḥ 'im sharḥ fil-'arabi* (Passover Haggadah in Judeo-Arabic), Jerusalem: Hosta'at Bakal, 1977. Arabic letters are from Émile Zola, *al-Mal, al-Mal, al-Mal* (Arabic translation of *L'Argent*, translated by the Lebanese Jewish journalist Esther Azhari Moyal), Cairo: Matba'at al-Shuri, 1907.

Cover design by Jason Alejandro

First paperback printing, 2017
Paperback ISBN 978-0-691-17609-3

Cloth ISBN 978-0-691-16248-5

Library of Congress Control Number: 2014935596

British Library Cataloging-in-Publication Data is available

This book has been composed in Gentium Plus, Berthold Akzidenz Grotesk, and Brioso Pro

Printed on acid-free paper ∞

Printed in the United States of America

For Ken and Jonah

Contents

Illustrations

Acknowledgments

This book represents nearly two decades of work on Mizraḥi and Palestinian literature in Israel. It was researched and written in New York, Jerusalem, Berkeley, Cairo, Tel Aviv, Princeton, Cambridge (MA), and Philadelphia. It began with an independent study of representations of Arabic-Hebrew relations in Israeli fiction, supervised by the late Magda al-Nowaihi (taken from us much too soon), whose example inspired me to become a scholar of literature. The following year, I embarked on a life-changing senior thesis on the poetry of Anton Shammas and Na'im 'Araidi, also under Magda's guidance. That project, the ideational kernel of this book, became my gateway to graduate study in comparative literature. I continued with independent research on Mizraḥi literature during a year in Jerusalem in 1997 and 1998. My abiding interest in the topic owes much to the passionately committed members of the Tsedek Ḥevrati (Social Justice) student organization at the Hebrew University. In spring 1998 we organized a panel on the "Mizraḥi voice" in Hebrew literature, with the participation of Amira Hess and Shimon Ballas, which sealed my decision to specialize in Mizraḥi writing. For their guidance and encouragement that formative year, I thank Nir Eyal, Ahuva Mu'alem, and Eli Bareket.

At UC Berkeley, I was blessed with an amazing cohort of fellow graduate students as well as excellent mentors. Every page before you bears the imprint of my advisors Robert Alter and Chana Kronfeld, unfailingly wise and generous teachers both. Their scholarship offered models of rigorous reading and elegant writing, and their graduate seminars were the grounds on which I developed much of the material for this book. Sections of chapters 2 through 5 were written from 1998 to 2004 for seminars with Chana Kronfeld, Robert Alter, and Ammiel Alcalay at Berkeley, and with Abbas al-Tonsi at the Center for Arabic Study Abroad in Cairo.

My befuddlement in the face of Columbia's interlibrary loan system had felicitous consequences, as it prompted me to contact Anton Shammas at Michigan in 1995 and ask him for a copy of his Arabic poetry collection. He became an informal mentor during my transition from undergraduate to graduate studies and, for nearly two decades now, has been a reliable and generous source of knowledge (not to mention a meticulous archivist), repeatedly saving the day. Early on in my graduate studies, Sasson Somekh took me under his wing, and he has followed my progress ever since. His inexhaustible knowledge and his support in matters large and small have made an immeasurable difference throughout this journey. Over the years, Michael Cooperson patiently assisted me with many and sundry matters related to Arabic language and literature, especially questions of translation. Almog Behar, a rare soul whose erudition is matched by his kindness, has been invariably collaborative rather than competitive in sharing his scholarship since we met.

In addition, this book could never have been written without my mentors, colleagues, and students, who shared sources, material, and expertise, acting as sounding boards for ideas, commenting on drafts of chapters, and proofing transliterations from the Hebrew and Arabic. For their invaluable help, I thank Shamma Boyarin, Kfir Cohen, Karen Grumberg, Liora Halperin, Kawthar Jaber, Yael Lehrer, Margaret Litvin, Chana Morgenstern, Michal Raizen, Tova Rosen, Lena Salaymeh, Raymond Scheindlin, Shaul Setter, Vered Shemtov, Deborah Starr, Sheera Talpaz, Riki Traum, Hamutal Tsamir, Dana Sajdi, Azzan Yadin, Yael Zerubavel, the numerous friends and colleagues who patiently answered question after question posted in cyberspace, and the two anonymous reviewers for Princeton University Press. I am also indebted to the audience members who provided feedback at annual meetings of the Middle East Studies Association, the Association for Jewish Studies, the American Comparative Literature Association, and the National Association for Professors of Hebrew, as well as at symposia or talks from 2007 to 2010 at UC Berkeley, Princeton, WIKO (Berlin), Harvard, Rutgers, NYU, Stanford, and UT Austin. Finally, I thank my wonderful colleagues at Princeton, especially Daniel Heller-Roazen, Eileen Reeves, Leonard Barkan, and Sandra Bermann, for their interest in the project and their support during my first years of teaching; and my editors Alison MacKeen, Anne Savarese, and Jenny Wolkowicki at Princeton University Press for seeing it through to its completion. The manuscript was developed during my final year at the Harvard Society of Fellows and completed thanks to the Robert Remsen Laidlaw '04 University Preceptorship in the Humanities at Princeton.

Earlier versions of material from chapters 2, 3, 4, and 5 appeared in the following publications: "Exchanging Words: Thematizations of Translation in Arabic Writing from Israel," *Comparative Studies of South Asia, Africa, and the Middle East* 23.1–2 (2003): 106–127 (reprinted by permission of Duke University Press); "From Baghdad to Bialik with Love: A Reappropriation of Modern Hebrew Poetry, 1933," *Comparative Literature Studies* 42.3 (2005): 125–154 (reprinted by permission of the Pennsylvania State University

Press); "Self and the City: Literary Representations of Jewish Baghdad," *Prooftexts* 26.1–2 (2006): 163–211 (reprinted by permission of Indiana University Press); and "Self-Portraits of the Other: Toward a Palestinian Poetics of Hebrew Verse," in *Transforming Loss into Beauty: Essays in Honor of Magda al-Nowaihi*, edited by Marle Hammond and Dana Sajdi (Cairo: American University in Cairo Press, 2008), 343–402 (reprinted by permission of the American University in Cairo Press). I thank all the publishers for permission to reprint.

How does one thank those for whom the seemingly unending process that culminates in a book has so many personal implications? My parents Joseph and Susan and my sister Roneet have patiently withstood my peripatetic life and long absences. I only wish I could be in two places at once so as to spend more time with them. In Philadelphia, we've been blessed with amazing friends who share in the mad adventure of dual-career parenting; this book would never have been completed without them. Whenever possible, Ken Reisman cooked dinner, reminded me to go to bed, pushed me to sharpen my arguments, and indulged my requests for the philosopher-scientist's take on excerpts of opaque literary criticism. To Jonah, *qurrat 'ayni wa-muna qalbi*, this is that book everyone kept telling you Ema had to write when you wanted to know why you couldn't play at home all day. Hopefully by the time you can read these words, you'll think it was a fairly reasonable trade-off, even if Ema really should have been helping you build those train tracks instead.

Note on Transliteration and Translation

This book addresses specialists, generalists, and comparatists, with or without any background in Hebrew or Arabic. Furthermore, as it happens, the book discusses two closely related languages with entirely unrelated transliteration systems. As such, I approach transliteration not as an exact science, but as a balancing act between scholarly accountability and overall readability. As a baseline, I follow the recommendations of the *International Journal of Middle Eastern Studies* for Arabic and the Library of Congress for Hebrew, with modifications. In attempting to maintain some general parity between the two transliteration systems, I dispensed with diacritical marks for the Arabic and with the final *h* for Hebrew *he sofit*, while using ʻ to represent *ʻayin* and ʼ for *hamza* in Arabic and *alef* in Hebrew. Given the large quantity of transliterated Hebrew, however, I eventually found it necessary to reinstate the subscript dot below *h* to distinguish *ḥet* from *he*; for *tsadi*, I use *ts* rather than *ẓ*. I also generally omit *e* for *shva naʻ* (e.g., *dvarim*, not *devarim*), except for biblical and rabbinic Hebrew and the texts in the Sephardi style discussed in chapter 2. For Arabic words and names embedded in Hebrew linguistic settings, in cases where the word has been absorbed into Hebrew (e.g., *aḥla*), I treat it as Hebrew; where the word is used as a foreign term in Hebrew (e.g., *fallahin*), I treat it as Arabic. For proper names, I defer to the author's preferred English spelling or the most frequently used variation (e.g., Saul Tchernichowsky, not Shaul Tsherniḥovski; Emile Habiby, not Imil Habibi; Sami Michael, not Sami Mikha'el). In the absence of preferred forms, I follow my transliteration practices. Where Arabic names are used in Hebrew contexts (e.g., Salman Masalha as a Hebrew writer), I still treat them as Arabic. Place-names are rendered in standard English.

For translations, I work with existing English translations where available but modify them as needed. Unless otherwise specified, all translations from the Hebrew and Arabic are mine.

Introduction

The No-Man's-Land of Language

> Two myths perish simultaneously: the myth of a language that presumes to be the only language, and the myth of a language that presumes to be completely unified.
>
> —MIKHAIL BAKHTIN[1]

> A language is therefore on the hither side of Literature.
>
> —ROLAND BARTHES[2]

What does it mean to write when you inhabit the fraught borderline between Hebrew and Arabic? Well, it depends on whom you ask. In a Hebrew poem insisting that strangers can be friends, the Palestinian Israeli poet Salman Masalha infuses the statement "Ani kotev 'ivrit," "I write Hebrew," with myriad shades of wonder and possibility.[3] In an opposing poetic maneuver, Sami Shalom Chetrit, a Moroccan-born Jewish Israeli, challenges his readers by declaring (in Hebrew), "Ani kotev la-khem shirim/be-lashon ashdodit/she-lo tavinu mila": "I write you poems in Ashdodian," a nonexistent language, "so you won't understand a word."[4] These antithetical gestures, that of the Palestinian Arab who embraces Hebrew and the Moroccan Jew who disavows it, are mirror images of one another, at once equal and opposite. Both are provocative in their unexpected disruption of the norms defining language, identity, and belonging in the State of Israel. More subtly, the two poetic declarations are tempered by the muteness of the other language, *Arabic*—the mother tongue of both poets, concealed but not absent. What is the place of Arabic in these two Hebrew poems, with their crisscrossings

1 Bakhtin, *Dialogic Imagination*, 68.

2 Barthes, *Writing Degree Zero*, 10.

3 Masalha, *Eḥad mi-kan*, 15–16.

4 *Ashdodit* (the "Ashdodian" language) is Chetrit's metonym for a nonstandard spoken Hebrew; see chapter 6. See Chetrit, *Shirim be-ashdodit*, 7.

of language and identity among Palestinian, Israeli, Arab, and Jew? More broadly, in the intensely politicized space of Israel/Palestine, how do Arabic and Hebrew interact, and how does their relationship come into play in literature by Jewish and Palestinian authors?[5]

This book asks and answers those questions in multiple ways, examining the lives and afterlives of Arabic and Hebrew in Israeli literature, culture, and society. Hebrew is the spiritual, historical, and ideological cornerstone of the State of Israel, and Hebrew literature, having accompanied the national project from its inception, is an integral part of Israeli society. Yet in its broader geopolitical context, Hebrew is the language of a small state that views itself as an embattled island in a hostile Arabic-language sea. Powerful social norms in Israel/Palestine assign Hebrew to Jews, Arabic to Arabs; notions of linguistic possession and transgression surround and pervade literary production in both languages. Writing across those borders is not only an aesthetic but also a distinctly political choice. What, then, does it mean for the idea of Hebrew as the eternal language of the Jewish people and as the national language of the Jewish state when Palestinian Arab citizens choose to write in Hebrew and Israeli Jewish citizens choose to write in Arabic? Alternatively, what does it mean for second- and third-generation Mizraḥi Jews, descendants of Arabic-speaking parents and grandparents, to write in a Hebrew that cannot elide the traces of the sticky Arabic-language past?

THE NO-MAN'S-LAND OF LANGUAGE: ARABIC AND HEBREW IN ISRAEL/PALESTINE

In 1979 Anton Shammas, then a young poet and now the most established Palestinian Israeli writer of Hebrew, titled his second Hebrew collection *Shetaḥ hefker* (*No-Man's-Land*). The volume closes with these lines:

> I do not know.
> A language beyond this,

5 In speaking of "Palestinians" here, I refer to Palestinian citizens of Israel. In Israel, "Jewish" and "Arab" are seen as "nationalities," not just ethnic tags. Although my analysis focuses on culture produced in the State of Israel, I use the term "Israel/Palestine" to acknowledge the de facto political, cultural, and linguistic realities of a binational collective, and also because the temporal range of my narrative incorporates the pre-state period. When I write "Israel and Palestine," I refer to the entire area encompassing the State of Israel, the West Bank, and the Gaza Strip, which includes Jewish and Palestinian citizens of Israel as well as Palestinians living under Israeli occupation without citizenship. In that case, my use of the term "Palestine" is meant to acknowledge the reality of this name and all it connotes for millions of Palestinians and others worldwide, not to map it onto any precise political borders; readers of different political persuasions may interpret it geographically as they wish.

And a language beyond this.
And I hallucinate in the no-man's-land.[6]

What is the "no-man's-land" of this hallucinating poet? In Hebrew, the term *shetaḥ hefker* (literally, "a territory of abandonment")[7] signified the partition dividing Jerusalem into Arab and Jewish sections before the 1967 war. As Gil Eyal notes, the word *hefker* itself is an intensely loaded term that in the Jewish tradition connotes lawlessness and loss. Linguistically, it is associated with *hitparkut*, becoming a non-Jew, "thus connoting a zone where identity dissolves, where the Jew merges into the Gentile."[8] In the literary context in question, the no-man's-land is at once a space *between* Hebrew and Arabic and a space *outside* the ethnocentric domain that equates Hebrew with "Jewish," Arabic with "Arab."[9] It is not a utopia; to the contrary, not knowing a language "beyond this"—beyond the politics of conflict and separation—Shammas is doomed to eternal wandering in the forsaken zone between two alienated languages. In the early 1980s, not long after the publication of his poem, Shammas had prophesized, "This whole thing is a kind of cultural trespassing, and the day may come when I will be punished for it."[10] Nonetheless, I argue, there is a redemptive side to this act of trespass. Through those very wanderings, we uncover a space of alternative poetic visions and cultural possibilities. This space emerges from the ground up through individual acts of translation and literary imagination; it provides a zone of passage for symbols and ideas to migrate between the two languages. In short, it is a space of poetic trespass, where writers transgress the boundaries of language and identity inscribed in the sociopolitical codes of the state.

Poetic Trespass charts the literary topography of this no-man's-land. It examines the interaction of Hebrew and Arabic in Israel/Palestine from the inception of Zionist settlement to the present, and limns the place of Arabic within the modern Hebrew imagination. In Israeli society, Hebrew

6 Shammas, "Yud-gimel drakhim le-histakel be-ze," *Shetaḥ hefker*, 46. For an analysis of the poem, see Levy, "Borderline Writers," and idem, "Self-Portraits of the Other"; also Grumberg, *Place and Ideology*, 123–127.

7 Grumberg, *Place and Ideology*, 127.

8 Eyal, *Disenchantment*, 7–8.

9 My concept of the no-man's-land as a zone between languages and outside nationalist-monolingual cultural space is influenced by Anuradha Dingwaney in Dingwaney and Maier, eds., *Between Languages and Cultures*; see chapter 4 in this book. Karen Grumberg observes that Shammas's deployment of the biblical construction *me-'ever mi-ze* ("beyond this") in the poem connotes the ancient conflicts over territory that defined the Israelite nation; as such, "Shammas's no-man's-land coalesces issues of language, place, and conflict" (*Place and Ideology*, 123–124). I borrow "a space between places" from Grumberg.

10 Shammas, "Diary," 29.

and Arabic are extremely potent cultural and political symbols, markers of identity, and repositories of past and future visions.[11] As one of the most politically resonant symbols of collective identity, language is not just the raw stuff of literature but can also be a literary topos, an object of representation, in its own right; as Mikhail Bakhtin would have it, language in literature is always both *represented* and *representing*.[12] Expanding upon this premise, the book investigates the multifaceted roles of Arabic within the past and present lives of Modern Hebrew literature and culture. How has Hebrew been invented, interrupted, reimagined, and then rewritten through the voice, the trace, and, at times, the conspicuous absence of Arabic? I closely examine how Jewish Israeli and Palestinian Israeli authors use literature as a space for representing language as a contested site of history, memory, and identity, and how they have reenvisioned both Arabic and Hebrew through a dialogue between the languages. One of the curious aspects of this phenomenon is that authors on both sides have contributed to the Hebrew-Arabic no-man's-land as a dynamic space of literary and cultural interaction even in the absence of a corresponding space of political dialogue, and despite the great incommensurability of resources devoted to Hebrew over Arabic.

As Israel's two official languages, Hebrew and Arabic coexist uneasily within a rigid political and social hierarchy. Israel was created as a Jewish state and a *Hebrew* state; the revival of Hebrew was the heart of the nation-building project. Today, Hebrew is the public language of state and society, while Arabic is largely relegated to private use behind closed doors.[13] Hebrew literature and culture are valued as spiritual and national assets, while Arabic, the language of the enemy, is viewed as a socially, politically, and culturally inferior tongue, valued mainly for its uses in the military and state security services. Finally, and perhaps most important, Hebrew is still viewed in Israel as a *Jewish* language, a language that may be used by Palestinian Arabs but is nonetheless the exclusive cultural "property" of the Jewish people; Arabic, a marker of Otherness, has been delegitimized as a "non-Jewish" language despite

11 Sociolinguist John Edwards explains that the distinction between the "communicative" and "symbolic" functions of language lies "in a differentiation between language in its ordinarily understood sense as an instrumental tool, and language as an emblem of groupness, a symbol, a psychosocial rallying-point" (*Language and Identity*, 55).

12 Bakhtin, "From the Prehistory of Novelistic Discourse," 45. I apply Bakhtin's insights about the represented and dialogical nature of language in the novel to literary discourse more generally.

13 Even within the Palestinian public sphere, Hebrew interference characterizes spoken Arabic (as detailed in chapter 1). The Israeli public sphere is dominated by Hebrew.

the long history of Jewish life in the Arabic-speaking world.[14] In theory, then, Hebrew and Arabic ought to have separate and clearly demarcated, if adjacent, lives within the State of Israel. Yet nearly 20 percent of Israel's citizens are bilingual Palestinian Arabs,[15] while roughly half of Israeli Jews have roots in Arabic-speaking countries.[16] Moreover, thousands of Palestinians in the West Bank and Gaza possess knowledge of Hebrew through labor in Israel or incarceration in Israeli prisons. Thus in reality, Modern Hebrew as a living language in Israel/Palestine has always been shaped through contact with Arabic, particularly colloquial Arabic but also classical (literary) Arabic. Their relationship has informed literature written in Israel/Palestine from the turn of the twentieth century to the present, and it is that little known side of Israeli literature that is this book's central concern.

Following a loosely chronological trajectory, and tying readings of selected literary texts into broader historical and sociological frameworks, *Poetic Trespass* also presents a historical counternarrative: an alternative story of the evolution of language and ideology in the Jewish state. The book takes a long historical perspective, beginning not in 1948 with the foundation of the state but rather at the turn of the century, with the early days of Zionist settlement in Palestine. I demonstrate how Arabic has been both a model and a foil for Modern Hebrew literature and, more broadly, for Hebrew culture, functioning first as a positive, defining presence at a time when Hebrew was mostly absent from the Palestinian landscape and then as the "presence of absence" after Hebrew consolidated its hegemony in Israel. While Arabic was excluded from the edifice, however, it became an important part of the proverbial cracks. As a result, this book tells two distinct, if interrelated, stories about the relationship of Hebrew and Arabic: one is a tale of ambivalent yet intimate entanglements, the other of the imagination that is born of distance. The tension between proximity and distance persists throughout the book and shapes the authors' myriad figurations of language, from Emile Habiby's *faux amis* to Anton Shammas's retreating "self-portrait" to Almog Behar's imminent yet intangible Arabic past.

14 Jews took part in Arabic culture from pre-Islamic times through the twentieth century. The ninth through thirteenth centuries were the apex of Jewish participation in Arabic literature. Small numbers of Jews also participated in the nineteenth- and early twentieth-century *nahda* or revival of Modern Arabic culture in the Levant, and Jews were well integrated into literary and cultural life in mid-twentieth-century Iraq and Egypt (Snir, "Arab-Jewish Culture," and Moreh, "Oriental Literature").

15 Palestinian citizens of Israel, often called "Israeli Arabs," number about 1.3 million.

16 In the 1950s, about half of Israel's Jewish population would have spoken Arabic as a first language.

The protagonists of this study belong to two distinct groups: Palestinian citizens of Israel (often called "Israeli Arabs"; I prefer the term "Palestinian Israelis," which acknowledges their hybrid identity) and "Mizraḥim," Israeli Jews with roots in Islamic lands. *Mizraḥi* (plural *mizraḥim*), Hebrew for "Easterner," refers to a collective identity created in Israel to distinguish the totality of Asian, African, and Southeastern European Jews from the population of Eastern, Western, and Central European Jews, collectively referred to as "Ashkenazim."[17] When referring to Jews who were born and came of age in the Arab world (not in Israel), I sometimes employ the term "Arab Jews."[18] I use all these terms with the awareness that they are social constructs; they are not givens, they are not transparent, and they do not imply essentialized or primordial identities.

The book's juxtaposition of literature written by Palestinian Israelis and Mizraḥim is not an entirely self-evident choice. I bring together writers from the two groups while paying heed to their different positions vis-à-vis the political and cultural centers of power in Israel, and, as follows, their different authorial objectives. Hybridity, it must be noted, does not imply an erasure of power discrepancies; Palestinian and Mizraḥi writing may be productively compared, but that does not mean that their activities take place on a level playing field. Palestinians in Israel enjoy fewer civil rights and less social prestige than do members of any Jewish sector.[19] Furthermore, in everyday life and practice, Palestinians and

17 The newer category "Mizraḥim" has also subsumed "Sephardim." Although often generalized to include all non-Ashkenazi Jews, "Sephardim" more accurately denotes descendants of Spanish exiles (many of whom settled throughout Greece, Turkey, Italy, and the Balkans and spoke Ladino rather than Arabic), as opposed to indigenous Asian and African Jewish communities. On the creation of "Mizraḥi" identity, see Shohat, "Invention of the Mizrahim." For the evolution of "Sephardi" and "Mizraḥi" in contemporary Israeli discourse, see Goldberg, "Sephardi to Mizrahi." See also my brief discussions in chapters 1 and 5. Finally, it should be noted that the influx of Ethiopian Jews to Israel beginning in the 1990s presented an additional challenge to the descriptive categories, Ethiopians being neither Ashkenazi, Sephardi, nor (arguably) even Mizraḥi.

18 Historically, Arabic-speaking Jews (with the exception of a small number of intellectuals) did not call themselves "Arabs." However, in recent years the term "Arab Jew" has acquired currency in academic discourse, thanks largely to the work of Ella Shohat and Sami Shalom Chetrit. The term avoids the anachronism of "Mizraḥim" in a pre-1948 context and retains the sense of a cultural and linguistic association with Arabic. For more on the idea of "Arab Jewish" identity, see Gottreich, "Historicizing the Concept of Arab Jews in the Maghrib" and Levy, "Historicizing the Concept of Arab Jews in the *Mashriq*"; see also idem, "Mi-hu ha-yehudi ha-'aravi."

19 Prior to the large wave of immigration from the former Soviet Union in the early 1990s, Mizraḥim constituted roughly half of Israel's Jewish population. Yet for all intents and purposes, they were perceived and treated as a minority group. Palestinians in Israel after 1948 became not only an ethnic but also a "national" minority and were placed under martial law until 1966. They are disadvantaged in virtually every aspect of public life in Israel.

Mizraḥim generally have little direct interaction; the common bond of the Arabic language is not strong enough to overcome the strident political and social forces separating "Jews" from "Arabs" in Israeli society, let alone in the occupied West Bank and Gaza. On the political front, although one can find expressions of solidarity and activism linking Mizraḥim and Palestinians from the earliest years of statehood,[20] they remained marginal and never developed into a popular movement. A strictly sociological approach to the question of language in the two groups would be comparative rather than integrative; this book argues that the realm of the literary imagination presents us with other possibilities.

In literature, the relationship between Hebrew and Arabic forms a coherent topic of analysis that transcends the Jewish-Arab divide. The "no-man's-land," much like the "borderlands" of Chicano literature, is a cultural-political space produced through literary bilingualism, translation, and creative manipulations of language—in this case, through the combined activities of writers from different ethnic, religious, and linguistic backgrounds.[21] For three generations now, from the 1950s to the present, a small number of authors on both sides of the divide have defied the sociopolitical strictures assigning Arabic to Arabs and Hebrew to Jews. They have done so either by choosing to write in the language of the Other (i.e., Arabs writing Hebrew, Jews writing Arabic), or by finding creative ways to rewrite the Hebrew language from within, often through an actual or imagined dialogue with Arabic. Potent historical and cultural symbols and themes migrate back and forth between writings by Palestinian and Mizraḥi authors, blurring the boundaries of cultural origins and linguistic ownership.[22] In a nation-state that places an ideological premium upon its language and literature, these transgressions can be deeply unsettling. What is at stake for Jewish and Palestinian authors in choosing to write in the language of the Other, or, in the case of young Mizraḥi writers, of symbolically reclaiming Arabic as a Jewish language? How have notions of language and identity been disputed through the

20 For examples in the realm of scholarship, see Shohat, "Sephardim in Israel" and Joseph Massad, "Zionism's Internal Others."

21 As much as it is a space of division and separation, the borderland is still a metaphor of human presence. As Gloria Anzaldúa and others have shown, even as the border enforces separation and difference, borderlands themselves become a fertile space of hybridity. The border has also been adopted as a metaphor for language and bilingualism in the Israeli/Palestinian context, in which so much of life is about space and control of space. In the work of bilingual Hebrew-Arabic writers, the border often presents itself as an existential condition.

22 Examples of symbols and themes utilized in both languages include *trees* (Bardenstein, "Threads of Memory"), *caves* (Levy, "Nation, Village, Cave"), and *muteness* (Khoury, "Rethinking the *Nakba*"). The "presence of absence" as a shared trope is discussed in part 3.

literary exchanges of Arabic and Hebrew? My exploration of these questions traverses a variety of texts, some of them well known, others virtually unknown, all of which I selected on the basis of their thematic concerns and linguistic strategies.

Although broader literary landscapes are mapped throughout the book, *Poetic Trespass* is not intended to be an inclusive survey of either Mizraḥi or Palestinian-Israeli writing, but rather a study of the questions I have posed, as examined through complementary literary and historical perspectives. Moreover, the book focuses on the multiple roles of Arabic in the imagination of Israeli Hebrew, rather than the question of Hebrew in Palestinian Arabic writing.[23] The preponderance of the book thus deals with literature written in Hebrew although every chapter contains discussion of Arabic, and chapter 3 is devoted entirely to Arabic-language prose. In addition to looking anew at Hebrew literature through the extracanonical perspective of minority writing, *Poetic Trespass* also reexamines the Hebrew literary "center" (represented by the canonical poets Bialik and Tchernichowsky) as read through Mizraḥi and Palestinian eyes. The Arabic language figures to a minor degree within Hebrew literature by some Ashkenazi Israelis, notably the novelist S. Yizhar and the poet Avot Yeshurun, as well as a small group of pre-state writers mentioned in the following chapter.[24] This book, however, does not address these writers, inasmuch as my focus is not simply on appearances or representations of Arabic language within Hebrew literature but rather on a sustained literary engagement with the *idea* of language as it is manifested in the Hebrew-Arabic no-man's-land—a topic I find most salient within the works of the writers I have included.

While *Poetic Trespass* reads these literary works in the context of Israeli society and culture, that is not their only possible point of entry. As will be discussed in chapter 3, it would be misleading to characterize a book such as Emile Habiby's *The Pessoptimist* as either a "Palestinian" or

23 Have Palestinian writers in Israel also found ways to rewrite the Arabic language from within; has their writing been influenced by Hebrew language, literature, and culture? Aside from my analysis of Habiby in chapter 3 and my brief discussion of Bialik and Palestinians in chapter 2, this important question lies beyond the purview of the book. The answer must incorporate the broader history of Palestinian Arabic literature from inside the 1948 borders, as represented by writers such as Riyad Baydas, Samih al-Qasim, Muhammad Naffa', Zaki Darwish, Hanna Ibrahim, and Muhammad 'Ali Taha. For more on this topic, see the numerous studies by Mahmud Ghanayim, and Mahmoud Kayyal. See also Elad-Bouskila, *Modern Palestinian Literature*, and Jayyusi, *Anthology of Modern Palestinian Literature*.

24 Yizhar and Yeshurun have been studied at length. For one study of Yeshurun's "Passover on Caves," which incorporates Arabic words alongside Ladino and Yiddish, see Gluzman, *Politics of Canonicity*, 141–180.

"Israeli" novel—or for that matter even solely as an "Arabic" novel, despite its having been published first in Arabic. My reading of texts with multiple linguistic and cultural affinities is, implicitly, a questioning of reductive framings of literary history; my treatment of any given text as "Israeli" or "Palestinian," "Hebrew" or "Arabic," is never meant to obscure the text's multiple cultural, political, and linguistic locations and affiliations.

The project's core idea of reenvisioning Arabic and Hebrew in Israel/Palestine through readings of Palestinian and Mizraḥi literature is deeply indebted to the groundbreaking work of Ammiel Alcalay, Ella Shohat, and Hannan Hever.[25] Collectively, their writings forged new pathways into the study of Israeli culture. They broke down social, cultural, and political barriers, formed alliances between discourse and praxis, and brought the insights of the global postcolonial experience to bear upon literary and cultural analysis in the context of Israel/Palestine. Building on their conceptual foundations of a counternarrative of Israeli literature and film recuperating Middle Eastern perspectives, this book offers a diachronic narrative of the Hebrew-Arabic "no-man's-land" that penetrates it more deeply on linguistic and historical levels. The first conceptual shift I undertake is to adopt an analytical frame based on ideas of *language*, to broaden the existing discursive preoccupation with questions of Mizraḥi/Sephardi, Arab Jewish, Palestinian, or Levantine identity in Hebrew literature and film. My second intervention entails bringing Arabic-language texts into direct conversation with Modern Hebrew literature and literary history. In Israel/Palestine, there now is a rich and ever-expanding body of print and visual culture oriented toward the history, memory, and contemporary experience of *ha-mizraḥ* (in Arabic, *al-sharq*), an umbrella term that can stand variously for the East, the Middle East, the Orient, and the Levant—not to mention pre-state Palestine, a time-bound space peopled by native, Arabic-speaking Muslims, Jews, and Christians. By following the interaction of Arabic and Hebrew from the critical period of Modern Hebrew's gestation into its maturity, and by utilizing that historical lens as a hermeneutic for reading contemporary literature and culture, we can investigate this expansive body of work on multiple levels reaching far beyond questions of identity. Toward these ends, I employ a deliberately eclectic methodology combining close readings with critical theory, sociolinguistics, and intellectual history to offer an interdisciplinary exploration of this cultural terrain.

25 See, in particular, Shohat, *Israeli Cinema*; Alcalay, *After Jews and Arabs*; and Hannan Hever's numerous articles on minority discourse in Israel, culminating in *Producing the Modern Hebrew Canon* and *Ha-Sipur ve-ha-le'om*.

In the historiographical arena, *Poetic Trespass* joins a broader scholarly effort to reclaim the diversity of language and experience within the history of modern Hebrew culture and to recover alternative histories for Israel/Palestine.[26] While the historic multilingualism of Modern Hebrew literature is a topic of growing interest, the scholarship has focused closely on Yiddish and European languages, paying scant attention to Ladino and virtually none to Arabic. On the other hand, some recent studies of contemporary Hebrew literature have addressed Palestinian writers of Hebrew and, to a lesser extent, Hebrew's connections to Palestinian literature; but they have not delved into the intricate work of Arabic within the Modern Hebrew literary imagination or the rich bilingual life of Arabic and Hebrew in Israel/Palestine.[27] Historically, Arabic was by no means the only Other of Modern Hebrew; as chapter 1 explains, before and during the formative years of Israeli statehood, all other languages spoken by Jewish immigrants were perceived as challengers to Hebrew, and suppressed. But in the current moment, with Hebrew a fully sovereign national language, Arabic has become Modern Hebrew's dialectical Other.

LANGUAGE AND ITS OTHERS: METALINGUISTIC DISCOURSE AND "HYPERLANGUAGE"

If this book serves as a counterhistory, reconstructing a genealogy of Modern Hebrew and Arabic in Israel/Palestine, its theoretical point of departure is literature's capacity to not only represent but *reimagine*—indeed, even recreate—language. To be sure, studies of literary bilingualism or multilingualism, particularly as they intersect with minority discourse, have explored the relationship of language and literature in depth.[28] What is perhaps distinct about the case of Hebrew and Arabic is the intensity and specificity of the political-historical context. The anxiety surrounding the relationship between Arabic and Hebrew, present and palpable in everyday life in Israel and Palestine, elicits what I call a "metalinguistic thematics": a hyperawareness of language, of its

26 See, for instance, Berg, *Exile from Exile*; Kronfeld, *On the Margins of Modernism*; Seidman, *A Marriage Made in Heaven*; Gluzman, *Politics of Canonicity*; Chaver, *What Must Be Forgotten*; LeVine, *Overthrowing Geography*; Peleg, *Orientalism and the Hebrew Imagination*; Shenhav, *Arab Jews*; Campos, *Ottoman Brothers*; Grumberg, *Place and Ideology*; Shimony, *'Al saf ha-ge'ula*; Starr, *Remembering Cosmopolitan Egypt*; Starr and Somekh, *Mongrels or Marvels*; Pinsker, *Literary Passports*; see also note 27 below.

27 See Brenner, *Inextricably Bonded*; Peleg, *Orientalism and the Hebrew Imagination*; Hochberg, *In Spite of Partition*; and Anidjar, *Semites.*

28 See Arteaga, *An Other Tongue*; Dingwaney and Maier, *Between Languages and Cultures*; the work of Doris Sommer, particularly *Bilingual Games* and *Bilingual Aesthetics*; Zabus, *African Palimpsest*; Ch'ien, *Weird English*; Miller, *Accented America*; and Yildiz, *Beyond the Mother Tongue.*

social and cultural meaning, negotiated within poetry, prose, cinema, and visual art. If, as the linguist Louis Hjelmslev proposed, "metalanguage" is a "language which takes another language as its object," then metalinguistic writing is that which takes its own uses of language as a thematic preoccupation.[29] In his 1923 essay "The Task of the Translator," Walter Benjamin famously contemplates how translation "powerfully affects" the source language and text, creating an "afterlife" of the original. Through an extended metaphor of a shattered vessel whose fragments are reassembled, Benjamin envisions translation as the liberation of "pure language" from its imprisonment in one form, followed by its transposition and reinscription (or, if you will, its reassemblage) into a different linguistic code. This process, Benjamin says, creates a reciprocal relationship between the translation and source text, while also revealing the essential kinship between languages.[30]

In a similar sense, in their current zone of contact, Arabic and Hebrew have "powerfully affected" one another, creating new forms of meaning on every level from the individual lexeme to the full text. Furthermore, when the very act of writing in one language versus another is a personal and political statement, the language of the text inevitably doubles as a metatextual discussion *about* language. Modern Hebrew literature in general is infused with a heightened awareness of its own language, as historically Modern Hebrew authors were also linguistic innovators. Given the current relations between Hebrew and Arabic, this kind of

29 As Patricia Waugh explains in *Metafiction*, "The linguist L. Hjelmslev developed the term 'metalanguage' (Hjelmslev 1961). He defined it as a language which, instead of referring to nonlinguistic events, situations or objects in the world, refers to another language: it is a language which takes another language as its object. Saussure's distinction between the signifier and the signified is relevant here. . . . A metalanguage is a language that functions as a signifier to *another language*, and this other language thus becomes its signified" (4, emphasis in original). Roman Jakobson also uses the term in his 1959 "Linguistic Aspects of Translation": "A faculty of speaking a given language implies a faculty of talking about this language. Such a 'metalinguistic' operation permits revision and redefinition of the vocabulary used" (234).

30 Benjamin, "Task of the Translator," 71–74, 78–81, my emphasis. By explaining translation in terms of fragmentation and the signification process, Benjamin took translation theory well beyond the old metaphors of fidelity and equivalence. But by decontextualizing language and consigning it to the realm of the metaphysical, Benjamin seems to assume that all languages enjoy equal status, and that the translator is unaffected by the forces governing relations between source and target language. He writes that the ultimate purpose of translation is "expressing the central reciprocal relationship between languages," and that languages are "a priori, and *apart from all historical relationships*, interrelated in what they want to express" (72, my emphasis). From the postcolonial perspective, the problem is that authors, readers, and translators cannot think, let alone write, in terms untainted by power relations; see also the related discussion in chapter 3.

creative tension around language is especially pronounced in writing from their no-man's-land. The cultural space of *in-betweenness*, encompassing contact zone and no-man's-land,[31] is "a fertile space, and disquieting, because . . . it proves to be a sphere (or zone) *in which one both abandons and assumes associations*"; it is the space of *transculturación*, where "the dominant language and culture is rewritten, inflected, subverted by the 'subaltern,' functions as a form of resistance."[32] To write in one language means contending with the shadow of the other, while contending with the other language often means reimagining the first. As with the case of English-Spanish "borderlands" poets, "No matter which language they write in, the 'other' language shines through producing, as it were, an effect of refraction."[33] In the works discussed in this book, both Arabic and Hebrew are employed in this translational mode of thought whereby the act of writing is an implicit negotiation of language itself.

As a result, I argue, in literature of the no-man's-land, Arabic and Hebrew are bound together in a continuous state of creative tension, generating metalinguistic discourses through performative deployments of language. The same negotiation of symbolic power that inevitably accompanies translation between two languages of unequal status is brought into the *original* writing process: a process of writing both *in* and *between* two languages, that links the political and the metaphysical. Hebrew and Arabic are each redefined through the other; in the process, they become dialogized. This is a case not just of linguistic hybridity, but of an aestheticized hyperawareness of the writing language in relation to its dialectical Other, while gesturing toward Benjamin's "pure language"—the essential part of meaning that resists expression in words.[34] Literary language of this type is highly performative, calling attention to itself and potentiating the thematic level of the text with another layer of meaning to tell a second story.[35] To denote such excessively performative, self-aware literary language, I use my own term, "hyperlanguage."

31 Mary Louise Pratt identifies "contact zones" as "social spaces where disparate cultures meet, clash, and grapple with each other, often in highly asymmetrical relations of domination and subordination" (*Imperial Eyes*, 4). To be sure, there are other contact zones in the linguistic and cultural history of Israel: Hebrew and Yiddish, Hebrew and Russian, Hebrew and Amharic, to name a few. The contact zone of Hebrew and Arabic is distinct in that it is the cultural meeting ground of Palestinian Israelis and Mizraḥi Jews.

32 Dingwaney, "Introduction: Translating 'Third World' Cultures," 8, my emphasis.

33 Savin, "Bilingualism and Dialogism," 217.

34 See Benjamin, "Task of the Translator," 79–80.

35 On performative language—language that serves to construct identity or an understanding of social reality—see Judith Butler, *Bodies That Matter*, and idem, *Excitable Speech*. The concept of "performative utterances" was developed by J. L. Austin; see *How to Do Things with Words*. See also Benjamin Lee, *Talking Heads*, for more on performativity and metalinguistics in the philosophy of language.

Deeply immersed in the politics of language, the authors in question must also overcome the political limitations of language as a discursive apparatus. Resisting the external constraints imposed upon language, they attempt to free it, using literature as a space to reinvent, reimagine, and rewrite language from within. This book examines such cogent negotiations of language by authors who create "double-voiced" discourses characterized by an ironic distance between language and meaning.[36] Some authors pen bilingual or multilingual texts, incorporating Arabic and other languages into their Hebrew poetry and prose by means of translation and transliteration. As an extreme example, the late Iraqi-Jewish author Samir Naqqash wrote dialogues in a Jewish dialect of Arabic and translated them into standard Arabic in the footnotes, producing margins that competed with the narrative for primacy over the printed page.[37] Other writers, while not technically bilingual, demonstrate a bilingual consciousness in their writing, bringing the absent language into their work through creative thematic devices. They may weave elaborate plots around concepts of language and translation, communication and miscommunication, and the loss of language. Some even create "pseudo-languages," such as Sami Shalom Chetrit's aforementioned "Ashdodian"; these act as foils to standard Modern Hebrew ("correct Hebrew" or *'ivrit tiknit*).

In all cases, what is at stake in these metalinguistic thematics is the hegemony of standard Modern Hebrew within Israeli public life and culture. As we shall see, for historical reasons to be explained in the following chapters, in Israel, "correct" or "grammatical" Hebrew and high Hebrew culture became socially encoded as Ashkenazi (European Jewish), prompting some Mizraḥi writers to explore other ways of writing Hebrew or, simply, other kinds of Hebrew. Thus, while this book focuses on representations and manipulations of Arabic and Hebrew within Israeli literature, it also considers other languages that have been strategically deployed in order to reenvision Modern Hebrew as a Middle Eastern language. In so doing, it challenges the predominant view of Israeli Hebrew as an anomalous Semitic-cum-European language severed from its regional history and ties.

Representing language pictorially as *script* introduces a visual dimension to the portrayal of the relationship between the two languages. Although Arabic and Hebrew are closely related Semitic languages with long and deep historical ties, and both are written from right to left,

36 Cf. Bakhtin, "Discourse in the Novel." This term is elaborated in chapter 3.

37 In this respect, Yoel Hoffman is an interesting Ashkenazi counterpoint to Naqqash; in both "The Book of Joseph" and "Katschen," Hoffman translates German and Yiddish (and in "Katschen" even Arabic) into Hebrew in the footnotes (see Hoffman, *Sefer Yosef*). Naqqash's use of footnotes, however, is much more extensive.

they employ different and easily differentiable scripts. This orthographic variation lends itself well to visual representations of linguistic identity, whether in visual art or in bilingual printed texts. National monolingualism and the suppression of Arabic as a Jewish language have been contested not only by writers but also by visual artists, and we will encounter some of their images alongside related readings of literature.

THE POLITICS OF POETICS

Given the political implications of writing in the Hebrew-Arabic no-man's-land, what is this book's connection to politics more broadly? This is a study of literature and language in which references to history, politics, sociology, and religion play supporting roles. I am interested in offering an analysis of literature and art, through which one might also glean historical, cultural, or sociological insights, rather than a prescription for Middle Eastern peace or a plea for reconciliation between Palestinian Arabs and Israeli Jews. When dealing with incendiary political contexts, it is easy to lose sight of what is unique about literature as a cultural practice. The connection between literature and reality is notoriously complex, and literature does not reflect reality in a direct, transparent manner; nor does social reality exist outside the conventions of language. Some of the literary texts discussed in this book offer critiques of historical and societal issues ranging from the dispossession of Palestinians to Israel's language policies to the exclusion of Mizraḥim from the cultural center. They do not offer solutions, suggest alternatives, or even represent these issues in exacting historical detail; that is not their purpose. In Israel, writers command public respect, and their extraliterary (political and social) views are taken very seriously, but they are not public officials or politicians (although a few of Israel's seminal writers, including S. Yizhar and Emile Habiby, did also serve as members of Parliament). Historically and in far many more contexts, authors have stood at the political vanguard of their societies. As such, their stories, novels, and poems are not always representative of mainstream public opinion, and their goals and methods are very different from those of journalists or historians.

That said, literature in both Israel and Palestine is an intensely political affair. Indeed, it is the political importance of language and literature that lends the current study its extraliterary significance. Literature historically played a prominent and important role both in the creation of Modern Hebrew and in the development of a national culture in Israel. Furthermore, while perhaps not as central to Israeli society today as during the early years of statehood, literature in Israel is still a discursive field of cultural negotiation as well as a barometer of social and cultural change. Even though this study concerns the Palestinian-Israeli conflict only insofar as it relates to literature and the use of language, we should not overlook the related question of literature's role in the conflict. Consider the fiasco that ensued in March 2000 when Yossi Sarid, then the Israeli minister of education and culture, attempted to introduce a few poems by the late Mahmoud Darwish, the Palestinian poet laureate, into the Israeli high school literature curriculum. After right-wing members of the Israeli parliament threatened a vote of no confidence, the then prime minister Ehud Barak (of the center-left Labor Party) concluded that Israel was "not ready" for the globally acclaimed poetry of Darwish. That a few poems were considered threatening enough to justify bringing down an entire government may give the reader some indication of just how sensitive a political matter literature can be in this intensely nationalist context. Nor is the political role of literature in Israel restricted to its placement within the educational system; the literary representation of sensitive historical topics such as the Holocaust, Israel's numerous wars and conflicts, and the Palestinian *nakba* continue to inspire passionate public debate, often around questions of historical accuracy and inclusion.[38] In this sense, the so-called republic of letters is not an autonomous realm; in contexts entrenched in nationalism and political conflict, literature is never very far removed from society.

The book is divided into three parts. The first part—Historical Visions and Elisions (chapters 1 and 2)—reframes the discussion of Palestinian and Mizraḥi writing in Israel/Palestine by revisiting the historical narratives surrounding the formation of Modern Hebrew language and literature. Chapter 1 recounts the role of Arabic in the revival of Modern Hebrew, considers the linguistic dilemmas of Palestinian Israelis and Mizraḥim, and closes with a discussion of literary bilingualism and translation between Arabic and Hebrew. This counternarrative elucidates the evolution of Zionist attitudes toward Arabic from the pre-state period to the present, following them from the early stage when Arabic was romanticized as a model of "authenticity" through its transformation into the "language of the enemy" and the instrumental language of military

38 For example, Elias Khoury, author of *Bab al-Shams* (*Gate of the Sun*), was publicly criticized by Israeli historian Tom Segev for exceeding the bounds of poetic license in his portrayal of the Israeli destruction of Palestinian villages in 1948. As Khoury notes, "Literature is not and cannot be a historical reference, and all the novels and poems, both Israeli and Palestinian, that relate fragments of the *nakba* can't be treated as documents, but they can be conceived as mirrors of trends in the ideological scene" ("Rethinking the *Nakba*," 252).

intelligence. Chapter 2 continues the historical critique by returning to a formative moment in the development of Modern Hebrew literature to illustrate how Israeli Hebrew was severed from the history and milieu of Arab Jews. The chapter reconstructs the multigenerational, star-crossed romance of Ḥ. N. Bialik, known as the "national poet" of the emerging Hebrew state, and the "Sephardim" (Sephardi, Mizraḥi, and Arab Jews). Its point of departure is a 1933 ode to Bialik by an Iraqi Jewish poet who portrays Modern Hebrew as the outgrowth of the Sephardi poetic tradition. I read the poem contrapuntally with Bialik's 1927 lecture contending that the "genius" of Hebrew literature had deserted the Sephardim for European Jews; this is followed by a discussion of Sephardi responses, including one in Arabic published by a Jewish newspaper in Cairo. The chapter concludes with contemporary Mizraḥi rereadings and rewritings of Bialik, in which Bialik himself becomes a literary trope: the emblem of the Ashkenazi-dominated Hebrew establishment that would define Mizraḥim as the "other," the "marginal," and the "minority." These two chapters provide the historical basis for my argument about texts that cross boundaries between Hebrew and Arabic. Reading such texts against the Eurocentric narrative of Hebrew modernity dooms them to the eternal status of a "minority literature" responding to a hegemonic cultural discourse, but these same texts can perform a very different kind of logic when read against a historical perspective grounded in their *own* cultural matrix, one suffused with the languages and historical memory of *ha-mizraḥ/al-sharq*, the "East."[39]

The following chapters in parts 2 and 3 engage the shared question of metalinguistic discourse in the literature of Israel/Palestine. The second part of the book—Bilingual Entanglements (chapters 3 and 4)—focuses on the Arabic and Hebrew work of Palestinian writers in the State of Israel, while drawing out the underappreciated significance of their bilingual and bicultural engagements. Chapter 3 juxtaposes the Arabic prose fiction of the Palestinian Israeli writer Emile Habiby (1922–1996) and the Iraqi Jewish writer Samir Naqqash (1938–2004). Habiby was a major figure in the Israeli political and cultural landscapes as well as in Modern Arabic

39 This argument builds upon Ammiel Alcalay's *After Jews and Arabs*, which seeks to resituate Hebrew literary production of Sephardi and Arab Jews within the space of the Levant, a space in which the Jew "*was* native, not a stranger but an absolute inhabitant of time and space" (1). While Alcalay does not make this argument per se in his book (whose temporal range is vast and exposition schematic), he anticipates it through his critique of the elision of Arab Jewish intellectuals from narratives of Jewish modernity (153–154; see also chapter 2 of this book) and of Israeli literature's characterization as a "European fiction" (252–253). See also Levy, "Reorienting Hebrew Literary History," for an expanded discussion of Hebrew literary historiography and Arab Jewish/Mizraḥi writers.

literature. Naqqash was the most important contemporary Jewish writer of Arabic, yet remains virtually unknown. As two native speakers of Arabic who wrote Arabic prose fiction in Israel, they offer an illuminating, if unorthodox, point of comparison. The chapter explores the poetics of misunderstanding in their fiction, elucidating how they thematize communicative failure as one means of contesting dominant historical narratives and undermining their faulty logic. It also offers the first comparative study of Habiby's critical reception in both Arabic and Hebrew, based on my bilingual reading of his masterpiece *al-Mutasha'il* (*The Pessoptimist*).

With chapter 4, we turn to the Hebrew poetics of Palestinian Arab writers. The discourse on this topic was long dominated by a single author and work, Anton Shammas's landmark 1986 novel *'Arabeskot* (*Arabesques*), now complemented by a growing interest in the Hebrew novels, journalism, and television writing of Sayed Kashua.[40] Yet the scholarship has overlooked the larger body of Hebrew poetry by Palestinian Israeli authors, including two volumes by Shammas. In this chapter I explore how three Palestinian poets engage the Jewish literary corpus and employ biblical allusion within their Hebrew verse—a process I dub "Palestinian midrash." Their Hebrew poetry self-consciously problematizes its own relationship to both Hebrew and Arabic, once again eliciting the phenomenological qualities of "language and its Others."

Part 3—Afterlives of Language (chapters 5 and 6)—addresses the question of language in the Hebrew poetry and prose of contemporary Mizraḥi writers, with attention to intersections of recent Mizraḥi and Palestinian Israeli discourses. This part of the book maps out the two main avenues of innovation in Mizraḥi uses of language. It explores Mizraḥi literature as a space of intervention in which writers have repeatedly challenged the hegemony of Modern (Israeli) Hebrew. At the same time, it traces a complementary process: the evolving role of Arabic in the Hebrew work of first-, second-, and third-generation Mizraḥi authors, in which Arabic is gradually transformed from an "instrumental" to a "symbolic" language. Chapter 5 addresses the prose fiction of first- and second-generation Mizraḥim, illustrating how first-generation authors, who were compelled to change their writing language from Arabic to Hebrew, use Hebrew to represent lost Arabic worlds; the second part

40 In the past decade, Sayed Kashua has attracted international attention for his gripping and sardonic novels concerning Palestinian life in Israel, as well as for his weekly satiric column in the Hebrew daily *Haaretz* and his weekly television drama *'Avoda 'aravit* (Arab Labor). The first program to present Palestinian characters speaking Arabic on Israeli prime time, it premiered in 2007. See Grumberg, *Place and Ideology*, chap. 3; Gil Hochberg, "To Be or Not to Be"; and Shimony, "Shaping Israeli-Arab Identity."

takes up second-generation Mizraḥi writers, who salvage the linguistic residue of the past to dialogize their representations of "immigrant Hebrew" and displace standard Hebrew (*'ivrit tiknit*) as the signifier of Israeli identity. Chapter 6 continues the discussion through readings of poetry and a transgeneric short story/prose poem. Focusing on the idea of the "presence of absence," I explore the imaginative ways second- and third-generation Mizraḥi authors use language not only to rewrite but to *un*write the idea of Israeli Hebrew, rejecting it altogether. Their ingenious linguistic prestidigitation entails devising "secret" languages as well as writing in archaic forms of Hebrew and in pseudo-languages, while Arabic eventually becomes a metaphor of sorts, a "place holder" for a sense of fragmented identity and the loss of origins. At the same time, the "presence of absence" informs Palestinian writing and art on the erasure of Arabic and of Palestinian memory. The chapter also incorporates visual representations of the Mizraḥi relationship to language. Collectively, these texts and images reimagine Israeli Hebrew as a language intimately intertwined with Arabic and other Middle Eastern languages.

The conclusion returns to Palestinian Hebrew writing with a poem by Salman Masalha and its intertextual invocation of a sonnet corona by the canonical early twentieth-century Hebrew poet Saul Tchernichowsky. Masalha's poem, provocatively titled "Ha-tikva" ("The Hope"), appropriates the name of Israel's national anthem while depicting the aftermath of a violent event, presumably a terror attack. I unravel the layers of meaning ensconced within the poem, which I read as a political and aesthetic intervention, to arrive at the fundamental questions implied by its act of bearing witness: How do we define the political agency of witnessing? How can the outsider, the Other, bear witness to violence and disaster; how can she or he be heard? The book concludes with these broader questions about the epistemological limits of representation in the no-man's-land of language.

In this book, then, I approach language as a multifaceted prism: language as a medium of communication; language as an object of desire, of possession, of control, and of resistance to control; language as a part of the social world, a subject of representation; and language as a kind of metaphysical excess, uncontainable, unrepresentable, and in some sense unknowable. What does it mean to write between Hebrew and Arabic—or Aramaic, or Judeo-Arabic, or a combination thereof—in Israel/Palestine? Through the explorations that follow, we will illuminate the poetics of the no-man's-land: a poetics of trespass.

Part 1

Historical Visions and Elisions

CHAPTER 1

From the "Hebrew Bedouin" to "Israeli Arabic"

Arabic, Hebrew, and the Creation of Israeli Culture

> When two languages meet, one of them is necessarily linked to animality. Speak like me or you are an animal.
>
> —ABDELFATTAH KILITO[1]

> So, if you want to really hurt me, talk badly about my language.
>
> —GLORIA ANZALDÚA[2]

Much more than just a medium of communication, language is a symbol of identity that impels people to hold referendums, bring down governments, and even go to war.[3] It is the *idea* of language, its meaning in this symbolic sense, that preoccupies the many works examined in this book. The encounter between Hebrew and Arabic did not begin with the Israeli-Palestinian conflict, but the conflict has irrevocably transformed their relationship. Indeed, one would be hard-pressed to find a current discussion of the two languages that is not framed by their present circumstances as languages on opposite sides of an enemy divide. Their current relationship in Israel/Palestine is the outgrowth of over a century of sociolinguistic, political, and cultural developments; though the two languages had shared a long and storied past, Zionism catalyzed their reunion in the context of modern nationalism. In this chapter I survey that historic landscape to offer a counternarrative of Israeli language and culture, arguing that Arabic has played a central, formative, yet paradoxical role in the self-definition of Modern Hebrew from the very outset. The repressed story of Arabic and

1 Kilito, "Dog Words," xxvii.

2 Anzaldúa, *Borderlands*, 81.

3 On many levels, Israel's nationalist language politics and its spillover into literature might be compared to numerous other cases such as Quebec, the former Yugoslavia, and the U.S./Mexico borderlands. See, for example, Sherry Simon on language politics and translation in Quebec; Gloria Anzaldúa on the U.S./Mexico borderlands; and Andrew Wachtel on Yugoslavia. For more on "borderlands" literature, see Miller, *Writing on the Edge* and Stavans, *Border Culture*.

Hebrew in Israel/Palestine is inseparable from the triangulated history of Ashkenazi Jews, Palestinian Arabs, and Mizraḥi Jews, each group having faced distinct yet interrelated dilemmas of language. In excavating this multilayered site of memory, I trace pre-state linguistic practices, the institutionalization of Modern Hebrew, and the continuing evolution of Hebrew and Arabic in the political scene, concluding with the question of literary translation between the two languages.

LANGUAGE AND IDENTITY: *'AJAMI* AND "ISRAELI ARABIC"

The relationship of Hebrew and Arabic in Israel/Palestine has always been a contest of power operating on an uneven playing field. Sociolinguists and linguistic anthropologists who study language in Israel/Palestine concur that the conflict has "conditioned the linguistic attitudes toward Arabic and Hebrew on both sides of the Arab-Israeli divide" such that "both parties look at the language of the Other as the language of the 'enemy.'"[4] If Jewish Israelis generally see Arabic as the language of their hostile neighbors and the "enemy within," then "[t]he Arabs, correspondingly, see Hebrew as the language of a foreign body that has been forcibly implanted in their midst, one that continues to occupy Arab lands."[5] Similarly, both sides tend to view ethnic or national identity in categorical and totalizing terms: conflict leaves little room for nuance. In everyday parlance, for example, most Palestinians (as well as other Arabs) do not distinguish between "Israelis" and "Jews," using the Arabic term *al-yahud*, "the Jews," when referring to Israelis. Jewish Israelis, in turn, usually say *'aravim*, Hebrew for "Arabs," rather than "Palestinians," typically without differentiating Palestinian citizens of Israel from residents of the West Bank and Gaza. Palestinians in Israel, however, challenge binary notions of language and identity. They speak Hebrew as a second language, using it in everyday interactions with Jewish Israelis—and, in a different manner, with each other, through the Hebrew absorbed into Palestinian-Israeli Arabic.[6]

4 Ibrahim, "Language and Politics," cited in Suleiman, *War of Words*, 139. See also Spolsky and Shohamy, *Languages of Israel*: "For most Israeli Jews, Arabic is first and foremost the language of the surrounding Arab states, many of which have been engaged in war with Israel since its establishment and which continue to be seen as threats to national survival. It is, second, the language of the Palestinians living in Gaza and the West Bank, the heirs and continuing supporters of a national liberation movement that has used terrorism to achieve its goals. It is, third, the language of a minority group within Israel, granted civil rights since the creation of the state, but feared as a potential fifth column in struggles either with the Palestinians or with other Arab states" (118).

5 Suleiman, *War of Words*, 141.

6 "As about 90% of the employed Palestinian population work outside the community and come into contact with the Jewish population on a daily basis, Palestinians are undergoing a far-reaching process of language and cultural exposure . . . and it is in this context that they have

The question of "Israeli Arabic"'s relationship to Hebrew came to the fore in the critically acclaimed 2009 film *'Ajami*, whose unflinching realism garnered local and international accolades.[7] The film itself and its reception among Jewish Israeli viewers and critics tell us much about the power dynamics of language and society in Israel/Palestine. Co-written and co-directed by a Palestinian Israeli and a Jewish Israeli, the film portrays the intertwined stories of Palestinians and Jews in a crime-ridden neighborhood of Jaffa, a historic Palestinian city on the outskirts of metropolitan Tel Aviv. *'Ajami* surprised Jewish Israeli viewers not only with its gritty, graphic depictions of social and political tensions and police violence, but also with its unprecedented (and in fact unscripted)[8] portrayal of a *linguistic* reality: the Hebrew-smattered Arabic of Palestinians in Israel.[9] Jewish Israelis, most of whom have little real-life exposure to Palestinian Israelis speaking among themselves, were startled by hearing familiar Hebrew idioms seamlessly interpolated within strings of otherwise unintelligible, fast-flowing Arabic speech. Some Hebrew words in the characters' speech are Arabicized (through Arabic suffixes or grammatical declensions) to the point of being unrecognizable to most Jewish Israelis; such hybrid constructions signal a pidgin or creole strain within local Arabic. At times, when Palestinian characters converse with or in the presence of Jewish characters, they switch to Hebrew. This is known as "code-switching," a linguistic phenomenon that refers to the "use of more than one language in the course of a single communicative episode" and that takes place in a context of asymmetrical political or social power relations between speakers.[10]

---

developed an 'Israeli-Palestinian' variety of Arabic characterized by frequent codeswitching and borrowing from Hebrew" (Ben-Rafael et al., "Linguistic Landscape," 13).

7 A low-budget film employing amateur actors, it won a number of prestigious awards. *'Ajami* was the first predominantly Arabic-language film submitted by Israel for the Academy Award for Best Foreign Language Film, for which it received a nomination.

8 Most of the actors were local amateurs recruited on location in Jaffa who underwent a ten-month acting workshop emphasizing improvisation. The directors had written the story line but did not use a script with dialogue, letting the actors improvise. The result captivated viewers and critics.

9 More specifically, the film portrays the Arabic of Jaffa. Jaffa's proximity to Tel Aviv and the characters' daily interactions with Hebrew-speaking Jewish Israelis account for the unusually high frequency of Hebrew words in their colloquial Arabic. As Rovik Rozental points out, in other Arab population centers in Israel, not only is linguistic interference or influence from Hebrew less prominent, but it tends to be concentrated in administrative terminology related to the state. By contrast, the Hebrew terms in *'Ajami* are primarily low-register slang. See Rozental, "Ha-zira ha-leshonit."

10 Heller, *Code-Switching*, 1, quoted in Suleiman, *War of Words*, 29. In code-switching, the speaker might switch into the higher prestige language or dialect when in the presence of the dominant social group or, conversely, may intentionally speak in the lower prestige "code" to preserve privacy or establish cultural boundaries, "as a sign of cultural solidarity or distance, and as an

Encountering everyday Israeli Hebrew expressions within Arabic speech is not an ordinary experience for the Jewish Israeli viewer. The language of the film occasioned widespread commentary in the Hebrew press and on blogs. Seeing themselves in the mirror of the Other, numerous Jewish Israeli viewers reported feeling a gratifying sense of self-recognition mixed with an unnerving sense of defamiliarization. One viewer found the experience of watching the film simultaneously scintillating and alienating, imagining herself a "foreigner" in relation to the Arabic speakers on the screen and in the audience: "How sexy to sit in the Ayalon Mall [near Tel Aviv], with your popcorn and diet cola, and watch a movie in Arabic along with a large number of Israeli Arabs. . . . There are also parts in the movie where the Arabs [in the audience] laugh. We don't. There are nuances that a foreigner will never understand."[11] Critics for Israel's major dailies celebrated the film and lavished praise on its language. As one wrote, the film's success in conveying an unmediated reality is due largely to "its very precise dialogues, in both Hebrew and Arabic, in which one feels no 'scriptorial' presence. . . . That's life, and this is language [*ele ha-ḥayim, ve-zot ha-safa*]." The article's subheading jauntily proclaims, "The movie *'Ajami* provides a peek at one of the most important linguistic phenomena in *our language*: Israeli Arabic."[12]

Statements such as "That's life, and this is language" and "a peek at . . . our language: Israeli Arabic" are anchored in underlying assumptions about community, identity, ownership, and power. Whose language, whose reality, are "we" speaking about? In context, the phrase "our language" (*ha-safa shelanu*) is intriguingly ambiguous. It subsumes the Arabic-Hebrew patois of *'Ajami*'s characters into an imagined national language that contains Hebrew *and* Arabic; at the same time, the lives of Arabic-speaking characters in Jaffa are recoded as a part of "Israeliness," potentially opening a new discursive space of representation. Yet here, as in many other postcolonial and minority contexts, such resignification, rather than reflecting an existing reality, is a form of symbolic appropriation: naming their hybridized language "Israeli Arabic" makes it safe for local consumption, while stripping it of Arab or Palestinian connotations.

---

act of (cultural) identity"; Kramsch, *Language and Culture*, 125. See also Bell, "In the Shadow of the Father Tongue" on code-switching and its representation in Creole fiction.

11 Feldman, "*'Ajami*, seret."

12 Rozental, "Ha-zira ha-leshonit," my emphasis. Similarly, Avirama Golan writes, "The film presents itself in simplicity as an Israeli story . . . and speaks in an Arabic that exists in only one place in the world—in Israel, because this is an Arabic that is mixed with Hebrew"; see "Bi-zkhut 'ajami." See also Shnitzer, "Be-shkhuna shelanu."

Given Palestinian Israelis' quotidian immersion in Hebrew, not to mention the fact that they are citizens of the state, one might expect that Israeli *Hebrew* would also be viewed as "their" language, just as the film critic could claim "Israeli Arabic" as a part of "our language." Or, to put it bluntly, why should a few Palestinian Israelis speaking Hebrew, or speaking Arabic mixed with Hebrew, be such a big deal? In practice, however, Hebrew's symbolic status is disconnected from the reality of its everyday usage. No matter how many Palestinian Arabs speak Hebrew and no matter how well they speak it, Israeli Hebrew remains an exclusively "Jewish" language in the eyes of the state, its Jewish citizens, its Arab citizens, and the world. Ideas of linguistic ownership and possession stop short of opening the gates of Hebrew to the Palestinian.[13]

Beyond all else, there is a stunning dissonance between the critics' celebratory embrace of "Israeli Arabic" and the disparaging attitudes toward Arabic (not to mention Arabs) that prevail in mainstream Israeli society. As members of the liberal elite, the critics see the creolized language of *'Ajami* as a sign of Arab cultural integration into the Hebrew-speaking Jewish majority, a welcome harbinger of coexistence. The film itself, however, does not promote this interpretation. While it demonstrates how the lives and fates of Jewish Israelis and Palestinians are closely intertwined, it offers very little by way of hope or redemption. In fact, from a sociolinguistic perspective, linguistic interference often indicates asymmetrical power relations, as in the case of "Spanglish" in the United States.[14] The Israeli film critics fail to recognize the interference of Hebrew in Palestinian Arabic as a sign of the ever-weakening status of Arabic in Israel—as evidence of what Anton Shammas, in writing about what he calls the "Arabebrew" of Haifa, has termed the "vanishing Arabic" of the mixed Arab-Jewish city. From his perspective as a bilingual Palestinian Israeli, "not only did the Hebrew language empty the land of its [Palestinian] inhabitants, but it also rendered their language captive."[15] In short, the critical responses to *'Ajami* are themselves expressions of majority-minority power relations. What springs to life in the language of the film is the conspicuous, unreciprocated influence of Hebrew on Arabic; what the criticism reveals is the majority's blindness to its own position of privilege. As members of the majority group, Jew-

13 With the large influx of foreign workers into Israel in recent decades, Palestinian Arabs are no longer the only non-Jewish speakers of Hebrew in Israel. However, as this book is concerned with relations between Hebrew and Arabic, the question of Hebrew in other contexts lies outside its scope.

14 Cf. Anzaldúa, "How to Tame a Wild Tongue."

15 Shammas, "Mixed as in Pidgin," 303–304.

ish Israelis can enjoy the uniqueness and authenticity of "Israeli Arabic" on the movie screen voyeuristically—from a safe distance, without venturing out of their linguistic home.

MODERN HEBREW: FROM IDEA TO LANGUAGE TO STATE

A century before the making of *'Ajami*, the picture of Arabic-Hebrew relations on location in Palestine was quite the opposite. An early twentieth-century ethnographer with a camera would have documented not the influence of Hebrew on Israeli Arabic, but the influence of Arabic on Palestinian Hebrew. The role of Arabic in the formation of Modern (Israeli) Hebrew, all but forgotten today, left its traces throughout the literary works discussed in this book. Although Israeli Hebrew is now a living, breathing national language, it began as an *idea*, and it has never quite stopped being one; Gilles Deleuze and Félix Guattari have called Hebrew "a mythic language," one that "still possesses the quality of an active dream."[16] The idea of Hebrew as the spiritual ether of the Jewish state goes back at least as far as 1879, when a Russian Jew named Eliezer Ben-Yehuda wrote an article called "A Burning Question" in which he fervently argued for the linkage between linguistic and national revival. Zionist settlement in Palestine had not yet commenced, and Ben-Yehuda's idea was so controversial that he struggled to find a publisher.[17] Paradoxically, the choice of Hebrew was predicated on its history as the language of the Bible, even though Zionism itself was a primarily secular movement that embraced the idea of a secularized Jewish language.[18]

Initially, Hebrew was not a universally popular or self-evident choice even among Zionists. Hebrew did not take hold as a spoken language in Palestine until the decade leading up to the First World War, with the wave of ideological Russian Jewish immigrants known as the Second *'Aliya*; its progress was incremental, realized largely through Hebrew-language primary education. As one old-timer recalls, "No, no, they [the parents] didn't speak Hebrew at home—they spoke Yiddish—but they would smack us kids if *we* didn't speak Hebrew. Our Hebrew in those days was a jumble:

16 Deleuze and Guattari, "What Is a Minor Literature?," 25.

17 See Harshav, *Language in Time of Revolution*, 84 and Stavans, *Resurrecting Hebrew*, 33.

18 The dueling secular and religious-national facets of Zionism and, subsequently, of Israel resulted in unresolved internal conflicts both vis-à-vis Israel's non-Jewish minorities and within its Jewish population. For example, Israeli society is split between those who support exemptions and special privileges for ultra-Orthodox Jewish communities versus those who demand that they serve in the armed forces and pay income taxes. Advocates of Jewish settlement in Palestinian territories often adopt theological terminology; some detractors invoke secular Zionist terms. In *The Arab Jews*, Yehouda Shenhav discusses the aporias of Zionist ideology in terms of its relation to religiosity as well as its Orientalist perceptions of Arab Jews.

a word in Turkish, a word in Hebrew, a word in Yiddish, a word in Arabic. But we called it Hebrew."[19] In the end, Ben-Yehuda's revolutionary vision succeeded beyond his wildest dreams. Less than half a century after the publication of his "burning question," the connection among land, language, and sovereignty became doctrinal, and a genuinely Hebrew-speaking society was formed. In present-day Israel, Hebrew is used in all aspects of public and private life. Poetry, street signs, café menus, textbooks, and military orders are all written in Hebrew; Hebrew is spoken at home, in the streets, in the army and the university, in board rooms and back rooms, and on television and radio. In short, Modern Hebrew seems nothing less than a miraculous success story, the tale of a language wrested from the jaws of historical oblivion and rejuvenated against all odds. Moreover, Hebrew is now spoken by nearly a million and a half Palestinian Israelis, in addition to thousands of foreign "guest" workers, making it impossible to define it as a strictly Jewish language.

Yet the blinding success of Modern Hebrew masks another, far less triumphant tale: the fate of all *other* languages in Israel. Hebrew hegemony was realized through the persistent stigmatization and suppression of "Diasporic" languages. In many respects, this scenario is not without historical precedent. In post-Enlightenment Europe, Romantic nationalist ideologues of the late eighteenth and nineteenth centuries championed the linkage between national identity and a single language, engendering policies of linguistic centralization.[20] The top-down creation of "national" languages usually entailed the repression of other languages or dialects.[21] Nonetheless, the story of Modern Hebrew is exceptional in the audacity of its vision and forcefulness of its realization. In the case of Hebrew, one could say that it was not even the state that created the language so much as the *language* that created the state. It entailed not only linguistic centralization or the privileging of one language or dialect over others, but the reinvention of a traditional, liturgical language as an all-encompassing, everyday spoken and written medium, carried out through the successful inculcation of nationalist monolingualism.[22]

19 Amos Oz, *Po va-sham be-erets yisra'el bi-stav 1982*, 155–156 and *In the Land of Israel*, 198, Goldberg-Bartura's translation.

20 Shohamy, *Language Policy*, 26. See also Safran, "Nationalism"; May, *Language and Minority Rights*; Bourdieu, *Language and Symbolic Power*, esp. chap. 1; Anderson, *Imagined Communities*, esp. chap. 5, "Old Languages, New Models"; and Yildiz, *Beyond the Mother Tongue*, 4–10.

21 May (2001) reports on the historical processes that made certain language varieties gain the status and prestige of national languages "while other languages have been 'minoritized' and, most often, 'stigmatized'" (May, *Language and Minority Rights* [2001], 127, cited in Shohamy, *Language Policy*, 27). It became accepted to perceive all "other" languages as threats.

22 See Segal, *New Sound*, 4.

The demise of Diasporic Jewish languages and literatures is most often associated with Yiddish, a tragic casualty of the Nazi genocide, Stalinist repression, the cultural assimilation of North American Jewry, and Israel's language policies.[23] Equally devastating, but hardly acknowledged, is the eradication of Arabic-based Jewish culture following the mass emigration of Jews from the Arab world. Although Arabic is nominally Israel's second official language, Israel was created not as a bilingual nation but as a monolingual *Hebrew* state.[24] In 1952, David Ben Gurion, Israel's first prime minister and the father figure of the state, declared in the Knesset (Israeli Parliament) that "the State of Israel is a Jewish state and this is indicated by the Law of Return and *by the Hebrew language*."[25] If anything, the second-class status of the Arabic language simply mirrored and marked that of Palestinian Arabs in Israel, who after 1948 were transformed into a national minority and second-class citizens. Israel's destruction of a large number of Palestinian villages during and after the 1948 war is a well-known historical fact. In the linguistic arena, this process of erasure continued well after 1948 with the gradual and ongoing removal of Arabic from the historic as well as the living map of the country. Concurrently, Israel's language policies systematically destroyed Arabic as a Jewish language, putting an abrupt and tragic end to the illustrious history of Jewish thought and creativity in Arabic—a history that reached back as far as pre-Islamic poetry.

This purposeful remapping of language and identity—Hebrew for Jews, Arabic for Arabs—continues to be enacted through social practices and the media as well as through separate residential patterns and educational systems for Jewish and Palestinian Israelis. It has been extraordinarily fateful, albeit in different ways, for both Palestinians and Mizraḥim, reinforcing a separate and politically subordinate identity for Palestinians in Israel while stripping Mizraḥi Jews of their identities and pasts. As Zvi Ben-Dor writes, "The founding fathers had two groups in mind: Hebrew-speaking Jews, and Arabic-speaking Arabs. Nothing was supposed to exist in the middle, between the two groups, and it was in this 'in-between' that Arabic speaking Jews found themselves."[26] That in-between space is

23 On the question of Yiddish and Hebrew in Palestine, see Chaver, *What Must Be Forgotten*.

24 The British mandate had specified English, Arabic, and Hebrew as the official languages of Palestine. In 1948, the new State of Israel took over the British regulation and dropped English, but "maintained a *de facto* role for English, after Hebrew but before Arabic" (Spolsky, "Situation of Arabic in Israel," 227). See also Suleiman, *War of Words*, 144; Spolsky and Shohamy, "Language in Israeli Society and Education," 101; and Kuzar, *Hebrew and Zionism*, 9.

25 Fisherman and Fishman, "'Official Languages' of Israel," 505, quoted in Suleiman, *War of Words*, 152, my emphasis.

26 Ben-Dor, "Eyb, hshuma, infajarat qunbula," 35, translation by oznik.com.

the no-man's-land, the space of cultural encounter whose history this book seeks to narrate.

HEBREW AND ARABIC IN PRE-STATE PALESTINE: HEBREW ORIENTALISM

For centuries prior to Zionist settlement, small communities composed of Sephardi, Moghrebi (North African), and Ashkenazi Jews resided in Ottoman Palestine, mainly in Jerusalem, Hebron, Safad, and Tiberias, and beginning in the mid-nineteenth century, in Jaffa as well.[27] Now known as the "old *yishuv*," these mixed communities of Jews were multilingual. Through commerce and other forms of social interaction, Yiddish-speaking Ashkenazi Jews acquired knowledge of Arabic and Judezmo (Judeo-Spanish), while Sephardi and Moghrebi Jews as well as Muslim and Christian Arabs often spoke a smattering of Yiddish.[28] At this point, Hebrew was not widely spoken in Palestine, although it did serve as a lingua franca between Jews of different ethnicities.[29] Jewish attitudes toward Arabic in Ottoman Palestine were neutral: Arabic was simply part of the social environment, just as Christian and Muslim Arabs were indigenous local inhabitants whose presence was assumed. In memoirs of both Jews and non-Jews from Ottoman Palestine and in Hebrew-language short stories and novellas by "native" Palestinian Jewish writers, relations between Sephardi and Moghrebi Jews and their Christian and Muslim neighbors are typically depicted as cordial or warm, replete with mutual exchanges of food and gifts on holidays, shared extrareligious customs and practices, and even shared wet nurses.[30]

The first wave of Zionist settlement in Palestine, referred to in Israeli historiography as the First *'Aliya* (literally, "ascent"), commenced in 1881–1882. This wave consisted mostly of Eastern European Jews, although it also included a religiously motivated group of Jews from Yemen.[31] It was during the Second *'Aliya* (1904–1914) that the "new *yishuv*," the emerging Jewish community in pre-state Palestine, underwent a genuine ideological

27 Justin McCarthy puts the Jewish population of Palestine as approximately 10,000 in the 1860s. In 1893 there were 18,000 to 29,000 Jews in Palestine; by World War I there were 55,000 to 60,000. See McCarthy, *Population of Palestine*, 13–34.

28 For more on the multilingual background of Ottoman Palestine, see Spolsky and Shohamy, "Language in Israeli Society and Education," 96–97.

29 Segal, *New Sound*, 26; Saposnik, *Becoming Hebrew*, 25, and Kuzar, *Hebrew and Zionism*, 7.

30 The most oft-cited of these memoirs is Eliyahu Eliachar, *Lihiyot 'im yehudim* (in English, Elie Eliachar, *Living with Jews*), but the writings of Ya'akov Yehoshua and others provide similar accounts. See Tamari, *Mountain against the Sea* and Alcalay, *After Jews and Arabs*.

31 See Shimony, *'Al saf ha-ge'ula*, 21; the book's introduction provides a good summary of Jewish-Arab relations during the first and second *'aliyot*.

transformation. The Zionist program was deeply indebted to the idea of the "new Jew" or "new Hebrew man," the antithesis of the Diaspora Jew.[32] This vision idealized the biblical past, a time when (in the Zionist imagination) Jews enjoyed political sovereignty, worked their own land, and spoke Hebrew. It portrayed Jewish history in the Diaspora as a dark era of oppression and suffering that precipitated spiritual and physical decline. Accordingly, Zionism privileged biblical Hebrew while denigrating Diasporic Jewish languages such as Yiddish, as well as postbiblical (rabbinic) Hebrew, which was heavily influenced by Aramaic.

To make themselves into "new Jews," however, the early Ashkenazi Zionists needed local models. Toward this end, they looked to the "natives," the Palestinian Arabs, romanticizing the *fellahin* (peasants) and Bedouin (nomadic shepherds) as personifications of the landscape.[33] Photographs from early twentieth-century Palestine often feature European Jews dressed in Bedouin shepherd garb or on horseback (see Figure 1).[34] As Yael Zerubavel observes, the hybrid figure of the "Hebrew Bedouin" was "one of the options that emerged out of this attempt to bridge over historical gaps and offer an alternative vision of the past and the future."[35] Some Ashkenazi Zionists also typecast Jewish immigrants from Yemen as living relics of their biblical forebears, telluric Jews with a natural connection to the land, who were encouraged to immigrate to Palestine to replace local Arab workers and provide "Hebrew labor."[36] Arabisms in Hebrew speech were a trend among the youth of the First and Second *'Aliya* and, in particular, among members of the *Ha-shomer* (the Guardsmen), a paramilitary underground organization formed in 1909.[37] In the words of one memoirist, "From the days of *Hashomer* to the *Palmach*—we were dying to be like them [the Arabs] . . . to talk like them, to walk like them, we imitated them in everything. . . . We regarded them as the model

32 See, for example, Harshav, *Language in Time of Revolution*, 17–23.

33 "This encounter began under the sign of a myth of autochthony, a project of inventing a new Hebrew culture, almost out of whole cloth, and for this very reason it required the mask of the Arab. The invention of the Hebrew went hand in hand together with the invention of the Arab, and therefore the characteristic experience of this new culture was of this imaginary yet coherent space that contained the two within it and that contemporaries recognized as 'the Orient'" (Eyal, *Disenchantment*, 2).

34 See Zerubavel, "Memory," 315; and Eyal, *Disenchantment*, 43.

35 See Zerubavel, "Memory," 316. Zionist settlers also adopted the cultural model of the Russian peasantry. Connecting the two, Itamar Even-Zohar attributes the first (Orientalist) trend in large part to nineteenth-century Romantic norms and "Oriental" stereotypes in Russia: "these were the options that an adjacent, accessible culture provided." See Even-Zohar, "Emergence," 180–181, and Saposnik, *Becoming Hebrew*, 183.

36 For example, see Saposnik, *Becoming Hebrew*, 173–177.

37 Zerubavel, "Memory," 325; and Saposnik, *Becoming Hebrew*, 162.

Figure 1. The Hebrew Bedouin: *Hashomer* men in the early twentieth century. Courtesy of the Pinchas Lavon Institute for Labour Movement Research, Tel Aviv.

of the native. . . . Anyone who knew how to chat in Arabic seemed more worthy in our eyes."[38]

During this early stage of nation building, Arabic words were "self-consciously deployed" in literary depictions of the new lives of Jewish laborers in Palestine to evoke an authentic, colloquial flavor.[39] Similarly, a number of leading Ashkenazi writers of Hebrew in Palestine (e.g., Brenner, Arielli, Frishman, Smilansky) idealized Arabs, their language, and their culture as paragons of native authenticity, producing a subgenre of Hebrew Orientalist literature.[40] These were complemented by translations of classical Arabic poetry into Hebrew by Palestinian Sephardim (members of the Arabic-speaking Sephardi elite of the old *yishuv*) such as Abraham Shalom Yahuda; many of their translations were published in the *Palestine Almanac* (*Lu'aḥ erets yisra'el*, Jerusalem, 1896–1916).[41] In the 1920s through 1940s, other Palestinian Sephardim including Yitzḥak Shami, Yehuda Burla, Shoshana Shababo, and Mordekhai Tabib wrote stories and novellas

38 Ben-Yehuda, *Beyn ha-sfirot*, 175, quoted in Zerubavel, "Memory," 325.

39 Saposnik, *Becoming Hebrew*, 162.

40 See Peleg, *Orientalism and the Hebrew Imagination*; Barzilay, "The Arab in Modern Hebrew Literature"; and Coffin, "Image of the Arab in Modern Hebrew Literature."

41 Amit-Kochavi, "Integrating Arab Culture," and idem, "Israeli Jewish Nation Building."

about the traditional lives of Palestinian Arabs and Sephardi Jews.[42] Pesaḥ Bar-Adon, a Polish Jewish painter and archaeologist who immigrated to Palestine in 1925, lived among Bedouin tribes and furthered the romantic view of the Arabs in his 1934 memoir.[43] Such examples indicate the varied ways Palestinian Arabs and the Arabic language figured in the Hebrew cultural and literary imagination from the earliest days of Zionist settlement in Palestine.

Admiration of Palestinian Arabs and of Arabic was a fixture in writings of Eliezer Ben-Yehuda himself. As Benjamin Harshav recounts, Ben-Yehuda was deeply impressed by the Arab passengers even on the ship to Palestine: "Tall, strong men . . . I sensed that they felt themselves citizens of that land," while "I come to that land as a stranger, a foreigner."[44] Ben-Yehuda extended his admiration to the old *yishuv*'s Palestinian Sephardim, whom he characterized as a "natural community," in contrast to the Orthodox Ashkenazim who were "not natural human beings" leading organic lives.[45] He confesses,

> Why should I deny it? It is a better, much nicer impression that was made on me by the Sephardim. Most of them were dignified, handsome, all were splendid in their Oriental clothing, their manner respectable, their behavior pleasant, almost all of them spoke Hebrew with the owner of [the journal] *Havatselet*, and their language was fluent, natural, rich in words, rich in fixed idioms of speech, and the dialect was so original, *so sweet and Oriental!*[46]

Later, he adds, "I mentioned this detail here incidentally because it is one of the reasons that influenced me later in my relationship toward Sephardim and Ashkenazim."[47] By this he meant the question of Modern Hebrew's projected character. The accent and pronunciation of Modern Hebrew were then the subject of heated debates—debates that, as Arieh Saposnik has argued, were part of Zionism's broader negotiation of

42 See Alcalay, *After Jews and Arabs*, 214; Hever, *Ha-sipur ve-ha-le'om*, chaps. 3 and 4; Tamari, "Ishaq Shami and the Predicament of the Arab Jew in Palestine," in *Mountain against the Sea*, 150–66; Halevy, *Bat ha-mizraḥ ha-ḥadasha*; and Peleg, *Orientalism and the Hebrew Imagination*, 37–39. Although he was Ashkenazi, as a member of the old *yishuv* who represented interethnic relations, Ya'akov Ḥurgin should also be studied with this group.

43 Bar-Adon, *Be-oheley midbar*, cited in Zerubavel, "Memory," 326.

44 Ben-Yehuda, *He-ḥalom*, 84, quoted in Harshav, *Language in Time of Revolution*, 158.

45 Ben-Yehuda, *He-ḥalom*, 95, quoted in Harshav, *Language in Time of Revolution*, 158.

46 Ben-Yehuda, *He-ḥalom*, 97, quoted in Harshav, *Language in Time of Revolution*, 158, emphasis in original.

47 Ben-Yehuda, *He-ḥalom*, 107, quoted in Harshav, *Language in Time of Revolution*, 159. Saposnik also quotes Ben-Yehuda's arguments in favor of the Sephardic accent ("the Sephardic accent is in any case more pleasing and proper"; *Becoming Hebrew*, 72).

"East" and "West" vis-à-vis the emerging national culture.[48] Should Modern Hebrew pronunciation be modeled on Ashkenazi Hebrew, Sephardi Hebrew, or a compromise between the two? In addition, there was the pressing issue of new coinages: should they be derived from roots in the existing Hebrew lexicon (and if so, exclusively from biblical Hebrew or from all layers of the language), adapted from European languages, or borrowed from Arabic?[49] Ben-Yehuda, who opposed non-Semitic influences on the language, argued for using all available Arabic roots to enrich Hebrew.[50] In the preface to his monumental Hebrew dictionary, he wrote,

> I particularly compared the roots of our language with those of Arabic . . . since this consistent similarity makes the reader realize how close these two languages are in nature and spirit, so much so that they are almost *one and the same*. It is this realization that explains and justifies my constant practice of borrowing handfuls of Arabic in order to fill the voids in our language wherever its vocabulary lacks some root from which the necessary word may smoothly be coined.[51]

When the newly reconfigured Language Committee reconvened in 1911 with the need for new coinages heading its agenda, it sought members "whose knowledge of both languages, Hebrew and Arabic, is beyond any doubt."[52] Its charter, written by Ben-Yehuda, approved by the scholar and educator David Yellin (whom we will encounter in chapter 2), and published in 1912, specified two goals: first, to prepare the language for the full range of quotidian demands and, second, to "preserve" its "Oriental quality."[53] It was later decided that all Jewish schools should employ a Hebrew "pronunciation" teacher from among the Arabic-speaking Syrian Jews of Aleppo, despite the fact that the vast majority of schoolchildren were of Ashkenazi origin.[54] However, "the Oriental nature of pronunciation [Ben-Yehuda] dreamed of was contrary to the whole mentality and intonations

48 Saposnik, *Becoming Hebrew*, esp. 160.

49 See Harshav, *Language in Time of Revolution*, chap. 27; and Segal, *New Sound*, chap. 2.

50 Harshav, *Language in Time of Revolution*, 160.

51 Ben-Yehuda, *Complete Dictionary of Ancient and Modern Hebrew*, 10, cited in Amit-Kochavi, "Integrating Arab Culture," 53; emphasis in original.

52 Harshav, *Language in Time of Revolution*, 84.

53 Academy of the Hebrew Language, *Collection of Documents*, 31, quoted in Harshav, *Language in Time of Revolution*, 159.

54 Ben-Yehuda, *He-ḥalom*, 207, quoted in Harshav, *Language in Time of Revolution*, 159. Segal notes that a preference for the Sephardic stress system was expressed as early as 1895, in the first documented discussion of the new accent for Hebrew by a group of pedagogues in Palestine (*New Sound*, 53). Even-Zohar claims that Ben-Yehuda (as he lay ill in a French hospital) was convinced of the preferred status of the Sephardi accent by a Christian priest; see "Emergence," 178–179.

of the new immigrants, and never took root."[55] From 1909 to 1913, a critical period of time between the Young Turk revolution and the First World War, the language question became a subject of vociferous contention between the Ashkenazi Zionist leadership and a small group of Arabic-speaking Sephardi notables. As native Palestinian Jews, the Sephardi leadership supported Zionist settlement but advocated equitable relations with Christian and Muslim Palestinians and argued that Ashkenazi immigrants to Palestine should adopt Arabic language and culture; their argument failed to divert the Ashkenazi leadership from its adamant Hebraism.[56]

Nonetheless, despite these unsuccessful proposals to make Modern Hebrew sound like Arabic, or to make Arabic the everyday language of the Jewish community, the Arabic language continued to serve the Hebrew revival as an ideal. As late as the 1930s and early 1940s, some Hebrew pedagogues in the *yishuv* argued that the study of Arabic grammar provided the best means for Jews to acquire a deeper knowledge and understanding of their own language, Hebrew.[57] Similar attitudes underscored the founding of the School of Oriental Studies at the Hebrew University in 1927; at a related meeting, David Yellin declared that "[t]he Hebrew language demands knowledge of the Semitic languages, the development of the Oriental spirit."[58] Meanwhile, native Palestinian Sephardim continued promoting Arabic as a counterpart to Hebrew in the *yishuv*. For example, the scholar Abraham Elmaleḥ (1885–1967) published a Hebrew translation of the Arabic classic *Kalila wa-dimna* (a medieval collection of animal fables) in 1926 and a Hebrew-Arabic dictionary in 1928.[59]

This is not to say that prior to the creation of the State of Israel in 1948 Zionist intellectuals and writers held uniformly positive views of Arabic language and culture, let alone of Arabs; Zionist attitudes toward Arabic were ambivalent and conflicted from the outset.[60] In contrast to Ben-Yehuda, who opposed lexical borrowing from non-Semitic languages, other members of the Language Council argued that "despite the fact that the

55 Harshav, *Language in Time of Revolution*, 160; see also Segal, *New Sound*, 4. Segal also clarifies that the so-called Sephardi accent was never truly Sephardi. From his comments from a 1903 meeting, it is evident that "Ben-Yehuda is proposing a Sephardic Hebrew but it is one that is based on an Ashkenazic perception. It is 'Sephardic' only to the ears of its Ashkenazic speakers" (*New Sound*, 62).

56 See Campos, *Ottoman Brothers*, esp. chap. 7; and Lital Levy, "Jewish Writers in the Arab East," esp. chap. 4. See also Saposnik, *Becoming Hebrew*, 178–180.

57 See Halperin, "Babel in Zion," chap. 5, esp. 34–39. Arabic-language instruction through the 1930s and 1940s was hindered by the dearth of adequate textbooks and did not emphasize knowledge of the regional colloquial language.

58 Halperin, "Babel in Zion," 35 (Halperin's translation).

59 See Elmaleḥ, *Sipurey kalila ve-dimna*, and idem, *Milon 'ivri-'aravi.*

60 For a comprehensive and nuanced discussion of early Zionists' conflicted attitudes toward East and West more generally, see Saposnik, *Becoming Hebrew*, chap. 7.

Arabic language is our sister language in the family of Semitic languages, it has no foundation in our psyche."[61] In 1912 and 1913 articles appeared in the Hebrew press dismissing the notion that Arabic culture could exert any real influence upon the emerging Hebrew culture, given the perceived cultural superiority of Jews to Arabs in Palestine; some writers went so far as to claim that there was no such thing as a true Arab culture.[62] One of the authors, the Hebrew publicist Ya'akov Rabinowitz, denounced the nineteenth-century Arabic-language Jewish Egyptian writer Ya'qub Sanu' (James Sanua) as a "blow to Hebrew nationalism."[63] Rabinowitz also targeted the activities of Nissim Malul (1892–1959), a Palestinian-born Sephardi writer of Arabic and Hebrew who promoted the teaching of Arabic in the *yishuv* as an integral part of the national revival.[64] In a heated three-part response to Rabinowitz, Malul presciently countered that should the Jewish community desist from teaching Arabic to its children, "we will become an isolated nation, separate from all other peoples living under Ottoman rule."[65] Years later, Vladimir (Ze'ev) Jabotinsky, the Russian-born ultranationalist writer and founder of right-wing Revisionist Zionism, stringently objected to the notion that Modern Hebrew should sound like Arabic. In a 1930 publication titled *The Hebrew Accent* he "claimed that the Semitic sounds of Arabic were but a series of noises without distinction or character. . . . Modern Hebrew, then, must rid itself of Arabic sounds and adopt the noble sounds of the Mediterranean languages."[66] In short, if many early twentieth-century Zionists romanticized Palestinian Arabs and the Arabic language as models for the Hebrew revival, others insisted that Arabic had no place in the emerging Hebrew state. Even in this early phase, attitudes toward Arabic were correlated with ideological positions on the political and cultural character of the projected state.

Later, in the early 1940s, the Young Hebrews, a small, informal group of artists and intellectuals better known as the "Canaanites," sought to redefine the emerging nation as a strictly "Hebrew" entity rooted in the ancient Middle East, rejecting its identity as "Jewish."[67] Initially inspired

61 Saulson, *Institutionalized Language Planning*, 134, quoted in Suleiman, *War of Words*, 140.

62 Saposnik, *Becoming Hebrew*, 269n17. Saposnik cites three articles from *Ha-po'el ha-tsa'ir*, by Avi Tsela, Ya'akov Rabinowitz, and Ben ha-Dor, respectively.

63 Campos, "A 'Shared Homeland,'" 358; see also Behar and Benite, *Modern Middle Eastern Jewish Thought*, 65. For more on Rabinowitz and his views toward the Orient and Sephardi Jewry, see Saposnik, *Becoming Hebrew*, 159, 172, and 269n17.

64 On Malul, see Levy, "Jewish Writers in the Arab East," 218–221; and Behar and Benite, *Modern Middle Eastern Jewish Thought*, 62–63.

65 Behar and Benite, *Modern Middle Eastern Jewish Thought*, 66.

66 Kaplan, "Between East and West," 133. See also Harshav, *Language in Time of Revolution*, 160. For the original, see Jabotinsky, *Ha-mivta ha-'ivri*.

67 Peleg, *Orientalism and the Hebrew Imagination*, 132; Kuzar, *Hebrew and Zionism*, 12–13 and chap. 4; Nocke, *Place of the Mediterranean*, 200–208; and Diamond, *Homeland or Holy Land*.

by European right-wing movements and particularly by Italian fascism, Canaanism viewed both Judaism and Islam as primitive forces at odds with secular enlightenment. The Canaanites (referring to the ancient pre-Israelite Canaanites of antiquity) rejected the idea of an Arab collective or Arab sovereignty while accepting Arabs as individuals. In a radicalization of mainstream Zionist themes, they advocated divestment of all remaining ties to the Jewish Diaspora and the creation of a new, pan-Semitic polity in the region that would unite various non-Muslim ethnic groups and "redeem" local Muslims from the purported darkness of Islam and from pan-Arabism. As opposed to the earlier ideal of the "Hebrew Bedouin," in this case the reimagining of Hebrew nativity was modeled not on but *around* "the Arabs," and supposedly in collaboration with them.

While the Canaanites' political vision failed, their artistic vision had a profound effect upon Israeli culture. Their calls for "the creation of a native, Hebrew art rooted in the local landscape and devoid of any foreign, especially diasporic, Jewish elements" and corresponding belief that the key to this art entailed a "pure" Hebrew vernacular, influenced the development of both visual art and literature in Israel. Israeli Hebrew culture embraced the "pre-Diasporic" biblical past and "post-Diasporic" contemporary Hebrew while suppressing layers of the language associated with Diasporic Judaism. The story of the Canaanites represents an ambiguous position toward Arabs and Arabic, as the Canaanites effectively attempted to Orientalize Hebrew language and culture while bypassing the Islamic character of the Arab Middle East—or perhaps more accurately, while reconfiguring it in a primordial manner as "Eastern."[68] Nonetheless, their idea of a true Hebrew culture was based upon the vision of a shared regional heritage, even if Arabic cultural influences were recoded as "Canaanite" or as "Eastern" rather than "Arab."

Views of Arabic in the pre-state period were thus complex and perhaps even self-contradictory in their Orientalism—a discursive split indicating the colonial nature of the Zionist project vis-à-vis "native" Arabs and "Oriental" Jews.[69] In the final analysis, however, those views were vastly more favorable than those that emerged during statehood. Even in 1946, as tensions between Palestinian Arabs and Zionists were reaching a climax, the noted European Jewish scholar Shlomo Dov Goiten wrote in a pamphlet that "Learning Arabic is a *part of Zionism*, a part of the return

68 Peleg, *Orientalism and the Hebrew Imagination*, 132.

69 Shenhav writes, "Zionism (like other colonial enterprises) created a politics of belonging and difference and spoke in a number of voices, yet, at the same time, declined to acknowledge the cultural ambivalences of its own creation and attempted to enfold it within closed binary distinctions" (*Arab Jews*, 71).

to the Hebrew language and to the Semitic Orient."[70] Given the historic role of Arabic in imagining the Hebrew national self, how did Arabic then come to be imagined as Hebrew's Other? How is it that the very language that elicited admiration and even envy from figures such as Ben-Yehuda is now viewed by Israelis in such disparaging terms? Although 1948 represents a major turning point in Arab-Jewish relations, the shift in popular perceptions of Arabic had commenced well before.

Broadly, the answer involves both the consolidation of Hebrew hegemony and the souring of relations between Palestinian Arabs and Zionist settlers as early as 1913 but especially from the late 1920s, with conflict intensifying after the 1936 Arab Revolt. As Palestinian-Jewish relations deteriorated and the integrationist option appeared increasingly unviable, the Arab/Palestinian gradually assumed the role of the Other in the Zionist imagination. In tandem, Arabic lost its appeal as a template for Hebrew. The establishment of the state in 1948 was the final straw inverting the balance of power between Arabic and Hebrew: Hebrew was now a sovereign national language, while Arabic became the language of a newly created national minority, the defeated remnant of Palestinian Arabs. In the years that followed, even when Arabic continued to serve as a model for Hebrew, for example by providing sources for Hebrew place-names, the establishment's approach to Arabic was no longer one of emulation, but one of appropriation and domination. At the same time, Arabic was also perceived as the language of the regional majority that threatened Israel's existence. Additional factors including the Holocaust, Jewish immigration from Arab lands, and the Cold War led Israel to turn increasingly to the West both politically and culturally, isolating the state from its regional environment.[71] On the international front, this turn was reflected in a decisive political alignment with the United States and Western Europe. Domestically, Israel's decisive turn to the West perpetuated the marginalization of Mizraḥi Jews by the Ashkenazi cultural and political elite.[72] As we shall see in later chapters, the impact of these choices still reverberates within Palestinian and Mizraḥi literature in Israel.

70 S. D. Goiten, *On the Teaching of Arabic*, 8, quoted in Halperin, "Orienting Language," 481, Halperin's translation and emphasis. As Halperin and numerous other scholars have pointed out, such attitudes were to some extent a continuation of the nineteenth- and early twentieth-century German Jewish scholarly fascination with, and reclamation of, the Sephardi intellectual legacy; I expand on this point in chapter 2.

71 Saposnik, *Becoming Hebrew*, 187–188. For more on how this decision played out over time and continued to be contested in Israeli public discourse and culture, see Levy, "Whirling Dervish."

72 Peleg, *Orientalism and the Hebrew Imagination*, 135.

STATEHOOD: ISRAEL'S LANGUAGE POLICIES AND MIZRAḤI IMMIGRATION

Prior to 1948, immigration to Palestine was dominated by Yiddish-speaking Ashkenazi Jews.[73] The struggle to establish Hebrew's primacy over Yiddish, German, Russian, and the other native languages of Zionist settlers was referred to in terms such as *kibush ha-safa* (conquering the language) and *milḥemet safot* (a war of languages). It was summarized in a popular "Speak Hebrew" campaign associated with the slogan *Yehudi, daber 'ivrit* (Jew, speak Hebrew!).[74] Hebrew eventually won the war, but for decades Yiddish was still seen as Hebrew's primary threat; evidence of the persecution of Yiddish could be found even into the 1970s.[75]

By 1948, Modern Hebrew was spoken by the majority of the Jewish population.[76] Then came statehood and soon after a flood of immigrants from Europe, Asia, and Africa. Sephardi and Middle Eastern Jews spoke a host of Jewish languages (Judeo-Arabic,[77] Judeo-Spanish/Judezmo, Judeo-Persian, and neo-Aramaic, among others), in addition to the standard languages spoken in their countries of origin, while European Jews usually spoke both Yiddish and standard European languages. In this modern-day Babel, Hebrew was viewed as a necessary instrument of social unification and the key to integration into the national collective. But the implementation of a monolingual ideology went well beyond questions of exigency.[78]

73 In the early decades of Zionist settlement, the German-speaking Ashkenazi intellectual elite advocated using German for higher education in Palestine. In a famous 1913 incident referred to as the Language War, Jewish students violently demonstrated against the proposal to use German in a technological school in Haifa. By 1918, the use of German in schools was banned. See Saposnik, *Becoming Hebrew*, 213–232; Segal, *New Sound*, 44–47; Spolsky and Shohamy, *Languages of Israel*, 198–199; idem, "Language in Israeli Society and Education," 98; and Suleiman, *War of Words*, 17.
74 See, for instance, Shohamy, *Language Policy*, 28. Another formulation was "'Ivri, daber 'ivrit!" (Hebrew [person], speak Hebrew!).
75 Spolsky, "Hebrew and Israeli Identity," 187.
76 Bachi, "Statistical Analysis," 179–247, cited in Spolsky and Shohamy, "Language in Israeli Society and Education," 99. See also Fishman, *Yiddish*, 406.
77 "Judeo-Arabic" denotes both the Jewish dialects of colloquial Arabic spoken by Jews in the Arab world (and by their descendants) and the written language employed by Jews in Arabic-speaking regions (for secular and religious purposes). Written Judeo-Arabic was based largely on classical Arabic, with numerous loanwords from Hebrew and Aramaic as well as influences from vernacular Arabic. Like Yiddish and Judeo-Spanish, it was written in Hebrew characters. For clarity, throughout this book I use "Judeo-Arabic" to denote the written variant only, referring to the spoken variants as Jewish colloquial dialects of Arabic.
78 Spolsky and Shohamy, "Language in Israeli Society and Education," 97, 100. The authors conclude, "The achievement of this ideology [of Hebrew monolingualism] has been high. . . . The cost too has been high. A once-multilingual population is on the way to becoming monolingual

After 1948, the native Jewish communities of the Arab world found themselves caught in the political crossfire of the conflict. Over the next two decades, under widely varying degrees of political, economic, and social pressure, some seven hundred thousand Jews from Arabic-speaking countries immigrated to Israel. They were joined by waves of impoverished European immigrants including Holocaust survivors and Jews fleeing communist Romania. The result was a dramatic, unprecedented encounter of Jewish communities with conflicting expectations of life in the new state. Intensifying their culture shock, they arrived during a chaotic period of economic austerity and of existential uncertainty under constant threat of war.

The Zionist ethos demanded a total replacement of the old with the new. All new immigrants, be they Ashkenazim, Sephardim, or Arab Jews, were expected to repudiate their erstwhile identities and adopt the singular language and culture of the state, emulating the "pioneers" from the earlier waves of immigration (*ha-'olim ha-vatikim*). The Ashkenazi newcomers generally accomplished this with greater ease due to the cultural background they shared with the old-timers and because as fellow Europeans, they were placed higher in the social hierarchy (with the ironic exception of Holocaust survivors, who were referred to as "human dust"). The Ashkenazi Zionists who arrived in Palestine in the late nineteenth and early twentieth centuries had been motivated by ideological factors; those who chose to stay in Palestine were more amenable to changing their languages and identities. For them, it was ultimately a matter of choice, even if, as Yael Chaver has shown, it was a prolonged process characterized by "profound personal and communal ambivalence."[79] Although European Jewish immigration during the Mandate period was driven less by Zionist ideology than by political and economic pressures, by then the *yishuv* was already established, its ideology becoming formalized. After 1948, the old-timers controlled the new state's major economic, social, political, and educational institutions, which they had founded during the Mandate. The new immigrants arriving in the 1950s thus found themselves latecomers to a society whose established rules and norms eluded them.

Most European Jews—like other Europeans of their time—believed that Europe was the seat of modern civilization and culture, and considered non-Europeans culturally backward. They did not exempt their

or at the best bilingual. The national capacity in language (Brecht et al. 1995) has been frittered away. The rich cultural heritage of the two thousand years of Jewish culture and life in the Diaspora has been undermined. The submersion program has produced serious watering-down of ideals and principles" (ibid., 100).

79 Chaver, *What Must Be Forgotten*, xiii.

co-religionists from this worldview. In the massive waves of immigration, craftsmen from tiny hamlets in the Atlas Mountains or Kurdistan arrived alongside educated, white-collar professionals from cosmopolitan Cairo and Beirut; the Ashkenazi-led establishment did not differentiate between them. Sephardi and Arab Jews were treated as social inferiors, collectively stigmatized as "Asiatics" and "Levantines."[80] Upon disembarking from planes, many were sprayed with DDT, a scene that has been replayed repeatedly in Mizraḥi literature. They typically spent months or years in squalid tent camps (*ma'abarot*) lacking electricity, running water, and basic sanitary conditions, from which many were assigned to "development towns" (remote settlements far from urban centers) or to slum-like urban neighborhoods. Lacking economic opportunity and plagued by unemployment and its corresponding social ailments, Mizraḥim found themselves on the bottom rung of Israel's Jewish hierarchy, with Palestinian Arabs just below them.

Furthermore, they faced a cultural impasse. Historically, Sephardi and Mizraḥi Jews were deeply connected to religious tradition, albeit of a moderate and forgiving variety. In the twentieth century, those who were no longer observant, among them many Iraqi and Egyptian Jews, were urban cosmopolitans who valued commerce and skilled professions while disdaining the agricultural labor so fetishized by Zionism. The new arrivals thus found that their values and practices clashed with those of Israel's secular, socialist society, often to their surprise and dismay—after all, this was the "Jewish" state. As for Arabic, not only was it now widely perceived as a backward and unharmonious language, but to make matters infinitely worse, it was the language of the enemy with whom the state was still at war. Arabic-speaking Jews thus threatened to collapse the distinction between Jews and Arabs.[81]

All of this explains the unique predicament of Jewish speakers of Arabic in Israel. While all new immigrants experienced hardships, while all Diasporic languages were suppressed, in practice, the dilemmas of Arabic speakers were compounded by the added misfortunes of arriving on the scene long after the Ashkenazi founders, of being socially marginalized and stigmatized as a minority population, and, worst of all, of being associated with the language and culture of the enemy—an utterly intractable problem. Thus, while Israel's language policy targeted all Diasporic Jewish languages, the implications differed from case to case. Having been

80 There is a significant body of scholarship on Mizraḥim in Israel, by Ella Shohat, Sami Shalom Chetrit, Yehouda Shenhav, Hannan Hever, and others. On the stigmatization of Mizraḥim in Israel as a sociological process, see Khazzoom, "Great Chain." On "Levantinism," see Hochberg, *In Spite of Partition*, 44–50.

81 See also Shenhav, *Arab Jews*, 193.

extirpated from mainstream Israeli society by the late 1970s, Yiddish has faded into the shadows of history, at least as far as secular Israelis are concerned. It is now perceived largely as an anachronism, a language spoken by the elderly or by hermetic ultra-Orthodox Jews living in cloistered communities.[82] On the other hand, now that it poses no threat, Yiddish no longer suffers from any major public stigma, and in recent years a small revival of interest in Yiddish and Ashkenazi culture has emerged on the cultural scene. Ladino has also been a focal point of (limited) government interest and support. Today, the history and demise of Arabic as a *Jewish* language barely registers in Israeli public consciousness.[83] Yet Arabic retains a strong presence, even a hyperpresence, within Israeli society as the "language of the Other."

The current relationship of Mizraḥim to Arabic is inseparable from the history of the Mizraḥim as a social category invented in Israel.[84] Upon arrival in Israel, Jewish immigrants from Asia and Africa were collectively and patronizingly labeled *'edot ha-mizraḥ* ("Oriental communities"), a "single category denoting an intra-Jewish ethnic group" that stripped them of ideologically unacceptable identifiers such "Arab" or "Persian."[85] Like members of "new ethnicities" in the United States, in time they "accepted the hegemonic image of identity and sameness and tried to imbue it with political meaning that was positive and assertive," becoming "Mizraḥim."[86] From the early decades of statehood, many Mizraḥim came to associate their poor treatment at the hands of the Ashkenazi elite with the governing Labor Party. Social protest movements developed in the 1970s, and the 1977 parliamentary elections resulted in the historic upset wherein Mizraḥi voters unseated the Labor Party after four decades of uninterrupted hegemony, voting in the right-wing Likud Party headed by Menahem Begin. This protest vote had more to do with the Labor Party's questionable treatment of Mizraḥim during its long reign than with the Likud Party's conservative economic, social, and political policies. Nonetheless, the party's Mizraḥi voter base also adopted its hard-line political views.

82 According to the Israeli government's official tourism website, there are currently more speakers of Judeo-Arabic dialects (300,000) than of Yiddish (200,000) in the country. See http://www.goisrael.com/Tourism_Eng/Tourist+Information/Discover+Israel/Population.htm.

83 Discussion of the issue is confined mainly to a tiny number of highbrow cultural publications such as *Ha-kivun mizraḥ* and *'Iton 77*.

84 See Shohat, "Invention of the Mizrahim."

85 Shenhav, *Arab Jews*, 193. The term *'eda* (pl. *'edot*) connotes an ethnic group or religious congregation, but in practice it is deployed exclusively in relation to Mizraḥi Jews. For more on the Hebrew terms corresponding to "race" or "ethnicity" and the struggle over Jewish identity in Israel, see Lefkowitz, *Words and Stones*, 15.

86 Ibid., 15; see also Shohat, "Invention of the Mizrahim."

Understanding these historical dynamics can help unravel the complicated tangle of Mizraḥi attitudes toward Arabs and the Arabic language. Mizraḥim are stereotypically viewed as hard-liners when it comes to relations with Palestinians and the Arab states, the "peace process," and territorial concessions, a trend that may seem counterintuitive given their origins in Arab countries. However, the stigmatization of Arabs and Arabness compelled Mizraḥim to differentiate themselves from Palestinians, often by adopting the anti-Arab sentiment already present in Israeli society.[87] This process produced inconsistent and conflicted attitudes toward Arabs and Arabness. Many first-generation Mizraḥim express ambivalent feelings toward their countries of origin, some emphasizing a high quality of life and close relations with non-Jewish neighbors and others accentuating their sense of betrayal by the Arab governments and, in some cases, by Arab publics that turned against their indigenous Jewish populations. Similarly, it is not uncommon for Mizraḥim to express affinity with aspects of Arab culture, while maintaining that "Arabs" (as a wholesale category) cannot be trusted as negotiating partners or that they are inherently intolerant of minorities—a position that, while not exclusive to Mizraḥim, has come to be associated with them in a stereotypical manner. One might see this process as a case of discourse creating its subjects, inasmuch as the performance of *mizraḥiyut* or Mizraḥi identity in Israel entailed the articulation of such attitudes. Furthermore, it should be emphasized that such viewpoints are common in Israeli society as a whole, not only among Mizraḥim, and that (as in any large sector) one finds among Mizraḥim the full spectrum of political views. Indeed, Mizraḥim have also led radical social movements; a number of leading left-wing activists in Israel are among those Sami Shalom Chetrit calls the "new Mizraḥim."[88] In short, the correlation between Mizraḥim and right-wing politics is a generalization, and even something of a cliché; but it is one with strong purchase in Israeli society and culture. I invoke it here in order to shed light upon the complicated and self-contradictory dynamics of the Mizraḥi relationship to Arabic.

87 See Chetrit, *Intra-Jewish Conflict*, 142–144. As Chetrit writes, "Over the years, Mizrahim were relabeled as right-wing warmongers, Arab-haters, and obstacles to peace—a ludicrous claim, since it was MAPAI [the Labor party] that had successfully carried out the negation of Arab Jews' Arabness. Likud simply plucked the ripe fruit." This identification with the right, as he says, "further deepened the Mizrahi-Jewish conflict of identity. Over three decades, the cultural socialization of the state had required the Mizrahim to strip away all Mizrahi and Arab cultural values and identity, perceived as the antithesis of European Zionist culture and identity; now, in return for the pact with Likud and for the dramatic rise in their national status, Mizrahim were required, and to take it upon themselves, to serve as front-line soldiers of Jewish nationalism" (ibid., 143).
88 Ibid., 202–234. See also Alcalay, *After Jews and Arabs*, 220–227.

In this vein, Zvi Ben-Dor argues that the relations of Mizraḥim to the Arabic language "are as problematic as their relations with the Arabs, perhaps even more so."[89] Among Jewish Israelis, the sound of spoken Arabic tends to connote the fear of terrorism or, at best, cheap labor associated with Palestinian day workers. The limited colloquial Arabic absorbed by Israeli Hebrew was restricted to low-register domains, most notoriously obscenities and curses, but also expressions in Israeli street slang (e.g., *sababa, 'al ha-kefak*) and names of popular foods (such as *falafel*). Very few Jewish Israelis are familiar with the high-register functions of Arabic in the literary tradition or in the Islamic *turath* (heritage), parallel to the role of Hebrew in Jewish textual culture. First-generation Arab Jews from the Levant (Iraq, Egypt, Syria, and Lebanon) are usually literate in classical Arabic, but their relationship to the language was distorted by the intense social pressure to repudiate their Arab identity. Again and again in literature, personal accounts, and scholarship, one encounters two distinct generational responses to this quandary. While the first generation of Arabic-speaking immigrants typically withered in defeated silence, many second-generation Mizraḥim purged their Hebrew of any Arabic influence and distanced themselves from Arabic culture; moreover, they were shamed by their parents' expressions of Arabness such as speaking Arabic in public or listening to Arabic music at home.

Nonetheless, despite the intense stigmatization of Arabic, many Mizraḥim continued to speak Jewish dialects of Arabic at home, and some, albeit a smaller number, still do today. As linguistic anthropologist Dan Lefkowitz observes, Mizraḥim in Israel often deflect the negative connotations and low prestige of Arabic by referring to their own dialects not as *'aravit* (Arabic), but rather as *moroka'it* ("Moroccan"), *'irakit* ("Iraqi"), and so on, disassociating them from the spoken language of Palestinian Arabs.[90] In certain social contexts, knowledge of Jewish dialects of Arabic may even foster a sense of ethnic solidarity and serve as a form of resistance to Ashkenazi hegemony over Israeli Hebrew.[91] The latent potential

89 Ben-Dor, "Eyb, hshuma, infajarat qunbula," 32, translation by oznik.com.

90 Alluding to these self-perceptions, Lefkowitz refers to the collective Jewish Arabic dialects spoken in Israel as "non-Arabic." Lefkowitz, "Conflict and Identity in Palestinian Narratives."

91 For example, in a 2001 study of Romema, a Moroccan Jewish settlement in the northern Negev desert, it was found that the community viewed Hebrew as the language of the state and therefore as the means of national inclusion, but also as the "language of the rulers" (Ashkenazi Jews) and an instrument of ethnic exclusion. While youths in the town routinely speak Hebrew with one another, they switch to Moroccan Judeo-Arabic in the presence of an Ashkenazi Jew or a member of another community whom they wish to exclude from the conversation. As such, "[t]his disjunction in the attitude towards Hebrew creates a third space into which Romemites inject [Judeo-] Arabic as a 'secret language' of intra-Jewish ethnic exclusion" (Suleiman, *War of Words*, 155).

of such linguistic "acts of identity"[92] is manifested with vital force in the Mizraḥi literature investigated in part 3 of this book.

MIZRAḤANUT AND MEDIA: ORIENTALISM, INSTRUMENTALISM, AND PRIME TIME

The official relationship toward Arabic continued to evolve after Israel's achievement of statehood in 1948. One important index of this relationship is the teaching of Arabic in Jewish schools. Arabic had been taught as a foreign language in Jewish schools even during the Mandate period.[93] From 1948 to 1967 the teaching of Arabic in Jewish schools declined; instead of training European Jews to speak Arabic, as in earlier years, the establishment relied upon the native knowledge of its new Arab Jewish immigrants to fulfill its propaganda, intelligence, and security needs. Iraqi Jews in particular served as a ready cadre of radio announcers on Israel Radio's Arabic-language broadcasts,[94] teachers of Arabic in both Arab and Jewish schools, journalists for Arabic-language Zionist newspapers, government officials assigned to work in the Arab population, and even recruits for the Mossad, Israel's spy agency.[95] Certainly, many were driven less by ideological motivations than by economic necessity, being shut out of other white-collar positions in an establishment dominated by Ashkenazi Jews. In short, Arab Jews were integral to the state apparatus when it needed their expertise in Arabic. This state of affairs produced a schizophrenic split in private and public identity; Arab Jews would listen to Egyptian singers on the radio and converse in Arabic at home while at work their intimate knowledge of Arabic was transformed into an expert familiarity with the language and culture of the enemy.[96]

Following the occupation of the West Bank and Gaza Strip in 1967, Arabic acquired new significance as the language of colonial administration

92 See Le Page and Tabouret-Keller, *Acts of Identity.*

93 Halperin, "Babel in Zion," chap. 5. As Halperin demonstrates, even in these early years, foreign language instruction in Arabic was oriented toward "'Knowing the Arab,' a methodology explicitly or implicitly tied to surveillance, control, and mastery" (28–29).

94 See Penslar, "Broadcast Orientalism," 183. Penslar notes that the Arabic-language service (which was directed at Israel's Arab population) was staffed by Iraqi Jews, but their Ashkenazi superiors would not authorize programming in the Iraqi Jewish dialect (ibid., 188).

95 See, for instance, Rejwan, *Outsider in the Promised Land*, and Shenhav, *Arab Jews*, 1–7. Gil Eyal also discusses the advisory roles played by Sephardi notables to the authorities prior to 1948; see *Disenchantment*, 48–50 and 141–144.

96 For example, Shenhav writes movingly of his father, who was recruited to work in Israeli intelligence, and his colleagues, who illustrated the ironies in Israeli policy, which stripped Arab Jews of their Arabness yet implored those working in intelligence "to go on living as Arabs by license" (*Arab Jews*, 3).

and intelligence, propelling the teaching of Arabic in Jewish schools.[97] At the same time, Arabic was and is still perceived as a low-prestige subject, its knowledge valued only for serving the state's security requirements. This "instrumentalist" agenda, rather than the aim of Arab-Jewish coexistence, let alone cultural appreciation of Mizraḥi heritage, has dictated the Israeli approach to Arabic education for decades. Writing of his own educational experiences in Israel, Zvi Ben-Dor recalls,

> The Arabic language was the most practical thing one could learn in high school—that is, if you weren't assigned to a mechanics school. The professional infrastructure for Intelligence-men-to-be was already laid out in junior high. . . . If you look at the Arabic textbook for the 7th and 8th grades . . . the very first pages will reveal brief passages about "infajarat qunbula" (a bomb exploded), or "helikubtar min thiraz 'sikurski'" (a Sikurski model helicopter). No special intelligence is needed to figure out what these particular words—and not, say, poetry by [the Syrian poet] Nizar Qabbani—are doing in a textbook for twelve year olds.[98]

The idea of Arabic as an instrumental language stands at the center of what Israelis call *mizraḥanut*—literally, "Orientalism"—in Hebrew, an umbrella term for the analysis of all subjects related to the past and present Middle East and Islamic world, including Arabic literature and culture, Islamic religion, civilization, and history, and contemporary politics.[99] For sociologist Gil Eyal, *mizraḥanut* is more than the study of the Arabo-Islamic word; it is a "complex of knowledges and practices that mediate [Israeli Jews'] encounter with the reality around them."[100] In the days before statehood, *mizraḥanut* was the provenance of old-style Orientalists such as the aforementioned Pesaḥ Bar-Adon, figures who produced the "Orient" as a kind of enchanted Arab-Jewish space. With the rise of the state, Eyal argues, just as the figure of the Arab "lost its capacity to mediate between old and new Jew, so too did Israeli *mizrahanut* turn separatist, and its knowledge now serves to confirm the cultural chasm between Israelis and their neighbors."[101] Today, he elaborates, Israelis apply the term *mizraḥan* (Orientalist) not only to academics

97 Mendel, "Arabic and Security."

98 Ben-Dor, "Eyb, hshuma, infajarat qunbula," 41–42, translation by oznik.com.

99 *Mizraḥanut* within the Israeli academy was the subject of A. B. Yehoshua's well-received novel *Ha-kala ha-meshaḥreret* (The Liberating Bride), discussed in chapter 6.

100 Eyal, *Disenchantment*, 2–3.

101 Ibid., 4.

> but also to all those government officials, army officers, journalists, and other experts who monitor the neighboring Arab countries, supervise the local Palestinian population, or participate in official and media debates about Arab, Islamic, and Middle Eastern affairs. . . . In this sense, *mizrahanut* is not merely a form of expertise but a core component of Israeli culture, of the way public discourse is conducted in Israel, of the way Israelis perceive the world around them, and of the manner in which they relate to themselves and define their own identity.[102]

The "instrumentalization" of Arabic, which dehumanizes the language in the public eye, was reinforced by the changing connotations of Arabic in Israeli media, particularly state television. Israel began television broadcasts only in the late 1960s; televisions entered Israeli homes en masse in the 1970s. For many Jewish Israelis, formative memories of television are associated positively with the state channel's Arabic news broadcasts and with the popular Friday night Arabic movies (subtitled in Hebrew) as well as Arabic-language children's programming. The first *Intifada* (Palestinian uprising), from 1987 to 1993, overlapped with the beginning of the media explosion in Israel (the opening of commercial channels, a second state channel, and cable television). Coverage of Palestinian protests and terror attacks during Israeli prime time transformed mainstream views of Arabic throughout the mid-late 1990s and into the period of the second *Intifada in* the 2000s; nostalgia for the Friday night Arabic movie and the children's show *Sami and Susu* was replaced in viewers' minds with terrible, threatening images of violence and destruction. Similarly, in the first decade or so following Israel's 1967 annexation of the West Bank and Gaza, Arabic had entered mainstream Jewish Israeli consciousness in a different way, as Palestinian laborers began working in Israel in large numbers, and Jewish tourists shopped in Arab markets or visited East Jerusalem. These temporary, arguably positive developments in perceptions of Arabic were reversed in the 1990s and 2000s with the closures of the West Bank and Gaza and other measures of enforced separation.

With the ongoing deterioration of Israeli-Palestinian relations, the prestige of Arabic has sunk to an all-time low, and antipathy toward the language has reached new heights. Right-wing Israeli parliamentarians attempted in 2008 and again in 2011 to make Hebrew the state's only official language, revoking Arabic's official status. In 2008, one of the bill's sponsors explained, "Precisely in these times, when there are radical groups of Israeli Arabs trying to turn the State of Israel into a binational state, it is most urgent to put into law the unique status of the language of

102 Ibid., 2–3.

the Bible—the Hebrew language."[103] In 2009, Avigdor Lieberman, the chairman of the far-right-wing Yisra'el Beytenu (Israel Is Our Home) party and Israel's foreign minister from 2009 to 2012, campaigned under the slogan *Rak Liberman mevin 'aravit* (Only Lieberman understands Arabic). In fact, the Russian-born Lieberman speaks no Arabic, but that hardly matters. The idiomatic translation is that Lieberman knows how to deal with the Arab enemy, to read between the lines of slippery Arabic double-talk. Lieberman ran successfully under this reprehensible slogan while Arabic was (and, despite the aforementioned efforts, remains) one of Israel's official languages and the language of one-fifth of its citizens, the Palestinian Israelis—whom a majority of the Jewish Israeli population now views with suspicion, and whose very citizenship, Lieberman proposes, should be made contingent upon an oath of loyalty to the state.[104] It is a far cry from the days when knowledge of spoken Arabic was valorized and coveted by young Zionists eager to strike roots in their adopted homeland.

PALESTINIANS AND ARABIC IN ISRAEL

Following statehood in 1948, even as Arabic-speaking Jewish immigrants began pouring into the new nation, the residual Palestinian population was held under martial law, lifted only eighteen years later.[105] During these years, Palestinians in Israel were subjected to daily harassments, including curfews and expulsions. Travel outside their villages and towns for any reason required permits that were granted at the whim of capricious military governors. Anton Shammas poignantly recalls how as a child he would accompany his father in waiting in line for hours at the local police station for a permit to travel from his village of Fassuta to the nearby city of Haifa—a permit that was written in Hebrew, a language his father did not understand:

> My father, those days, was continuously and pensively struggling with the new language that had invaded his small world and ours, imposing upon him confusion and a new type of illiteracy. He needed a special

103 See Ilan, "MKs," and Lis, "Lawmakers Seek to Drop Arabic."

104 See, for example, Weymouth, "Interview with Avigdor Lieberman"; Ravid, "Lieberman." Lieberman's election and proposal of "no loyalty–no citizenship" were brilliantly satirized by Sayed Kashua in *Haaretz*; see Kashua, "Gdolim yoter mi-Bar Rafaeli" (More popular than [the fashion model] Bar Rafaeli).

105 Statistics on the number of Palestinians in Israel in 1948 vary from about 120,000 to 160,000. Today, they constitute close to 20 percent of Israel's population, or 1.2 million of the 6.3 million citizens of the state; see Kimmerling and Migdal, *Palestinian People*, 170–172. For other estimates, see Hareven, *Every Sixth Israeli*, 4; Jiryis, *Arabs in Israel*, 289; and Pappé, *Forgotten Palestinians*, 18.

> permit, like all the fathers of his generation, to move around in the scenes of his homeland which had turned overnight into "the homeland of the Jewish people"; but no such permits were available for moving around in the cultural scenes.
>
> The permits to travel to Haifa from Fasuta, under the military administration of the 1950s, were written in Hebrew. Wanting to decipher his limits, as it were, he was learning Hebrew for beginners . . . with the aid of books which were illustrated with water towers and plowed furrows, depicting a lifestyle in which he had no share, depicting a new set of arcane symbols whose signification were beyond his grasp and beyond his horizon.
>
> I remember standing in line with him in the scorching sun in front of the nearby police station, for hours on end, waiting for his travel permit to Haifa to be issued inside. . . . I do remember the silent, scolding looks of my father, blaming me for having so much fun out of a dubious, extremely tedious, humiliating trip. And I do remember that around that time I started to realize the utter importance of paper.[106]

Ironically, the vocation of the Palestinian Israeli Hebrew writer seems to begin here, in this humiliating encounter with the documents of the state. His recognition of the importance of paper as the medium of bureaucratic control and state oppression is later met by his realization of the power of writing. This insight is coupled with his own paradoxical position as someone who, unlike his father, speaks Hebrew fluently, and can therefore use it at will—not to comply with the demands of the state, but to expose and contest them.

In the aftermath of the war, the new state continued consolidating Jewish control over Arab land, most notably through the Absentee Property Law of 1950. This law also created the notorious and absurd category of "present absentees" (*nifkadim nokheḥim*), which denoted Palestinians who left their property during the 1948 war but remained within the borders of Israel. Although they became citizens of the state, they were not permitted to return to their homes or reclaim their property. These internal refugees still constitute about a quarter of the one million Palestinian citizens of Israel.[107] As David Grossman, a leading Israeli author, observes, "[T]he Jewish majority in Israel treats all its Palestinian citizens as present absentees. . . . If in 1948 the Palestinians in Israel were 'those that are not but actually are,' over the years they turned into 'those who are but

106 Shammas, "At Half Mast," 220–221.

107 See Kimmerling and Migdal, *Palestinian People*, 171–173; and Masalha, "Present Absentees," 256–257.

actually are not.'"[108] The idea of the present absentee, or more broadly, of the *presence of absence*, has evolved into a powerful trope in both Arabic and Hebrew literature of Israel/Palestine, as we will find in chapter 6. The early 1950s witnessed the establishment of the state educational system, which determined that Arab primary and secondary students would be educated separately from Jewish students, with an Arabic-based curriculum that emphasized Zionist and Jewish topics and themes in an effort to promote civic loyalty and to discourage identification with the Arab world. During these fateful years the Palestinian community, still traumatized by the events of 1948 and cowed by martial law, was politically submissive.

These were also particularly difficult years for Arabic writing in Israel. Under military rule, Arabic publications were strictly monitored and writings considered disloyal or subversive were censored.[109] Arab Jews and Palestinians who wished to publish in Arabic did so through small, local publishing houses or in journals, primarily those affiliated with the different branches of the Israeli Communist Party. Between 1948 and 1967, moreover, Palestinians in Israel were isolated from the rest of the Palestinian population in the West Bank (then under Jordanian control) and Gaza (under Egyptian control) as well as from the broader Arab world. This meant too that no new Arabic literature could flow in or out of Israel, a major barrier for Palestinian writers as well as newly arrived Jewish writers of Arabic.

The June 1967 war brought about a number of dramatic changes. With Israel's conquest of the West Bank and the Gaza Strip, their borders were opened and Palestinians within Israel's 1948 lines were able to reestablish contact with family members and former neighbors now living as refugees on the other side. Likewise, this development facilitated access to Arabic-language materials from the outside. In the 1970s Palestinians in Israel became more politically assertive, as demonstrated by a 1976 protest against land expropriations in which six Arab citizens were shot and killed by Israeli police, an event still commemorated annually in Palestinian communities. However, institutionalized discrimination against Palestinians in Israel never abated, as has been amply documented by scholars and journalists.[110]

In tandem with its policy of expropriating Palestinian lands, the state systematically Hebraicized the nation through policies of renaming and through Hebrew signage. Throughout the Galilee, Jewish towns and

108 See Grossman, *Sleeping on a Wire*, 295, my translation adapted from Watzman's.

109 Kayyal, "Intercultural Relations," 55.

110 The literature on the topic is extensive. For just two examples, see Grossman, *Sleeping on a Wire*, 298–303, and Pappé, *Forgotten Palestinians*.

settlements were constructed atop or alongside abandoned and evicted Palestinian villages, many of which had been razed to preclude their inhabitants' return. These were dubbed with Hebrew names that were often loose translations or approximate Hebraicizations of their erstwhile Arabic titles; in some cases, biblical place-names were revived. This policy of renaming obscured the recent Palestinian Arab presence and its Arabic-encoded history, manufacturing an unbroken continuity between biblical antiquity and the Israeli present: a translational cartography that masked the process of converting historic Palestine into the new State of Israel. Within mixed cities such as Haifa and Jerusalem, many old streets were renamed, their Mandate-era British and Arabic names replaced with Hebrew titles evoking the goals and identity of the state.[111] Emile Habiby, the leading Palestinian Israeli writer and statesman of his day, wryly revisits this phenomenon in his 1985 novel *Ikhtiyya* (*What a Shame!*):

> [O]ur Jewish brothers changed many of the long-standing Arab street names in the city [into Hebrew]. Thus El-Nasra [Nazareth] Street became Israel Bar Yehuda Street; and King Faisal Square, opposite the Hijazi Train Station, became the Ḥativat Golani (Golani Brigade) Street. But on the street sign they misspelled it in Arabic, so it came out "khatibat Julani," which in Arabic means "Julani's fiancées." And I, until I acquired the requisite military knowledge, was of the impression that this Julani was a Hebrew Don Juan with many mistresses, whom out of politeness were called his "fiancées."[112]

The violence of translation (let alone faulty translation), countered with misreading as resistance, became recurring themes in Habiby's writings, as elaborated in chapter 3.

The net result of Israel's renaming policies was the Hebraicization of the linguistic landscape (linguistic objects marking public space, such as road signs and billboards) and the gradual disappearance of Arabic from public space.[113] Aside from its presence on shop signs in Palestinian communities, Arabic is consistently printed only on highway signs, Israeli currency, and postage stamps; its public presence is hardly perceptible.

111 See, again, Shammas's commentary on this form of linguistic cannibalism in "Mixed as in Pidgin."

112 Habiby, *Ikhtiyya*, 23–24. See also Hever, *Producing the Modern Hebrew Canon*, 210.

113 Ben-Rafael et al., "Linguistic Landscape," 7. Their study concluded that the linguistic landscape of the Jewish sector is dominated by Hebrew, followed by a highly visible English, with Arabic in a barely perceptible third place; in the Palestinian sector (excluding East Jerusalem), Arabic is most common, closely followed by Hebrew (26). Spolsky concurs that English maintains a greater public presence than Arabic in Israel and that, de facto, Arabic "is regularly discriminated against" (Spolsky, "Situation of Arabic in Israel," 228).

These attributes of the linguistic landscape reinforce the proscribed separation between Palestinians and Jews.[114] Furthermore, Arabic is broadcast in limited Arabic-language programming on public radio and television; many public services have no Arabic-speaking employees, and national events are held in Hebrew only.[115]

Arabic remains the language of instruction in Palestinian-sector schools, where Hebrew is a compulsory subject from the third through twelfth grades.[116] Yasir Suleiman argues that these educational policies, rather than acting as a medium of reconciliation, exacerbate the tensions between Palestinian youth and their national surroundings.[117] In Hebrew-speaking schools, Arabic is compulsory only at the junior high level, for three years, and is optional thereafter; some schools bypass the requirement altogether.[118] As such, despite the code-switching that characterizes Israeli Arabic, "[t]here is little bilingualism in this officially bilingual country. Arabic and Hebrew coexist as dual languages, as paired languages, as opposed languages. Although many Palestinians speak Hebrew fluently, none do so in the home. Nowhere do Arab children speak to their parents in Hebrew."[119] Conversely, Hebrew is spoken by Palestinians in any social interaction that includes a Jewish Israeli, regardless of how many Palestinians are present.[120] Even among some Palestinian Israelis, particularly those living in mixed Hebrew-Arabic environments such as Jaffa, Arabic is perceived as an inferior language.[121] Palestinian Israelis have also expressed fear of speaking Arabic in the presence of Jewish Israelis during politically

114 Lefkowitz, "Conflict and Identity."

115 Ben-Rafael et al., "Linguistic Landscape," 12–13.

116 Spolsky, "Situation of Arabic in Israel," 230.

117 In his words, "Educating the Arab youth in Hebrew is conceived as a means of imparting to them an understanding of the dominant culture and its national ideology, in so far as this revolves around Judaism as a religion and Zionism as a political movement. Instead of reducing the conflict between Jews and Palestinians in Israel, this policy antagonizes the Arab youth and causes them to look for alternative sources of information, outside the school environment, on aspects of their national culture" (Suleiman, *War of Words*, 151).

118 Spolsky and Shohamy, "Language in Israeli Society and Education," 108. Arabic education in Jewish schools has been seen as a "problem" since before the founding of the state (Spolsky, "Situation of Arabic in Israel," 231). In August 2010, *Haaretz* reported that a new government program will make Arabic language classes compulsory in Israel's Jewish schools beginning in the fifth grade; the program has not yet been implemented. See "Arabic Studies to Become Compulsory." In recent years additional pilot programs aiming to reform Arabic study in Jewish schools have been introduced but thus far have gained little traction, largely because individual schools have a wide berth for determining their curriculum.

119 Lefkowitz, *Words and Stones*, 149.

120 Ibid., 152.

121 See Ḥalutz, "Language Is My Anchor" (interview with Ayman Sikseck).

sensitive moments.[122] Paradoxically, Arabic's low prestige enables Palestinians in Israel to maintain a separate national identity.[123]

What of Palestinians without Israeli citizenship—those in East Jerusalem, the West Bank, and the Gaza Strip? Following the withdrawal of Israeli forces from Bethlehem after the 1993 Oslo Accord agreements, informants in a study expressed the viewpoint that Israeli Jewish knowledge of Arabic "means continuing their occupation and control over us" and that it is "normal" for Israeli Jews not to use Arabic, because Palestinians "need" Israeli Jews (employers or military personnel) but not vice versa.[124] In short, language is perceived as an instrument of power and control; Palestinian perceptions of Hebrew, like Jewish Israeli perceptions of Arabic, cannot be divorced from the occupation and political struggle.

ARABIC-HEBREW BILINGUALISM AND THE POLITICS OF TRANSLATION

Thus far I have traced the forces that work to separate Arabic from Hebrew. Yet the literature of the no-man's-land emerges from the past and present of literary bilingualism and translation between the two languages; indeed, most of the bilingual authors discussed in this book are also translators. In the 1950s, Jewish writers newly arrived from Iraq published in Arabic, primarily in journals of the Israeli Communist Party. Over time, most switched to Hebrew. Of the handful who continued publishing Arabic books in Israel, the most prominent, Samir Naqqash, died in 2004, leaving a void in his wake; Jewish writing in Arabic has since virtually ceased. On the other hand, since the late 1960s a small number of Palestinian Israelis have chosen to write in Hebrew. Thus, Arab Jews born before the mid-1950s and Palestinian Israelis embody the modern phenomenon of Arabic-Hebrew literary bilingualism. They are the only writers in recent times with a *choice* of writing in Hebrew or Arabic—a choice that no longer exists for Jewish writers, and that is rare even for Palestinian Israelis. With few exceptions, Israeli-educated Mizraḥim are not literate in Arabic. Arabic influences on their Hebrew work are thus derived from the colloquial Arabic of the home, a limitation that paradoxically creates a space for literary innovation, as will be discussed in part 3. For fully monolingual Mizraḥi Hebrew writers, the final loss of Arabic

122 For example, see Grossman, *Sleeping on a Wire*, 168.
123 Suleiman, *War of Words*, 152.
124 Spolsky et al., "Language, Education, and Identity," cited in Suleiman, *War of Words*, 142.

occasions imaginative forms of compensation; themes of haunting and memory abound in the works of these "post-Arabic" Hebrew writers.[125]

Historically, Hebrew-Arabic bilingualism and translation date back at least to the tenth century CE.[126] The interplay of the two languages was a defining feature of Sephardi Jewish civilization, as will be detailed in chapter 2. But whereas the earlier translation activity had been entirely belletristic and religious in nature, in the contemporary context of Israel/Palestine, translation between Arabic and Hebrew serves very different purposes. While an enormous amount of Hebrew to Arabic translation activity in the Arab world has been concerned with politics and military intelligence, in Israel most Hebrew to Arabic translations were carried out for practical purposes such as advertisements and textbooks.[127] Due to limited institutional support and commercial interest, the amount of *literary* translation has been negligible.

HEBREW TO ARABIC TRANSLATION

If translation always operates on an uneven field, in this case the field is positioned directly over a fault line. As Mahmoud Kayyal, a specialist in Hebrew to Arabic translation, points out, Hebrew to Arabic translation activity has been an "antagonistic dialogue"—polemical, guided primarily by political considerations, and fraught with stereotypes—such that translations were seen as "documents reflecting the culture of the other," their purpose "ideological rather than literary."[128] Furthermore, while the number of translated works in both directions (Hebrew to Arabic and Arabic to Hebrew) is quite small, there is a disproportionate imbalance in favor of Hebrew to Arabic translations (here we may also keep in mind that most Palestinian Israelis read Hebrew, while only a tiny fraction of

125 Michal Raizen coined the suggestive term "post-Arabic"; I thank her for allowing me to use it.

126 Soon after the Islamic conquests of the seventh century, Arabic supplanted Aramaic as the spoken language of Jews in the newly conquered regions. The first notable example of Hebrew-Arabic translation is thought to be the Egyptian-born Babylonian Jewish scholar Sa'adia Gaon's tenth-century translation of the Bible into Arabic. The tenth- to twelfth-century Hebrew poets and philosophers of al-Andalus (Islamic Iberia) were highly literate in Arabic, and their Hebrew works are famously polyglossic; some, such as the *maqamat* of Judah al-Ḥarizi, are largely creative translations from the Arabic. More on al-Andalus follows in chapter 2.

127 Robinson, "Israeli Market Needs for Arabic Translations," cited in Kayyal, "Intercultural Relations," 58. Mahmoud Kayyal, Mahmud Ghanayim, and Hannah Amit-Kochavi have carried out most of the research on translation and direct literary contact between Arabic and Hebrew.

128 Kayyal, "Intercultural Relations," 53. For a comprehensive study of the topic, see Kayyal, *Targum be-tsel ha-'imut.*

Jewish Israelis read Arabic). In a 2009 collection of interviews with Israeli and Palestinian authors, Palestinian writers in the West Bank note this imbalance and add that they have no stable publishing houses, with the partial exception of the Ramallah-based Ogarit Publishers, which has operated only in recent years.[129] They also repeatedly express the sentiment that Israelis are not interested in Palestinian literature and culture, nor in Arabic literature more generally.[130] This observation is echoed on the other side of the divide by Dorit Rabinyan, an Israeli Hebrew writer of Iranian Jewish heritage:

> [Rabinyan:] The problem with Palestinian literature in Israel is that so few of us know anything about it.
> [Runo Isaksen:] Did you ever read any Palestinian literature in the course of your schooling?
> [Rabinyan:] No, they thought it would be more useful for us to read James Joyce than the literature of our neighbors. I think it is in fact an Israeli policy *not* to translate Arabic literature. There is a hostile attitude that is being transferred from one generation to the next. The truth is that we do not have insight into their personal and cultural life.[131]

In the early years of the state, from 1948 to 1967, the Labor Party–led establishment had supported cultural activity concerned with Arab-Jewish understanding; within this framework, there was considerable Hebrew to Arabic translation activity in the Arabic-language publications founded or supported by the state.[132] However, the direct involvement of the state in Arabic cultural activity diminished after 1967. Outside Israel, Arab intellectuals after 1948 devoted translational efforts to discrediting Israeli culture by portraying it as racist, anti-Arab, or anti-Islam. Limited knowledge of Hebrew language and culture led to distorted readings and imprecise renderings as well as reliance on foreign stereotypes.[133]

129 Isaksen, *Literature and War*, 121, 157, 165.

130 Ibid., 116–117, 155, 167, 175, 187, 200.

131 Ibid., 108.

132 Kayyal, "Intercultural Relations," 55. "Officially supported translation activity took place mainly in Establishment frameworks, particularly the newspapers *al-Yaum* (1948–1968) and *Haqiqat al-Amr* (1937–1959), which were written in Arabic but unequivocally reflected the views of the Establishment; or in the publications of Arab circles close to the Establishment, such as *al-Mujtama‘* (1949–1954), published in Nazareth" (ibid., 60). All in all, there were about half a dozen Arabic-language magazines (official, semiofficial, and independent) published by Jews and Palestinians in the 1950s and 1960s, in addition to Dar al-Nashr al-‘Arabi, the Arabic-language publishing wing of the Histadrut (Israel's Labor Federation, aligned with the governing Labor Party).

133 Kayyal, "Intercultural Relations," 56, and Kayyal, "Hebrew-Arabic Translations," 4.

The 1967 war, an ideological turning point in Arab culture, stimulated interest in Hebrew literature as one of the best means of learning about Israeli society. Research institutes and departments of Hebrew emerged throughout the Arab world, especially in Egypt. However, as before, the interest in Hebrew literature was motivated more by political than literary or aesthetic concerns. The late 1990s saw limited cooperation between Israeli translators and publishers in the Arab world, but this development slowed following the beginning of the second *Intifada* in 2000. On the other hand, increased Hebrew proficiency has improved the quality of translations carried out in the Arab world.[134] Translations of Hebrew stories and poems have continued to be published in cultural magazines in Ramallah.[135]

The large and established department of Hebrew at 'Ain Shams University in Cairo has produced scholars and translators of Hebrew literature. Two of the department's graduates, Nael El-Toukhy and Mohammad 'Abud, represent a new face of Hebrew to Arabic translation. Bypassing the difficult political circumstances concerning the translation of novels, which entails obtaining copyrights from Israeli publishers and cooperating with Israeli cultural institutions,[136] they draw on sources readily available through the Internet. Translating short stories and poetry, they also tend to publish their work in the public domain, in media such as blogs and online journals or newspapers.[137] 'Abud translated Almog Behar's short story "Ana min al-yahud" ("I Am of the Jews"), which won the *Haaretz* short story prize in 2005, and published his translation with an introduction the following year in the prestigious Arabic journal *al-Hilal* (the story is analyzed at length in chapter 6).[138] El-Toukhy's translations of selected poems from the 2009 antiwar anthology *Latset!* (*Get Out!*) were published in

134 Kayyal, "Intercultural Relations," 64.

135 Isaksen, *Literature and War*, 116–117.

136 Although Egypt and Israel are technically at peace, Egyptian intellectuals by and large oppose "normalization" of relations with Israel, which would entail cooperation with Israeli institutions. On that note, the Israeli Academic Center in Cairo, which was opened following the 1978 Camp David Accords, was intended as a major node of cultural contact, endowed with a large library of Hebrew works and a host of prominent visiting authors and academics from Israel. But it has been largely boycotted by Egyptians and subject to prolonged closures.

137 Raizen, "Cairo as Translation Zone." I thank Michael Raizen for drawing my attention to these two figures and to their work as translators of and commentators on Hebrew literature and culture, as well as to their utilization of online media.

138 'Abud, "Shazaya al-qahr al-thaqafi"; Raizen also notes that 'Abud is currently writing his doctoral dissertation at 'Ain Shams on the *Haaretz* short story contest (Raizen, "Cairo as Translation Zone").

a Lebanese online journal, and in print in Egypt; he is currently translating Behar's novel *Tchaḥla ve-Ḥezkel* (*Rachel and Ezekiel*).[139]

After 1967, most Hebrew to Arabic translation activity was carried out by independent institutions operating with state support. From the 1970s on, especially after the closure of the Arabic-language Labor Party establishment newspapers, independent left-wing groups and organizations began publishing translated works. In this phase, the active translators were mainly young Palestinians educated within the Israeli system.[140] The amount of literary translation increased in this period, as translation became viewed as an important vehicle of mutual understanding; some Hebrew authors initiated and even financed the translation of their own work into Arabic. Still, from 1948 to 2000, only thirty-one literary titles were translated from Hebrew into Arabic outside Israel, and fifty within Israel (with poetry more widely translated than novels). According to Kayyal, these translations gained little status within the target population of Arabic readers.[141]

A number of Hebrew works have also been translated into Arabic and published by Arab presses outside Israel/Palestine. Manshurat al-Jamal, a small Iraqi expatriate press that has operated in Cologne, Beirut, and more recently Baghdad, has published titles originally written in French, Hebrew, and Arabic by Iraqi Jewish authors such as Shimon Ballas and Sami Michael, in addition to a few titles by Israel's most internationally recognized writer, Amos Oz.[142] In 2005 it published Samir Naqqash's

139 See *Alghaoon* 12 (February 2009): 8–9, cited in Jacobs, "From IDF to .PDF," 162, 166n47. In Cairo, another Hebrew novel by an Iraqi Jewish author, Eli Amir's 2005 *Yasmin*, was translated by Hussein Sarag, deputy editor of *October* magazine, and published in 2007.

140 Kayyal, "Intercultural Relations," 62–63, and "Hebrew-Arabic Translations," 8.

141 Kayyal, "Intercultural Relations," 59–61, 62. Notably, from the late 1960s through the late 1980s, about half the translations were carried out by three Palestinian-Israeli translators: Mahmud 'Abbasi (b. 1935), Anton Shammas (b. 1950), and Muhammad Hamzah Ghanayim (1953–2004). The latter two largely ceased their Hebrew-to-Arabic translation activities in the 1980s (although at the same time they continued to translate Arabic literature into Hebrew, and to publish their own fiction and poetry; Kayyal, "Intercultural Relations," 63, and "Hebrew-Arabic Translations," 7). More recently, Salman Natour (b. 1949) has translated Hebrew works by leading Israeli writers including David Grossman, Amos Oz, A. B. Yehoshua, Etgar Keret, and Orly Castel-Bloom; the Palestinian poet Samih al-Qasim translated and edited a 1991 anthology of Hebrew poetry.

142 Manshurat al-Jamal was founded in Cologne in 1983; in 1995 it opened a branch in Beirut and another in Baghdad in 2005. Since 2008 it has been based in Beirut. I thank Khalid al-Maaly for information about the press. The press published an Arabic translation of Oz's celebrated autobiography *Sipur 'al ahava ve-ḥoshekh* (*A Tale of Love and Darkness*) in Beirut; see *Qissa 'an al-hubb wa-l-zalam*. The translation, by Palestinian Israeli Jamal Ghnaim, was funded by a Palestinian family from East Jerusalem to honor their son, a Hebrew University law student, who was fatally

Arabic translation of Sami Michael's *Victoria*, an important novel dealing with Jewish life in Baghdad, discussed in chapter 5.[143]

ARABIC TO HEBREW TRANSLATION

Literary translation in the other direction, from Arabic to Hebrew, has been even more restricted in scope; as of 2005, out of over 7,000 titles translated into Hebrew, only 123 were from Arabic.[144] Very few of the major works of Modern Arabic fiction are available in Hebrew. In the early decades of the state, translations of Palestinian literature were overseen almost entirely by the Israeli security forces and in the spirit of "Know thy enemy" rather than "Know thy neighbor."[145] From the 1950s to the 1990s, works of Palestinian Israeli poets such as Samih al-Qasim and Siham Daoud were sporadically translated by Sasson Somekh, a leading Israeli scholar of Arabic literature, and published in literary journals, cultural supplements of newspapers, and books; Shimon Ballas published the first Hebrew translation of short stories by Palestinian writers.[146] But as Somekh observes, the cultural life of Palestinians in Israel was "beyond the sight and curiosity of the majority of the Hebrew reading public. It is as though the hundreds of thousands of Arab citizens (today one million) had no part in the cultural life of the country."[147] A momentary breakthrough was achieved with the popular translations of Emile Habiby's writings into Hebrew by Anton Shammas, which led to Habiby's controversial acceptance of the Israel Prize for Arabic literature in 1992 (see chapter 3). The major Arabic to Hebrew translators in the 1990s were Shammas and Muhammad Hamzah Ghanayim, whose critically acclaimed translations are widely considered to have enriched Hebrew literature; others included the poets Na'im 'Araidi and Salman Masalha (the subjects of chapter 4). In addition, the Cairo Trilogy of Nobel Prize–winning Egyptian author Naguib Mahfouz was translated into Hebrew by Sami Michael.[148] Still, as Somekh himself noted in 1993, there were no full-time Arabic to Hebrew translators in Israel, nor was there any governmental or nongovernmental institution encouraging the growth of this

---

shot in 2004 while jogging on the university campus; the assassins mistook him for an Israeli Jew. See "Beirut Publisher Releases Translation of Amos Oz Autobiography."

143 Michael, *Fiktorya: Riwaya.*

144 To be precise, these included thirty-three novels, thirty-three plays, and fifty-seven anthologies (Amit-Kochavi, "Israeli Jewish Nation Building," 102).

145 Amit-Kochavi, "Hebrew Translations of Palestinian Literature," 57.

146 Ballas, *Sipurim palestiniyim.*

147 Somekh, "Reconciling Two Great Loves," 18–19.

148 Somekh, *Targum be-tsidey ha-derekh*, 5, 7.

translation activity.[149] All in all, as Hannah Amit-Kochavi summates, the translation of Arabic literature into Hebrew demonstrates

> a high level of perseverance on the part of a small group of [both Arab and Jewish] translators and scholars working within an unsympathetic cultural environment. Translations have been undertaken and published largely by a small number of influential Israelis, who used their personal standing within academic and literary circles to promote Arabic literature in translation. . . . Examples abound of the rise—and sometimes fall—of literary projects exclusively devoted to the translation of Arabic literature into Hebrew.[150]

In 1999 an unprecedented step toward expanding Arabic literature in Hebrew translation was undertaken as a private, independent initiative by Yael Lerer, founder and operator of Andalus Publishing. Founded with private money and a small seed grant from the European Union, the press operated from 2000 to 2007. During those seven years, Andalus commissioned and published Hebrew translations of eighteen acclaimed Arabic titles by major writers such as Mahmoud Darwish, Elias Khoury, al-Tayyeb Salih, Huda Barakat, and Jabra Ibrahim Jabra, with the full consent of the authors.[151] When the enterprise came under attack in the Egyptian press in 2001, it garnered support from leading Arab writers and intellectuals including Edward Said, Darwish, and Khoury.[152] Andalus's Hebrew translations received rave reviews in the Israeli press, but sluggish sales forced the closure of the publishing house in 2008. In Lerer's own assessment, "As a cultural enterprise it has left its illustrious mark: rave reviews, diehard fans, grateful happenstance readers. As an economic venture it is a complete failure: supply without demand."[153] The case of Andalus Publishing corroborates Palestinian writers' complaints about the lack of Israeli interest in Arabic or Palestinian culture. As Lerer notes elsewhere, while the Israeli intelligentsia feels a cultural obligation to consume Western

149 Ibid., 5–6. See also Alcalay, *Keys to the Garden*, 57.

150 Amit-Kochavi, "Israeli Arabic Literature," 34–35. One such example is *Mifgash/Liqa'* (Meeting or Encounter), a bilingual Hebrew-Arabic literary magazine that printed original and translated texts side by side. It was first launched in the 1960s, and its publication resumed in the 1980s and continued through 1997.

151 Lerer, "Andalus Test"; idem, "De l'autre côté."

152 Lerer, "Andalus Test." Lerer adds that the controversy began with the Egyptian journal *Akhbar al-adam*, after which the leading international Arabic-language newspaper *al-Hayat* picked up the story and published a long debate (comprising some sixty separate contributions!) on the question of translating Arabic literature into Hebrew. Other related features appeared in Egyptian newspapers as well (Lerer, personal correspondence, October 17, 2010).

153 Lerer, "Andalus Test."

literature, whether in the original or in Hebrew translation, it does not see knowledge of Arabic literature as part of its cultural mandate. In Israel and beyond, she writes, people "simply can't imagine that Arab writers can write beautiful, even overwhelmingly powerful books."[154]

On a more hopeful note, the collaborative model of Palestinian and Arab Jewish intelligentsia from the early 1950s has been revived by a small but energetic group of third-generation Palestinian and Jewish Israelis—most of them scholar-activists—who publish together both online and in print, producing bilingual editions such as *Shira mefareket ḥoma/Shi'r yuhattimu al-jidar* (*Poetry Dismantling Walls*, 2010) and the online journal *La-roḥav/Maqta' 'ardi* (*Crosswise/Wide Crossing*), inaugurated in 2012.[155] Almog Behar, a prominent presence in these ventures, is (at the time of this writing) co-editing a bilingual anthology of young Jewish and Palestinian writers. Where first-generation Arab Jews and Palestinian Israelis had once held literary discussions and published poems and stories in the cultural journal *al-Jadid*, over fifty years later new voices are renewing a transformed discussion and vision of cultural alternatives for Israel/Palestine.[156]

All in all, the enterprise of literary translation between the two languages illustrates the dynamics of cultural negotiation in a tight political clamp. From the early photographs of the "Hebrew Bedouin" to the recent cinematic representation of "Israeli Arabic," the relationship of Arabic and Hebrew in Israel/Palestine has always been politically fraught. It has, moreover, been formed in and by a triangular web of relations among Palestinians, Ashkenazi Jews, and Mizraḥim, with each group being forced to define itself linguistically, culturally, and politically in relation to the others. If the Palestinian relationship to Hebrew as depicted in *'Ajami* is murky, the Mizraḥi relationship to Arabic is mired in seemingly paralyzing contradictions. Nor has translation activity between the two languages enhanced cultural familiarity and understanding on a meaningful scale. And yet writers from both sides have found creative strategies for reclaiming language from the vise of the conflict and the strictures of the state and for making it their own, whether writing in Hebrew, in Arabic, or in a multilingual idiom. In the chapters that follow, we will explore these strategies in depth, following the negotiation of self, society, and language in literature and art from the Hebrew-Arabic no-man's-land.

154 Lerer, "Publishing Arabic Literature in Hebrew."

155 The journal is published online and available for download; see http://www.gerila.co.il/wide01/ and http://www.gerila.co.il/he/?iid=380&p=1.

156 *Al-Jadid* was an Arabic-language monthly journal associated with the Israeli Communist Party. Founded in 1952, it was originally edited by Emile Habiby and Jabra Nicola; it survived until the early 1990s. See Somekh, "Reconciling Two Great Loves," 3.

CHAPTER 2

Bialik and the Sephardim

The Ethnic Encoding of Modern Hebrew Literature

> Israel is geographically part of the Middle East . . . [but] for literary purposes, the Israeli sensibility is incontrovertibly a Euro-American sensibility. Very little about Israeli belles-lettres can be called Levantine, even though a sizable proportion of the Israeli population . . . has Levantine or Oriental antecedents. From a Middle Eastern perspective, then, all Israelis, even those of Moroccan or Persian or Yemenite origin, are European; their literature is European; their outlook is alien or external to the Middle East.
>
> —*Israeli Poetry: A Contemporary Anthology*[1]

What exactly was new about *ha-sifrut ha-'ivrit ha-ḥadasha*, the "new" or "modern" Hebrew literature?[2] Where and when does it begin? For Robert Alter, the "new" literature begins in Enlightenment Germany with an underlying ideological transformation, a "programmatic negotiation of the terms of Jewish collective identity."[3] More recently, Dan Miron has questioned the premise of a clean break between the "new" and "old" Hebrew literatures, noting that the so-called "old" literature, such as the Sephardic Golden Age poetry

1 Bargad and Chyet, *Israeli Poetry*, 3; quoted also in Alcalay, *After Jews and Arabs*, 253.

2 In Hebrew, "new" (*ḥadash*) is often used idiomatically in the sense of "modern," rather than the Latinate calque *moderni* (modern). Hence *ha-sifut ha-'ivrit ha-ḥadasha* can be translated either as "the Modern Hebrew literature" or "the new Hebrew literature."

3 For Alter, "[t]he newness of modern Hebrew literature has long been a subject of debate among Hebrew literary historians because the supposed emergence of the modern movement in eighteenth-century Germany was preceded by eight consecutive centuries of secular belletristic writing in Hebrew, first in Spain, then in Italy and northern Europe. . . . But the new movement that surfaced in Enlightenment Germany was, I think, different in kind from its predecessor because of its fundamentally ideological character. That is to say, by the late eighteenth century European Jewry was launching on that process of radical historical transformation we call modernization, and what was at issue now in the act of writing Hebrew was not just an aesthetic pursuit but a programmatic negotiation of the terms of Jewish collective identity" (*Invention of Hebrew Prose*, 3; see also idem, *Hebrew and Modernity*, esp. chap. 1).

on the human condition, may not be as "dramatically different" from its successors as historians had previously imagined.[4] Gil Anidjar, a younger scholar, goes further, seeing the narrative of Modern Hebrew literature as a "schizoid" history "in which no strict or even desirable autonomy has ever been established, either of the Hebrew vis-à-vis the Jewish, or of the Jewish vis-à-vis the non-Jewish, or of the literary vis-à-vis the nonliterary." For Anidjar, "Hebrew literature" is no more a separate, autonomous, monolingual literature than its history is a unified, monolingual history.[5] In short, Alter asserts newness, Miron equivocates, Anidjar denies. But why must the question revolve solely around whether the Hebrew writing we call "modern" emerged from an Enlightenment-inspired break with the multilingual Jewish past, or through a more gradual evolutionary process that took a radically nationalist turn in Israel?

What I would like to suggest in this chapter about the idea of Modern Hebrew literature is that when we invoke the language of "new" and "old," we are bringing more than a distinction of periodization, style, or even philosophical outlook to bear. We are also invoking an *ethnic* distinction. Because of the way Hebrew literary history was both imagined and written, Modern Hebrew literature becomes inseparable from Jewish modernity writ large. There is one kind of modernity; it is European. There is one kind of Hebrew that is "new," "modern," autonomous, and enlightened; there is another one that does not successfully separate from its Diasporic, multilingual, and premodern past. There is one group of Jews that makes the big collective leap to "modernity"; there is one group that does not.

In the previous chapter I followed the vicissitudes of Hebrew and Arabic throughout a century of interaction in Israel/Palestine, limning the shifting positions of Arabic within Modern Hebrew literature and culture. In fact, the pre-1948 interaction of Modern Arabic and Hebrew reached well beyond Palestine's borders, encompassing a transnational network of Jewish communities in the Arab Levant. These communities were home to scholars, polemicists, and poets who are unknown today, in contrast to the well-known Ashkenazi (European) Jewish writers universally recognized as the protagonists of Modern Hebrew.[6] This chapter reexamines the

4 Miron, *From Continuity to Contiguity*, 6. It is worth looking at the set of questions with which Miron opens his tome, which he presents as the culmination of his career as a Hebrew literary historian.

5 Anidjar, *Semites*, 81.

6 On Jewish intellectuals and the transnational cultural space of the Levant, see Alcalay, *After Jews and Arabs*. Although Ladino is outside the purview of this study, it should be noted that the Arab Jewish intellectual network in the Levant was paralleled by a Mediterranean intellectual network of Ladino-speaking Sephardim stretching from Istanbul to Southeastern Europe. See Cohen and Stein, "Sephardic Scholarly Worlds."

history and indeed the *idea* of Modern Hebrew literature through the tension between its dominant narrative, associated with Ashkenazi Jews, and the suppressed perspectives that emerge from the literary and scholarly activities of Arab Jews and Mizraḥim both before and after the founding of the state. Since everyone loves a love story, and since there is no better way to tell a story than by means of another, I illustrate this history through the saga of a multigenerational affair: the passionate and conflicted romance of the so-called Sephardim (Sephardi, Mizraḥi, and Arab Jews) with Modern Hebrew literature's leading persona, Ḥayim Naḥman Bialik. Their story takes us from the 1920s to 1930s Levant—Baghdad, Jerusalem, and Cairo—to present-day Israel/Palestine, with the spirit of *al-Andalus* (Islamic Spain) accompanying us all along the way.

FROM BAGHDAD TO BIALIK WITH LOVE

We begin this tale with the meeting of two literary figures of vastly incommensurate stature: one a minor and now forgotten Hebrew poet and scholar in Baghdad, the other Bialik, a Russian Jew, the most famous and widely venerated Modern Hebrew poet to this day. In 1933, an Iraqi Jew by the name of Dahud ben Sleyman Semaḥ (David Tsemaḥ)[7] sent Bialik a sixtieth birthday present. Bialik was already Modern Hebrew's leading light, referred to as *ha-meshorer ha-le'umi*, the "national poet" of what was to become the Hebrew state. Appropriately enough, the gift was a poem extolling Bialik as the "father" of Modern Hebrew verse (see Figure 2).[8] Composed in the medieval style of the Hebrew Golden Age of Sepharad (the Hebrew term for Islamic Spain),[9] the poem is a virtuosic tour de force. Its opening lines stage an intricate homophonic wordplay leading swiftly to an extended metaphor: a beautiful maiden, the embodiment of Hebrew poetry. Yet no sooner do we meet this lovely maiden

7 Transliterated from the Modern Hebrew pronunciation, his last name is Tsemaḥ; the trilingual (Arabic, Hebrew, English) letterhead on his stationery renders him in English as "Hakham David Saimah."

8 The poem was printed with editor notes in Ben Ya'akov, *Shira u-fiyut*, 420. The poem also appeared more recently with a brief interpretation in Lev Hakak, *Nitsaney ha-yetsira*, 184–186.

9 Muslim Spain has as many different names as it has legacies. These include Spain and Iberia, or in older usage "Moorish" Spain; in Arabic, it is al-Andalus, and in the Hebrew tradition, it is Sepharad—also Modern Hebrew's name for contemporary Spain. I generally refer to the Hebrew poets of al-Andalus as "Sephardi" (or "Sephardic") poets, as they are traditionally known in Hebrew and in Jewish scholarship. The descendants of the Jewish exiles from Spain are also known as Sephardim. With the establishment of the State of Israel, the term was generalized to refer to all Middle Eastern Jews, most of whom do not trace roots to Spain or speak Ladino (the language of Sephardim, also known as Judeo-Spanish). Bialik's controversial statements about "the Sephardim" discussed below pertain to *all* Asian and African Jews. See also note 17 of the introduction.

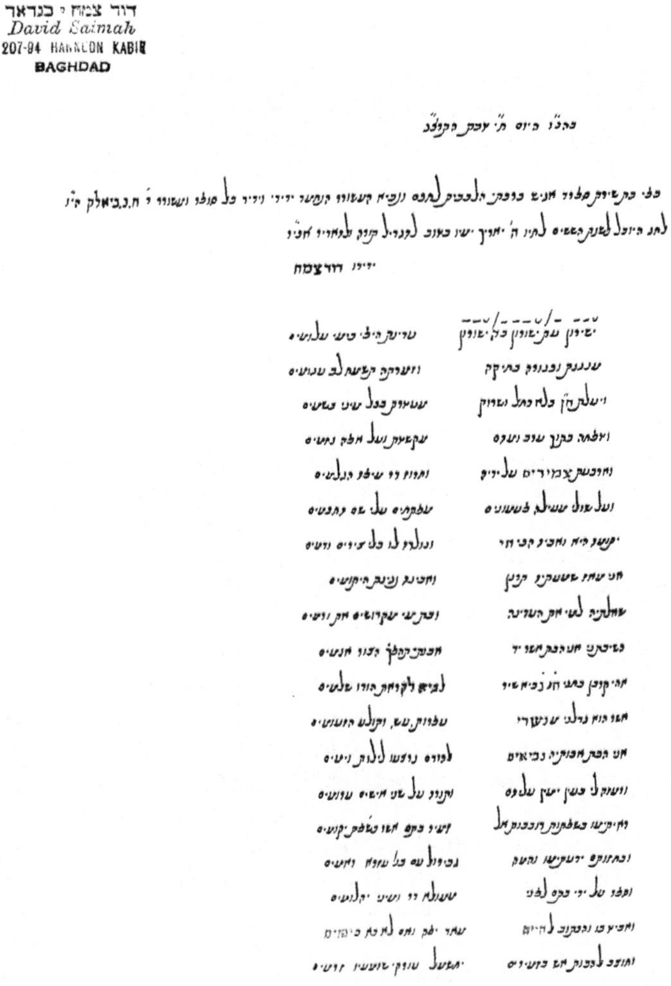

Figure 2. The birthday poem in Semaḥ's own hand: Letter to Bialik dated 18 Tevet 5693 (January 16, 1933). Courtesy of the Babylonian Jewry Heritage Center, Or Yehuda.

than we are told that she was "nurtured by Arab civilization" (*tupaḥa be-tokh 'arav*). Her identity grows ever more perplexing: at first the poem implies that Bialik is her father, but when directly questioned as to her patrilineage (*le-mi at, ha-'adina?*), the maiden points to two men, who turn out be none other than the medieval Hebrew poets Solomon ibn Gabirol and Moses ibn 'Ezra—two of the great Jewish luminaries of Sepharad. By this point, the poem has taken on the performative quality of a paternity suit, challenging its contenders: Will the "real father" of Modern Hebrew literature please stand up? Why would a poem celebrating Bialik as the "savior" and "rejuvenator" of Hebrew emphasize the beautiful maiden's *Arab* roots—and shift the spotlight away from Bialik, its panegyric subject, back to two medieval Sephardi poets lurking in the wings?

What is at stake in this poetic conundrum is the cultural identity of Hebrew literature at that historic juncture. The answer rests both upon the enormity of Bialik's cultural cache in Israel and upon the historiographical understanding of Modern Hebrew literature. Geographically speaking, Modern Hebrew literature has been mapped as a continuum from Eastern (and, to a lesser degree, Western) Europe to Palestine; from the late eighteenth- and nineteenth-century Jewish Enlightenment (in Hebrew, the *haskala*) to the migration of important European Hebrew writers such as Bialik to Palestine in the early twentieth century. And because of the belated and compressed nature of Hebrew cultural modernity, in many cases the litterateurs themselves doubled as the scholars, critics, and historians, codifying and commenting upon the cultural edifice even as they penned its poems, stories, and novels.

This was certainly the case for Bialik. Born in 1873 in Ukraine, writing from the 1890s until his death in 1934, Bialik is widely credited with the creation of a Modern Hebrew poetic idiom. Bialik's literary career spanned Odessa, Berlin, and Tel Aviv. For decades he dominated the Hebrew literary scene, and his name still elicits veneration. His lengthy, romantic, often anguished poems are mandatory reading in the Israeli educational system, and many of them have been adapted for music and absorbed into Israeli popular culture. Moreover, not only is Bialik the uber-canonical literary figurehead of Modern Hebrew literature; he was, in his own lifetime, the self-appointed arbiter and curator of the Hebrew canon. This was a massive project of textual recovery, editing, and anthologizing he titled *mif'al ha-kinus*, the project or enterprise of "gathering" or "convening"—the textual equivalent of the famous "ingathering of the exiles" that characterized the Zionist project of immigration.

The story of Modern Hebrew literature has in fact been told as the story of Bialik and of his immediate precursors and successors, all of whom had in common one important attribute: they were Eastern European Jews, working in what Hebrew literary critic and historian Benjamin Harshav has called a "time of revolution" sparked by the Russian pogroms of 1881–1882.[10] These figures were preceded by the *maskilim*

10 Harshav, *Language in Time of Revolution*, vii–x, 3–9. A few notable exceptions were Western European (German) Jews, but for the most part the major Hebrew literary figures from this period were born in Russia, Ukraine, Poland, and Lithuania.

(proponents of the *haskala*, the Hebrew Enlightenment), the first generation of Jewish writers to break away (in varying degrees) from Orthodoxy and refashion Hebrew into a neoclassical literary language. In Europe, Modern Hebrew and Yiddish literatures developed symbiotically from the 1880s through the 1930s in sites such as Odessa and Plonsk, Vilna and Warsaw, Berlin and Paris, eventually moving eastward and westward to Tel Aviv and New York.[11]

Hebrew and other multilingual writings from the rest of the Jewish world—North Africa, the Levant, Turkey, Iran, Yemen, Central Asia, India, the Balkans—during this formative period have not been included in histories of Hebrew literature. The recent work of Sephardi, Mizraḥi, and Arab Jewish writers in Israel (from the 1970s to the present) has been treated as a kind of offshoot of the mainstream Hebrew literature, as a late and secondary chapter; the cultural echo chamber of Modern Hebrew is still seen as strictly European.[12] What, then, were the rest of the world's Jews doing while European Jews were "inventing" Modern Hebrew in the nineteenth and early twentieth centuries? What were they reading, writing, thinking? The general assumption, both popular and academic, has been that they were still laboring in darkness and waiting for the European Jewish enlightenment and, later, for political Zionism to usher them into modernity.[13]

As it turns out, Jews in the multilingual Ottoman Empire and other parts of the Islamic world were producing texts reflecting a vast range of influences and interests, from cultural sources that were Jewish and Muslim, Middle Eastern and European.[14] In the late nineteenth and early twentieth centuries, the region we now call the Middle East underwent accelerated processes of modernization, secularization, and cultural liberalization that reconfigured the basis of identity from the religious-communal to the civic and the national. The latter half of the nineteenth century witnessed the many and varied activities of modernizing Arab writers and intellectuals, later collectively construed as a movement

11 For two recent works related to the European geography of Hebrew and Yiddish modernity, see Schachter, *Diasporic Modernisms*, and Pinsker, *Literary Passports*.

12 For example, in *Hebrew and Modernity*, Alter writes, "To begin with, Hebrew literature, though now created preponderously in the Middle East, resolutely remains a Western literature, looking to formal and even sometimes stylistic models in English, German, and to a lesser degree, Russian, French, and Spanish" (7).

13 Ammiel Alcalay's groundbreaking book *After Jews and Arabs* challenged some of these long-standing suppositions by means of a mammoth inventory of Middle Eastern cultural production, from Dunash ben Labrat's famous tenth-century wine poem—the first to adapt Arabic metrics to Hebrew—to contemporary Mizraḥi writing in Israel.

14 See Levy, "Jewish Writers in the Arab East," and idem, "Reorienting Hebrew Literary History."

called *al-nahda* (the Arabic "renaissance").[15] The spirit of the times swept the Jews along in its path, and in not quite fifty years, Jews in the Levant who availed themselves of the burgeoning new educational opportunities learned classical Arabic as well as European languages,[16] and began producing journalistic writing, short stories, poetry, and plays in Arabic, Hebrew, English, and French, in addition to Judeo-Arabic and Judeo-Spanish (Ladino).[17]

Some decades later, in the 1920s to 1940s, Jews in Baghdad, Beirut, and Cairo published newspapers in which aspiring authors tried their hand at poetry and short stories. This period of accelerated integration and acculturation facilitated the enthusiastic entry of Iraqi Jews into the world of modern Arabic literature.[18] Baghdad became the center of Middle Eastern Jewish creativity as a newly educated stratum of young professionals, having discovered the riches of world literature and the Arabic literary heritage, published poetry, short stories, essays, and novellas in presses throughout the Arab East.[19] Others devoted their creative energies to Hebrew, or translated Hebrew works into literary Arabic, simultaneously participating in the revival of both languages. These translation projects resulted in fascinating examples of cultural transfer: in 1945 the Iraqi Jewish writer Ezra Haddad translated *The Journey of Benjamin of Tudela*, a famous medieval Hebrew travel narrative, and

15 The term *nahda* is most often translated in scholarly literature as "renaissance," occasionally as "awakening" or "revival," all of which convey an ideological metanarrative. Literally, the term means "rising," "getting up" (as in rising from a sitting or lying position).

16 The Arab world is historically viewed as consisting of two regions: the *maghrib*, or West, known in English as "North Africa" (Morocco, Tunisia, Algeria, and Libya), and the *mashriq*, or East, which extends from Egypt to Iraq and encompasses the entire Levant. The cultural ties within each section are stronger than those across them, such that each is considered not just a geographical but to some degree also a cultural entity. Jewish writers of the *maghrib* would have belonged to a different cultural sphere, one that had come under particularly strong French influence during the French colonization of North Africa.

17 On Judeo-Arabic see chapter 1, note 77.

18 The exceptional prominence of Jewish intellectuals in Iraq has much to do with the unique character and contours of Iraq's Jewish community, often called the oldest Jewish Diaspora, which many believe dates to the first Babylonian exile some twenty-five hundred years earlier. In 1917, Jews formed the largest single ethnic or religious group in the city. By 1950, about a quarter of Baghdadis were Jewish. Baghdad's Jews held an important and visible role in the economic, social, and cultural life of the city: commerce in the city operated largely on a Jewish calendar, with entire business sectors closing on the Sabbath and other Jewish holy days. The Jewish community of Iraq numbered 140,000 to 150,000 (about 2.5 percent of the overall population). See Berg, *Exile from Exile*, 19; Rejwan, *Jews of Iraq*; and Bashkin, *New Babylonians.*

19 See Moreh, *al-Qissa al-qasira*, esp. the introduction; Snir, "Tmura tarbutit" and idem, "We Were Like Those Who Dream"; Somekh, "Lost Voices" (1989) and idem, "Lost Voices" (1994) (not identical essays).

published it in Arabic with an introduction by a prominent Muslim Iraqi historian; two years later, he translated a number of Omar al-Khayyam's *Rubaiyyat* from Persian to Hebrew. Haddad also wrote secular Hebrew poetry and instructional Hebrew books and was the principal of a Jewish secondary school, yet he declared in 1936, "*Nahnu 'arab qabla an nakun yahudan*": "We are Arabs before we are Jews."[20] In his writings as well as his statements, Haddad embodied the intercultural world of the Iraqi-Jewish intelligentsia.[21]

From the mid-1930s onward, the competing forces of Zionism and Arab nationalism were to put these writers in a tug-of-war with one inevitable outcome: following the creation of the State of Israel in 1948, the rope itself would break, its long-intertwined strands unraveling with unanticipated celerity. Caught in the political fallout of the conflict, Middle Eastern Jews were accused of being fifth columns. From the 1950s through the 1970s, the great majority of the Jews in Arab countries left what, for most, were their ancestral lands, for Israel and the West; some 90 percent of Iraq's inveterate Jewish community departed in 1950–1951 alone. By the end of the twentieth century, Jews like Haddad, who considered themselves part of the Arab collective, would be no more than a historic anachronism, and Iraqi and Egyptian Jewish writers no more than a quickly fading memory in their lands of origin. As historic subjects who fit neither the master narrative of Zionism nor that of Arab nationalism, their contributions to Modern Hebrew and Arabic literatures languish unrecognized, indeed virtually unknown.

THE LEGACY OF SEPHARAD

As a Hebrew writer in Baghdad of 1933, Semaḥ represents the twilight of Hebrew cultural production in Iraq. His poem to Bialik all but closes the curtain on a drama that began exactly seventy years earlier with the establishment of a Hebrew printing press in his city, an event that would briefly make Baghdad the modern center of Hebrew culture in the Arab East. By 1933, Modern Hebrew had been claimed by the Hebrew literary establishment (by now firmly ensconced in pre-state Palestine) as the progeny of the European *haskala* and its successor movement, the *teḥiya*. But for Arab Jews such as Haddad or Semaḥ, modern Hebrew literary history had commenced not with the *haskala*, but with the poetic revolution

20 Rejwan, *Jews of Iraq*, 219.

21 Haddad was the headmaster of al-Wataniyya (National) School from its founding in the 1920s (or, according to Ben Ya'akov, in 1933) until his emigration to Israel in 1951. See also Levy, "Haddad, Ezra," and idem, "Historicizing the Concept of Arab Jews in the *Mashriq*."

of the Sephardi Golden Age. The two-hundred-year Golden Age of Hebrew poetry in Muslim Spain (950–1150) opens with the arrival in Cordoba of another Baghdadi Jewish poet, Dunash ben Labrat, who is credited with the adaptation of Arabic metrics for use in Hebrew verse; it comes to a close with the dislocation of Jewish life under Almohad rule.[22] Remembered primarily for its intermingling of religions and cultures (Arabic, Hebrew, Romance/Mozarabic, Berber, and others), al-Andalus has been much idealized in modern times as a model of coexistence and of creative synthesis among the three monotheistic faiths. Nostalgia notwithstanding, the Andalusian amalgamation engendered remarkable texts by a new class of Jewish courtier elites who wrote in both Hebrew and Arabic—and whose Hebrew poetry constitutes a unique sociocultural phenomenon in the history of Hebrew literature.[23] Their choice of Hebrew (as opposed to Arabic) for writing poetry has been characterized as ethnocentric, yet the literary and linguistic ideology informing this "ethnocentric" poetry was derived entirely from the *host* culture.[24] The result of this somewhat paradoxical situation is, in Ross Brann's collocation, a "literary discourse designed to mediate cultural ambiguity."[25]

For centuries following the catastrophic expulsion from Spain, Sephardi Hebrew poetry remained an important model of creative expression for Middle Eastern Jews, many of whom were themselves descendants of the Sephardi exiles. By 1933, however, the influence of "new" Hebrew poetry was such that very few writers (even among Sephardi and Middle Eastern Jews) were still writing in this style. The Sephardi poetic tradition from al-Andalus, with its rigid prosody and stylistic conventions, was not considered a source for the renewal of Hebrew poetry. Moreover, younger Ashkenazi Hebrew poets were even then rebelling

22 See Brann, "Arabized Jews," 440; also Schirmann, *Toldot ha-shira*, 526–527; and idem, *Ha-shira ha-'ivrit*, 2:24, 55.

23 Ross Brann attributes the adoption of Arabic poetic norms by the elite of Spanish Jewry to the interrelated processes of urbanization and Arabization that accompanied the spread of Islamic civilization beginning in the eighth century. In writing Hebrew poetry, courtier rabbis in Islamic Spain retained Hebrew as their linguistic medium, but adopted Arabic poetic conventions of style, prosody, and content. The innovative aspect of their writing was its use of biblical language and allusion for the secular ends of entertainment and persuasion, such that "a startling fusion of the sacred and the profane became the touchstone of Andalusian Jewish culture" (*Compunctious Poet*, 6, 11).

24 López-Morillas calls it "a new prestige literature" and suggests that Jews looked upon biblical Hebrew as their own classical literary language, the functional equivalent of classical Arabic (the language of poetry and of the Qur'an) ("Language," 43–44). Brann calls the Sephardi Hebrew poetry an expression of "cultural nationalism" (*Compunctious Poet*, 14) and a "subversive appropriation of Arabic culture for Jewish ideological purposes" ("Arabized Jews," 451).

25 Brann, *Compunctious Poet*, 24.

against Bialik's chokehold on Hebrew letters and developing their own modernism, utilizing newer and freer styles, but from within a distinctly Euro-American stylistic frame of reference. Semaḥ's poems, written as a hobby, reflect his scholarly and personal identification with Sepharad; his poem to Bialik must be read in the context of their mutual interest in restoring the literary treasures of the Golden Age.

Semaḥ appears throughout studies of Baghdadi Jewry variously as a rabbi, a poet, and a scholar.[26] Born in 1902, Semaḥ was educated at the French-run Alliance Israélite Universelle school.[27] Unlike most of his Alliance classmates, however, Semaḥ also received religious instruction at Baghdad's modern *yeshiva* (seminary), for which he earned the title *rav* (rabbi). From his youth he was drawn to medieval Hebrew poetry, and he composed poems in Hebrew and Arabic about the horrors of the First World War, which the Ottoman Empire had entered on the German side.[28] He eventually became a bookseller, scholar, and poet. Semaḥ continued to write Hebrew poetry and criticism, as well as a number of collections of *mashal* literature (popular philosophical sayings, folktales, stories, and poems) in Judeo-Arabic, drawing upon sources in Hebrew, Arabic, English, and French.[29]

The archives hold a voluminous correspondence between Semaḥ, the Baghdadi-Jewish poet, and David Yellin (1864–1941), the native Jerusalemite and eminent Hebrew scholar who lived his entire life in Palestine.[30] Along with Eliezer ben Yehuda, Yellin had played a determinative role

26 For the scholarship on Semaḥ, see Avishur, "Sidud ma'arakhot," 4; idem, *Ha-sipur ha-'amami*, 16; Hill, "Hebrew Printing in Baghdad"; and Moreh, "Ha-shira ve-ha-sifrut ha-yafa." Most of the biographical information on Semaḥ presented above is from Ben Ya'akov, *Shira u-fiyut*, 420, and idem, *Yehudey bavel*, 305.

27 Founded in Baghdad in 1864, the Alliance produced the first generation of modern Iraqi Jewish intellectuals and paved the way for the emergence of other secular schools. During the last decade of Ottoman rule, the number of secular educational institutions in Baghdad soared, giving rise to the generation of acculturated Iraqi Jewish writers closely associated with the creation of modern Iraqi fiction.

28 Semaḥ's seminary instructor wanted to publish the collection, but when Semaḥ's father objected on the grounds that it was likely to invoke the wrath of the Ottoman authorities, the instructor burned the collection instead; Ben Ya'akov, *Shira u-fiyut*, 420.

29 See Semaḥ, *Kitab wurud al-da'udiya* and idem, *Amthal al-da'udiya*. Semaḥ's utilization of foreign sources in his *Amthal al-da'udiya* is discussed by Avishur in "Sidud ma'arakhot," 252.

30 The correspondence, by post between Jerusalem and Baghdad, is extensive; most of it dates to 1931–1932, although it continues through 1936. Semaḥ annotates several of his comments about Hebrew poetry with references to Arabic poetry, in beautiful Arabic penmanship (Yellin appears to be able to read it, but does not reply with Arabic writing in his own hand). It is also worth noting that while Semaḥ writes Yellin in the Hebrew script employed by Baghdadi Jews (a cursive Rashi script), when writing Bialik his Hebrew cursive is square, with the exception of the poetry he sends Bialik, for which he uses Rashi script.

in Hebrew's linguistic modernization. He also shared Semaḥ's passion for Sephardi Hebrew poetry, and his *Torat ha-shira ha-sfaradit* (*Introduction to the Hebrew Poetry of the Spanish Period*, 1940) was for many years the authoritative work on the subject. Writing to the Palestinian Sephardi rabbi Benzion Uziel, Yellin described Semaḥ as "one of our people's greatest sages in the [Hebrew] poetry of Spain and the knowledge of Arabic literature and poetry."[31] In his letters to Yellin, Semaḥ would often append a poem, in full rhyme and meter, whose thematic content reflected (or perhaps refracted) the letter's subject matter. Yellin also visited Semaḥ in Baghdad (see Figure 3). During a visit to Palestine in 1932, Semaḥ was Bialik's guest, after which the two poets exchanged letters.[32] Semaḥ also sent Bialik numerous comments on the poems of Solomon ibn Gabirol,[33] whose works Bialik had begun to reissue in the late 1920s. At Yellin's behest, Semaḥ returned to Palestine in 1935 to work at the Institute for the Study of Medieval Hebrew Poetry, where he assisted Yellin with the preparation of the poems of Todros Abu al-'Afiya (Abulafia)[34] for publication. In 1949, following the Palestinian-Arab defeat and creation of Israel, and in the midst of the ensuing deterioration of Jewish life in Iraq, Semaḥ immigrated to Israel. There, he continued to publish scholarly criticism of Sephardi Hebrew poetry, and also published his own poetry in Israeli newspapers and cultural journals.[35]

Semaḥ wrote the birthday poem shortly after his visit to Palestine, and one year before Bialik's death.[36] In light of the respect, indeed celebrity,

31 Ben Ya'akov, *Shira u-fiyut*, 420. Benzion Uziel (1880–1953) served as the chief Sephardic rabbi in British mandatory Palestine (later the State of Israel) from 1938 to 1953; during the period in which Yellin wrote him, he was the chief rabbi of Tel Aviv.

32 The archives contain a copy of a letter from Semaḥ to Bialik dated December 7, 1932, in which Semaḥ refers to a letter sent some months earlier. In it he also includes another poem in Sephardi style (which appears to also be of his own composition, pertaining to his visit to Palestine), which he annotates himself.

33 Solomon ibn Gabirol was an important and prolific Hebrew poet and philosopher, ca. 1021–1058. He penned over four hundred known Hebrew poems and sought to reconcile Jewish thought with Neoplatonism.

34 Another Hebrew poet from Toledo, ca. 1247–1306. Toledo was part of Islamic Iberia until 1085; by Todros Abulafia's lifetime it was part of Castile. Todros Abulafia was, however, still strongly influenced by Arabic literature and by Andalusi Hebrew poetry.

35 I have found his poetry and scholarship in *Moznayim*, 8 Av/July 22, 1931, 1–12; *Haaretz*, 11 Adar 5694/February 26, 1934, 4–5; *Maḥberet* 66–68 (Kislev 5718/December 1957): 8; and *Tarbits*, Tishrey 5721/October 1961, 72–83. He apparently also published in the journals *Ha-hed* and *Mizraḥ u-ma'arav*.

36 Yellin had written Semaḥ the week before Bialik's sixtieth birthday, informing him of the upcoming celebration. Perhaps this prompted Semaḥ to write the poem. It was apparently published in the journal *Moznayim*, presumably in commemoration of the departed "national poet." The poem was later reprinted in a 1959 anthology of poems dedicated to Bialik, *Shir ha-sharim*

Figure 3. Meeting of Yellin (third from left) and Semaḥ (fourth from left), Baghdad, winter 1932–1933. Courtesy of the Central Zionist Archives, Jerusalem.

Bialik commanded by then, one would expect nothing less than a paean to this "prince of poetry," as the poem calls him. And indeed, Semaḥ's poem delivers praise of the highest order—but not only of Bialik. Through a multilayered, deeply intertextual mesh of references, the poem creates a nuanced picture of Modern Hebrew poetry that is in dialogue *both* with the Sephardi tradition and with the revolutionary poetics spearheaded by Bialik. It celebrates yet decenters Bialik's persona as the modern-day "prophet" of poetry by locating the cultural origins of Modern Hebrew poetry in *'arav*, a term used in postbiblical Hebrew to connote Arabo-Islamic civilization. Between the lines, Semaḥ may have been quietly establishing his own role as a successor to the Sephardi Hebrew poets in the revival of Hebrew letters.

le-Ḥ. N. Biyalik; more on this anthology to follow. In the anthology, it appears under the title "Bat shirat sefarad taḥog ḥag yovel ha-shishim" (lit., The daughter of the poetry of Sepharad celebrates the sixtieth jubilee). It appears without title in Ben Ya'akov, *Shira u-fiyut*, 422.

ליובל הששים של המשורר חיים נחמן ביאליק

יְשִׁירוּן עֵת יְשׁוּרוּן בּוֹ יְשׁוּרוּן   עֲדִינַת הַיָּפִי בִּימֵי עֲלוּמִים
מְנַגֶּנֶת וְכִנּוֹרָהּ בְּחֵיקָהּ   וְזִמְרָתָהּ תְּשַׂמַּח לֵב עֲגוּמִים
וְיַעֲלַת חֵן בְּלֹא כָחֹל וְשָׂרֹק   מְעֻטֶּרֶת בְּכָל מִינֵי בְשָׂמִים
וְטַפָּחָה בְתוֹךְ עֲרָב וּמֵהֶם   מְקֻשֶּׁטֶת וְעַל אַפָּהּ נְזָמִים
וְאַרְבַּעַת צְמִידִים עַל יָדֶיהָ   וְחָרוּז דַּר מְיַפֶּה הַגְּלָמִים
וְעַל שׁוּלֵי מְעִילָהּ פַּעֲמוֹנִים   מְצַלְצְלִים עֲלֵי שֵׁם הַחֲכָמִים
יְתוֹמָה הִיא וְאָבִיהָ הֲכִי חַי   וְנוֹלְדָה לוֹ בְלִי צִירִים וְדָמִים ?
אֲנִי מֵאָז שְׁמַעְתִּיהָ תְּרַנֵּן   וְאָבִינָה נְגִינַת הַיְתוֹמִים
שְׁאַלְתִּיהָ : לְמִי אַתְּ הָעֲדִינָה   וּבַת מִי מִקְּדוֹשִׁים אַתְּ וְרָמִים ?
הֱשִׁיבַתְנִי : אֲנִי הַבַּת אֲשֶׁר יַד   אֲבוֹתַי תַּהֲפֹךְ הַצּוּר אֲגַמִּים
אָבִיא קָרְבָּן בְּחָגֵּי חַג נְבִיא שִׁיר   לְהָבִיא לִקְרַאת הוֹדוֹ שְׁלָמִים
אֲשֶׁר הוּא גִדְּלַנִי מִנְּעוּרַי   עֲפְרוֹת עָשׁ וְתוֹלָע, הַזְּעוּמִים
אֲנִי הַבַּת אֲבוֹתֶיהָ נְבִיאִים   לְהוֹדָם נִרְצְעוּ לֵילוֹת וְיָמִים.
וְרָמְזָה לִי בְעֵין יָמִין עֲלֵיהֶם   וְתוֹרֶה עַל שְׁנֵי אִישִׁים עֲרֵמִים
רְאִיתִימוֹ בְשִׂפְתוֹת דוֹבְבוֹת אֶל   זְמִיר בְּתֻם אֲשֶׁר בִּשְׂפַת יְקוּמִים
וּבַחֲזוֹתָם יְדַעְתִּימוֹ וְהֵמָּה   גְּבִירוֹל עִם בְּנוֹ עֶזְרָא רְאֵמִים
וְסֵפֶר עַל יְדֵי בִתָּם לְפָנַי   מְמֻלָּא דַר וּמִינֵי יַהֲלֹמִים
וְאַבִּיט בּוֹ וְהַכָּתוּב לְחַיִּים   מְאֹד יָפֶה וְאִם לֹא בָא בְיָמִים
וְחוֹצֵב לַהֲבוֹת אֵשׁ בִּזְמִירִים   יְחַשְׁמֵל עוֹרְקֵי שׁוֹמְעָיו וְרָמִים
יְחִיד הַדּוֹר וְאַבִּיר שִׁיר הֲלֹא הוּא   בְדוֹרֵנוּ וּמַחְמַדָּיו עֲצוּמִים
וְחַטֹּאת הַזְּמַן רַבּוּ בְּאָבְדוֹ   שְׂפַת עַמִּי וְנִתְמַלָּא אֲשָׁמִים
עֲדֵי בָא הוּא וְהֶחְיָה אֶת שְׂפָתָם   וְאֵין עוֹד בַּזְּמַן חַטָּאת וּמוּמִים
לְכָךְ חַיִּים קְרָאוּהוּ אֲבוֹתָיו   וְחִיָּה אֶת שְׂפַת תּוֹרַת תְּמִימִים
וְלִפְעָמִים יְהוּא קָשִׁים חֲכָמִים   וְהוּא נֹחַ וְאִישׁ צַדִּיק וְתָמִים
אֲהוּב הַכֹּל וְהַכֹּל נֶאֱהָבָיו   וּמַחְמַדָּיו בְּלֵב יַמִּים רְשׁוּמִים
אֲבָרְכֶנּוּ בְחַג שִׁשִּׁים וְיִמְעַט   בְּעֵינַי לוֹ מְלֹא עוֹלָם שְׁלוּמִים.

Transliteration of "La-yovel ha-shishim shel Ḥayim Naḥman Biyalik"[37]

1	*yeshirun ‘et yeshurun bo yeshurun*	*‘adinat ha-yofi bimey ‘alumim*
2	*menagenet ve-khinora be-ḥeykah*	*ve-zimrata tesamaḥ lev ‘agumim*
3	*ve-ya‘lat ḥen be-lo khahol ve-saroq*	*me‘uteret be-khol miney besamim*
4	*ve-tupaḥa be-tokh ‘arav u-me-hem*	*mequshetet ve-‘al apa nezamim*
5	*ve-arba‘at tsemidim ‘al yadeha*	*ve-ḥaruz dar meyape ha-gelamim*
6	*ve-‘al shuley me‘ila pa‘amonim metsaltselim*	*‘aley shem ha-ḥakhamim*
7	*yetoma hi ve-aviha hakhi ḥay*	*ve-nolda lo bli tsirim ve-damim?*
8	*ani me’az shema‘tiha teranen*	*ve-avina neginat ha-yetomim*
9	*she’altiha: le-mi at ha-‘adina*	*u-vat mi mi-qedoshim at ve-ramim?*
10	*heshivatni: ani ha-bat asher yad*	*avotay tahafokh ha-tsur agamim*
11	*avi qorban ba-ḥogi ḥag*	*le-havi li-krat hodo shelamim*
12	*asher hu gidlani mi-ne‘uray nevi shir*	*‘afrot ‘ash ve-tola‘a, ha-ze‘umim*
13	*ani ha-bat avoteha nevi’im*	*le-hodam nirtsa‘u leylot ve-yamim.*
14	*ve-ramza li be-‘eyn yamin ‘aleyhem*	*ve-tore ‘al shney ishim ‘arumim*
15	*ra’itimo be-siftot dovevot el*	*zamir bitam asher bi-sefat yequmim*
16	*u-vaḥzotam yada‘timo ve-heyma*	*gevirol ‘im bno ‘ezra re’emim*
17	*ve-sefer ‘al yadey vitam lefanay*	*memula dar u-miney yahalumim*
18	*ve-abit bo ve-ha-katuv le-ḥayim*	*me’od yafe ve-im lo ba ve-yamim*
19	*ve-ḥotsev lahavot esh ba-zmirim*	*yeḥashmel ‘orqey shom‘av zeramim*
20	*yaḥid ha-dor ve-abir shir ha-lo hu*	*ba-doreynu u-maḥmadav ‘atsumim*
21	*ve-ḥatot ha-zeman rabu be-abdo*	*sefat ‘ami ve-nitmala ashemim*
22	*‘adey ba hu ve-heḥya et sefatam*	*ve-eyn ‘od ba-zman ḥatat u-mumim*
23	*le-khakh ḥa’yim qera’uhu avotav*	*ve-ḥiya et sefat torat temimim*
24	*ve-lif‘amim yehu qashim ḥakhamim*	*ve-hu no’aḥ ve-ish tsadiq ve-tamim*
25	*ahuv ha-kol ve-ha-kol ne’ehavav*	*u-maḥmadav be-lev yamim reshumim*
26	*avarkhenu be-ḥag shishim ve-yim‘at*	*be-‘eynay lo malo ‘olam shelomim.*

37 Ben Ya‘akov, *Shira u-fiyut*, 422, with corrections of minor errors. My translation takes minimal poetic license for the purpose of rendering in comprehensible English what is a highly mannered, stylized Hebrew. In the interests of English syntax, I dispense with the break between hemistiches. Nearly every line of the poem contains at least one rich metaphor or bilingual pun; here I mention only those relevant to this chapter's central concerns. For this poem only, I transliterate *quf* as *q* rather than *k*, to reflect both Sephardi pronunciation and proximity to Arabic. I thank Tova Rosen and Raymond Scheindlin for their generous assistance with the poem's transliteration and translation, including corrections of Ben Ya‘akov's errors. For a more detailed close reading of the poem, see Levy, "From Baghdad to Bialik."

Translation of "For the Sixtieth Jubilee of the Poet Ḥayim Naḥman Bialik"

1 Yeshurun sings, when in him it sees a delicate beauty in the bloom of her youth[38]
2 playing the lyre in her bosom's embrace, her song gladdening the sorrowful heart.
3 A charming doe[39] [even] without kohl or rouge, perfumed[40] with all kinds of fragrances,
4 she was cultivated amongst the Arabs, and from them she is adorned with nose-rings
5 and [with] four bracelets on her arms and a mother-of-pearl necklace[41] that embellishes the body.
6 On the hems of her cloak bells tinkle the names of the sages [great rabbis].
7 She is an orphan, and yet her father indeed lives, and she was born to him without labor pains or blood!
8 I had heard her sing long ago, and understood this as the song of orphans,
9 [and so] I asked her: "Whose are you, delicate one, whose daughter from amongst the holy and exalted?"
10 She answered me: "I am the daughter whose forefathers' hand turned the rock into water.
11 I will bring a sacrifice in celebration of the festival of the prophet of poetry[42] to honor him with a perfect offering,[43]
12 he who raised me from my youth of loathsome dust, moth and worm.
13 I am the daughter whose forefathers were prophets, and to whose glory nights and days are enslaved."
14 And with her right eye she winked to show me two wise men.
15 I saw them with their lips moving to the song of their daughter, which was in the mouths of all people.
16 Upon seeing them, I recognized them, and they were Gabirol with ibn 'Ezra, the giants[44]

38 Literally, "in the days of youth."

39 Literally, "a charming ibex."

40 *Me'uteret be-khol miney besamim*: *me'uteret* is a loan word from the Arabic *'itr* (fragrance or perfume).

41 *Ḥaruz dar*: literally, a mother-of-pearl bead; probably a necklace made of beads.

42 Puns with "the festival on which we bring poetry."

43 Literally, "bring to his splendor a whole [perfect] offering." Here the term *shelamim* refers to a sacrifice translated as a "peace offering" or "whole offering," often used in celebration.

44 Literally, "rams" or "wild oxen."

17 and before me was a book in the hands of their daughter, filled with all kinds of precious pearls and diamonds
18 and I looked at it and the book written by Ḥayim[45] and it was very beautiful, even if not ancient,
19 striking sparks of fire with the poems[46] and electrifying the flow of blood in its listeners' veins.
20 Verily, he is unique in his generation, a knight of poetry, and his virtues are great!
21 The sins of Time[47] waxed great when it destroyed the language of my people and it [the language] became full of sin[48]
22 until he came and revived their language, so that Time's guilt was removed.[49]
23 And therefore his parents called him Ḥayim [life]: because he completely rejuvenated the language of Torah.
24 Though sages may be harsh at times, he is a mild, righteous, and blameless man,
25 everyone's darling, friend to all, so that his virtues are inscribed in the heart of time.[50]
26 I'll congratulate him on the festival of his sixtieth [birthday], and in my eyes a whole world of congratulations would be too small for him.

A MYSTERIOUS MAIDEN

The poem begins with an extended metaphor, introducing the "delicate beauty in the bloom of her youth" (line 1). Who is this mysterious maiden? The phrase *ve-ya'lat ḥen be-lo khaḥol ve-saroq*, "a charming doe (even) without kohl or rouge," invoked in line 3 idiomatically means "the real thing."[51] In the poem, the phrase personifies the maiden and represents Hebrew

45 Puns with "dedicated to life."

46 Alternatively, "hews flames of fire out of songs."

47 In medieval Hebrew and Arabic, "time" also connotes "fate" or "destiny."

48 I.e., Time was filled with blame.

49 I.e., Time has ruined Hebrew, but Bialik has rebuilt what Time ruined.

50 Literally "the days." This use of *yamim* (days) is a personification of time (used invoked in the sense of fate); in medieval Hebrew and Arabic, saying someone's virtues were inscribed on your heart was a term of affection. Here, the speaker's affection for Bialik is inscribed not on his own heart, but on the heart of time, as if to say that time itself has recognized his virtues and embraced him.

51 In the Babylonian Talmud, it is mentioned in the context of wedding rituals, as a song sung in Palestine of antiquity to celebrate the beauty of the bride; in Aramaic, *la-kaḥal ve-la saraq ve-la pirkus—ve-ya'lat ḥen* (Tractate Ketubot 17a), while its Modern Hebrew derivative is *le-lo keḥal u-sraq*. See under *kaḥal* in Even-Shoshan, *Ha-milon he-ḥadash*, 730.

poetry as an art whose beauty is innate and genuine, not cosmetic.[52] But then, in lines 4 and 5, we learn that the beautiful maiden was "cultivated amongst the Arabs, and from them she is adorned with nose-rings," with "four bracelets on her arms and a mother-of-pearl bead" (*ḥaruz*, punning on "bead" and "rhyme") that embellishes the body—in other words, that endows the poem with aesthetic form.[53] The medieval Sephardi poets frequently compared Hebrew language or poetry to a beautiful woman, and this modern poet leaves no doubt as to the maiden's cultural identity. She is the embodiment of Hebrew verse, but her meter, structure, and intercultural references are Arabic in origin, and she was nurtured, developed, and cultivated in the Arab cultural milieu. Thus, while the *essence* of her beauty is Hebrew (Hebrew, as the language of God and Torah, is innately beautiful), her style, her appearance, her character—indeed, all the external adornments that endow her innate loveliness with a distinct aesthetic form—are *Arabic*.

As to her parentage, however, the poet still has a few tricks up his sleeve. Line 7 introduces the riddle *yetoma hi ve-aviha hakhi ḥay / ve-nolda lo bli tsirim ve-damim?* (She is an orphan, yet her father lives! And she was born to him without labor pains or blood?) Through this paradox, Semaḥ invokes the well-known medieval genre of riddle poems, but with a deliciously subversive twist. The poem intimates the maiden's paternity through the words *hakhi ḥay*, punning on Bialik's first name, Ḥayim (life). The phrase "without labor pains or blood" recalls Bialik's seminal essay "Ḥevley lashon" ("Language Pangs," 1905), in which Bialik argues that to put an end to Modern Hebrew's "labor pains," Hebrew must acquire a truly "living," spoken register.[54] The phrase is also a nod to the classical Arabic tradition that great poetry is produced effortlessly, either by

52 This in turn recalls the classical Arabic polemic over *kadhib* and *sidq* (untruth and truth) in poetry. According to Mansour Ajami, most medieval critics conceived of truthful language as that which conforms to "reality and to the poet's intent," according to which "the best poetry obtains by the logical ordering of words and meanings." Untrue poetry, on the other hand, is that which employs excessive metaphor, exaggeration, or hyperbole. See Ajami, *Alchemy of Glory*, 1–2.

53 The Hebrew word *ḥaruz* (bead) puns with "rhyme"; see editor's note, Ben Ya'akov, *Shira u-fiyut*, 422. This "bead" endows the poem with its aesthetic form (much as jewelry embellishes the body). I believe the four bracelets on the maiden's arms might also refer to a particular metric scheme or other structural feature of Andalusian Hebrew poetry. Jonathan Decter suggests that the word *tsemidim* (bracelets) is similar to the word *tsimudim*, *tsimud* being a Hebrew technical term created by David Yellin to designate the Arabic *tajnis* or *jinas* ("paronomasia": wordplay, often alliterative or assonant, based on shared roots), a rhetorical figure applied by the Sephardi poets to their Hebrew verse (Decter, personal communication, March 25, 2005).

54 Bialik, "Ḥevley lashon," in *Kol kitvey Biyalik*, 197–198. As for the essay's date of publication, according to Chana Kronfeld, while it is usually attributed to *Ha-shiloaḥ* 18 (1907), it first appeared two years earlier in a special edition of *'Ivriya*; see Kronfeld, *On the Margins of Modernism*, 248. I borrow the translation "Language Pangs" from Kronfeld.

daemonic inspiration or by natural talent—an idea that dovetails both with the ancient Latin term *poeta vates* and with the Romantic trope of poet as prophet, which Bialik embraced, and which is made explicit in line 11, where Bialik is called the "prophet of poetry."[55] Together, lines 7 and 11 suggest that the maiden is the singular daughter of Bialik, whose poetic greatness is such as to have produced her in an immaculate birth of sorts, an idea that is a common trope of Andalusian Arabic and Hebrew writing.

But—and here is the twist—even as line 7 hints that the father is Bialik, the same line also destabilizes this reading by invoking at least two important medieval intertexts whose readings suggest an entirely different solution to the riddle. The first intertext is the famous "Shira yetoma" (literally, "Orphaned Poem"; idiomatically, "Singular Song") of Yosef ibn Ḥasday: *arusa at—ve-hi la-'ad betula, / ve-im la av—ve-hineyha yetoma* (She is betrothed to you—yet forever a virgin, / and she has a father, but is an orphan).[56] The "Shira yetoma" was composed by ibn Ḥasday for his friend, the great Hebrew poet and prime minister of Granada Samuel ibn Naghrila (ha-Nagid, 993–1056); in the poem, ibn Ḥasday boasts of his personal role in reviving Hebrew through his poetic labor. Bialik, moreover, had also penned a poem he called "Shira yetoma" in 1900. And the plot thickens: we find an even closer textual match to those lines about the orphan in the introductory *maqama* of Yehuda al-Ḥarizi's thirteenth-century masterpiece, *Taḥkemoni*.[57]

The *Taḥkemoni* begins with the speaker's long lament about the deplorable condition of Hebrew and the faithlessness of all those Jewish poets who have been seduced by Hagar (Arabic), leaving Saray (Hebrew) barren. The speaker will thus take it upon himself to find the Hebrew language (in the guise of a beautiful woman, of course) and to have intercourse with her; their offspring will be the *maqamat* that follow in the collection. In a reenactment of the biblical story of the first encounter with Rebecca,[58] the speaker meets a beautiful maiden at the well, and inquires,

55 Reuven Shoham argues that while both the *haskala* and the Hebrew poetry of Sepharad utilized biblical rhetorical/thematic models such as that of prophecy, Sephardi poetry did not use this trope (or the Bible in general) to try to "reform the normative cultural system of the Jews," whereas the *haskala* "embraced the Bible and the image of the prophet as part of its overt and covert struggle to change values in the Jewish world." Concerning Bialik's use of the "prophetic I," it is believed that he derived it from models in Russian (and other) Romantic poetry, particularly from Pushkin. See Shoham, *Poetry and Prophecy*, 1–3; and Miron, *Prophetic Mode*.

56 The "Singular Song" is a translation of the title suggested by Brann (*Compunctious Poet*, 49). See Schirmann, *Ha-shira ha-'ivrit*, 1:175.

57 A *maqama* is an Arabic genre of narrative in rhymed prose, often recounting the adventures of a narrator and his trickster counterpart. The genre was invented by Badi' al-Zaman al-Hamadhani in the tenth century in the Muslim East and became popular in al-Andalus, where it was also adapted into Hebrew by such writers as al-Ḥarizi. See also Drory, "Maqama," 190–210.

58 See Genesis 24:10-20 (*Tanakh*, 43).

"Whose daughter are you? And from what quarry were you hewn?" She replies, "I am an orphan yet my father lives [*ani yetoma ve-avi ḥay*]. . . . I am the Holy Tongue, your mistress. And if I be pleasing in your eyes, I will be your companion."[59] The *Taḥkemoni*'s speaker describes the maiden as adorned with the "jewelry" of his own poetic gifts: "the earrings of my praises are in her ears and the necklace of my verses around her neck"—"ornaments" with modern echoes in lines 4 and 5 of Semaḥ's poem.

Together, Semaḥ's orphan, necklace, and bead form a cluster of poetic associations that date back to the tenth and eleventh centuries. One of the classical Arabic terms for poetry is *nazm* or *manzum*, meaning "strung" (as in the sense of beads or pearls arranged and strung on a thread).[60] In such a necklace, the centerpiece, which has no counterpart on left or right and is hence unique, is often called the *yatima*, the female orphan.[61] All these interrelated elements appear in both Semaḥ's poem and the *Taḥkemoni*: the unique, beautiful "daughter" who is Hebrew poetry, and who is also an orphan; the "bead" that is also a rhyme (*ḥaruz*); and the necklace that, in its aesthetic conjoining of these individual "beads," is the poem. But what is more telling is that in both the "Shira yetoma" and the *Taḥkemoni*, the speaker (who in both cases also identifies himself as the text's author) sees *himself* as the savior and rejuvenator of Hebrew.[62]

59 Yehuda al-Ḥarizi, *Taḥkemoni*, 72–73; translation adapted from Reichert, 1:33–34.

60 In the opening of *Taḥkemoni*'s introductory *maqama*, for instance, the speaker says, "ve-haya ka-'anak la-shir" (he was as a necklace for poetry) (al-Ḥarizi, *Taḥkemoni*, 63).

61 The Andalusian scholar ibn 'Abd Rabbihi even modeled his anthology of poetry *al-'Iqd al-farid* (The unique necklace) on this pattern, such that each chapter is named after a stone and hence doubled, except for the "centerpiece" chapter, which is called the *farida* (the feminine form of "unique one," similar to *yatima*). The Hebrew word *yetoma* (female orphan), first mentioned in line 7 of Semaḥ's poem, immediately evokes its Arabic cognate and counterpart, *yatima*. While it, too, literally means (female) orphan, in the Arabic tradition it connotes a unique line of poetry, whose uniqueness is such that it is incapable of being reworked by other poets in their verse. For example, the title of al-Tha'libi's eleventh-century anthology of poetry, *Yatimat al-dahr* (The unique one of the age), illustrates how the word *yatima* comes to signify poetic uniqueness. In terms of the ibn Ḥasday–ha-Nagid correspondence, although ha-Nagid is the more famous poet, ibn Ḥasday's "Shira yetoma" is considered the finest poem of that period, hence the title (which may been decided long after its composition, as happened with medieval works). In this literary tradition, the poem is the "daughter" of the poet; the more excellent this daughter, the more she becomes "barren," because truly great poetry can neither reproduce nor be reproduced. This concept underscores the line from "Shira yetoma," inasmuch as the maiden (here, self-referentially representing the poem) will remain "forever a virgin." See also Kilito, *Author and His Doubles*, esp. 19–20, 28–31. I thank Michael Cooperson and Shamma Boyarin for bringing these connections to my attention.

62 One minor distinction: In ibn Ḥasday's "Shira yetoma," as in Semaḥ's poem, the beautiful maiden is identified directly with Hebrew poetry; in al-Ḥarizi's *Taḥkemoni*, she is the Hebrew *language* itself.

Thus we have two possible "fathers": Bialik and the speaker. Then, to complicate matters further, in lines 14–16, the maiden indicates that she is in fact the daughter of the two "wise men," the Sephardi Hebrew poets Solomon ibn Gabirol and Moses ibn 'Ezra, whose works Bialik had recently co-edited and published; in line 17, the speaker also calls her "their daughter."[63] Throughout the poem, then, lineage and paternity are blurred. The poem implies a line of succession from the Sephardi poets to Bialik, naturalizing Bialik into a tradition of belletristic Hebrew writing that began in *Sefarad.* Bialik would by no means have opposed such a linkage, which affirmed his own master narrative of Hebrew creativity as a semicontinuous, autonomous tradition spanning antiquity to modernity, whose common thread of "Hebrew genius" connected discrete historical moments, and to which he considered himself heir.[64] Indeed, in 1918 Bialik had said that the title *ha-meshorer ha-le'umi*, the national poet, by which he was already known, should be attributed first to Judah ha-Levi.[65] However, as we will see shortly, Bialik held a different view of the historical origins of Modern Hebrew literature.

Finally, there is the book in the maiden's hands, which, upon closer inspection, the speaker attributes to Bialik ("Ḥayim"). Bialik's book is not only beautiful, but powerful, striking sparks of fire with its poems and electrifying the blood in its listeners' veins.[66] Line 19 sweeps from antiquity to modernity: it begins with the biblical metaphor of rock and fire, and culminates in a distinctly modern metaphor through the word *ḥashmal*, a mystical term from Ezekiel newly refurbished to mean "electricity" in Modern Hebrew, and which Semaḥ uses in a very contemporary

63 Editor's note, Ben Ya'akov, *Shira u-fiyut*, 422. Bialik wrote in a letter that there was more "modernism" in the poems of Moses ibn 'Ezra than in much recent Hebrew poetry, though he hastened to add, "but do not understand from this that I, God forbid, belittle our fledgling poetry!" See Bialik, *Igarot Biyalik*, 4:25, quoted in "Eyn ani mevin keytsad melamdim ha-sfaradim mi-tokh sifrey limud shel ashkenazim," H-1. Regarding Moses ibn 'Ezra, Raymond Scheindlin sees him as the quintessential Andalusian Jewish intellectual precisely *because* of his simultaneous Arabness and Jewishness: "Of all the Arabized poets of the Hebrew Golden Age in al-Andalus, Moses (Abu Harun) Ibn 'Ezra is the one whose poetry most resembles that of an Arab poet. . . . The interplay of Arabo-Islamic and Jewish elements . . . is so fully developed in him as to render him a model case of an Andalusian Jewish intellectual" ("Moses Ibn 'Ezra," 252).

64 Bialik uses the term "Hebrew genius" in "Teḥiyat ha-sfaradim," his lecture on the revival of the Sephardim, discussed at length below.

65 This is according to a student of Bialik's in Odessa, in his 1918 notes on Bialik's lectures on Sephardi Hebrew literature. See "Toldot ha-sifrut ha-'ivrit" (signed in Cyrillic script) in the Education Archives at Tel Aviv University.

66 The biblical descriptive phrase *ḥotsev lahavot esh* (literally, "quarrying flames") has come idiomatically to connote a rousing speech; to a traditional reader, it suggests revelation. The phrase originates in Psalm 29; it is rendered in one translation as "the voice of the Lord kindles flames of fire" (*Tanakh*, 1138).

way (*le-ḥashmel*, "to electrify," in the sense of "enthrall"). The line links the medieval Hebrew idiom of the poem with the Modern Hebrew represented by Bialik.

With all these possible fathers, how can we determine the paternity of Modern Hebrew poetry? In lines 21 to 24, Semaḥ focuses overtly on Bialik's colossal role in revitalizing the Hebrew language. Yet Semaḥ places Bialik's own book in the hands of the daughter of the great Sephardi poets ibn 'Ezra and ibn Gabirol—thereby locating the revival of Hebrew and creation of secular poetry within the Sephardi tradition. Moreover, through its intertextual allusions, Semaḥ's poem overtly praises Bialik while covertly asserting its own composer's status in Hebrew letters. This kind of play between text and subtext was a familiar poetic convention of al-Andalus/Sepharad: poets would trade praise poems among themselves, each working to outdo the other in their poetic virtuosity and therefore implicitly flattering not the subject of the poem so much as themselves (recall that ibn Ḥasday used his "Shira yetoma," written for his friend ha-Nagid, as an opportunity for self-promotion). Similarly, through his panegyric, Semaḥ may have sought to establish a relationship with Bialik akin to that of ibn Ḥasday and ha-Nagid: a relationship of peers and of equals. But in the hierarchical structure of modern East-West relations, was such a relationship really possible?

FROM JERUSALEM TO CAIRO: THE "REVIVAL OF THE SEPHARDIM"

We know very little about the relationship between these two figures other than the fact that they had corresponded and that Bialik had hosted Semaḥ during his 1932 visit. As discussed in the previous chapter, European Jewish immigrants to Palestine, like many Europeans of their time, considered themselves culturally and intellectually superior to non-Europeans. In Palestine, "Sephardic" (Southeastern European, Asian, and African) Jews were often referred to disparagingly as "Asiatics" or "Levantines." This brings us to the popular perception that Bialik himself held an aversion to Middle Eastern Jews, and had said he detested *frenkim* (a derogatory term for Sephardi and Middle Eastern Jews) because they reminded him of Arabs—a charge that Bialik himself vehemently denied. In 2004 the literary supplement of the Israeli daily newspaper *Haaretz* ran an article attempting to end the controversy surrounding the alleged remark.[67] Its author questioned how Bialik could have devoted a decade of

67 The alleged statement appears in two formulations. The first, "I hate Arabs because they're like the Sephardim" or "I hate Arabs because they're like the *frenkim*" is referred to in Avineri, "Bialik ve-'edot ha-mizraḥ," H-1. Elsewhere the statement is inverted as "I hate *frenkim*

his life to Sephardi poetry, calling it the greatest creation since the Bible and Talmud, if he abhorred contemporary Sephardim.[68] (Unfortunately, the article served less to exonerate Bialik than to reinforce the offensive assumption that being likened to an Arab is an unequivocal affront.)[69]

While the alleged comment is probably apocryphal, Bialik had in fact discussed contemporary "Sephardim" (by which he meant all non-European Jews) in highly patronizing, if ostensibly sympathetic, terms. In 1927, Bialik delivered a lengthy lecture in Jerusalem at the invitation of Histadrut Ḥalutsey ha-Mizraḥ (Association of Mizraḥi Pioneers), a group of young Sephardi natives of Palestine who sought to affiliate themselves with the burgeoning Zionist movement. The lecture was titled "Teḥiyat ha-sfaradim" ("The Revival of the Sephardim"), and it called upon Sephardi Jewry to awake from its state of torpor and reclaim its legacy of cultural grandeur. While Sephardi Jews were the leading creative force for the entire Jewish people during the Spanish Golden Age, says Bialik, they have fallen into deep decline for the past five hundred years. Why, wonders Bialik, did the Divine Spirit (*ruaḥ ha-kodesh*) abandon the Sephardim, and where did it go?[70]

Bialik begins by establishing his own credentials in Sephardi matters as a scholar of Golden Age Hebrew literature, then tells his audience that it "is not so easy to penetrate and comprehend the soul of the Sephardi

---

because they remind me of Arabs" or variations thereof. Ammiel Alcalay, for instance, writes that Bialik "couldn't abide Sephardic Jews because they reminded him of Arabs"; *After Jews and Arabs*, 154 (Alcalay's reference is Naḥum Menaḥem, *Metaḥim ve-aflaya 'adatit be-yisra'el*, 83; Alcalay, *After Jews and Arabs*, 307n69).

68 In the introduction to his edition of ibn Gabirol's poetry, Bialik states, "After the Holy Scriptures and the *aggada* of the Talmud and Midrash, without a doubt there is no greater creative endeavor throughout the generations than that of Sephardic poetry. The 'greats,' of great and lofty spirit all, toiled for its composition" (Bialik, "Introduction," vii).

69 The article's main point is that since Bialik really *liked* Sephardim, he couldn't possibly have put them in the same category as *Arabs*! The author, Shmuel Avineri, quotes a letter from an offended author writing to the Israeli daily *Yediot aḥaronot* in 1969: "By putting us in the same category as Arabs, Bialik has become a symbol of schism and fraternal hatred in the eyes of Sephardim and Mizraḥim." Avineri defends Bialik against the charges of anti-Sephardi racism rather than addressing the overt anti-Arab racism of this writer's complaint. This irony was not lost on the article's readers, as one sees in the letters from the following week (*Haaretz*, January 9, 2004, H3). In his article, Avineri endeavors to clear Bialik's name first by showing how much Bialik admired the Sephardi poets, then by relating anecdotal, third-party reminiscences of Bialik vehemently denying any connection to the infamous statement, and finally by attributing the statement to someone else. To convey Bialik's depth of admiration for the Sephardim, Avineri employs patronizing language ("Bialik's words about the weakness that had visited itself upon the Sephardi community in the present [were] said in a loving spirit and as an impetus for reform") as well as Orientalist assertions ("Bialik didn't deprive himself from enjoying the beauty of the daughters of the Oriental Jewish communities")—delivering, in short, the proverbial apology that is worse than the insult. See Avineri, "Bialik ve-'edot ha-mizraḥ," H-4.

70 Bialik, "Teḥiyat ha-sfaradim," 111.

tribe [*nefesh ha-shevet ha-sfaradi*], which due to historical and other circumstances became a special tribe [*ne'asa le-shevet meyuḥad*]."[71] Having thus summarily defined his own listeners as impenetrable, inscrutable, and exotic, he asks them,

> And this tribe [the Sephardim], which contained nearly the whole of the Hebrew genius in the Diaspora for hundreds of years, and which was the creative force for the entire [Jewish] nation, both in its own time and for generations to come—how is it possible that after this glory, a time of spiritual and creative decline befell it, until it became entirely estranged from Hebrew creativity and was left, if I may dare to say it, a dry branch, or at least not a branch that bears fruit?[72]

From there, Bialik launches into a detailed historical explanation. The European Enlightenment, he postulates, actuated a radical, wide-scale spiritual and psychological transformation of European Jewry (the *teḥiya* or revival), leading ineluctably to the national revival.[73] This transformative force eluded the rest of the Jewish world, leaving the Sephardim untouched by modernity and the spirit of revival. Bialik even informs his Sephardi audience that their incorporation into the national revival in Palestine presents him with an unusual challenge: "And when one comes to an organization of Sephardi Jewry in order to insert them into the framework of the Hebrew *teḥiya* (revival), let us not delude ourselves that this is at all easy or that it can be done superficially."[74] He declares that the hope for the Sephardi revival is to be found in their glorious literary past, their only "banner." "I believe in full faith," he exhorts his

71 Ibid., 110. Modern Hebrew has no neutral words for race or ethnicity; as noted in chapter 1, the term *'eda* (ethnic or religious community) is used widely in the collocation *'edot ha-mizraḥ* to characterize contemporary Sephardi and Mizraḥi Jews, but is never applied to Ashkenazi Jews (see also chapter 1, note 85). Here Bialik, an Ashkenazi Jew, deploys the biblical word *shevet* (tribe) to describe modern Sephardi and Mizraḥi Jews, with no irony.

72 He continues, "There is no denying that the hegemony [*ha-hegemonya*] passed on to other communities and groups, and that during the previous centuries, in terms of its national [Jewish] creative power, Sephardi Jewry stood on a lower rung than the rest of the Russian-Polish Jews known as Ashkenazim, and that the contribution of the Sephardim was trifling compared to the creative output of the rest of the Jewish people [*ha-uma*]. I asked myself how to explain this; where did this tribe's Divine Spirit [*ru'aḥ ha-kodesh*] escape, and where did its creative spirit flee when the time came for the revival of the Jewish people [*teḥiya le-yisra'el*]? . . . Why didn't the spirit of revival touch them and awaken them from their lethargic slumber, and shake their soul and renew their creative power?" (ibid., 111).

73 The revival (*teḥiya*) of Ashkenazi Jewry and that of the Hebrew language, says Bialik, were preceded by a century and a half of psychological or spiritual "shocks" (*za'zu'im nafshi'im pnimi'im*) that paved the way for the *teḥiya*; ibid., 111.

74 Ibid., 111.

listeners, "that your revival needs to begin there. You must renew your relationship to that past, which in my opinion begins after the redaction of the Talmud"; hence the recovery of the Sephardi literary corpus is an absolute precondition of the desired revival.[75] In addition, he continues, the Sephardim must take pains to safeguard and preserve their folk heritage.[76] Finally, Bialik suggests educational reforms, advocating new textbooks that would include the Sephardi cultural heritage.[77]

Bialik's view that the Sephardim had been left untouched by the Enlightenment and by modernity and were frozen in a state of spiritual lethargy both reflected commonplace Ashkenazi views of non-European Jewry and helped reinforce those views in the *yishuv*, the Jewish community of Palestine. This view quickly became social doctrine in the forming state. Bialik was unaware that revolutionary changes were at work in the Middle East in the late nineteenth century and even at the very moment of his lecture, engendering a public sphere, a professional middle class, and a burgeoning print culture, and transforming cultural and social norms along the way. The fecund atmosphere of the *nahda* had inspired a small renaissance of secular Jewish creativity, primarily in literary Arabic and in Judeo-Arabic but also in Hebrew, French, Ladino, and other languages. None of this would register in the dominant narrative of Ashkenazi revival and Sephardi decline, or the precipitous fall of the Sephardim since their expulsion from Spain—a direct transposition of Hegel's claim that the "Oriental world" had fallen "out" of history.

Bialik's ahistorical characterization of the Sephardim pertains not only to their present but also to their past. Whereas Bialik contextualizes the *teḥiya* as a Jewish response to "external" (extrinsic) factors—namely, the Enlightenment—his characterization of the Spanish Golden Age is without context. Entirely disregarding the Arab culture and civilization of which it was part, Bialik discusses the medieval Sephardi tradition solely in Hebrew and Jewish literary terms, as if it were an autonomous

75 Ibid., 115.
76 Ibid., 116.
77 Ibid., 115. Here, one actually wishes his words had been heeded. Bialik proposes that one educational template cannot be used for all Jewish communities; the education of each "tribe" (*shevet*) must be carried out in accordance with its special character. Later, in the reply to his detractors, he adds, "I have no idea how Sephardim are taught from the schoolbooks of Ashkenazim" (*eyn ani mevin keytsad melamdim ha-sfaradim mi-tokh sifrey limud shel ashkenazim*; Bialik, "Teḥiyat ha-sfaradim," 117). In this case, Bialik's recognition of the different needs of different Jewish communities seems perspicacious. The question is how Bialik could have a pluralistic view of Jewish cultural character and educational needs but not of contemporary contributions to Jewish scholarship. See also Chetrit, "Revisiting Bialik," 20.

phenomenon that emerged ex nihilo.[78] Despite his great admiration for the Sephardi poets, Bialik was oblivious to who they really were: Arabized Jews. For him, they were simply the keepers of the torch of "Hebrew genius" during that period of history. At the same time, however, Bialik sees this moment as constituting the beginning of "Hebrew literature" in the sense of a literature authored by known, historically recognizable individuals, as opposed to the collective works of a society, such as the Bible and Talmud. It was also in Spain, he recounts, that Jewish learning was categorized scientifically through the taxonomies of philosophy, grammar, and so forth. "Suddenly," he says, "they [the Sephardim] discovered another way, and a new spirit."[79] Yet Bialik does not recognize these categories of knowledge as markers of the Greco-Arabic tradition: they were not actually "discovered" by the Sephardim, but were the current paradigms of Islamic science and learning, adapted by Sephardim to Jewish languages. By effacing the Arab component of Sephardi culture and identity both in al-Andalus and in the contemporary Levant, Bialik robs Sephardim of their place in history.[80]

As for Modern Hebrew literature, Bialik's position is unequivocal: "The new Hebrew literature began with the *haskala*. . . . Afterwards came the second period, the heir to the first, the period of nationalism, which went hand in hand with the *teḥiya*."[81] Noting the influence of the Sephardi legacy on the Wissenschaft des Judentums, he clarifies that even if the *inspiration* for the *teḥiya* belongs partly to Sepharad, its execution belongs solely to Ashkenaz:

> If the Ashkenazim found themselves still within the most collective mode of literary creation, here too it was the Sephardi Jews' personal

78 There is one exception. In his 1907 essay "Our Young Poetry" ("Shirateynu ha-tse'ira"), speaking of what he calls *piyut le'umi* (national *piyyut*), Bialik notes with a tinge of regret that "in the days of Rabbi Judah ha-Levi, its clear voice and its throat once more sounded gems such as 'Zion, Will You Not Ask,' but the seam of this renewed *tallith* was *slightly Arabic* (*ela she-ha-tefer shel talito ha-meḥudeshet 'aravi haya be-miktstat*)"; my emphasis. For Bialik, this brief concession to the enormous influence of Arabic on medieval Hebrew letters amounts to the recognition of an unfortunate flaw in the otherwise perfect *tallith* (prayer shawl) representing the masterpieces of the Sephardi Golden Age.

79 "And see this wondrous thing, that all those collective works . . . were all unnamed and in no chronological order—and here in Spain they suddenly discovered another way, and a new spirit"; Bialik, "Teḥiyat ha-sfaradim," 114.

80 Chetrit also picks up on this point. In his incisive reading, "Bialik did not say a single word about Arabness, which for him was a different world that had no connection to Jews. By speaking always of Sephardicness [*sic*] without Arabness, Bialik acts as a pioneer of the de-Arabization of Arab Jews and their culture, a trend that would grow evermore deeply entrenched in Israel's official policy toward Mizrahi Jews" (Chetrit, "Revisiting Bialik," 19–20).

81 Bialik, "Teḥiyat ha-sfaradim," 112.

> mode of creation that became the active and influential force during the period of the *teḥiya*, from [Moses] Mendelssohn to this day. The wondrous thing is that ever since, the creative faction of the Jewish people [*ha-uma*] has followed the path of Sepharad. We know the role played by the Sephardi [Golden Age] during the time of renewal in the *haskala* period. . . . The Hebrew scholarship of the *haskala* period was centered on these [medieval Sephardi literary] personalities, from whom they [the Ashkenazi Jews] learned how to revive the Hebrew language, thought, and spirit. That [revival] was among the Ashkenazi Jews. To our great sorrow, the Sephardim were the last to know their own roots, the roots of their spirit. And their own heritage, their assets.[82]

Moreover, in Bialik's introduction to the works of Solomon ibn Gabirol, published in the same year (1927), he not only reiterates this judgment but also draws a totalizing dichotomy whereby scholarship and intellectual inquiry are a purely *Western* endeavor, whose special charge it is to study its aesthetic object: the Hebrew writing of the East, portrayed here as the *unheimlich* place that is self and yet other, at once alive and dead:

> Even if we make an exception for the invaluable undertakings of Samuel David Luzzatto[83] and Ḥayim Brody (mentioned above), who were alone in their time, still before us will stretch the field of research on Sephardi [Hebrew] poetry, by all appearances a desolate valley full of dry bones, sowed with the stones of ruination from all the parts of the Temple, a sad testimony to the weakness of spirit and to the impotency of the current generation [of Sephardim], a generation distinguished by its [legacy of] wisdom and national spirit, but that has not found amongst its own a redeemer of the splendor of its forefathers' spirit, which cries out to this generation from the grave.[84] Who is to blame for this matter? There is no doubt that the source of this evil needs again to be sought in that same iron wall that stands these many years as a barrier separating our scholarly work in the Western countries from the Hebrew creative works, alive and continuous, in the countries of the East. Research and inquiry into the poems of our ancestors, as one of the branches of the wisdom of Israel born in the West, experienced

82 Ibid., 114–115.

83 Samuel David Luzzatto (1800–1865), an important Italian Jewish scholar, poet, and member of the Wissenschaft des Judentums. According to the Jewish Orientalist Yosef Yoel Rivlin, Bialik also demonstrated his admiration for Sephardi literature in his article "The Fellow from Padua" about another member of the Luzzatto family, Moses Ḥayim Luzzato (1707–1746), a prominent Italian Jewish kabbalist and philosopher; see Rivlin, "Ha-mizraḥ bi-yetsirotav shel Biyalik," 7.

84 In Hebrew, *dor she-mitgader be-ḥokhmato u-ve-le'umiyuto, ve-lo matsa be-tokho go'el le-tif'eret ruaḥ avotav, ha-tso'eket elav min ha-kvarim* (Bialik, "Introduction," *Shirey ibn Gabirol*, viii).

> its birth and growth primarily outside of the borders of the revival of Hebrew and its governance [i.e., Palestine].[85]

Read against this last passage, the correspondence between Semaḥ and Bialik becomes all the more intriguing. What was Semaḥ doing, if not "research and inquiry" on Sephardi poetry? From the archives, we know that Semaḥ had corresponded with Bialik, with Yellin, and with the Austrian Jewish Orientalist Benjamin Menaḥem Klar, whom he had hosted in Baghdad in 1928.[86] Even if Bialik had, at the time of writing, been unaware of Semaḥ's activity, he must have known about other Arab Jewish scholars and writers. For example, half a century earlier, another Baghdadi-born Jew, Sha'ul 'Abdallah Yosef of Hong Kong (1849–1906)—also a poet in his own right—was a preeminent scholar of Sephardi poetry. Yosef discovered and elucidated the manuscript of the aforementioned Todros ha-Levi Abulafia's *Gan ha-mashalim ve-ha-ḥidot* (later edited by Yellin with the assistance of Semaḥ) and also wrote commentary on Judah ha-Levi and Moses ibn 'Ezra.[87] Yosef had also corresponded on these matters with Ḥayim Brody (whom Bialik mentions above).[88] This selective blindness, however, was not unique to Bialik. Indeed, it continued the pattern established by Wissenschaft scholars decades earlier. As Ammiel Alcalay aptly summates,

85 Ibid.

86 Klar (1901–1948) was a leading scholar of Hebrew and Arabic who worked primarily on medieval and early modern topics in Hebrew, particularly language and poetry. He was involved in the early twentieth-century debates about the historical development of Hebrew pronunciation. He is remembered for his critical, annotated, and vocalized edition of *Megilat Aḥimaz*, a historical chronicle about a southern Italian Jewish family. In the 1930s he wrote a book in German about Bialik, and he was also close to David Yellin. He was killed in 1948 in the Hadassah convoy attack; his collected studies were published posthumously in 1954. The archives hold two letters from Klar to Semaḥ, one from September 1928 thanking Semaḥ for hosting him during his stay in Baghdad and discussing payment for rare books he had purchased from him, and another from September 1929 discussing an exchange of medieval manuscripts of the Rambam and Radak.

87 See also Hakak, *Nitsaney ha-yetsira*, 235.

88 Furthermore, as Sami Shalom Chetrit points out, any contemporary Sephardi prayer book or collection of liturgical poems (*piyyut*) would have given Bialik ample evidence of the abiding connection to the Sephardi past: "Sephardim from Morocco to Iraq never stopped disseminating the poetry of the Sephardi greats. Moreover, writing in the Sephardi tradition continued to be produced until the 'new' poetry came along and put an end to it" (Chetrit, "Revisiting Bialik," 18). Dan Miron also notes that "the medieval Spanish (actually, Andalusian) Hebrew poetry, in both its main genres, the sacred and the secular, has in reality been continued—in North Africa, Iraq, and other centers in the Middle East—alongside, and totally independently, of the contemporary new literature, well into the twentieth century" (*From Continuity to Contiguity*, 4). For examples of modern Sephardi poetry, see Ḥazan, *Ha-shira ha-'ivrit bi-tsfon afrika*; Ben Ya'akov, *Shira u-fiyut*; and Hakak, *Nitsaney ha-yetsira*.

> For all the invaluable and pioneering work done by Enlightenment Hebrew scholars, the deeper connection between an imagined Andalusia held up as an example of "successful" Jewish assimilation and the continued living tradition of Levantine rabbis and poets was never really made, despite contact and ample opportunities for such an exchange. . . . A progressive curve tracing this rift can be drawn from an eighteenth-century figure such as Hayim David Azulai, to nineteenth- and twentieth-century figures such as Hayim Palaggi, Giuseppe Almanzi, Eliahu Ben-amozeg, Shaul Abdullah Yoseph, A.S. Yahuda, and Moise Ventura, to mention only some. All of these people had extensive contact with European Jewish intellectuals and institutions, yet a reading of almost any general history of modern Jewish thought would leave one with the impression that none of these persons ever existed, that the Levantine and Arab world remained plunged in darkness, totally unaware of what was taking place outside it.[89]

Bialik's views on the Sephardim, the Hebrew revival, and Jewish modernity became received wisdom and, before long, social doctrine. This we know. The side of the equation that has not yet been considered is the reception of Bialik's views by the Sephardim themselves. There appears to have been some opposition to his speech among members of the audience. His printed reply to them is apologetic, at times defensive, stating that his intentions were misunderstood, and that intellectual languor is hardly exclusive to Sephardim; moreover, he adds, only a tiny number of Russian and German Jews took part in the *haskala* and the *teḥiya.*[90] The critical response of the young Sephardim seems to have caught Bialik off guard, convinced as he was of their "intellectual weakness" or scholarly lassitude.[91] However, the Sephardi response to his lecture did not stop at the doors of the lecture hall, or even at the gates of the city. In fact, Bialik's lecture before the "Mizraḥi Pioneers" was headline news for three straight weeks in *Isra'il*, the Arabic edition of a trilingual (Hebrew/Arabic/French) Egyptian Jewish newspaper, which printed a slightly abridged version of the lecture in Arabic translation followed by a three-part response (see Figure 4).[92] According to *Isra'il*, Bialik's lecture was attended by a large flank of local Sephardi notables as well as members of the "Sephardi federation"

89 Alcalay, *After Jews and Arabs*, 153–154.

90 Bialik, "Teḥiyat ha-sfaradim," 16, 18.

91 Chetrit, "Revisiting Bialik," 19.

92 The lecture itself took up the full first page of the newspaper, and part 1 of Malki's comments took up almost another full page. See "Muhadarat Biyalik 'an nahdat al-yahud al-safaradim (1)"; Malki, "Nahdat al-yahud al-safaradim (2)"; and idem, "Nahdat al-yahud al-safaradim (3)." On the newspaper and Malki, see Hillel, *"Yisra'el" be-kahir*; Landau, "Israël (Cairo)"; and Levy, "Shams (Cairo), al-."

السنة الثامنة

Huitieme anne No. 11

أسرائيل

صاحب الجريدة ومديرها
الدكتور البرت موصيري
الادارة : شارع البنك الوطني رقم ٨
بمصر
صندوق البوسته نمرة ١٤٨١

الاشتراك
١٠٠ صـ عن سنة داخل القطر
١٢٥ عن سنة خارج القطر
الاعلانات يتفق عليها مع الادارة رأساً
تليفون نمرة ٣٨٤٦ عتبة

يوم الجمعة ١٨ مارس سنة ١٩٢٧ — جريدة حرة أسبوعية — ١٤ آذار ثاني ٥٦٨٧

محاضرة بياليك

عن نهضة اليهود السفارديم

في نادي سالوصيه ها مزراح في القدس

Figure 4. Front page article on Bialik's lecture, in *Isra'il*, March 18, 1927.

(*al-Ittihad al-safaradi*) in Jerusalem.[93] Sa'd Malki, the Arabic-language editor of the newspaper, was not stinting in his praise: a "brilliant lecture," he effuses, in which Bialik "reached the heart of the matter, free of error."[94] Perhaps anticipating criticism from his readers or responding to earlier criticisms, Malki defends Bialik's position:

> On the other hand, Biliak did not give this lecture to win the approval and satisfaction of the Sephardi Jews. . . . Rather, he delivered his lecture to redeem the literary eloquence [*al-fashiyya*] of his brethren in creed and denomination; to revive them after their lethargy and rouse them to enter the arena of nationalism with their imagination and with their feet, carrying the pearls of the Sephardi literary revival.
>
> In all truth, Bialik gave their situation an expert and learned description, showing them [the Sephardim] their celebrated past greatness, that glowing civilized past whose praises are sung by Ashkenazim and Sephardim alike. . . . But one regrets that the Sephardim have cut all ties with that great past and were scattered to the four winds, and have not regained their solidarity or community . . . while our Ashkenazi brothers today are at the vanguard and are the ones who demonstrate and protest in the name of the Jewish people one and all, whereas the Sephardim don't move a finger, and don't even bother to publicize their views on national and political matters.

Bialik, Malki continues, didn't stop at describing the glorious Sephardi past but also put forth the "cure," a plan for the recovery of their lost prestige in Hebrew letters and learning. In closing, Malki extends heartfelt thanks to the "national poet" (*sha'ir al-umma*), concluding that the lecture could not be more timely: "For every Sephardi sorrows when he sees himself behind his Ashkenazi brethren in respect to letters and culture [*min al-wijha al-adabiyya*], and wishes for revival. But he is in a state of regression because he lacks the means of revival, the most important being internal Sephardi unity and the formation of strong national ties." This unification, Malki emphasizes, is what will restore the linkage between the Sephardi past and present.[95]

To his readers, Malki's response would have come as no great surprise. Bialik's speech dovetailed with Malki's own agenda of cultural and social

93 "Muhadarat Biyalik 'an nahdat al-yahud al-safaradim (1)," 1. The article provides other details as well, noting that the lecture was supposed to focus on their *literary* revival, and that the meeting was chaired by one "Dr. Levi," who also introduced Bialik. The organization identified is most likely the Hitaḥdut 'Olamit shel ha-Yehudim ha-Sfaradim, established by Avraham Elmaliaḥ in Jerusalem a few years earlier.

94 "Nahdat al-yahud al-safaradim (1)," 3.

95 Ibid.

reform among his readership at home in Egypt. Both in *Isra'il* and later in its successor paper *al-Shams*, he relentlessly lambasted the Egyptian Jewish community for what he viewed as its apathy to the cultural and political causes he championed; it was no wonder he took the speech as an occasion to beat the drum of Sephardi unity and mobilization. In the second segment of his three-part response, Malki returns briefly to Bialik's comments on Sephardi education, this time as a launching pad for a lengthy critique of Jewish education in Egypt; he calls for Sephardi schools in Egypt to add Hebrew to the existing instruction in French and Arabic, and for other (presumably Ashkenazi) Jewish schools with Hebrew instruction to teach the language in the Sephardi style and to incorporate Sephardi literature and history. (From his remarks, one surmises that ironically, at a time when Modern Hebrew was being revived in Palestine on a supposedly "Sephardi" model, in the heart of Egypt it was being taught exclusively in an Ashkenazi style.)[96] In the last installment, Malki bemoans the absence of local Sephardi associations that would promote and support the printing of Hebrew literature in general, and of Sephardi literature in particular, pointing to the active patronage of the Ashkenazi community in Egypt and elsewhere. Here he ties his discussion back to the ongoing Modern Hebrew revival in Palestine:

> And to this matter we attribute the presence of distinguished people in the arts and sciences and other fields. After their emigration to Palestine they engendered there a Hebrew literary revival [*nahda*], the likes of which Palestine had not seen since the Jews had left it. And the truth is that the *nahda* of our Ashkenazi brethren did not come suddenly or by chance, but rather by virtue of the great effort they invested in the study and investigation of Hebrew literature; their efforts reaped fruit when they experienced a great revival. Thanks to these efforts . . . , they became the vanguard of the [Jewish] people [*umma*].[97]

As opposed to the young members of the Mizraḥi organization in Jerusalem, Malki had internalized the narrative of Sephardi decline. He was most likely unaware of native Palestinian Sephardi writers of Hebrew such as Yitzḥak Shami and Yehuda Burla, who began publishing books only

96 Malki says further that the Sephardi Jewish schools do not include Sephardi history or literature in their curriculum, but teach French history, literature, and culture as if they are French schools. He advocates retaining French as the language of instruction, but calls for representation of Sephardi history and culture in order to inculcate a sense of pride in the students' cultural identity; he blames "the public" (*al-jumhur*; probably the Jewish community) for neglecting the matter. See Malki, "Nahdat al-yahud al-safaradim (2)," 1.

97 Malki, "Nahdat al-yahud al-safaradim" (3). He adapts the Arabic term *umma*, used throughout the history of Islam to refer to the Islamic community or "nation," to the Jewish people/community/nation.

in the late 1920s. Conversely, he was well aware of the activity of other Arabic-language Jewish writers in the Levant, as their writing appeared regularly in *Isra'il*. Throughout his career, Malki argued for a large-scale Egyptian Jewish cultural revival in both Hebrew and Arabic (a quixotic mission given the strong Francophone orientation of the Egyptian Jewish middle and upper classes); he therefore invoked the Ashkenazi revival of Hebrew as a model for emulation.

The significance of his engagement with Bialik for the purposes of our discussion is twofold. First, his translation and publication of the speech in Arabic for an Egyptian Jewish readership illustrates my contention that the story of Hebrew and Arabic during the formative period of the 1920s to 1950s must encompass the Arab Jewish intellectual network in the Levant.[98] Second, Malki's response demonstrates that while he may have internalized the argument that he was culturally subordinate to the Ashkenazim, in practice he was concerned primarily with his own agenda, which had much less to do with the idea of modern Hebrew culture and much more to do with the creation of a modern "Sephardi" cultural identity that would comprise Arabic, Hebrew, and European elements. His primary concern was that his community, whose identity was becoming dominated by French language and culture, would find a way to draw on the Sephardi past and the ongoing Hebrew renaissance while also embracing Arabic and taking an active role in the Egyptian national community. For the next twenty years or so, Malki would relentlessly promote this dual agenda; the rise of Zionism and creation of Israel eventually derailed it. On May 14, 1948, the day the State of Israel declared its independence, an Egyptian official arrived at the office of *al-Shams*, Malki's newspaper, to inform him of the government's decision to close it down. A few months later, Malki left behind his life's work in Cairo and immigrated to Israel.[99]

"THE NATIONAL POET OF THE ASHKENAZIM": MIZRAḤIM WRITE BACK TO BIALIK

Even before Bialik gave his speech on the revival of the Sephardim, Arab Jews were reading and writing about his poetry. In 1924, a rabbi in Aleppo by the name of Isaac Dayyan published an essay on Jewish enlightenment in which he invokes the "national poet." In the context of a polemic against modern Jewish intellectuals who abandon their culture, Dayyan quotes from the medieval Sephardi poets Judah ha-Levi and Abraham

98 This network is the central concern of my next book, *Partitioned Pasts*, on the intellectual history of Arab Jews from 1863–1948.

99 See Naḥmias, "Al-Shams."

ibn 'Ezra, followed by a quote from Bialik's poem "Surely the People Is Grass"; elsewhere he quotes Bialik's "Surely This Too." For Dayyan, "Bialik is both the 'national poet' and a source of cultural spiritual 'authority,' functionally parallel to Rabbi Yehuda HaLevy and to Rabbi ibn Ezra."[100] A decade later, in 1933, a few months before Bialik's death, a schoolboy in Tripoli wrote a poem called "Ha-yeled ve-ha-tsipor" ("The Child and the Bird") modeled after Bialik's famous poem "El ha-tsipor" ("To the Bird")—indicating that Bialik's poems were already being taught in some North African Jewish schools.[101]

By the time of his death, Bialik was already a national hero in what was not yet a nation-state. A few decades later, at the height of the mass immigration of Arab Jews to the newly established State of Israel, studying the poetry of Bialik became a formative experience for children from countries such as Morocco and Iraq. Moroccan-born Sami Shalom Chetrit revisits his childhood acculturation to Israeli society and Zionist ideology through schoolroom instruction in Bialik's poetry, beginning with his famous poem "Ken la-tsipor" ("A Nest for the Bird"): "When the teacher told us about Bialik, it was clear to me that he was one of ours, a sort of grandfatherly figure producing poems for his many grandchildren. What can I say? It was love at first sound. This was the first poem I learned to sing and recite in Israel."[102] Perhaps not surprisingly, decades later, when these Mizraḥi intellectuals, poets, and artists came of age, they returned to Bialik, often rewriting his lines within their own verse. One such poem by Iraqi-born Yossi Alfi portrays the ideological indoctrination of Mizraḥi children and erasure of Mizraḥi identity by Israeli pedagogy. His poem also references Bialik's main contender Saul Tchernichowsky, another Ukrainian-born Hebrew poet:

When I was little
A little poet
Tchernichowsky was a god
and Ukrainian fields my past.
And Bialik brought me a nest for the bird [*ken la-tsipor*]
From the warm lands to the cold of my yesterday.
And when I grew up I understood
there are no fields within me
and the Ukraine is not my home

100 Zvi Zohar, "A 'Maskil' in Aleppo," 101, 103. Rabbi Dayyan's essay "The Torah of Israel and the People of Israel" was printed at the beginning of a book that appeared in Aleppo in 1924. Zohar says the essay "aims to ground a conception of Jewish education, which includes Jewish and general studies within a framework which gives primacy to Jewish studies," including Hebrew poetry (95).

101 Chetrit, "Revisiting Bialik," 16.

102 Ibid., 1. Erez Bitton also rewrites "Ken la-tsipor" in his early work.

and a nest for the bird in the desert
without trees
did not lay in my mind
its three eggs.[103]

The end of the poem alludes to the same children's song "Ken la-tsipor" ("A Nest for the Bird") mentioned by Chetrit as the first poem he learned in school in Israel (and whose lines rhyme charmingly in the original):

The bird has a nest
among the trees [*ha-'etsim*]
and in the nest
she has three eggs [*betsim*].

But surely, one might protest, Bialik did not intend for his poetry to be used in this way—after all, in his 1927 speech, he himself had advocated teaching Sephardi literature and culture to Sephardi schoolchildren. Returning to the controversy surrounding his alleged remark, Bialik may have been a victim of his own success; for, regardless of what he personally believed about Sephardi and Mizraḥi Jews, he set himself up to become the icon of the Ashkenazi cultural establishment, which controlled the pedagogical apparatus of the state. Bialik's name thus still has the symbolic power to evoke an entire milieu that, collectively, was less than welcoming of Middle Eastern Jews and their cultures. As a reader's letter to *Haaretz* put it, "Bialik symbolizes much more than one unimportant utterance—rather, he symbolizes the repressive Israeli cultural center, which occluded the Arab culture of the Mizraḥim."[104] Over, the years, the tension between Bialik and the "Sephardim" was reified in the collective consciousness of Israeli public culture. The article in *Haaretz* identified three literary references to Bialik's perceived antagonism toward Mizraḥi Jews in Israeli fiction published in 2002 alone. In Moshe Pinto's story collection *Ha-meshorer ha-le'umi* (*The National Poet*), Bialik screams in comically literary Hebrew at his Yemeni Jewish gardener, "You son of an Arab . . . why didn't you stay in your hinterlands [*ben 'arav shekamotkha . . . madu'a lo nisharta bi-nidḥoteykha*]? Oh 'Other' one [*ho aḥer*], for what purpose did you come? To interlope? To rob? To ruin?"[105] In a memoir by Yossi Sucary, the narrator confesses that when he read Bialik's poetry, "I couldn't relate directly to the words, because his unforgettable

103 Yossi Alfi, in Chetrit and Eskhol-Mikhlin, *Me'a shanim, me'a yotsrim*, 88. Translation by Jessica Cohen with modifications (Chetrit, "Revisiting Bialik," 11). Tchernichowsky figures centrally in this book's conclusion.

104 'Ivri, Letter to the editor, H3.

105 Pinto, *Ha-meshorer ha-le'umi*, 12–13.

statement—I hate the Arabs because they remind me of the Mizraḥim—was stationed on the edge of my linguistic reservoir like an austere guard who wouldn't let them in."[106] And in Kobi Oz's satiric novel *'Avaryan tsa'atsu'a* (*Petty Thief*), the Mizraḥi narrator imagines his grandfather shouting at Bialik from an adjacent balcony as the national poet pens a love poem to matsoh balls ("Haḥziki li be-kneydelakh"). "But it didn't disturb Bialik one bit. For him, my grandfather was nothing but air. A piece of the landscape. How did they used to say it—just a *frenk*."[107] A similar sentiment underscores Eytan Naḥmias Glass's 1995 "ode" to Bialik:

> The national poet of the Ashkenazim [*ha-meshorer ha-le'umi shel ha-ashkenazim*],
> Ḥayim Naḥman Bialik hated us
> the blacks, the Sephardim, the Mizraḥim
> and with pomp and circumstance was this sensitive man
> lowered into the grave.
> But what can I do, still I love his poems—
> my heart blazes for his words, yet does not forgive.
> Take me under your wing, you son of a bitch![108]

"My heart blazes for his words, yet does not forgive" (*libi nisraf le-milotav, ve-lo sole'aḥ*) captures the speaker's intensely conflicted feelings about the "national poet of the Ashkenazim." The poem's powerful last line represents this ambivalence linguistically by mixing Hebrew and Arabic as well as high and low registers: "Hakhnisini taḥat knafekh, ben sharmuta!" (Take me under your wing, you son of a bitch!) "Take Me under Your Wing" is the title of Bialik's best known and most well-loved poem, which is widely taught in Israeli schools and has at least two musical renditions by Israeli pop stars.[109] The phrase is culturally elevated both in its high-register grammatical structure (the elegant *hakhnisini*, where colloquial Hebrew would use *takhnisi oti*) and in its religious and cultural connotations, evoking spirituality and the Hebrew *shekhina* (the feminine aspect of the Divine). Nothing could be more distant in style or spirit than the two words adjoining it in Glass's rendition: *ben sharmuta*, a hybrid Hebrew-Arabic curse from the Arabic *ibn sharmuta* (son of a whore). This is a prime example of how Arabic words, absorbed into Israeli Hebrew for curses and other low-register linguistic strata, become perceived as a "low" form of Hebrew often associated with Mizraḥim. (It is also the kind of Hebrew that Chetrit playfully calls "Ashdodian," as we shall see

106 Sucary, *Emilya u-melaḥ ha-arets*, 80.
107 Oz, *'Avaryan tsa'atsu'a*, 48–49.
108 Glass, *Ani Simon Naḥmias*, 21.
109 See Bialik, *Kol shirey*, 178.

in chapter 6.) On one level, then, the poem rejects Bialik by throwing the title of his most famous poem back at him along with a curse. But the metatext conveys a more mixed message. The combination of the two phrases "take me under your wing" and "you son of a bitch" reiterates the speaker's reluctant admiration of Bialik's poetry but is also a performance of the speaker's Mizraḥi identity (*mizraḥiyut*) through the foil of Bialik. The line is a perfect illustration of "language and its Other," of the simultaneous selfing and othering of language implicit in the act of writing in and between Hebrew and Arabic, or between standard Hebrew and Mizraḥi Hebrew (more examples to follow in part 3). Ultimately, Glass's poem, like Semaḥ's ode some sixty years earlier, is about language as the vehicle of identity. Glass exploits the linguistic tension between Bialik's highbrow Hebrew and the "street" Hebrew of curses and slang as a metaphor for the ethnic tensions between the Hebrew cultural elite and the Mizraḥim, subtly alluding to Bialik's alleged remark.[110] At the same time, reading Glass's "ode" to Bialik in juxtaposition with Semaḥ's poem seems to tell the whole story of the transformation of native Sephardi and Arab Jews into second- and third-generation Mizraḥi immigrants. Whereas Semaḥ embodies the end of a long-standing tradition, Glass represents a generation of deracinated young writers defining themselves in opposition to the Ashkenazi cultural center yet cut off from their own cultural roots, more of whom we will encounter in chapters 5 and 6.

Ronny Someck, a leading Israeli poet born in Baghdad, takes a different childhood experience of Bialik as the subject of his poem "*Khawaja* Bialik" ("Mister Bialik," 1996). Someck's poem alludes to the cultural conflicts of Palestinian Israelis in the Israeli educational system, where Bialik's poetry is a required subject. The familiarity of Palestinian Israelis with Bialik is well established; Mahmoud Darwish was influenced by him, and Rashid Husayn (another major Palestinian poet) translated his work into Arabic.[111] (Indeed, the story of Bialik and the Palestinians could take up a chapter of its own.[112]) The term *khawaja* in the poem's title is an Arabic

110 Eytan Naḥmias Glass (b. 1968, Tel Aviv) is of mixed heritage, with a German-born father and a Yugoslavian-Sephardi mother. *Ani Simon Naḥmias* (*I Am Simon Naḥmias*) is his first book. The title is an implicit reclamation of Sephardi or Mizraḥi identity, as it sounds like the name of a Sephardi old-timer from Greece or the Balkans.

111 On Darwish and Bialik, see Rifaʿi, *Athar al-thaqafa al-ʿibriyya* and Zonshteyn, "Biyalik ve-Darwish mazhirim."

112 In *El yafo* (*To Jaffa*), a 2010 novel by the young Palestinian Israeli writer Ayman Sikseck, a Palestinian Israeli student of literature attends a reading of Bialik's poetry in Tel Aviv. The influence of Bialik's poetry on a Palestinian schoolboy in Israel was depicted by A. B. Yehoshua in *The Lover*; see Yehoshua, *Ha-me'ahev*. See also Chetrit, "Revisiting Bialik," where Chetrit discusses how it was a Palestinian student in his university who first prompted him to reread Bialik from a radical political perspective. For a bilingual Hebrew-Arabic edition of Bialik's poetry, see *Leket shirim/Mukhtar min diwan Hayim Nahman Biyalik*.

form of address usually reserved for foreigners; the title itself conveys a certain irony, representing Bialik from a Palestinian perspective while also recalling the Orientalism of the pre-state era, when an Ashkenazi Hebrew writer such as Moshe Smilansky could refer to himself as "*Khawaja* Musa."

KHAWAJA BIALIK

An Arab girl sings a song by Bialik
and the wings of the bus shade the olive trees black
by the twists and turns of Wadi 'Ara.
No mother, no sister and her eyes roll
from eyelid to eyelid at the starry deceits
of *Khawaja* Bialik.
. . .
The sun that burned up in flame dots the blue
undershirts of the laborers with sweat
and the far-flung voice of the *muezzin* stretches
out like a worn-out carpet on the back of a donkey
who's lost his horsepower.[113]

The poem is replete with intertextuality: "no mother, no sister," the "starry deceits," and "the sun that burned up in flame" are all references to Bialik's aforementioned poem "Take Me under Your Wing." In a brilliant and unexpected move, Someck thus rewrites Bialik's most emblematic poem to reflect not the desperation of a Russian Jew in 1905, but the impoverished reality of a Palestinian girl in contemporary Israel, drawing a subtle comparison. In 2004, Someck expanded his concept of "*Khawaja* Bialik" in an art exhibit by the same title, which he mounted in the Chanan Rozen Museum of Israeli Art in Ramat Gan (a suburb of Tel Aviv).[114] The exhibit consisted of Someck's original poem, in addition to ten leaves of Bialik's poetry torn from a yellowed volume, over which Someck scribbled, doodled, scrawled, and splotched black ink—taking the idea of "rewriting" Bialik to a literal extreme (see Figures 5, 6, and 7).

On the image titled *Khawaja Bialik*, directly beneath the defaced photo portrait of the poet we see a splotchy phrase, *la-sim* (illegible word) *'al Bialik*. The Israeli viewer knows that the blacked-out word is most likely *zayin* (penis), alluding to the vulgar Hebrew slang expression *la-sim zayin 'al*—literally, to "put a penis on" someone or something; figuratively, "to hell with" or even "fuck" (someone, something). However, the elision of

113 Someck, *Gan 'eden le-orez*, 96.
114 See the catalog *Roni Somek—Khawaja Biyalik.*

Figure 5. Ronny Someck, "Khawaja Bialik," 2004. Courtesy of the Chanan Rozen Museum of Israel Art, Ramat Gan.

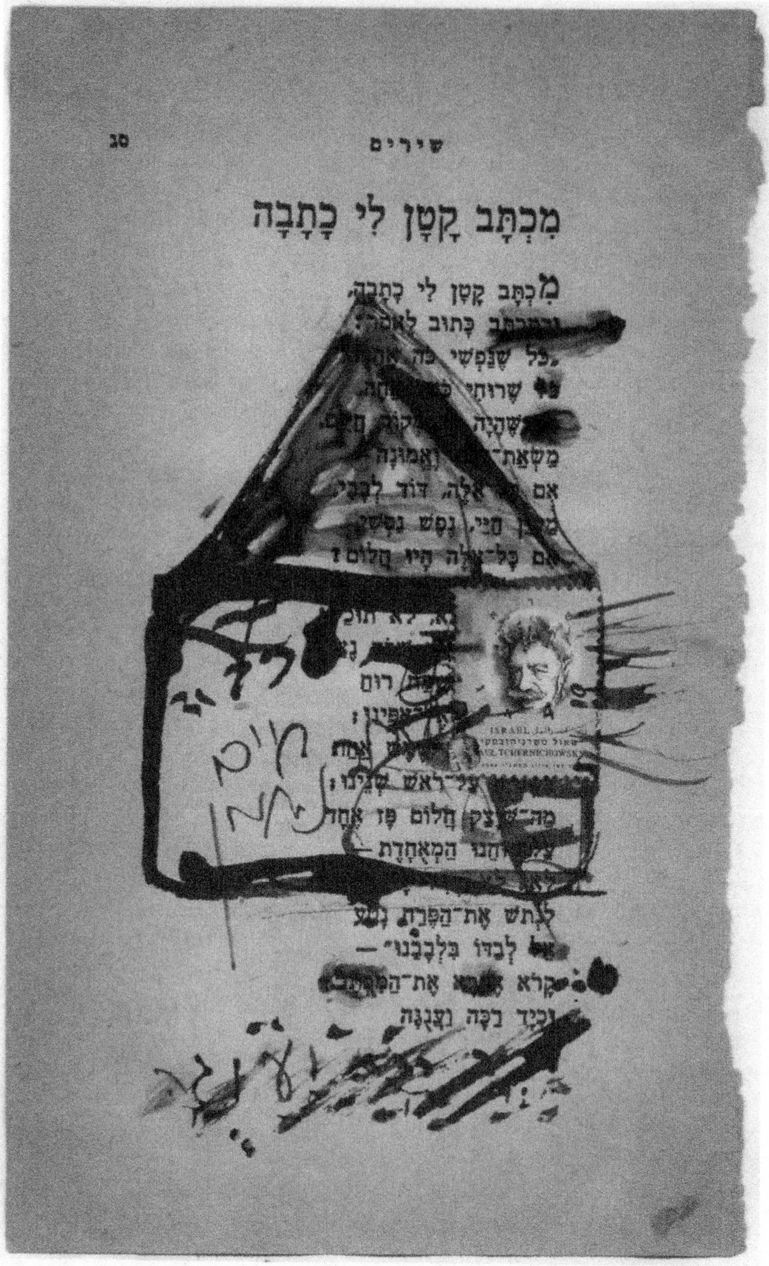

Figure 6. Ronny Someck, "Mikhtav katan li katva" ("She Wrote Me a Little Letter"), 2004. Courtesy of the Chanan Rozen Museum of Israeli Art, Ramat Gan.

Figure 7. Ronny Someck, "El ha-tsipor" ("To the Bird"), 2004. Courtesy of the Chanan Rozen Museum of Israeli Art, Ramat Gan.

zayin renders the sentence simply *la-sim . . . 'al Bialik*—literally, "putting [something] on Bialik"—which is exactly what the artist does by putting the ink blots and strokes "on" Bialik, thereby giving this "caption" a pointed double meaning. Like Glass's "ode," Someck's series of images simultaneously pays homage to the national poet while disfiguring and otherwise doing violence to him and his poems—producing an ambiguous and ambivalent reading of the "national poet" as a cultural symbol. In the second image, "She Wrote Me a Little Letter," Someck draws the outline of an envelope over the text of the poem. In a comic touch, the envelope, addressed to "Ḥayim Naḥman," bears a commemorative postage stamp of Tchernichowsky pasted directly over the poem! Through this gesture, Someck conflates the two great poets of the Modern Hebrew renaissance, implying that they are part of the same state-sanctioned cultural edifice, while the sketch of the envelope also resembles a house, imparting another layer of meaning to this idea of "edifice." Because the Jewish state was mythologized by Zionist ideology as *ha-bayit ha-le'umi*, "the national home," the *bayit* (house or home) is never far removed from the idea of the nation in the modern Hebrew cultural memory. Thus another Sephardi poet, Shelley Elkayyam, writes,

Let us open the house to the East
so that, at high morning,
into its bones
will enter
sun.[115]

Pervasive tropes of Israeli culture such as the "national poet" and the "national home" may verge on clichés, yet still command discursive authority. In his double-layered images of Bialik and Bialik's poems, Someck closes the distance between doctrine and cliché, overwriting the solemnity of icon with the irreverence of graffiti.

THE TRAJECTORY OF HEBREW MODERNITY

Let us return to 1933 and to Baghdad, where Semaḥ sits in his house composing verses for the national poet, thinking of how to impress him in the language they both love. Semaḥ's poem is a virtuoso performance of literary erudition and style in a Hebrew poetic tradition long identified with Middle Eastern Jewry. But it is also much more than a neoclassical display of lexical razzle-dazzle. Like the jack-in-the-box masquerading as an

115 Elkayyam, *Mi-tokh shirat ha-arkhitekt*, 37. See Levy, Salaymeh, and Valencia, "Poetic Structures on Contested Space."

innocent birthday gift, this praise poem is quite literally "riddled" with ambiguities and double entendres. As a metalinguistic discourse on the identity of Modern Hebrew literature, it celebrates the scope of Bialik's contribution, but locates Hebrew poetry in the legacy of al-Andalus, as opposed to the European Jewish *haskala.* As an ethereal cultural space, the poem is a theater in which the speaker, Bialik, the Sephardi greats ibn 'Ezra and ibn Gabirol, and, finally, the female "spirit" of Hebrew Poetry all appear as characters, interacting with one another in the ongoing drama of Hebrew literature. One imagines, in center stage, the figure of Hebrew Poetry—the beautiful, bejeweled, and bell-tinkling belle—holding in her hands the book by Bialik and looking pointedly at the venerable figures of ibn 'Ezra and ibn Gabirol, resurrected from their Andalusian pasts, perhaps still in grave-dusty robes. In collapsing historical time and cultural distance to bring these figures together, the poem becomes a nexus of the different historical moments and places they occupied.

What was Semaḥ hoping to achieve by presenting so many different "fathers" in this lyric paternity suit? Was he expounding a genealogy of Hebrew poetry that he assumed Bialik would embrace? Or was he trying to make a point about the role of Arab civilization in Hebrew culture, the very history that Bialik so blatantly overlooked in both his 1927 speech and his editions of Sephardi poetry? It is unknown whether Semaḥ read the text of the speech, or what he knew of Bialik's views on Hebrew modernity. But in raising the ghosts of the great Sephardi poets, Semaḥ seems also to have transferred something of the Sephardi legacy of "cultural ambiguity." Here, the ambiguity follows not from the interaction of medieval Jewish courtiers with a non-Jewish host culture, but rather from a twentieth-century Arab Jew's negotiation of the intellectual rights to his own tradition. In this light, Semaḥ's panegyric to Bialik can also be read as an artifact of the correspondence between two contemporary Hebrew poets, and as a social text about an Iraqi Jew facing the burgeoning European Jewish hegemony over Hebrew culture. In hindsight, the poem becomes an insignia of this unhappily imbalanced relationship, one produced at nearly the last moment before history became historiography, so to speak, and the narrative of Modern Hebrew literature was codified. Written at a critical point in the development of Modern Hebrew literature, it represents a different kind of Hebrew modernity—one whose trajectory passes from al-Andalus to Baghdad and Jerusalem.

While we are left to speculate about Semaḥ's intentions, we can affirm that the same invisibility that plagued Sephardi and Arab Jewish intellectuals such as Semaḥ during those formative years of modern Hebrew letters persists to the present day. Just as Bialik elided Sha'ul 'Abdallah Yosef from his purview of Sephardi scholars, contemporary histories of

Hebrew letters continue to efface Semaḥ and his Middle Eastern Jewish peers, such as the aforementioned Ezra Haddad and Sa'd Malki.[116] As historian Gabriel Piterberg observes, "The pattern through which Orientalism determined the representation of the Oriental Jews and integrated them, through the denial of their own memory and culture, into the Zionist/Israeli narrative was formed in the first period (1930s–50s) and . . . has not fundamentally changed until today."[117]

The story of Bialik and the Sephardim illustrates how Modern Hebrew literature was severed from the history and culture of Arabic-speaking Jews, and how the Hebrew cultural establishment became associated with the exclusion of Sephardi, Mizraḥi, and Arab Jews. If Bialik had objectified the "Sephardim" as the Ashkenazi cultural "Other," seven or eight decades later Mizraḥi writers returned the favor by making Bialik a symbol of their cultural occlusion. The name "Bialik" became a nodal point or signpost in the Mizraḥi discourse of difference, whence Bialik was transformed from "the national poet" to "the national poet of the Ashkenazim." In this regard, the mutual love-hate relationship of Bialik and the Sephardim can be taken as an object lesson in the perils of cultural essentialization.

116 For that matter, neither Semaḥ nor David Yellin is mentioned in *Biyalik ve-sofrey doro* (Bialik and his Contemporaries)—an extensive, "authorized" 1974 collection of papers exchanged between Bialik and the Hebrew writers and scholars of his time. Moshe Ungerfeld, the volume's editor and the caretaker of Bialik's archives, certainly knew of their tripartite correspondence, as he himself had included Semaḥ's poem in *Shir ha-sharim* (1959), a collection of poems dedicated to Bialik by admirers from throughout the world. The implication is that while an Iraqi Jewish writer such as Semaḥ could be considered one of Bialik's exotic worldwide devotees, he could not be considered one of his "contemporaries"—a modern Hebrew writer, scholar, or interlocutor of any stature—in his own right. Ungerfeld (1898–1983) was the director of Beyt Biyalik, the "Bialik house" museum in Tel Aviv, for some forty-five years.

117 Piterberg, "Domestic Orientalism," 135.

Part 2

Bilingual Entanglements

CHAPTER 3

Exchanging Words

Arabic Writing in Israel and the Poetics of Misunderstanding

The acclaimed Israeli film *Bikur ha-tizmoret* (*The Band's Visit*, 2007) tells the story of a small ceremonial police orchestra from Egypt invited to perform in the Israeli town of Petaḥ Tikva. Due to a minor mispronunciation—the band leader's substitution of "B" for "P," as Arabic has no "P" sound—the band is misdirected to the fictional location "Beyt ha-Tikva," a dusty, forsaken desert outpost. The night that follows is all about misunderstanding as well as understanding on the deepest levels, as the town's inhabitants—themselves lost in the ignominy and obscurity of Israel's impoverished peripheries—and the band's members warily accommodate themselves to one another, communicating primarily in broken English. Ultimately, the band makes it out of the desert in time for its engagement, but not before having shared an unarticulated lesson in the commonalities and incommensurabilities of human pain and loneliness, in hospitality and its limits. This lesson is driven entirely by a translingual misunderstanding, which on one level might amount to the subtle difference between a "P" and a "B," but on another level is a social and political chasm that cannot be crossed directly, only by means of a shaky English-language bridge. If this is the poetics of misunderstanding, it is a particular kind of truth that resides in the interstices of meaning: in neither what is said nor what is not said, but in the spaces between what is said, what is meant, and what is ultimately understood *and* misunderstood.

The poetics of misunderstanding lead us to the present chapter, in which we find ourselves again in Baghdad, Palestine, and Israel, but this time in order to read contemporary Arabic fiction from a (post)colonial perspective. Whereas earlier we encountered a period of open borders, here we find a literature shaped by the oppressiveness of borders, and by writers' oppositional relationships to the discourse of the state. The Palestinian Emile Habiby (1922–1996)[1] and Iraqi-Israeli Samir Naqqash (1938–2004), both native speakers of Arabic, both writing in Israel, both

1 Habiby's year of birth is given by some sources as 1921, by others as 1922.

drawing on what are essentially vanished histories in Palestine and Iraq, both using language to insist on an identity rendered impossible by the logic of the State of Israel—and more broadly by the tortured logic of the (post)colonial Middle East with its unassailable binarisms of Hebrew and Arabic, Arab and Jew—engage the indeterminacy of meaning implicit in linguistic exchange as a mode of resistance to authority. How does literature written between languages, dialects, or registers negotiate its linguistic status? How might this process itself become a thematic concern? My readings probe how the two writers represent the language of authority in order to disrupt the authority of language.

TRANSLATION AND THE BILINGUAL TEXT

In chapter 1, I explored the asymmetrical relations of power between Arabic and Hebrew in Israel/Palestine and their ramifications for bilingualism, translation, and literary production in the two languages. The power differential that *must already exist* in any situation of bilingualism informs studies of translation across a wide range of (post)colonial contexts, generally between "third-world" and "metropolitan" languages.[2] These studies have radically reevaluated the relationship between text and translation, interrogating the standard metaphors of fidelity and equivalence and opening the field up to consideration of the empirical power relations imbricated in any linguistic or cultural exchange.[3] If Walter Benjamin's 1923 essay situated translation in the lofty realm of the metaphysical, emphasizing the always fragmentary nature of any one language in relation to his ideal of a "greater" or "pure" language,[4] these works are concerned with the gritty relations between those different fragments, the here-and-now of social, economic, and political uses and functions of language. Language in this body of scholarship is never distant from the dialectic of authority and resistance: the meeting (or clash) of languages

2 The relationship of language and power in postcolonial contexts has been extensively theorized (see Emily Apter, Alfred Arteaga, Homi Bhabha, Jacques Derrida, Anuradha Dingwaney, Lydia Liu, Trinh T. Minh-ha, Tejaswini Niranjana, and many others). For extensive reflections on minor and major languages within transnational translation studies, see *Public Culture* 13.1 (Winter 2001).

3 Tejaswini Niranjana and Samia Mehrez point out in their respective studies that George Steiner and other critics who locate translation within the ostensibly universal tradition of "humanism" overlook the inequities of exchange in colonial paradigms, in which translation operates to the material benefit of the dominant (colonial or imperial) power. See Niranjana, *Siting Translation*, 59; Mehrez, "Translation and the Postcolonial Experience," 121; and Liu, *Tokens of Exchange*, esp. 1–12.

4 Benjamin, "Task of the Translator."

in colonial and postcolonial conditions has been widely credited with producing hybridized literature that breaks down the "monologized" discourse of nationalism and cracks its authority.

Those studies, however, focus on the politics of translation as a process applied *to* a text rather than a process that takes place *within* it. Some readings of Benjamin stress that *any* act of writing is already a translation, a transposition of pure meaning into a single linguistic form. In Paul de Man's view, the poet must convey a meaning that exists outside of language, whereas the translator is concerned not with extralinguistic meaning but simply with the functional relationship between languages.[5] For Octavio Paz, while translation and poetic creation are mutually enriching "twin processes," translation is the inverse of poetic creation.[6] Ultimately, both approaches see translation in the traditional sense of *transfer*, as moving thought into language, or moving thought from one language to another, rather than as an internal process, where translation plays a dynamic role *within* the creation of meaning.

On the other hand, scholars of hybrid or bilingual texts in colonial and postcolonial literatures have looked more closely at the functions of translation in *narrative*, but with an eye to disclosing the tensions and relations of power between major and minor languages. They tend to discuss Francophone and Anglophone writing as an intervention in the major language and culture, rather than focusing on other aspects of interlinguistic negotiations taking place within the narrative fabric.[7] Samia Mehrez draws attention to the intratextual role of translation in Arab Francophone writing, asserting that "by drawing on more than one culture, more than one language, more than one world experience, within the confines of the same text, postcolonial anglophone and francophone [*sic*] literature very often defies our notions of an 'original' work and its translation." To describe such works she proposes the notion of the "double" text, one that can be decoded only by the bilingual reader conversant in both cultures and traditions, and whose reading can therefore be "none but a perpetual translation."[8] But while Mehrez adduces the translation process as essential to reception—the *de*coding of the "double" text—she

5 De Man, "Conclusions." For de Man, then, the original text is already translated, "disarticulated," and "dead" (84); once something is in language, it is no longer original. Translation itself is a nonvital process of repetition.

6 Paz, "Translation," 159. Paz agrees with Benjamin that the translation is not a "copy" but a "transmutation" (160).

7 In her *Fantasia*, author Assia Djebar ruminates at length upon her own relationship with the French language and what it means to be "writing the enemy's language" (213–217) but does not discuss the presence of Arabic within the French of her narrative (see, e.g., 202).

8 Mehrez, "Translation and the Postcolonial Experience," 122–124.

does not read it into the *production* of the narrative code. Moreover, as is so often the case, she does not consider the reverse possibility of how a text written in a non-metropolitan language, for instance an Arabic novel incorporating traces of English or French, might be read as a hybrid or "double" text.

What happens when translation (and mistranslation) becomes part of the story itself? This chapter considers narratives that engage and problematize their own linguistic hybridity by explicitly thematizing the negotiation between different linguistic strands. In such works, bilingualism is a strategic tool for scrutinizing the role of language in colonial structures of power. In colonial situations, "[t]he colonizer's language and discourse are elevated to the status or arbiter of truth and reality; the world comes to be as the authoritative discourse says."[9] This is only too true in the Israeli-Palestinian context, with its competing realities and truths (Israel or Palestine? War of Independence or *nakba*? Terrorism or resistance?). Both Emile Habiby's *al-Mutasha'il* (*The Pessoptimist*) and Samir Naqqash's *Ana wa-ha'ula' wa-l-fisam* (*I, They, and the Split*) take on the problems of authority and identity at the heart of (post)colonial discourses. As Bourdieu teaches us, "The language of authority never governs without the collaboration of those it governs, without . . . misrecognition, which is the basis of all authority."[10] By "misrecognition," Bourdieu means a community's shared belief in the legitimacy of power, which mistakes the arbitrary for the inevitable. In Habiby and Naqqash's narratives, this "normal" state of misrecognition is reversed through the characters' strategic misrecognitions, which demystify the mechanisms of authority. These two texts thus symbolically invert discursive power through deliberate moments of communicative slippage that result from mistranslation and misinterpretation. Translation becomes a mode of consciousness, a state of mind, producing the self-aware quality of hyperlanguage in the narrative. Here the no-man's-land is the space not just between languages, but between message intended and message received: for the author, it is a space of maneuver and of latent resistance.

My readings limn the poetics of misunderstanding in this no-man's-land, following representations of translation and code-switching to see how misunderstanding provides insight into a higher truth. The characters' faulty attempts at grappling with the unfamiliar and translating it into their own idiom elicit the narrative's metatext, to be decoded by the reader who can read between the lines. By making so much of their meaning contingent on communicative *failure*—in other words, by intentionally

9 Arteaga, "An Other Tongue," 16.
10 Bourdieu, *Language and Symbolic Power*, 113.

obstructing the transparency of language within the narrative—these texts also demonstrate how the referential or mimetic function of language may be meaningfully destabilized in contexts where languages (and language choice) are ideologically fraught. Ultimately, translation and interlinguistic tensions serve as vehicles for disrupting the dominant discourse and for contesting history both as event and as narrative; they enable the writers to reclaim their repressed histories, transcending the cultural and political barriers placed between them and their pasts.

HABIBY AND NAQQASH IN A COLONIAL CONTEXT

Studies of translation in (post)colonial contexts usually focus on interactions of hegemonic metropolitan languages with "minor" or indigenous languages. Theoretical scholarship on the bilingual text in particular has been based primarily on Anglophone and Francophone literatures and, to a lesser degree, on minority writing in the Americas, Caribbean writing in Dutch, and Turkish writing in German, among other configurations of European and non-European languages. The literature of Israel/Palestine departs from the "X-ophone" model in numerous respects. To begin with, Israel's de facto policy of cultural separation enforces Arabic for Arabs and Hebrew for Jews, differentiating it from cases where the native population was forced to adopt the colonizer's language, as in Francophone North Africa.[11] Furthermore, unlike European and non-European languages, Hebrew and Arabic are closely related descendants of the same Semitic language family with many shared cognates, a point that will prove central to my analysis of Habiby's novel. Finally, Jews and Arabs have a shared history and culture, as exemplified by the history of al-Andalus discussed in chapter 2. Thus, in another departure from the X-ophone model, the meeting of Hebrew and Arabic did not begin with the colonial moment; rather, as with the case of Japanese and Korean, the colonial encounter transformed a long-standing historic relationship. This chapter brings to light the particularities of bilingual writing in the Israeli-Palestinian context, which, I argue, can lead us to a more nuanced theoretical understanding of the dynamics of translation and bilingualism in (post)colonial literature. With their philological kinship and joint literary past, Hebrew and Arabic offer bilingual writers exceptionally rich thematic possibilities. The idea of a deceptive *closeness* (as opposed to the sense of remoteness that generally characterizes relations between

11 Or in the Japanese occupation of Korea, which is all the more interesting given that in most other respects, the colonial relationship of Japanese and Korean resembles that of Hebrew and Arabic.

colonial and indigenous languages) permeates Habiby's work and is also indicative of the actual, physical proximity between speakers of Hebrew and Arabic in Israel/Palestine. Similarly, the Jewish religious and cultural connection to the biblical Land of Israel generates a wealth of literary references and allusions that are often mobilized in the service of Zionism but which our two authors tap for ironic or subversive purposes. For Naqqash, working between two different forms of Arabic within a Hebrew environment produces a highly unusual form of literary bilingualism.

The question of Israel/Palestine as a colonial paradigm is itself complex and not entirely analogous to the North African, South Asian, or Caribbean contexts. Within its 1948 borders, Israel never employed the absentee landlord model on which postcolonial theory was based. Scholars have argued variously that the State of Israel represents a "'postcolonial' colony," meaning a settler colonialism that also exercises direct rule over another, foreign territory,[12] an "adulterated colonialism" that is simultaneously national and colonial in character,[13] and an "eccentric" form of settler colonialism set apart by paradoxical lines of continuity with anticolonial nationalisms.[14] The Palestinian Habiby and Iraqi Naqqash occupy different positions within this already complex colonial framework and its politics of language. As noted in previous chapters, Arabic literature in Israel has been written by Palestinian Israelis, such as Habiby,[15] and, until Naqqash's death in 2004, also by a smaller group of Arab Jewish writers, mainly from Iraq.[16] Although both were Arabic-language writers in Israel, Habiby and Naqqash faced different challenges. Habiby, who remained in his native Haifa and became an Israeli citizen after 1948, represented

12 Joseph Massad discusses the simultaneity of the colonial and postcolonial phases within Israel/Palestine in terms of a "settler colonialism" that "presents us with different spatialities and temporalities as regards a diachronic schema of colonialism, then post-colonialism." He points to South Africa, the U.S., and Rhodesia as other examples "where settler-colonists declared themselves independent [initiating the "postcolonial" phase] while maintaining colonial privileges for themselves over the conquered population [extending the "colonial" phase]" (Massad, "'Post-Colonial' Colony," 311).

13 "Adulterated colonialism" is Ilan Pappé's term, cited in Shenhav, *Arab Jews*, 34. Shenhav provides a synthesis of arguments by Israeli "New Historians" to the effect that Zionism is a fusion of territorial nationalism and colonialism, citing writings of Kimmerling, Shafir, Pappé, and others (34–36); elsewhere, Shenhav calls it "Zionist exceptionalism" because it is a "unique hybrid" that is "quintessentially European, yet materializes in the Middle East; arguably secular, yet imbued with theology; modern, yet relying on ancient roots" (80).

14 See Penslar, *Israel in History*, 6; see also chap. 5, "Is Zionism a Colonial Movement," 90–111.

15 For a detailed discussion of "Arab-Israeli" or "Palestinian-Israeli" writers, including the questions of audience, politics of publishing, and marketing, see Elad-Bouskila, *Modern Palestinian Literature*, esp. chaps. 1–2.

16 Jewish writers of Arabic include Anwar Shaul, Shalom Darwish, Yitzḥak Bar-Moshe, and Sasson Somekh, in addition to Naqqash; see Berg, *Exile from Exile*.

the Israeli Communist Party as a member of Parliament for two decades. His acceptance of the 1992 Israel Prize, the State of Israel's highest honor for writers and academics, was criticized harshly throughout the Arab world.[17] Yet Habiby never ceased to identify with Palestine as a personal history and a political cause. Whether we locate his writing within the rubric of "colonial" or "postcolonial" literature, it portrays an unambiguously colonial dynamic of Israeli military and political domination of Palestinians.

Naqqash's case is more complex: on the one hand, as a Jewish writer in the Jewish state, he ostensibly shared the majority's privileges. The reality, however, is that as a self-declared "Arab Jew" writing in Arabic, he fell far and deep between two chairs. In Israel he had almost no reading public, and hence no interested commercial publishers; yet as a Jewish Israeli, he lacked access to publishers in the Arab world.[18] Virtually unknown both within Israel and abroad, Naqqash lacked any measure of institutional support or public recognition (while Habiby enjoyed widespread recognition, critical acclaim, and—perhaps most important of all—access to Arab publishers and readers). Naqqash himself rejected the ideological basis of Israeli identity by claiming that he was in exile from Iraq, which warrants viewing his oeuvre as a literature of exile. Some scholars consider Mizraḥim in Israel "internally colonized"; Naqqash's work reminds us that the dislocation of Arab Jews was itself the joint result of Zionism and European colonial politics. As an Iraqi, moreover, Naqqash was colonized by the British even before he was brought to Israel.[19] Naqqash can therefore be discussed in multiple and overlapping frameworks as a Jew in Iraq, as an Iraqi in Israel, and as an Arab Jew in a polarized Middle East. In short, while bearing in mind the disparities between Palestinians and Jews in Israel, both Naqqash and Habiby occupy anomalous positions

17 Jarrar characterizes the reaction as a "storm of protests" among Arab intellectuals that "overwhelmed the Arabic press" and lasted until Habiby's death in 1996 ("A Narration of 'Deterritorialization,'" 16 and 25n9). The prize was controversial in Israel as well; see note 78 below.

18 As a result, Naqqash had to self-publish his first book. Many of his later works were published by the Association of Jewish Academics from Iraq (a noncommercial press). A few of his works, including his major novel *Shlumu al-Kurdi wa-ana wa-l-zaman* (Shlomo the Kurd, Myself, and Time, 2004), were published by Manshurat al-Jamal, the Cologne-based Iraqi press discussed in chapter 1. See note 92 below for his publications.

19 On Mizraḥim as "internally colonized," see Massad, "Zionism's Internal Others" and Shohat, "Sephardim in Israel." Although scholars are aware of the "external" colonization of Arab Jews before 1948, this issue has generally taken a backseat to the study of Mizraḥim in Israel. In *The Arab Jews*, Shenhav examines the direct collusion of British colonial interests and Zionism as pertains to Iraqi Jews working in the oil industry in 1942, against the background of the developing plan to bring world Jewry to Israel.

within the Israeli literary landscape and can be read in a (post)colonial framework.

In juxtaposing the two writers, I thus imply a connection between their respective projects that transcends questions of political and social status. The foremost point of tangency is their decision to write in Arabic, in a context in which it had become a minority language; both possessed sufficient mastery of Hebrew to have utilized it for fiction if so desired. This choice was particularly fraught for Naqqash. As a Jew writing in Arabic in the post-1948 Middle East, Naqqash defied the dominant cultural order of both Israel and the Arab world; well aware of this, he repeatedly insisted on his right to continue writing in his native language.[20] Habiby's novel begins with the moment of transformation from Palestine to Israel; Naqqash's narrative begins in Iraq and ends in Israel. Hence both works, while written in Israel, reflect transnational contexts in which Arabic, the language of the narrative, undergoes a dramatic reversal in status from a majority to a minority language within the time of the narrative. In terms of the postcolonial literary model, these two writers are analogous neither to the Algerian writer of French, who uses the language of the Other, nor to the Algerian writer of Arabic, who uses the native majority language. Their writing also complicates the model of "minor literature" theorized by Deleuze and Guattari, inasmuch as neither Habiby nor Naqqash writes in Hebrew, the majority language in Israel (itself a minority language in the global context).[21]

Thus these two (post)colonial works, written in Israel but informed by memories of Palestine and Iraq respectively, both deal with the transition from an Arabic-language society to Hebrew-dominated Israel and with the process of "translation" the protagonists themselves undergo in order to cope with life in exile (external exile for Naqqash and internal exile

20 An interview with Naqqash appears in Alcalay, *Keys to the Garden*, 100–111. Naqqash enumerates his reasons for writing in Arabic, then adds, "A Jew who writes in Arabic presents all kinds of problems to everyone, yet I am simply continuing to write in my own language" (110). Elsewhere he writes that Arabic "is a language known for its perfection and rich heritage; if we compare it to Hebrew, which was dormant for thousands of years, then revived and returned to development a short time ago, we find that it [Arabic] is more beautiful and richer by several fold" (Elad-Bouskila, "Arabic and/or Hebrew," 138).

21 See Deleuze and Guattari, "What Is a Minor Literature?" While privileging "minor literature" as "revolutionary," Deleuze and Guattari restrict "minor" literature to works written in the "major" (majority) language by a "minor" (minority) writer. For an extended critique of the model, see Kronfeld, *On the Margins of Modernism*, 5–14. As Rachel Weissbrod germanely points out, "While some of the languages used by Israel's minorities belong to the most widespread languages on earth, its dominant language, Hebrew, is a minority language in a global context" ("Implications of Israeli Mutilingualism," 52–53).

for Habiby).[22] As works written in the self-aware, metalinguistic mode of literary "hyperlanguage," both texts bring the mind-set of translation into the language of the text, and demand it of the reader.

FALSE FRIENDS: MISTRANSLATION AS STRATAGEM

Habiby is best known for his first novel, *al-Waqa'i' al-ghariba fi ikhtifa' Sa'id Abi al-Nahs al-Mutasha'il* (*The Strange Facts in the Disappearance of Sa'id the Ill-fated Pessoptimist*; henceforth *The Pessoptimist*), a major work in the modern Arabic canon.[23] The five works of his oeuvre, published between 1969 and 1991, can be read as a cumulative project driven by the desire to give a voice to the Palestinian experience in Israel.[24] Habiby saw himself as a representative of Palestinian society in Israel, which in the aftermath of the 1967 war regained access to the Arab world from which it had been isolated for almost two decades.[25] *The Pessoptimist* focuses on the period before the opening of borders: on "the 'cryptic,' 'missed' years" during which Palestinians in Israel remained under martial law.[26] As Hannah Amit-Kochavi observes, it depicts their psychological trauma and social shock as they confronted their loss of freedom, their separation from exiled members of their family and community, and their isolation as a disadvantaged minority. In short, the novel portrays their struggle for spiritual and material survival as well the challenges of defining personal and national identity in this impossible situation.[27]

22 Vicente Rafael describes translation in this sense as "'involv[ing] not simply the ability to speak in a language other than one's own but the capacity to reshape one's thoughts and actions in accordance with accepted forms,' a process that involves 'either affirmation or evasion of the social order'" (Rafael, *Contracting Colonialism*, 210–211, cited in Evans, "Metaphor of Translation," 149).

23 The book was originally published in 1974; all citations below are to the 2006 edition (Haifa: Dar 'arabask).

24 As Rachel Feldhay Brenner relates, "When asked about the Israel Prize award, Habiby related that his literary career started as a response to the denigrating comment made by Yig'al Alon, then the minister of education in the Israeli cabinet: 'Had there been a Palestinian people, it surely would have had a literary legacy.' It was at that moment that . . . 'I became determined to create in this country a Palestinian literature that would outlive both me and him.'" See the interview with Dalia Karfel, "Emil ve-ha-mashmitsim" (Emile and the slanderers), cited in Brenner, *Inextricably Bonded*, 113, 313n5. Over the course of his literary career, Habiby published five major works: *Sudasiyyat al-ayyam al-sitta*, 1969; *al-Mutasha'il*, 1974; *Luka' ibn Luka'*, 1980; *Ikhtiyya* (alternatively spelled *Ikhtayyi*), 1985; and *Khurafiyyat Saraya bint al-ghul*, 1991. He first gained fame in the Arab world for his *Sudasiyyat*, but it was his *Pessoptimist* that won him the greatest acclaim. See Jayyusi, "Introduction," in Habiby, *Secret Life*, xii; see also Heath, "Creativity in the Novels of Emile Habiby," 158.

25 Neuwirth, "Traditions and Counter-Traditions," 198–199.

26 Ibid., 199.

27 Amit-Kochavi, "Israeli Arabic Literature," 38; I use her language (modified slightly) in the two sentences above.

The tragedy and absurdity of Palestinian life in Israel are satirized through the misadventures of the hapless hero Sa'id, who relays his story in a series of letters.[28] A deliberate rewriting of Voltaire's *Candide* and the picaresque medieval Arabic genre of the *maqama*, the novel alternates between the perspectives of the naïve narrator and the canny critic.[29] Like its title "Pessoptimist," the novel is a study in contradictions and paradox: Sa'id (whose name means "happy") is happy and unhappy, is lucky and unlucky, lives in reality and in fantasy, and is both witless and wise.[30] Above all, the novel's exposition of antithesis is anchored in a profound resignification of language.

For Habiby, language becomes a stage for the performance of political meaning. His contrapuntal interweaving of the different layers and styles of classical and colloquial Arabic, which began in earnest in *The Pessoptimist* and persisted throughout his later novels, broke down boundaries between "high" and "low" registers of Arabic and constituted a radical break from the literal and often didactic style of his predecessors. The hallmark of Habiby's innovative approach was his diegetic thematization of language; his narrators' humorous digressions on matters of language are arguably the centerpiece of his novels.[31] Again, the very title of *The*

28 The identity of the letter's recipients is unclear, as is Sa'id's fate after being rescued from his impossible situation by space aliens. But "through scattered passages in which the recipient is addressed directly, the reader learns that the recipient is somehow connected to *al-Ittihad*, the newspaper of the CPI"; see Coffin, "Reading Inside and Out," 29–30. An epilogue adds that the letters bore an Acre postmark, which leads the recipient to a mental asylum in the city. The hospital's records turn up a similar name: "Sa'di Nahhas [the Ill-fated Optimist] known as Abu al-Thum [Mr. Garlic], and called Abu al-Shu'm [Mr. Pessimist] by some," who died a year earlier (Habiby, *al-Mutasha'il*, 225). In another play on translation and on double meanings, *thum* is the Arabic for "garlic" and *shum* its Hebrew cognate, which in Hebrew can also mean "none" or "nonesuch"—i.e., "Abu al-Shum" may not really exist. The novel then closes with a parable about a lawyer and a madman, about reality and lunacy.

29 Neuwirth, "Traditions and Counter-Traditions," 200; Allen, *Arabic Novel*, 213; and Abisaab, "*The Pessoptimist*"; Abisaab refers to the text as a "modern *maqama*" (2). *Maqamat* (in the plural), which first emerged in the tenth century, are "collections of short independent narratives written in an ornamental rhymed prose (*saj'*) with verse insertions, and share a common plot-scheme and two constant protagonists: the narrator and the hero. Each narrative (*maqama*) usually chooses one familiar adab-topos for elaboration" (Drory, "Maqama," 190). See also note 48 below.

30 Ghanayim, "Dream of Severance," 205.

31 Numerous critics have written about Habiby's creation of a new style or perhaps even subgenre of Arabic writing through his ironic thematizations of Arabic language. Akram Khater writes that in Habiby's work, "language is not only a simple mirror that reflects, but one that charges the reflection *with meanings which reside in several layers*. It is the intentional, yet unpretentious, depth of these layers—which is greatest in *Ikhtayyi*—that separate Habibi's work from most Palestinian novels" ("Emile Habibi," 88, my emphasis); his "irreverent approach to grammar and linguistic order is not just innovative, but it also reclaims the Arabic language from the tradition. In sum, Habiby's linguistic devices and language innovations form the elements of his vision of Palestinian identity" (ibid., 90). See also note 71 below.

Pessoptimist—in Arabic, *al-Mutasha'il*, a combination of *mutafa'il* (optimist) and *mutasha'im* (pessimist)—reflects the centrality of this kind of wordplay to his writing. That bilingual wordplay between Hebrew and Arabic also forms an important element of his novelistic and political project has not gone unnoticed by critics, yet this aspect of his work has not been analyzed in depth, most likely because very few critics of Habiby are versed in both languages.[32]

Habiby himself was a Palestinian who became one of Israel's political and literary luminaries; who wrote in both Hebrew and Arabic but maintained a linguistic division of labor, using Hebrew for his journalism and political essays and Arabic for his fiction.[33] While written in literary Arabic and sprinkled with the colloquial Palestinian dialect, *The Pessoptimist* depends heavily on a Hebrew backdrop for its meaning. Sa'id's conversations are often interlaced with references to Israeli society and material culture;[34] the narrator also addresses the reader directly with witty observations about Hebrew terms and their usage in Palestinian society, whose humor thinly cloaks biting social or political commentary. While these digressions may have been born of necessity, as Habiby needed a way to "translate" his material for the Arab reader outside Israel/Palestine, he transforms them into a critical element of his broader project: exposing the dismal reality of Palestine (and of the Arab world more generally) through the liberation of language from authority, be it the authority of *tradition* or an oppressive *political* authority.[35] Finally, one of

32 The role of Hebrew in Habiby's Arabic writing is briefly discussed in Somekh, "Ha-opsimist ve-ha-pesimist"; Khater, "Emile Habibi"; and Neuwirth, "Traditions and Counter-Traditions"; see also Ghanayim, "Magic Journey."

33 A founding member of the Israeli Communist Party and a leading Arab journalist, Habiby served three terms in the Knesset on the Communist list and was editor-in-chief of *al-Ittihad* (Unity), Israel's leading Arabic periodical.

34 For example, in a chapter called "The Story of the Golden Fish," Sa'id recalls, "Since I realized that birth control was a proof of loyalty, we had no more children. And whenever our secret became too heavy to bear, I declared my loyalty, whether I was asked to or not. I had regarded myself as an introvert until they sent us in a delegation to Europe and had us take along lots of *tembel* hats [in Arabic, *qubba'at "tambal"*] to present to our Jewish brothers there, along with talk of milk and honey, the marrying of spinsters, and the cure for cancer. I presented them with my shirt, pants, and all my underwear, keeping nothing hidden but my secret" (Habiby, *al-Mutasha'il*, 134, and *Secret Life*, 97, translation adapted from Le Gassick). This passage cannot be fully appreciated without familiarity with the *kova' tembel* (which Le Gassick mistakenly transliterates from the Hebrew as *tambal*). This floppy, brimless hat became an iconic symbol of "pioneering" life in Israel the early years of statehood. (The word *tembel* idiomatically means "fool," "dunce," or "idiot" in Israeli Hebrew). Habiby brilliantly weaves this cultural symbol into his parodic passage detailing Sa'id's loyalty to the state.

35 Ghanayim notes that in Habiby's first literary work, *Sudasiyyat al-ayyam al-sitta*, which was published as a book in Israel in 1970 (two years after its initial publication in a Lebanese journal), there are only six references addressed to readers outside Israel ("Magic Journey," 207). In his

the "strange facts" about the social life of the text is that it has been read both as a major Palestinian novel written for a broader Arabic-reading audience and as a striking example of minority literature in the Israeli canon (more on this will follow). I read *The Pessoptimist* as a "double text" *both* in that it is a bilingual work and in that it has followed separate trajectories in the Arabic and Hebrew literary fields.

The chronicle of Saʻid's "strange facts" commences shortly after the 1948 war, when he decides to return from his exile in Lebanon to the "inside." After infiltrating the border, Saʻid presents himself before the Israeli military authorities, claiming sanctuary in the name of an Israeli official with whom his father, killed in the war, had previously collaborated. The authorities detain Saʻid overnight in an Acre mosque crowded with Palestinian refugees from destroyed villages who are about to be deported the following day. There, Saʻid encounters his erstwhile headmaster, who gives him an impromptu "history lesson" on the numerous conquests of Palestine. The following day, an Israeli army driver conveys Saʻid to his hometown, ushering him into his new life with the words *ahlan wa-sahlan fi medinat yisra'el* (welcome to the *medina* of Israel), which our protagonist misinterprets to mean that the Israelis have changed his beloved city's name from "Haifa" to "Israel."[36] Only much later does he come to understand the source of his error: the word *ma-DI-na* means "city" in Arabic, but in Hebrew the same word, with a slight vowel change and shift in stress (*me-di-NA*), connotes "state."[37]

The trenchant irony of an Israeli using the standard Arabic greeting *ahlan wa-sahlan* to "welcome" a Palestinian refugee to his own, now-occupied land is compounded by Saʻid's misinterpretation. In the narrative, this blunder characterizes Saʻid's extreme naïveté, but the same blunder plays out in the metanarrative as a strategic communication aimed directly at the reader. Saʻid's mistranslation subtly transforms the message of the driver into the message of the author—the latter, of course, bearing the real truth value within the novel's economy of meaning. Throughout the novel, it is not the portrayal of the Israelis so much

view, "Habiby's orientation towards the Arab world intensified after *Sudasiyya* achieved critical acclaim" (ibid., 207). This evolution is "apparent in *al-Mutasha'il*, published six years later, in which the author presents his readers with a far larger number of remarks, explanatory notes and references whose content is obviously not directed towards Arab readers in Israel"; many of these references "take on an ironic tone . . . becoming an inseparable part of the literary work itself" (ibid., 207–208). In Khater's view, Habiby's thematization of translation between Hebrew and Arabic is more pronounced in *Ikhtiyya* than in *The Pessoptimist*; in "*Ikhtayyi*, as opposed to the earlier novels, translation between language and cultures emerges as a very real problem for the Palestinians living in Israel, complicating life even further" (Khater, "Emile Habibi," 86).

36 Habiby, *al-Mutasha'il*, 60.

37 See also Mehrez, "al-Mufaraqa," 46.

as Sa'id's failure to understand them that conveys the essence of his new colonial reality. Habiby's manipulation of the cognate *madina/medina* exemplifies his narrative strategy: from here, the tale that unfolds is one of slight shifts, of double entendres, in which appearances of familiarity are misleading. As an opening example, then, this brief vignette of Sa'id and the Israeli driver humorously but pointedly introduces the new Israeli state from a Palestinian perspective, alludes to Israel's very real policy of changing place-names from Arabic to Hebrew, and nods to the deceptive proximity between Hebrew and Arabic that is central to the spirit of the novel.

While such moments of "play" between Hebrew and Arabic are interspersed throughout the novel, in each case it is not simply language but survival that is at stake: these verbal exchanges are power plays as much as they are wordplays. Representing translation and mistranslation becomes an *internal* literary strategy, deployed to expose the colonial mechanisms of power, and then to subvert them. In any work of literature written under bilingual conditions and in a (post)colonial context, translation between the two languages cannot take place without some degree of political confrontation. At the same time, the relationship established between Hebrew and Arabic in this novel is not one-dimensional. Habiby repeatedly emphasizes the proximity and interrelation of the two languages, and the transactions between them are multivalent and often deeply ironic.

One could, in fact, see the false cognate as the operative metaphor of this book. The *madina/medina* confusion is a classic example of *faux amis*, that is, false friends—and indeed, *The Pessoptimist* as a whole is rife with false friends, not restricted to the linguistic variety. Co-opted into the Israeli security apparatus as an informer, Sa'id soon finds himself surrounded by a league of such "friends": the secret service agent *Adon* Safsarshik, Sa'id's would-be savior; Sa'id's own boss Ya'qub, an Arab Jew; and the little "Big Man" to whom both Sa'id and Ya'qub answer. As for the army driver who welcomes Sa'id to *medinat yisra'el*, this fellow further tells Sa'id that he volunteered for the army in order to "fight feudalism," that he "likes Arabs," and that when the war is over, the state will build *kibbutzim* for Arabs, which, he says, will "rely on liberated young men like [Sa'id] who speak a civilized [human] language."[38] To this remarkable declaration, the driver adds the Hebrew greeting *shalom*, which

38 In Arabic, *sa-yuqimun li-na kibutsat ya'tamidun fi-ha 'ala amthali min al-shubban al-mutaharririn al-ladhina yutqinun lugha insaniyya*; Habiby, *al-Mutasha'il*, 59. In Le Gassick's translation, "They would depend heavily on 'liberal' young men like myself who knew a civilized language well" (*Secret Life*, 41). *Lugha insaniyya* can be translated as a "human," "civilized," or "humanistic" language; in the Arabic text it conveys something of all three.

Sa'id promptly translates into the English "peace," thereby "proving my humanity." The driver then laughs and translates "peace" back into Arabic as *salam, salam*—charitably extending the linguistic boundaries of humanity so as to include the Arabic-speaking (though apparently "liberated") Sa'id.[39]

Of course, Habiby's representation of such discourse mimics the double talk and hypocrisy of the establishment. But this kind of verbal chicanery presumes transparency both of the language and of the implicit rules of the game—an assumption that Sa'id repeatedly foils. Instead, he takes the rulers at their very literal word. In one such scene, set at the conclusion of the 1967 war, the Voice of Israel broadcast calls for all "defeated Arabs" (*al-'arab al-mahzumin*)[40] to fly white flags from their houses. The announcer obviously is addressing the inhabitants of the newly conquered West Bank, but Sa'id, listening in Haifa, is just a bit unsure *which* "defeated Arabs" he means: those defeated in 1967 or those defeated in 1948, such as himself? To be on the safe side, he ties his white bed sheet to a broomstick and props it up on his roof, convinced that would attest to his "white" (clear) conscience.[41] When his Jewish boss Ya'qub furiously demands an explanation, Sa'id protests that he meant only to demonstrate his loyalty to the state. Ya'qub retorts that the higher-ups have interpreted his action as an insurrection: "That announcer was telling the West Bank Arabs to raise white flags in surrender to the Israeli occupation. What did you think you were up to, doing that in the very heart of the state of Israel, in Haifa, which no one regards as a city under occupation?"—to which Sa'id indignantly replies "Ziyadat al-khayr khayr!" (You can't have too much of a good thing!).[42] His self-declared patriotism notwithstanding, Sa'id's misinterpretation of the announcer's directives quickly lands him in prison.

Through such faulty and overly literal interpretations, Sa'id inverts the official state discourse so that it ends up meaning the opposite of what its spokespersons intend. His linguistic failures are a symbolic corrective: by not performing the desired translation, our hapless hero exposes the warped reality around him. Moreover, in keeping with the literary tradition of the fool who doubles as prophet, his linguistic tomfoolery doubles

39 Habiby, *al-Mutasha'il*, 59–60. In Le Gassick's translation, "He said, 'Shalom,' and I answered, 'Peace,' showing how civilized I was" (*Secret Life*, 42).

40 Habiby, *al-Mutasha'il*, 167.

41 Many of the expressions and words in the passage have double meanings, and Habiby also plays on expressions invoking the root *b-y-d* (clear or white) such as "my clear conscience" (*bayad tawiyati*), "my bed sheet" (*bayad firashi*), and the "white [*abyad*] flag," among several other wordplays (Ghanayim, "Dream of Severance," 207).

42 Habiby, *al-Mutasha'il*, 169–170, and *Secret Life*, 122; Le Gassick's translation.

as ethical critique. Anuradha Dingwaney pinpoints the subversive potential of mistranslation when she describes the "between" space of translation and cross-cultural texts as "that space from within which the (colonized) native deliberately (mis)translates the colonial script, alienating and undermining its authority."[43] But what distinguishes many of Sa'id's mistranslations, as illustrated by the *madina/medina* example, is that they are paradoxically a result of the close relationship between the languages. For Habiby, a cognate such as *madina/medina* offers itself up as a "hybrid construction":

> one that, while uttered by a single speaker, contains two manners of speech, two styles, two "languages," two semantic and axiological systems. Bakhtin . . . showed that frequently even one and the same word belongs simultaneously to two languages or two belief systems that intersect in a hybrid construction. *It is through this hybrid construction that one voice is able to unmask the other within a single discourse. It is at this point that authoritative discourse becomes undone.*[44]

The thematic potential of the hybrid construction is milked by Habiby repeatedly to make a point not only about Palestinian life under Israeli rule, but about the instability of language itself, particularly when it is pressed into the service of essentializing or totalizing discourses. Not only can language "mean" something other than what the speaker intends, but cognates and shared roots can cross the delineating boundaries of language and national identity, bringing us readers into the no-man's-land between borders. We see this point illustrated again in a passage spoofing the hyperbole of nationalistic and militaristic language in both Hebrew *and* Arabic. During Sa'id's overnight detention in the famous Jazzar mosque in 'Akka (Acre), where he is surrounded by Palestinian refugees from destroyed villages, his former headmaster gives him a brief history lesson on the numerous conquests of Palestine. Reminding Sa'id that Acre was liberated from the Crusaders by a Mamluk leader, he adds, "His military title was al-Alfi, meaning 'the Thousander.'"[45] When Sa'id asks if the rank of *aluf* for Israeli generals is derived from that title, the headmaster replies, in an outright mimicry of the Zionist narrative, "God forbid, my son. No. That [*aluf*] is derived from the word for a leader of a thousand

43 Dingwaney, "Introduction: Translating 'Third World' Cultures," 9.

44 Wolf, "*Third Space*," 133, my emphasis. By "authoritative discourse," Wolf (following Bakhtin) means not the literally authoritative discourse of a political authority, but rather the authority of any monological discourse; however, as Bakhtin shows us, the two often go hand in hand. See Bakhtin, *Dialogic Imagination*, 304–305.

45 Habiby, *al-Mutasha'il*, 36, and *Secret Life*, 24, Le Gassick's translation.

men, a term used in the Bible. Oh, no! These aren't Mamluks or Crusaders. These are people returning to their country after an absence of two thousand years." The headmaster then concludes, "'Ala kulli hal, ya buni, dhalla al-hadith yajri, mundhu **alfay** sana, 'ala l-**uluf**, qadatun **alfiyun**, aw **alufiyun**, wa-qatla bi-l-**uluf**. Laysa hunaka 'ala l-ard aqdas min dam al-insan, ya buni, wa-lidhalika summiyat biladuna bi-l-muqaddasa" (Anyway, my son, people have been talking for two thousand years in terms of thousands—generals of a thousand men, men slain by the thousands, the Alfi's and the Aluf's and so on. There is nothing on earth more holy than human blood. That is why our country is called the Holy Land).[46]

The irony in this passage is palpable, but its stylistic punch takes its power from the fast and furious repetition of the shared triliteral root *alif-lam-fa* (Arabic)/*alef-lamed-feh* (Hebrew), associated primarily with a "thousand." While this type of wordplay and sound play within Arabic is characteristic of Habiby's writing, here he plays with a single root shared by the two languages, in two similar yet antithetical contexts—one, the Mamluk router of the Crusaders; the other, the term for an Israeli general. In the Arabic original, this fast-paced and highly exaggerated repetition of the *a-l-f* root comically defamiliarizes it and renders both the Arabic *alfi* and the Hebrew *aluf* absurd—all the more so when read aloud. By satirizing such hyperbolic, overblown language ("thousands and thousands of . . ."), Habiby also highlights its complicity in the recent military conquests that have produced the human misery surrounding Sa'id and the headmaster even as they are conversing about history in abstract terms. Most pointedly, Habiby invokes the trope of two thousand years (*alfay sana*) so central to Zionism's narrative of return. The headmaster's discourse on history, with his musings on the idea of "thousands," does not directly negate the Zionist narrative; in a more subtle and oblique manner, it resizes the State of Israel as just one particular moment (as opposed to *the* defining moment) within a grand historical panorama of conquerors, undoing the *teleology* of Zionism. Likewise, by telling Sa'id that the blood of the anonymous victims of history put the "Holy" into the Holy Land, the headmaster redefines this trope, intervening in Zionism's assumption of a unique claim to the biblical identity of the land. "[S]ince the facts of 'history' are inescapable for the post-colonial, since attention to history is in a sense demanded by the post-colonial situation, post-colonial theory has to formulate a narrativizing strategy in addition to a deconstructive one," writes Niranjana.[47] As we have just seen, such narrativizing strategies of history are already implicit within (post)colonial fiction. Here Habiby reanimates the shared

46 Habiby, *al-Mutasha'il*, 36–37, and *Secret Life*, 24, Le Gassick's translation, with additions.
47 Niranjana, *Siting Translation*, 37–38.

linguistic past of Arabic and Hebrew to parody (and thus interrupt) all absolute claims to the land or its history.[48] But to decode the passage's ideological subtext, to grasp this (re)narrativizing strategy, requires familiarity with the cultural discourses of both Arabic and Hebrew.[49]

The text's doubleness is underscored in another chapter titled "First Lesson in Hebrew" ("al-Dars al-awwal fi al-lugha al-'ibriyya").[50] Here, Sa'id relates two more incidents from his early days in the State of Israel, both of which involve misunderstandings based on the pronunciation of a single letter. In the first, his aunt, mistaking him for a government agent taking the census, exclaims, "'I am *mahsiyya!*,'' meaning, "I have already been counted in the census!" But, as Sa'id tells us, "she pronounced it *makhsiyya* (castrated) as the soldiers pronounce it."[51] Habiby's comment alludes to the Ashkenazi pronunciation of the Hebrew letter *ḥet* (ח) and Arabic *ha* (ح) as a hard *kh* (خ). As in the confusion of "P" and "B" in *The Band's Visit*, here too the mispronunciation of a single letter gestures toward a reality of dissonance: "The play on words *mahsiyya* and *makhsiyya*—pronounced as it is differently by the oppressor and the oppressed—hints at the political impotence of Palestinians living in Israel when it equates being counted in the census of the state with castration."[52] Later in the same chapter, wanting to know whether he can still catch a bus, Sa'id asks a Jewish passerby for the time; the man shouts back a word Sa'id mistakenly hears as "Acht." Sa'id recalls, "I was no dummy and remembered that acht means 'eight' in German."[53] Although in this instance Habiby does not gloss the

48 Angelika Neuwirth interprets this scene differently, as an ironic inversion of the Zionist objective of *kibbuts ha-galuyot* (ingathering of the exiles), where Habiby transposes the idea to the Palestinian refugees whose "expulsion and dispersion is the price to be paid for the attainment of the Messianic goal." She points out that the headmaster indeed refers to it as a *jam' shaml* (bringing together the dispersed), in a travesty of the original concept. Moreover, "the role of language . . . in this context seems not merely to be pointless but indeed a medium of deception. By modeling the scene on the classical *maqama* [where the headmaster plays the role of the trickster], Habibi marks it as a cynical farce for his readers, who are able to grasp the intertextual foil" (Neuwirth, "Traditions and Counter-Traditions," 208–209).

49 Anton Shammas's translation approximates the sound of the Arabic, but the effect is less robust in Hebrew due to Hebrew's different vowel patterns and the interchange between the letters *fe* and *pe*: *'Al kol panim, bni, be-meshekh* ***alpayim*** *shana shava mila zo,* ***'alf,*** *ve-'alta le-lo heref: mefakdey ha-****alafim****, ha-****alufim****,* ***alfey*** *harugim. Eyn davar kadosh yoter 'al-pney ha-adama mi-dmo shel ha-adam, bni, 'al ken yikra'u la-erets zo shelanu erets ha-kodesh* (Habiby, *Ha-opsimist*, 30).

50 Habiby, *al-Mutasha'il*, 66.

51 In Arabic, *'Ana mahsiyya ya khawaban!' Wa-lafazatha 'makhsiyya' kema yalfazha al-'askar* (Habiby, *al-Mutasha'il*, 67). See also Neuwirth, "Traditions and Counter-Traditions," 202, Neuwirth's translation.

52 Khater, "Emile Habibi," 86.

53 Habiby, *al-Mutasha'il*, 69, and *Secret Life*, 48; Le Gassick's translation, with modifications (Le Gassick mistransliterates the name of the neighborhood as "Wadi Nasnas").

passage with a translingual explanation, the reader who knows Hebrew immediately identifies the source of Sa'id's error: *eḥat* (pronounced by most Israelis as *ekhat*), meaning "one," could easily be confused by a non-Hebrew speaker with the German *acht*. In this instance, the unannotated joke would be lost on the monolingual *Arabic* reader.[54]

From such episodes Sa'id appears not so much an unreliable as an *uninformed* narrator. In his theory of novelistic discourse, Bakhtin analyzes the dialogical tension between the narrator's speech and the discourse of the author, which he terms the "nondirect speaking" of the narrator conducted "through a refraction of authorial intentions."[55] Habiby's use of Sa'id's voice to express his authorial intentions exemplifies such "double-voiced" discourse. To reconcile the discourse of the author (Habiby) with the language of the uninformed narrator (Sa'id), we must be informed readers who can fill in the gaps of language and logic in Sa'id's narration. In the previous passage, the text requires us to work backward from Sa'id's mistranslation (*acht*) to reconstruct the original Hebrew (*eḥat*). In other cases (such as that of the white flag incident), our privileged knowledge is of the message the authorities intend to convey. In this case, the reader negotiates between official discourse and Sa'id's faulty interpretation: between the message sent and the message received. It is in that no-man's-land between them that the message of the *author* is voiced.

At other moments in the narrative, Sa'id slips out of his dimwitted role and assumes the sharp-witted, highly "informed" voice of the author. Here too we may turn to Bakhtin: "The author is not to be found in the language of the narrator . . . but rather, the author utilizes now one language, now another, in order to avoid giving himself up wholly to either of them."[56] For example, Habiby continues Sa'id's narration of the *acht* incident by explaining how Sa'id teaches himself Hebrew; it takes over ten years, he tells us, before he is able to deliver a public address. Habiby then adds,

> But what is strange is that now a quarter century later [with the occupation of the West Bank in 1967], the soapmakers of Nablus mastered Hebrew in less than two years. When one of them switched to the

54 In fact, it is lost on Le Gassick, the novel's translator; see *Secret Life*, 48.

55 Bakhtin, "Discourse in the Novel," 313. Bakhtin continues, "Behind the narrator's story we read a second story, the author's story; he is the one who tells us how the narrator tells stories, and also tells us about the narrator himself. We acutely sense two levels at each moment in the story; one, the level of the narrator, a belief system filled with his objects, meanings, and emotional expressions, and the other, the level of the author, who speaks (albeit in a refracted way) by means of this story and through this story" (ibid., 314).

56 Ibid., 314.

> manufacture of marble tiles he hung up a sign in clear Kufic script [of Arabic], saying that his premises made *shayesh*, followed by his own magnificently prolix and distinctively Arab name: *shayesh* is the Hebrew word for marble. This is not merely a case of necessity being the mother of invention; it is also a matter of the financial interests of a country's elite who cared so little who ruled them politically that they applied in practice the Arabic proverb: Anyone who marries my mother becomes my stepfather.[57]

The marked change of tone (from loony to levelheaded, confounded to critical) signals a shift from narrator's to author's voice, and with this slippage the representation of language and translation takes on a different valence. Elsewhere, Sa'id/Habiby acknowledges that translation is a means of material survival; in a disquisition on the "virtues of the Oriental imagination," the speaker cites Arab waiters in Tel Aviv hotels who "translate" their names into Hebrew.[58] But in the soapmaker story, translation into Hebrew is depicted as a gratuitous measure reflecting no more than unabashed opportunism. The authorial voice links language directly to national identity, and essentializes it as either pure (loyal) or impure (disloyal). Translation in this passage is the offender; the Arabic proverb highlights the fidelity-infidelity metaphor embedded in the entire passage.

In addition to using direct authorial intervention to counterpose Sa'id's gullibility and passivity, Habiby also offers an alternative in the form of Sa'id's son "Wala'."[59] Whereas Sa'id uses (mis)translation to adapt and survive, his son Wala' rejects his father's complicity and instead joins the *fida'iyyin* (guerrilla fighters). Eventually, trapped in an ambush by the state security forces, he walks into the sea and disappears, followed by his mother. Even the opposition between father and son is represented through a minor linguistic switch: the *fida'iyyin* with whom Wala' throws in his lot, popularly viewed as the hope for the Palestinian liberation,

57 Habiby, *al-Mutasha'il*, 70 and *Secret Life*, 49, translation adapted from Le Gassick.

58 *Wa-l-nadal Shlomo, fi afkham fanadiq til abib, a-laysa huwwa Sulayman bin Munira, ibn haritna? Wa-Dudi, a-laysa huwwa Mahmud? Wa-Moshe, a-laysa huwwa Musa bin 'Abd al-Masih? Fa-kayfa la yartaziq ha'ula fi funduq aw fi mata'm aw fi mahatat benzin, law-la al-khayal al-sharqi?* (And Shlomo, a waiter in one of Tel Aviv's finest hotels—isn't he really Sulayman, son of Munira, from our neighborhood? And "Dudi," isn't he really Mahmud? And "Moshe," too; isn't his real name Musa, son of 'Abd al-Masih? How could they earn a living in a hotel, restaurant, or gas station, if not for the Oriental imagination?; Habiby, *al-Mutasha'il*, 140).

59 The name Wala' means "loyalty" or "fidelity," while Sa'id means "happy." In the story, Sa'id chooses the name Wala' to please his Israeli boss, who disapproves of the name Fathi ("victorious") originally proposed by the mother; see Habiby, *al-Mutasha'il*, 134; and Allen, *Arabic Novel*, 217.

are translated into the *fada'iyyin*, or extraterrestrial beings, who come to rescue Sa'id from his own impossible situation. All in all, the difference between salvation through active, real-life resistance and through passive fantasy/insanity turns out to be a matter of switching the soft *dal* (د) to the velarized *dad* (ض) and *i* to *a*.[60]

Language is also thematized throughout the novel in other ways, with revealing chapter headings such as "Sa'id Changes into a Cat That Meows"[61] and "The Ultimate Tale: The Fish That Understand All Languages."[62] The latter comes as a comment following Sa'id's narration of his son's escape into the sea and presumed suicide. After the loss of Wala' and his wife, Sa'id returns to the site regularly to fish and to silently call to his son, "hoping always for some response." On one such occasion, he relates,

> One day a Jewish boy who had sat down unnoticed beside me surprised me with the question:
> "In what language are you speaking, Uncle?"
> "In Arabic."
> "With whom?"
> "With the fish."
> "Do the fish understand only Arabic?"
> "Yes, the old fish, the ones that were here when the Arabs were."
> "And the young fish, do they understand Hebrew?"
> "They understand Hebrew, Arabic, and all languages. The seas are wide and flow together. They have no borders and have room enough for all fish."[63]

Here Sa'id depicts freedom as a kind of linguistic universality in which translation is rendered obsolete. All told, translation in the novel is a necessary evil; at best it is a means of survival, and at worst it is selling out. This begs the question of Habiby's attitude toward *literary* translation, given that all his major works were translated into Hebrew by Anton Shammas.[64] Habiby did not write in a translatable idiom; much to the contrary, he prided himself on the complexity of his Arabic and its resistance to translation. In his last novel, *Saraya bint al-ghul* (*Saraya, the Ogre's Daughter*, 1991), Habiby even addresses Shammas directly in the body of

60 See also Allen, *Arabic Novel*, 214; and Neuwirth, "Traditions and Counter-Traditions," 204.

61 The chapter reads, "How often I yelled at those about me, 'Please, everyone! I groan at the burden of the great secret I bear on my shoulders! Please help me!' But all that came from beneath my moustache was a meowing sound, like that of a cat" (Habiby, *al-Mutasha'il*, 108, and *Secret Life*, 76, Le Gassick's translation).

62 Habiby, *al-Mutasha'il*, 148, and *Secret Life*, 108, Le Gassick's translation.

63 Habiby, *al-Mutasha'il*, 158–159, and *Secret Life*, 114, Le Gassick's translation.

64 On Habiby and Shammas, see Somekh, "Ha-opsimist ve-ha-pesimist."

the narrative, challenging him to translate his Arabic wordplay (*al-tabaq wa-l-janas*) "into any near or distant language" as compensation for what the Israelis "took from us and from our language."[65]

If Habiby's relationship to translation seems fraught, we must remember that not only does *The Pessoptimist* read as a "double text," but it has led a double life within the Arabic and Hebrew literary fields, belonging at once to two modern literary canons. *The Pessoptimist* occupies a prominent place in the modern Arabic canon and entered the Israeli canon via Hebrew translation, where it "created a consciousness of Palestinian literature as part of the Israeli literary landscape."[66] As Nancy Coffin observes, "Perhaps one of the most striking features of Habibi's novel is the fact that it was enjoyed on both sides of the 1948 borders of Israel, even during the heyday of Arab literary commitment."[67] In this regard, the novel is probably unique, and the social life of the text on both sides of the political and linguistic divide deserves further exploration. The double life of *The Pessoptimist* also raises the question of the bilingual text without bilingual readers, as so few readers are equipped to appreciate the novel's full cultural and linguistic range.[68] As I have argued, this novel embodies a bilingual consciousness and generates meaning through translingual worldplay. That does not imply that it fails to create meaning for monolingual

65 The passage reads, "I challenge Anton Shammas to see if he can translate these antithetical expressions and paranomasia [*al-tabaq wa-l-janas*] into any near or distant language, first and foremost into the kind of flea-bitten language [*lughat 'akaluni al-baragith'*] our [Arabic] press uses to its shame, as if in compensation for what they [Israeli Jews] have taken from us and from our language: *manqal* for barbeque; *kassah* for roughhousing; *dakheelak* for please; *tislam* for thank you; our folk dance, the *dabka*; even *mabsut*, our word for happy, has been Hebraized for gender and number, with the plurals *mabsutim* and *mabsutot*." Habiby glosses Shammas's name with a footnote that reads, "A well-known, skillful scholar and author who translated my novels *al-Mutasha'il* and *Ikhtiyya* into Hebrew. Experts in the twin languages claim that he has enriched the Hebrew language—the author" (Habiby, *Khurafiyyat Saraya bint al-ghul*, 151, and Habiby, *Saraya, the Ogre's Daughter*, 178, translation adapted from Ghanayim's and Theroux's). Elsewhere in the novel, Habiby also mentions the Iraqi-born Israeli writer Sami Michael and addresses his comments to him; *Saraya, the Ogre's Daughter*, 212–213. See also Ghanayim, "Dream of Severance," 212; Somekh, "Anton Shamas," 41; idem, "Ha-opsimist ve-ha-pesimist," 66; and Hever, "Of Refugee Gals and Refugee Guys," 225–226.

66 Brenner, "Search for Identity," 96.

67 Coffin, "Reading Inside and Out," 26.

68 Yasemin Yildiz explores a similar problem in relation to the bilingual Japanese-German writer Yoko Tawada, whose work presents "a bilingualism addressing itself to 'monolinguals' . . . confronting them with perspectives gained in an unfamiliar language"—in this case by refusing hybridity and the possibility of translation between languages. Instead, Tawada thematizes translation of language into nonverbal communication, in the process offering monolinguals the momentary "heightened metalinguistic awareness of bilinguals" (*Beyond the Mother Tongue*, 115–119).

readers—only that the meaning created may diverge quite profoundly in its respective reading communities.

The Pessoptimist was originally serialized in *al-Ittihad*, the Israeli Communist Party newspaper edited by Habiby; with its 1974 publication in book form in Beirut, it "proved wildly popular throughout the Arab world." As Coffin explains, "[I]ts lavish blend of puns, word play, and literary and historical allusions has helped to set it apart from the spare, pared-down, and 'ultra-realist' Arabic prose that was typical of the late 1960s and early 1970s."[69] This distinctive style is described by Coffin as a "rich Brechtian tapestry of literary montage [created] by combining passages of almost journalistically documentary language with allegory, satire, puns, archaisms, and elements of the fantastic, as well as quotations from and allusions to both Arabic and non-Arabic historical and literary works."[70] The novel's extensive and intensive dialogue with Arabic sources from the *turath* or classical tradition, including frequent and liberal references to poets such as al-Mutanabbi, al-Maʿarri, and ibn ʿArabi, as well as modern poets such as Samih al-Qasim, not to mention popular culture, has been thoroughly parsed.[71] Habiby himself supplies many of the intertextual references through footnotes in the text, mimicking (and often mocking) the classical Arabic style of annotation.[72] Arabic literary critics have focused largely on Habiby's language, stylistic influences, and use of irony in the novel; they also discuss the novel's characters and plot, all in relation to Habiby's implicit goal of representing the Palestinian experience. For the most part, they have downplayed the Hebrew linguistic and Israeli cultural dimensions of the text.[73]

69 Coffin, "Reading Inside and Out," 26. The book was published in book form in Haifa in 1974, then in Beirut the same year, with a third edition appearing in Jerusalem in 1977 (Allen, *Arabic Novel*, 210).

70 Coffin, "Reading Inside and Out," 27.

71 Critics have noted the influences of a vast array of classical and popular sources in the text, collectively including the language and style of the Qur'an, of al-Jahiz, al-Hamadhani, al-Hariri, Sufism, and the Ismaʿili heritage, *Kitab alf layla wa-layla* (the *Thousand and One Nights*), folktales and folk songs, and newspapers issued by the Palestinian Communist Party. "From the outset, then, Habibi is to lead his readers into an intertextual maze, one involving not only the great cultural heritage of the classical past but a variety of transcultural references" (Allen, *Arabic Novel*, 213). Khater observes that Habiby uses traditional linguistic structures such as rhymed prose (*saj'*) "in ways that seem to bring out the absurd as much in the style as in the image" ("Emile Habibi," 90). See also Ghanayim, "Dream of Severance," 206, and Somekh, "Anton Shamas," 42. Allen discusses Habiby's use of digressions in the forms of jokes, chapters dedicated to footnotes, etc. as a "modern adaptation of the classical Arabic trope of *istirad*" (*Arabic Novel*, 215). See also note 31 above.

72 Ghanayim, "Magic Journey," 209.

73 For example, Samia Mehrez, who argues convincingly for the "double" status of the Francophone Maghrebi text, does not make this connection regarding *The Pessoptimist* in her own (albeit considerably earlier) study of the novel; see Mehrez, "al-Mufaraqa." Le Gassick and

On the other hand, Hebrew literary critics treat *The Pessoptimist* as part of the Hebrew canon, focusing on its transmission into Israeli culture via Hebrew translation. In 1984, ten years after the original Arabic publication, Shammas's celebrated Hebrew translation was published under the title *Ha-opsimist* by a small, radical Israeli publishing house specializing in translations from Arabic.[74] In the same year, the Palestinian Israeli actor Muhammad Bakri adapted the novel as a one-man play, which he staged in both Arabic and Hebrew for Palestinian and Jewish audiences throughout Israel.[75] Highly successful, the play was performed in both languages for about ten years, in professional theaters as well as Jewish and Arab schools, community centers, and open-air venues.[76] In the late 1980s, Jewish high school students saw the Hebrew version that included a post-performance discussion with Bakri. The novel, however, has never been part of the curriculum for either Hebrew or Arabic literature in Israeli schools.[77] When Habiby won the Israeli Prize in 1992, *The Pessoptimist* was widely discussed in the Israeli media.[78] Both the play and the prize instilled the novel in Israeli cultural consciousness. The only best-selling Hebrew book translated from Arabic, it was republished in 1995 by one of Israel's central publishing houses, and while less widely known today, it is still in print.[79]

Although they are aware of *Ha-opsimist*'s status as a translated work, most Hebrew literary critics (of varied political leanings) have overlooked the novel's importance in the Arabic canon as well as its relationship to the Arabic literary and historical traditions.[80] Yet all mention the influence of

---

Jayyusi's translation contains numerous errors in transliteration of Hebrew terms, and consistently omits Habiby's explanations of these terms or any other Hebrew references.

74 Habiby, *Ha-opsimist.*

75 "The Hebrew version played by Bakri, prepared by Rami Livneh, made use of Shammas' translation, with some modifications necessary to let Bakri play different characters, including women, as well as Sa'id, the hero and narrator of the play" (Amit-Kochavi, "Performing Arabic Plays," 179).

76 Ibid.

77 Since 2006, *Ha-opsimist* has been included on a list of optional or "additional" (not obligatory) readings for students in Jewish schools completing the highest (elective) level of literature studies for the Israeli equivalent of the A-level exams. In 2012, the Ministry of Education produced a new literature program for Arab schools in which the novel can be included as an optional text, again for those completing the highest level literature exam, but it has not yet been approved. I thank Kawthar Jaber for this information.

78 Amit-Kochavi, "Israeli Arabic Literature," 39. In the wake of the prize, strong political reactions, both negative and positive, followed; an Israel Prize laureate announced he was giving up his own award in protest (ibid.).

79 Amit-Kochavi sees Habiby's positive reception in Israel as an exception to the rule, explained by Shammas's translations and by Bakri's performance of the stage adaptation ("Israeli Arabic Literature," 27).

80 Here I refer to scholars who work primarily or exclusively on Hebrew literature; this observation does not apply to the Israeli scholars Sasson Somekh, Mahmud Ghanayim, and Hannah

Candide, a work of the Western canon, which in their view transforms *The Pessoptimist* from a provincial third-world novel to a "universal" literary work or, to paraphrase Pierre Bourdieu and Pascale Casanova, raises its value in the literary market.[81] In the months leading up to the controversial decision to award Habiby the Israel Prize, Israeli critics generally gave the novel a benign reading that was jarringly oblivious to the book's sardonic, intensely critical tone; celebrating its "universalism" and "humanism," the critics denuded it of its particularism and whitewashed its subversive political content. In recent scholarship, Rachel Feldhay Brenner and Hannan Hever cogently critiqued this misreading of Habiby's work by earlier Israeli critics.[82] Yet their own studies tend to focus rather myopically on questions of minority-majority relations and the politics of canonicity in the Israeli system, at times assuming that the text is addressed to the Israeli reader. For example, Brenner writes,

> Habiby's determination to create Arabic-written Palestinian literature in Israel and then deliberately have it translated into the language of the Zionist oppressor leaves no doubt about his cultural and national self-identification as an Israeli Arab. The highly critical *oeuvre* in Hebrew *clearly targets an Israeli Jewish readership.* In this sense, the political signification of Habiby's literary work reflects a demand for the recognition and acceptance—no matter how critical—of the Arab minority on the Israeli Jewish cultural scene.[83]

Amit-Kochavi, who specialize in Arabic literature or in translation between Arabic and Hebrew, and who are attuned to all the cultural, linguistic, and historical features of the work as an Arabic text.

81 Cf. Bourdieu, *Language and Symbolic Power*, and idem, *Field of Cultural Production*; Casanova, *World Republic of Letters*.

82 See Brenner, "Hidden Transcripts," 93. As she explains elsewhere, this is more or less the Israeli literary establishment's approach toward Palestinian fiction in Israel in general (Brenner, *Inextricably Bonded*, 123, 128–131). Hever also writes that *The Pessoptimist* and *Ikhtiyya* were, by and large, well received by Israeli critics, as was Bakri's dramatic adaptation of *The Pessoptimist*. The "reaction of the majority culture emphasized the universal element common to Jews and Arabs in these works. . . . The emphasis on the artistic achievement as universal has obliterated and repressed the fact that what is being shown is a power relationship between an oppressive majority and an oppressed minority" (*Producing the Modern Hebrew Canon*, 213). Yet Hever also sees the novel as expressing a certain "universalist ethic," largely through Habiby's female characters and attention to women's issues (ibid., 222). In Hever's reading, Habiby uses universal humanism as a smoke screen disguising his criticism of the state. Brenner disputes Hever's reading, pointing out that Habiby's criticism of the state's oppressive policies is anything but disguised (*Inextricably Bonded*, 129–130).

83 Brenner, *Inextricably Bonded*, 114, my emphasis. This viewpoint is not supported by any of the criticism from scholars of Arabic literature; for example, Nancy Coffin reads the novel's political subtext as a debate about power and the question of the armed struggle after the 1967 war (largely through the aforementioned *fada'i-fida'i* connection) (Coffin, "Reading Inside and Out"). See also note 35 above.

Hever frames his reading in terms of a discussion of Palestinian works in the Israeli Hebrew literary canon, which he sees as a "national minority literature." He acknowledges their doubleness, noting that "Palestinian works that have been written in Israel conduct a relationship both with Arabic literature and culture and, in translation, with Hebrew literature and culture."[84] Thus in his view, Habiby

> can be read by the Hebrew reader both internally and externally, both as part of the Israeli canon and as external to it. Whether conscious or not, his writing is designed to attack the shifting boundaries of the Israeli canon, which Habibi's writings in translation have been instrumental in opening up. The way Habibi infiltrates the majority culture and literature as a minority author is through his activity in the linguistic/cultural heart of majority culture.[85]

Influenced by Deleuze and Guattari's theory of minor literature, Hever construes Habiby as a minor writer using the major language (Hebrew) to penetrate the national canon. Habiby's visibility in Israeli cultural and political life until his death in 1996,[86] along with the fact that the Hebrew translations of *Ikhtiyya* and *Saraya* were published within just a few years of the Arabic originals, support Hever's reading of Habiby as a minority author in Israel. Moreover, it has been suggested Habiby did have the Israeli reader (in addition to Arab audiences abroad) in mind during the writing of *Saraya*, his last novel.[87] Yet Habiby's status as a major Arab writer is obscured in these discussions of his role in the Hebrew canon, when it should be brought into those discussions.[88] How, for example, does Habiby's double status and movement between the major and the minor complicate Deleuze and Guattari's model of "minor literature," which assumes a single, fixed relationship among author, language, and nation?

84 Hever, *Producing the Modern Hebrew Canon*, 208.

85 Ibid., 227–228.

86 In addition to Habiby's role as a parliamentarian in Israel, as Ami Elad-Bouskila points out, Habiby wrote for the Hebrew press, gave frequent interviews in Hebrew on Israeli radio and television, and appeared in literary evenings and interviews on myriad subjects, not restricted to literature. See Elad-Bouskila, *Modern Palestinian Literature*, 39.

87 Ghanayim, "Dream of Severance," 210; Hever, *Producing the Modern Hebrew Canon*, 225–226.

88 See, for instance, Brenner, "Hidden Transcripts," and idem, "Search for Identity," both of which discuss the works of Atallah Mansour, Anton Shammas, and Emile Habiby. While Brenner focuses on the transmission of Habiby's writing into Israeli culture and its critical reception in Israel (which she discusses with acute insight), she does not engage the question of its linguistic hybridity as a translated oeuvre. She notes that Habiby had an "outstanding reputation in the Arab world before his literary talents were acknowledged in Hebrew" ("Search for Identity," 95), yet she groups Habiby's writing with works by Shammas and Mansour as "published in Hebrew" without considering how its translational status may differentiate it from the work of Palestinians who choose to write in Hebrew (see Brenner, "Hidden Transcripts," 89).

How do Shammas's masterful translations of Habiby's "untranslatable" idioms and expressions push the boundaries of the Hebrew language, or reveal connections between the two languages?[89] Does Shammas's Hebrew translation of Sa'id's mistranslations of Hebrew render the language "foreign" to its own speakers in the way that *'Ajami* foreignized Hebrew for its Jewish viewers (see chapter 1)?[90]

Ultimately, the Hebrew translation of *The Pessoptimist* took on a social and cultural life of its own; as such one might question whether the critics on both sides of the divide are even addressing the "same" text. Critics on either side of the Arabic-Hebrew divide read Habiby's works not only in different languages, but in relation to different literary systems, each with its own internal politics, histories, and codes of interpretation. Arab critics might read Habiby in juxtaposition with other innovative contemporary Arab novelists as part of a new wave of post-1967 Arabic literature, or in relation to other Palestinian writers of Arabic (such as Ghassan Kanafani), while Hebrew critics group Habiby with other Palestinian writers in Israel (usually Shammas and Atallah Mansour). The interpretive code-switching connected with Habiby's works blurs the distinction between original and translation, taking us back to Walter Benjamin's foundational observations about translation not as replication but as a new form of life for a work of art; "kinship," he reasons, "does not necessarily involve likeness."[91] Like other "double" texts, then, *The Pessoptimist* poses something of a predicament for the monolingual reader. Yet even if the vast majority of a text's readers are not bilingual, awareness of its double status can help the reader move beyond monocultural reading practices in which comparison (if undertaken at all) is conducted on one culture's terms and through its interpretive codes, toward an understanding of the text as a hybrid creation negotiating among different languages, cultures, and audiences.

NAQQASH AND DOUBLE MARGINALIZATION

Of the Arab Jewish authors who continued writing in Arabic after immigrating to Israel, Samir Naqqash was the youngest and most prolific, with about a dozen plays, novels, and short story collections to his name.[92]

89 For a fascinating exposition of Shammas's linguistic techniques in translating Habiby's intricate wordplay into Hebrew, see Sasson Somekh, "Anton Shamas"; as Somekh notes, his brief study is not comprehensive or systematic, and a fuller study would incorporate additional questions of style, allusion, and the problem of translations of "culturally specific textemes" (50).

90 On such "foreignizing" effects, see also Mehrez, "Translation and the Postcolonial Experience," 130.

91 See Benjamin, "Task of the Translator," 73–74.

92 In addition to *I, They, and the Split*, Naqqash's other works include the plays, novels, and story collections *al-Khata'* (1972); *Hiyakat kull zaman wa-makan* (1978); *Yawma habilat wa-ajhadat al-dunya*

Naqqash left Baghdad in 1951 at age thirteen, and made no secret of his sense of alienation in Israel.[93] In fact, we find far less Hebrew in Naqqash's works than we do in Habiby's. However, Habiby was a vigorous participant in Israeli political and cultural life, whereas the virtually unknown Naqqash rejected the Israeli linguistic and cultural milieu in order to preserve the integrity of his Iraqi identity. As such, the bilingual energy in Naqqash's writing is channelled toward the colloquial Baghdadi dialects of Arabic (henceforth *'amiyya*) and standard literary Arabic (henceforth *fusha*, pronounced "foos-ha"). In contradistinction to *The Pessoptimist*, here we are dealing with a case of *native* bilingualism, or more precisely, a situation of diglossia.

Until the mid-twentieth century, Iraq was the site of an "unusually profound and sharply delineated dialectical cleavage" corresponding to Muslims, Jews, and Christians.[94] The Jewish dialect is largely (though not entirely) comprehensible to a Muslim or Christian Iraqi; it is marked by a noticeably different phonology and by its myriad loan words and expressions from Hebrew, Aramaic, Persian, and Turkish. For centuries it functioned as the private language of the Jews of Iraq, but with the community's dispersion to Israel and the West in 1950–1951, its last embers are now fading. In the double interest of mimesis and linguistic preservation, Naqqash transcribes the dialect when depicting his Jewish characters' speech; he also takes pains to represent the Muslim and Christian dialects. This literary deployment of the multiple Baghdadi dialects, remarkable in its verisimilitude and attention to detail, is the distinguishing characteristic of Naqqash's oeuvre.[95] To the general reader of Arabic, however, it poses a formidable challenge. In response, Naqqash devised an extensive system of annotation: every appearance of Baghdadi dialect is glossed with a translation into *fusha*, very often with additional commentary, on the bottom of the page. At time, these footnotes climb to perilous heights on the page. (This elaborate text-commentary structure is also vaguely reminiscent of Jewish and Muslim scriptures, with their

---

(1980); *Fi ghiyabih* (1981); *Nuzulu wa-khayt al-shaytan* (1986); *al-Rijs* (1987); *Awrat al-mala'ika* (1991); *Nubu'at rajul majnun fi madina mal'una* (1995); *Shlumu al-kurdi wa-ana wa-l-zaman* (2004); and *Fuwa ya dam!* (1987/2011).

93 Alcalay, *Keys to the Garden*, 107–108.

94 Blanc, *Communal Dialects in Baghdad*, 3.

95 Within the Arabic literary tradition, the representation of dialogue has long been a contentious topic. Arabic prose narrative is nearly always written in *fusha*, which is standard throughout the Arab world, but the myriad Arabic vernacular dialects differ from region to region, which challenges the Arab writer who aims for both authenticity and legibility. Attempted solutions have ranged from writing the dialogue in literary Arabic to utilizing the vernaculars to adopting a combination of literary and spoken Arabic. On the general problem of translating nonstandard vernacular language and texts that employ code-switching, see Bell, "In the Shadow of the Father Tongue."

marginal commentaries.) The glosses, while of uneven helpfulness,[96] offer another example of authorial intervention in the narrative, bringing to mind Habiby's open challenge to Shammas in *Saraya*. Collectively, the footnotes become a kind of third space in the text that mediates between the world of the narrative and world of the reader; to invoke Genette's term, they are a paratext.[97] In addition to his radical system of annotation, Naqqash frequently thematizes interlinguistic tensions. Translation thus has dual functions in Naqqash's writing, serving a thematic purpose at the textual level (inside the narrative), and a pragmatic purpose at the paratextual level (in the footnotes). The footnotes frame the text as a "posthistory": as the depiction of a lost world, whose literary reconstitution necessitates extreme extradiegetic measures. One could say that Naqqash, a self-defined Arab Jew, takes his symbolic revenge on the forces of history by putting the marginalized Jewish dialect in the narrative and its standard Arabic translation in the margin. Alternatively, he might have utilized in-text translation strategies, perhaps compromising on a written language of dialogue that would retain the flavor of local *'amiyya* expressions while remaining accessible to the general Arabic reader. But Naqqash made no such concessions, refusing to translate himself into a more marketable idiom and demanding instead that his reader use his notes in the margin to translate—a remarkable instantiation of Mehrez's claim that the reading of a hybrid text is itself an act of translation.

His autobiographical novella *Ana wa-ha'ula' wa-l-fisam* (*I, They, and the Split*)[98] follows the narrator, a young Jewish boy in Baghdad, through the

96 Nancy Berg opines that "[t]he gloss does not necessarily make [Naqqash's] text accessible to the Iraqi, much less the non-Iraqi. Naqqash's fellow Iraqi-born writers have expressed their own difficulties in reading his work. . . . Yitzhak Bar-Moshe [another Iraqi-Jewish writer of Arabic] declares his colleague's work to be 'unreadable' and 'not enjoyable,' due to the effort it demands" (*Exile from Exile*, 55). Of his choice to deploy dialogue in the narrative and long translations in the margin, Naqqash explains, "Spoken dialogue is much more trustworthy and exact than dialogue written in literary language. And this is one of the difficulties that makes some of my work virtually unreadable. So that I find myself forced to add translations below the dialogues. I myself don't even know how I got to this point of being able to use the language of each character, regardless of their social standing. . . . [O]ur house [in Baghdad] was a kind of meeting place for many different kinds of women and men . . . so I had the opportunity to hear and absorb all of these different dialects and styles" (Alcalay, *Keys to the Garden*, 107).

97 Genette describes the paratext as a "threshold," an "'undefined zone' between the inside and the outside. . . . Indeed, this fringe, always the conveyor of a commentary that is authorial or more or less legitimated by the author, constitutes a zone between text and off-text, a zone not only of transition but also of *transaction*: a privileged place of pragmatics and a strategy" (*Paratexts*, 2, emphasis in original).

98 The term *fisam* literally means "split" or "fissure," but the same root in a different morphological pattern (*infisam*) denotes schizophrenia. Naqqash's usage conveys something of both meanings: he is discussing both the split between Muslims and Jews in Iraq that develops during

gradual deterioration of Jewish life in Iraq during the late 1940s and his unwilling emigration from Baghdad to Israel in 1951.[99] Language in this novella is profoundly linked to communal identity, first that of the Jews in Iraq and then that of the Iraqi immigrants in Israel. The first half of the story, set in Baghdad, pivots around a cast of secondary characters at whose center lurks the idiosyncratic Gurji Chilwiyyi, the narrator's feared and hated religion tutor. The teacher's repeated command of "Iqa'!"[100] (Read!) is a menacing trope in this part of text (and of the narrator's life). In the midst of describing one of the dreaded religion lessons, the narrator digresses, "I read; about the Promised Land I read. But I am in Iraq and it is here that I live and breathe and learn and dream, and plan for the future. And during the holidays, there is the shaking of hands, and the murmuring of lips: 'Tizku le-shanim rabuth. Inshallah sana alakh a-bi-rushalim' (footnote 26)."[101] Turning to footnote 26, we read, "A traditional greeting exchanged by Iraqi Jews since time immemorial, which means: may you live long and may we celebrate next year in Jerusalem." We then return to the narrative, which continues, "Even our partner Husayn al-'Alaywi, who has been speaking of the impending liberation of Palestine, heard this holiday greeting from my uncle's naïve wife and scowled, checking his rage in a circumspect silence."[102]

This passage exemplifies the story's stratified linguistic texture as well as its thematization of language and identity; I have translated the *fusha* into English and left the *'amiyya* in the original in order to replicate the reader's experience. The Jewish Baghdadi Arabic dialogue also contains a Hebrew holiday greeting shared by many Jewish cultures (*tizku le-shanim rabot*, the last word pronounced by Iraqi Jews as *rabuth*). In Jewish society, anyone, no matter how secular, would recognize the phrase "Next year in Jerusalem." Hearing this sentence in Arabic, the Muslim business partner understands its literal meaning but fails to translate it correctly: he

---

the time period of the story, and the sense of rupture in the narrator's identity, as expressed in the following passage: "And I, eleven years old, hear the [anti-Jewish] cries and taste bitterness. The struggle taking place inside me, between the two men of different opinions, intensifies. The crack of the *fisam* widens and its lines are bloody, [but they] melt away overnight" (*Ana wa-ha'ula'*, 167). Later, after the narrator's family has registered to leave, we read, "And we are fragments (*shatat*) being pulled by the two sides of the *fisam*: belonging and not belonging (*intima' wa-la intima'*)" (ibid., 182).

99 For a summary of the historical developments that form the backdrop of the novella, including the *farhud* and events precipitating the mass Jewish emigration from Iraq, see Tripp, *History of Iraq*, 105–106, 124–146, and Bashkin, *New Babylonians*, esp. 112–125, 187–202.

100 The imperative "Read!" would be "Iqra'!" in standard Arabic, but in the Iraqi Jewish dialect the *ray* is pronounced as *ghayn* and in this word it merges with the *qaf*.

101 Naqqash, *Ana wa-ha'ula'*, 131–132.

102 Ibid.

interprets it not as an innocuous holiday greeting or figure of speech, but as a Zionist slogan. Here, a mistranslation serves to dramatize the rise in intercommunal tensions that eventually leads to the narrator's ejection from his native city. There is a double irony in that the expression's banality is lost not only on the Muslim character, but presumably on the reader; hence the explanation in the margins. Naqqash's footnote may also serve as an implicit criticism of the Zionist project, which did, in fact, perform the ultimate overliteralization of this traditional figure of speech. Translation in the margins thus works in tandem with the narrative to represent the Baghdadi Jewish dialect, and through it, Iraqi Jewish life.

As the narrative continues, things grow steadily worse. As but one anti-Jewish measure adopted by the Iraqi government, teaching Hebrew is outlawed, and so Gurji Chilwiyyi is arrested. The situation becomes increasingly intolerable until the narrator's family finally reaches the devastating conclusion that "there is really no future for Jews here [in Iraq]."[103] Reluctantly, they register for the *tasqit* (the denaturalization of Jews registering for emigration),[104] poignantly depicted by Naqqash in a passage remarkable for its portrayal of the contradictory reactions by both Jews and Muslims:

> We take our nationality to the Meir Tweig synagogue and sign our names. There the bureau for denaturalization crouches in wait. The high-ranking officer sits on a table, carrying out orders. The people lose their identities—they dispense of them voluntarily. No . . . rather, they leave them to be torn up against their will. And once again the puzzle is solved and made insoluble. Only a bit of time has elapsed and we have already become people without nationality or identity. The officer who has just stripped us of our *intima'* and torn us up by the roots gazes at us somberly, asking "Haven't you heard the news?"
>
> "No, why, did something happen?"
>
> With a grim face, as brother complaining to brother: "What? You haven't heard yet? Queen Alia died."

103 In Arabic, *Ma di-yitla' darb. Rah nisaqqat wi-nimshi. Fi'alan ma khallu li-l-yahudi ba'd 'aysha hina* (There's no way around it [literally, no path will appear]. We'll sign up and go. They really haven't left any life for a Jew here). This utterance is in the Muslim dialect, as a member of the narrator's family converses with a Muslim family friend; Naqqash, *Ana wa-ha'ula'*, 168.

104 The *tasqit* refers to the forfeiture of citizenship under the Denaturalization Law, passed by the Iraqi parliament on March 2, 1950, which gave Iraqi Jews one year to register to leave the country legally provided they forfeit their Iraqi citizenship. The day after its expiration, the Iraqi parliament in secret session passed another law decreeing that all the possessions, holdings, and assets of Jews who had signed up were to be "frozen," i.e., nationalized. This relatively wealthy community of 130,000 to 140,000 was rendered destitute overnight.

> Stripped of identity . . . yet the faces grieve. And the *intima'* sticks its neck out from deep within the guts and weeps over the contradiction's human remains.[105]

Intima', a word without an exact English equivalent, connotes the feeling of affiliation with and belonging to a collectivity. Naqqash invokes the term twice in a passage depicting the officer's incongruous appeal to the Jewish family as members of the "imagined community"[106] during the *very moment* of their denaturalization. Even as the officer strips the Jews of their citizenship, he addresses them "as brother . . . to brother"; conversely, even in their disenfranchised condition the now-stateless Jews still feel part of the nation. Yet the narrator also recognizes the paradox of their deeply ingrained *intima'* (as Iraqis) in a nation that has rejected them (as Jews). At the end of the passage, it is not the denaturalized Jewish citizens who are weeping for their departed queen, but the *intima'* itself that weeps over its abandoned subjects, the Iraqi Jews. Their identities fragmented by this paradox, the people are reduced to *ashla'* (disjointed parts of corpses) in the construct *ashla' al-munaqada* (the human remains of the contradiction). Once again, meaning emerges in the gap between the message sent and the message received; in this case, not through a misunderstanding on the part of the listener, but on the part of the *speaker*. The officer's message to the Jewish family is based on the mistaken premise that they are still Iraqi citizens, naturally expected to identify with national symbols such as the monarchy. In this light, his statement becomes empty.

FALSE EQUIVALENCES

It is in this spirit of becoming empty that the narrator watches as one by one, the entire cast of secondary characters who peopled the earlier part of the story (and his childhood) leaves for Israel: "Baghdad is being emptied of her Jews. The synagogues are emptied of their worshippers; the schools, of their pupils, and the hospital of its visitors and patients. And the clubs and playgrounds and prophets' tombs, all are empty and deserted. The city is sad and gloomy in her stillness, and her silence speaks the most eloquent of languages."[107] The story follows the narrator and his family through their own final moments in Baghdad, resuming with their arrival in Israel. From this point on, it is infused with the narrator's bitter

105 Naqqash, *Ana wa-ha'ula'*, 168.
106 Cf. Anderson, *Imagined Communities.*
107 Naqqash, *Ana wa-ha'ula'*, 170.

disappointment as he encounters former neighbors and acquaintances from Baghdad and tells of each one's dramatic fall. This process of disillusionment culminates in the rediscovery of Gurji Chilwiyyi, the erstwhile religion instructor, as a bum on the streets of Jerusalem, with which the story ends. In one passage narrated entirely in Jewish Baghdadi dialect, "Albert" (French pronunciation), a formerly prosperous merchant in Baghdad, explains how he became a beggar in Tel Aviv:

> "I can't stand being hungry and not having something to eat. One day I was walking around in Tel Aviv. I went into a restaurant and said, bring me a fish. He said, head or tail? So I said, what's this head or tail business? Just bring the whole fish! He brought me a fish just about as long as my hand, and I finished it off in one bite. *Yaba*, how much? He said 'sixteen *lira*.' A fish the size of my hand, sixteen *lira*—sixteen *dinars*! Two or three months go by like this, and my money runs out. I want meat, there's no meat . . . no chicken . . . no eggs. And I'm hungry, and I want to eat! Some Ashkenazi near us [in the transit camp] was raising a couple o' chickens . . . I don't know where the *mamzer* got them from. I open the door of my hut and I gather a little barley and call out to the chickens. This one walks inside and I shut the door and grab her. The knife is ready. No sooner is she in my hand than I dispatch her. Then I say to my wife Hanina, 'Hanina my girl, don't be sad—today fate has brought us something good to eat.'"
>
> "So . . . ? How did you become a beggar?"
>
> "One day I was walking down the road. It was in the winter and was raining—you haven't yet seen the rain here. It rains like crazy. I ducked into an alley to wait for it to stop. I just happened to put out my hand to see whether or not it had stopped raining, and a coin falls in my palm! So I left my hand right where it was until it filled up with coins. Then I came home and said, 'Hanina, I found myself some nice work. Better than sitting around doing nothing.'"[108]

Thus far I have analyzed passages written primarily in *fusha*, with brief interpolations in *'amiyya*. In this last passage, however, the entire narration is written in the Jewish Baghdadi dialect. An incredibly literal rendition of the dialect's idioms and cadences, Albert's speech is transcribed so phonetically that it makes little sense until read aloud and, at many points, until compared with the *fusha* translation. Without pathos, and with only a modicum of irony, Albert explains his new "profession" as the product of a *misunderstanding*. The entire monologue hinges on the cultural and social disorientation of the newly arrived Iraqi Jews, which Albert shares with his listeners.

108 Ibid., 185–186.

For example, Albert, who has been in Israel longer than the narrator's family, translates the Israeli *lira* (pound) into the Arabic *dinar* (the currency used in Iraq) for his listeners, emphasizing the inordinate expense of food in the new country. Thus, while the exchange rate in Albert's explanation ("sixteen lira—sixteen dinars") is a one-to-one, exact equivalence, it is also a false equivalence, in the sense that the buying power of the *dinar* in Iraq is so much greater than that of the *lira* in Israel. The logic of this "false equivalent" in Albert's translation of monetary values recalls the logic of the false cognate: even (or especially) when things seem to be familiar—to *make sense*—they are essentially different, thus they trick and confound.[109]

How does Naqqash attempt to convey the cultural nuances of Albert's colloquial language in the *fusha* translation in the margins? In reference to the Ashkenazi neighbor, the *'amiyya* version reads, "Aku fed wehid ashkenazi jighanu amghabi kam jiji. Maghaf minayn jibu il-mamzer" (There's an Ashkenazi nearby who was raising some chickens. I don't know where the *mamzer* got them from). Here, two Hebrew terms are embedded within the colloquial Arabic: *ashkenazi* and *mamzer* (bastard). In the Jewish Baghdadi dialect, *mamzer* is a traditional term of disparagement, linked to its original, religious-legal meaning; in Israeli Hebrew usage it connotes something closer to "scoundrel," often uttered with an undertone of admiration for the subject's wiliness. The non-Jewish Arab reader would be unfamiliar with the term. When we look at the *fusha* translation of those two sentences, we find, *Yujid bi-jiwar sarifatina al-khamiyya, rajul shiknazi yurabbi 'adadan min ad-dajaj. La adri al-laqit min ayna ati bi-him*—a fairly exact translation into a higher register, except that the *fusha* translation adds *sarifatina al-khamiyya* (our makeshift hut),[110] which the original leaves implicit. But in the translation, *ashkenazi* is rendered *shiknazi*, which has a slightly derogatory connotation; had he been aiming for more neutral language, Naqqash could have written *rajul yahudi urubi* (European Jewish man) or something similar. Finally, *mamzer* is translated as *laqit*, the classical Arabic epithet for "foundling." The register of this word is oddly formal and elevated in comparison with *mamzer*; although *laqit* was sometimes used in the sense of "bastard" in classical literature, it is not a term of

109 When Albert refers to his "money" running out, the *'amiyya* version uses *flus* (money), while the translation refers to *darahim* (the plural of *dirham*, in many countries a smaller denomination than the *dinar*); later on, referring to the coins that drop into his hand, both versions use *qirsh*, a linguistic relic of the Ottoman era (source of the Hebrew *grush*). These terms locate the passage within a distinctly Arab material frame of reference (but interestingly, not one associated directly with Iraq; the Iraqi equivalent would have been *fils*).

110 *Khamiyya* is an unusual adjective, perhaps invented by Naqqash; it appears to be derived from *kham*, meaning "unworked, unprocessed" or "linen, calico." See Wehr, *Dictionary of Modern Arabic*, 224.

disparagement in contemporary parlance. In short, Naqqash's choices are inconsistent: *shiknazi* lowers the register, while *laqit* raises it considerably and fails to convey the nuances of the term *mamzer* in either Jewish Baghdadi dialect or in Hebrew. What we *can* say is that these various adaptations underscore the narration's astounding degree of verisimilitude as well as the efforts that Naqqash expends in accommodating the reader through linguistic and cultural translation. This is truly a "double text" not only in that it straddles two worlds, but also in that it is literally both written and read in two different languages: the dying colloquial dialect of a forgotten Diasporic community, and the written language shared by millions of Arabic readers worldwide.

TRANSLATION, MISUNDERSTANDING, AND THE DESIRE FOR HISTORY

We have seen how *The Pessoptimist* and *I, They, and the Split* serve as historical counternarratives, reflecting the "post-colonial desire for 'history.'"[111] The writings of Habiby and Naqqash challenge official Zionist historiography. They contest hegemonic narratives that hold Palestinians accountable for their own displacement and suffering, and that deny or downplay the historicity and normalcy of Jewish life in Arab countries, as well as the multiple levels of loss experienced by Arab Jews in Israel. In both texts, the key to this recovery process is the author's creative use of language and of languages. For Habiby, language is a means of breaking through the repression of authority, be it cultural or political in nature. Finding new ways of using Arabic is crucial for the author's ability to effectively represent a new political order. For Naqqash, inscribing the language of Iraqi Jews in the edifice of Arabic fiction becomes a means of contesting the erasure of Arab Jews from historical memory. Furthermore, both Habiby and Naqqash depict the strategies of life in exile as a kind of auto-translation or code-switching in a hostile world, recalling Niranjana's equation of "hybridity" with "living in translation."[112]

Yet these two texts also demonstrate meaningful differences in their authors' relationships to language, which stem from their respective relationships with the past and with the decisive moment of rupture. *The Pessoptimist* takes place ex post facto, with 1948 as the turning point; the "before" is understood as a period of harmony between Sa'id and his human and linguistic environment, shattered by the cruel lunacy of the "after" period the narrative depicts. By contrast, Naqqash's story takes

111 See Niranjana, *Siting Translation*, 39–42.
112 Ibid., 40.

place both in Baghdad and in Israel, and traces the deteriorating status of the Jews in Iraq prior to emigration. Naqqash therefore portrays linguistic tensions in both the "before" and "after" periods: in Iraq, learning Hebrew is forbidden, and the Jewish dialect of Arabic is misunderstood or derided by the Muslim majority, whereas in Israel, Arabic becomes a scorned and repudiated tongue.

As a result, translation within these texts takes different forms. In Naqqash's story, extreme heteroglossia and the thick texture of cultural references necessitate extensive annotation. Openly acknowledging the opacity of his language, Naqqash flaunts literary convention to valorize the historically pluralistic character of Baghdad. His obsession with recording the linguistic minutia of this vanished world verges on fetishization. In the face of Israeli discourse, his writing is not post-Zionist but rather nostalgically "pre-Zionist,"[113] intent on resuscitating the Iraqi-Jewish ambiance in its fullness—and on not admitting the present into this re-created world, but for the margins. Habiby's novel elicits a pronounced interaction between Arabic and Hebrew, emphasizing not linguistic equivalence, but mistranslation. Through the "in-between" spaces of the narrative, *The Pessoptimist* rewrites Israel's language of authority from a Palestinian insider's perspective. At the same time, even as he reveals the myriad ways in which the Israeli military and security services brutalize, dispossess, and exploit the remaining Palestinian population, Habiby's thematic uses of translation and wordplay between Arabic and Hebrew all conclusively demonstrate one point: the two peoples, like their histories, cultures, and languages, are irrevocably intertwined. This is not necessarily a hopeful (or even an original) observation, but it is an incontrovertible reality.

These works utilize translation as a critical element of the narrative, generating both plot and meaning. They suggest a theory of translation in which it is not equivalence, but the lack thereof, that yields a statement's truth value. In them, language is a metaphor for itself,[114] an inside joke between author and reader, delivered at the character's expense. In particular, Habiby's use of misunderstanding is also a project of destabilizing linguistic referentiality. Meaning in his narrative is conveyed *not* through the successful delivery of the message from speaker

113 I use the term "post-Zionism" in the sense of an epistemological discourse rather than a chronological ordering.

114 The hyperlanguage of these texts is infused with a meta-awareness of itself as language, one that is largely ironic, which I see as a metaphorical distance. A self-conscious idiom that "knows" its shortcomings, that recognizes its own function in the signification process, is a *metaphor* for language that performs its referential function transparently.

to addressee, but through its failure.[115] In the thematic representation of communicative breakdown, we see language recognizing its own inevitable fiction, acknowledging how tenuous is the link between signifier and signified, how easily it is obstructed. This kind of disruption in the signifying function can intervene not only in authoritative discourses (as exemplified by the targeted rewriting of hegemonic historical narratives), but also in any monolithic understanding of language. In these and doubtless many other bilingual texts, translation works *inside* the narrative to negotiate between different languages and cultures, between author and reader, and even between the conflicting layers of affiliation and identity that the author brings to the text.

115 Jakobson, "Closing Statement," 13.

CHAPTER 4

Palestinian Midrash

Toward a Postnational Poetics of Hebrew Verse

When I speak to you in your language, what happens to mine? Does my language continue to speak, but in silence? Because it's never eliminated from these moments. When I speak to you, I feel the flow of my mother tongue divide into two streams: one is gutturally silent, the other, running on empty, unmakes itself with an implosion into the order of bilingualism. . . . It's then that I lose my words, forgetting which one belongs to which language.

—ABDELKEBIR KHATIBI[1]

In 1986, a Hebrew-language novel called *'Arabeskot* (*Arabesques*) took the Israeli literary scene by storm. For the Hebrew cultural establishment, the appearance of this sophisticated narrative work by a Palestinian Arab author was a seismic event whose aftershocks still register a quarter century later. It was not the first time a Palestinian Arab had published in Hebrew;[2] in fact the author, Anton Shammas, was already known in Israel as a journalist and poet before the novel established him as a writer of international renown. *Arabesques* became a watershed in the history of Hebrew literature due to its elegant style, its virtuosic use of Hebrew, its sustained thematic engagement with Palestinian and Israeli identities and cultures, and not least of all its status as a critic's text that lends itself to a seemingly endless array of interpretations.[3] What underscores the myriad readings of the novel is an abiding preoccupation with "*the* issue": the question of Hebrew in an Arab hand, with all its attendant

1 Khatibi, *Love in Two Languages*, 41.

2 That distinction belongs to Atallah Mansour, author of *Be-or ḥadash* (In a new light, 1966).

3 See, for instance, Hever, "Hebrew in an Israeli Arab Hand" (reprinted in *Producing the Modern Hebrew Canon*); Snir, "Hebrew as the Language of Grace"; Brenner, "Hidden Transcripts," and idem, *Intextricably Bonded*; Feldman, "Postcolonial Memory, Postmodern Intertextuality"; Hochberg, "Dispossession of Hebrew," and idem, *In Spite of Partition*; and Gluzman, "Politics of Intertextuality." As for Arabic criticism, see al-'Id, *Tikniyyat al-sard al-riwa'i*; idem, "Arabesques"; and Siddiq, "al-Kitaba bi-l-'ibriyya al-fusha."

political and cultural ramifications. Faced with an undeniably accomplished and powerful work, Hebrew readers and critics were confronted with the same dilemma of self-definition that has long plagued metropolitan literatures in a (post)colonial age: is a literature defined by its contemporary community of readers and writers or by its dominant cultural tradition? For Modern Hebrew literature, this dilemma is compounded by Hebrew's profound connection with Judaism and Jewish identity. Hebrew, it seemed, could no longer be considered simply a "Jewish language," nor Hebrew literature a "Jewish literature"—a revelation discomfiting for its opening to the unknown, yet exciting for its potential. The novel stoked the fires of a heated public polemic: is Modern Hebrew a Jewish language, or the national language of *all* its speakers, regardless of their religion or ethnicity? When Amos Oz, Israel's best known novelist, was asked if he considered *Arabesques* to be a "turning point in Israeli society," he replied, "I think of this as a triumph, not necessarily for Israeli society, but for the Hebrew language. If the Hebrew language is becoming attractive enough for a non-Jewish Israeli to write in, then we have arrived."[4] Just the previous year, another leading Israeli novelist, A. B. Yehoshua, had notoriously advised Shammas to pick up and "move a hundred meters to the east" (i.e., to East Jerusalem) in order to realize his Palestinian identity, sparking a bitter debate with Shammas over the State of Israel's identity as Jewish or democratic.[5] From such remarks, one need not exercise too much imagination to fathom the persistence of scholarly infatuation with the Gordian knot of Palestinian Hebrew writing.

Yet the plethora of scholarship and criticism on the topic overlooks an integral part of this literary phenomenon: the three volumes of poetry, two in Hebrew and one in Arabic, published by Shammas a decade before his novel.[6] Nor is more than passing mention given to other Palestinian poets in Israel, most of whom have also published bilingually in Hebrew

4 Twersky, "An Interview with Amos Oz," 26, cited in Hever, "Hebrew in an Israeli Arab Hand," 264–265. As Hever notes, "Oz is presenting the Hebrew language in two lights: as the language of the ruling majority and as the language of a minority compelled to fight for cultural and political recognition" (ibid., 265); reprinted in Hever, *Producing the Modern Hebrew Canon*, 1. See also Levy, "Borderline Writers," 74.

5 Yehoshua's "advice" to Shammas has appeared in multiple sources, including Yehoshua, *Ha-kir ve-ha-har*, 188, and (in English) Horn, *Facing the Fires*, 48. Shammas's response originally appeared in his weekly column in *Kol ha-'ir*, September 13, 1985. See Levy, "Self-Portraits of the Other," 356. In 2005, Yeshoshua engaged in a similar exchange with Sayed Kashua; see Halpern, "Overstepping Boundaries."

6 To the best of my knowledge, the only criticism of Palestinian Israeli writers of Hebrew that addresses poetry (in this case, the poetry of Shammas and 'Araidi) and also refers to their Arabic creative production is Snir, "Hebrew as the Language of Grace."

and Arabic.[7] The present chapter addresses this lacuna through a close reading of poetry by Shammas and his contemporaries Salman Masalha and Na'im 'Araidi.[8] Their poetry, I argue, offers us a different window onto the question of Hebrew writing in a Palestinian hand. I read their Hebrew verse as a poetics formed *between* languages, cultures, and national traditions, replacing the hermeneutics of antithesis (Palestinian or Israeli? Israeli or Jewish?) with one of "in-betweenness."[9] Furthermore, I move away from debating the identitarian definition of Hebrew to explore the nuanced relationship of Palestinian writers with Hebrew's cultural heritage and with the traditional Jewish modes of reading and interpretation embedded therein. Through an analysis of allusion and metalinguistic discourse in Palestinian Hebrew poetry, I will illustrate the intertextual practice I call "Palestinian midrash."[10]

PALESTINIAN OR ISRAELI? ISRAELI OR JEWISH?

Where chapter 2 dealt with the genealogy of Modern Hebrew literature and its ethnic encoding as Ashkenazi, and chapter 3 with Arabic's resignification as a minority language in the new State of Israel, here I examine Hebrew as an ethnoreligious minority language turned national majority language, uneasily confronting its identity and privilege vis-à-vis its *own* minorities.[11] Is Palestinian writing in Israel a minority discourse within Israeli literature or an offshoot of Palestinian literature, or something of both? To what degree does this categorization of Palestinian Israeli writing

7 When Shammas is discussed alongside other writers, those are nearly always Emile Habiby and Atallah Mansour (with the aforementioned exception of Snir, "Hebrew as the Language of Grace").

8 Due to considerations of length, this chapter does not discuss the works of two other contemporary Palestinian poets in Israel: Siham Daoud, who writes in Hebrew and Arabic, and Nidaa Khoury, who writes in Arabic but has been published in bilingual editions and in Hebrew and English translation. For more on Daoud and her poetry, see Levy, Salaymeh, and Valencia, "Poetic Structures on Contested Space." See also Elad-Bouskila, *Modern Palestinian Literature*. Concerning the transliteration of 'Araidi's name, standard transliteration rules would render it 'Araydi; 'Araidi himself and most of the criticism spell it alternately Araide or 'Araidi, so I have compromised on the latter.

9 My understanding of "in-betweenness" builds upon different articulations of this hermeneutic in critical work on bilingualism, translation theory, and cultural studies in postcolonial contexts; for example, see Niranjana, *Siting Translation*; Arteaga, *An Other Tongue*; Dingwaney and Maier, *Between Languages and Cultures*; and Simon and St. Pierre, *Changing the Terms*.

10 For an explanation of "midrash," see note 46 below.

11 Hannan Hever has thoroughly explored the question of majority-minority relations in Hebrew literature, elucidating what he sees as the confusion of a majority language/literature adopting the rhetoric and psychology of a minority. See "Hebrew in an Israeli Arab Hand," and idem, *Producing the Modern Hebrew Canon*; see also note 4 above.

depend on language choice? In ʿAraidi's own view, even *Arabic* literature written in Israel "cannot be considered 'Palestinian' because it was not created in a Palestinian state and was not influenced by the tradition of Palestinian literature in the pre-1948 era, when Palestine did exist." ʿAraidi adds that many of the Arabic-language writers in Israel were educated in the Israeli system and that their formative reading experiences were largely in Hebrew, giving Arabic literature in Israel an "Israeli" character.[12] His claim concerning the lack of continuity between pre-1948 and post-1948 Arabic literature in Israel/Palestine deserves further scrutiny, but his broader point—that Palestinian writers in Israel are inevitably influenced by the hegemonic language and culture—is highly relevant. All three of the writers discussed in this chapter were born within five years of statehood (ʿAraidi in 1948, Shammas in 1950, and Masalha in 1953). From 1948 to 1967, Palestinians in Israel were isolated from the larger Arab world and its cultural output; this barrier, compounded by immersion in the Israeli educational system, would have oriented young writers of that generation toward Hebrew literature. And in fact, one of Shammas's major influences was the Jewish Israeli poet Amir Gilboa,[13] while Naʿim ʿAraidi wrote his doctoral dissertation on the ultra-nationalist poet Uri Tsvi Greenberg, to whom he dedicated a poem.[14] At the same time, all three writers are also writers and scholars of Arabic literature (in contradistinction to their younger colleague Sayed Kashua, who lacks the requisite mastery of literary Arabic, and publishes exclusively in Hebrew).[15] While there is no doubt that the bilingual Palestinian author who chooses to write in Hebrew must have an Israeli Jewish reader in mind, this does not render his or her writing exclusively "Israeli."[16] ʿAraidi's argument overlooks the significance of

12 Ramras-Rauch, *Arab in Israeli Literature*, 194.

13 Shammas dedicates a poem to Gilboa in his first Hebrew collection. See "Korida," in *Krikha kasha*, 13.

14 See ʿAraidi's poem "Uri Tsvi Greenberg," a pastiche of biblical intertexts and allusions (e.g., *talit she-kula tekhelet*; *hu haya baḥur va-tov / adom ha-seʿar*; and *eyn ḥadash taḥat ha-shemesh*), in *Ulay zo ahava*, 24. Shammas also alludes to Greenberg in a poem discussed below.

15 This chapter does not address the work of Kashua, an important Palestinian Israeli journalist, television writer, and novelist, because he publishes only prose and exclusively in Hebrew; educated in a Jewish high school in Jerusalem, he lacks sufficient command of literary Arabic to publish in it. See also note 40 of the introduction.

16 Of course, their readership potentially includes other Palestinians in Israel, but given that this group (many of whom prefer to read in Arabic) comprises a small minority of readers within an already limited target audience, it is safe to assume that Shammas, ʿAraidi, Masalha, and other Palestinian Israeli authors write in Hebrew for a Jewish readership. This is corroborated both internally, through the use of canonically Jewish allusions (and the relative paucity of Palestinian, Arabic, Muslim, and Christian cultural sources and references) in their Hebrew writing, and externally, through footnotes explaining culturally foreign references to the reader, e.g.,

bilingualism and biculturalism; Palestinians writing in Israel can be compared to writers in the Palestinian Diaspora who also live and work under the hegemony of another language and culture, such as the Palestinian-American poet Naomi Shihab Nye.

'Araidi's position also begs the question of what factors, aside from language, contribute to the characterization of a literature along national lines. The prevalence of particular themes and the recurrence of symbols and topoi in a body of writing will lead an interpretive community to expect them. For decades, Palestinian Arabic poetry has reified "Palestine" both as a geographical homeland and as the collective Palestinian memory. The references to stock objects and symbols (oranges, roses, rifles, olive trees or branches, migrating birds) served a unifying function, creating a shared metaphorical language of "homeland" signifiers that could substitute for the signified in face of dispersion and exile. Masalha, 'Araidi, and Shammas straddle a fence overlooking both this tradition and the Israeli poetic tradition, whose roots are entwined with Jewish nationalism in its various manifestations, including Revisionist Zionism (as exemplified by Uri Tsvi Greenberg). Modern Hebrew in the early to mid-twentieth century often positioned the lyrical self within the collective national memory and identity, creating a language of reference that assumed a common experience of poet and reader. For nationalist poets such as Greenberg, *place* represented redemption from exile, the link between the biblical Land of Israel and the modern-day State of Israel.[17] Hence we have two different poetic traditions laying claim to the same land. And yet both these histories—if not the land itself—are strikingly

---

'Araidi's poem "Farid al-Atrash," whose footnote identifies the subject as "One of the great Arab composers and singers" when Farid al-Atrash is universally known among the Arab public; see 'Araidi, *Ḥazarti el ha-kfar*, 15. Similarly, 'Araidi glosses a reference to the medieval philosopher and poet al-Ma'ari; see "Bo'i nedaber al-zeyt ha-arets" ("Let's Talk about the Olive of the Land"), in *Kol ha-'onot*, 135.

17 For instance, Greenberg published these verses in 1954:

> Outside—Jerusalem . . . and the moaning of God's trees
> Cut down there by enemies in all generations . . .
> Heavy-rivered clouds: within them lightnings
> And thunderings, that to me on a night of rain are tidings
> From the mouth of the Almighty till the end of generations.

See Greenberg, "Be-leyl geshem bi-rushalayim" ("On a Night of Rain in Jerusalem"), trans. Arieh Sachs, in Burnshaw et al., *Modern Hebrew Poem Itself*, 62–63. But Greenberg represents only one strain within Modern Hebrew poetry; other Hebrew poets of Greenberg's generation (and earlier) wrote poems of place in far less inflated, symbolic, or nationalist terms (e.g., Leah Goldberg's "Tel Aviv 1935," also anthologized in *Modern Hebrew Poem Itself*, 130).

absent from the poetry of 'Araidi, Masalha, and Shammas, whose poetic geographies are intimate, personal, and often abstract.

Rejection of Israel's allegories of land and language does not lead these writers to embrace a Palestinian mode of territorialization in their poetry. They remain islands unto themselves; in another of Shammas's poems, the speaker refers to himself as a "self-resident" (*toshav 'atsmi*).[18] All three also write poems to or about Jerusalem, the most symbolic of places for Palestinians and Israelis, but here too, it is a personal rather than a collectively symbolic Jerusalem. Shammas and Masalha lived in Jerusalem while writing and publishing their poetry, and this lived experience is reflected in their verse. In his first collection, Shammas pens a series of love poems called "Five Gates of Jerusalem" that intertwine traits of the city, canonical Jewish allusions, and erotic imagery so freely that we cannot tell if we are reading a metaphor of the city as woman or of the woman as city.[19] Similarly, Masalha composes sensual poems about Jerusalem expressing the minutia of color, sound, and sensation while walking or driving in the city, observing his surroundings and remembering private moments,[20] while 'Araidi writes numerous odes to Jerusalem; one of them describes "my Jerusalem" as a "sad melody," a "poem" and a "note."[21] These intensely "private Jerusalems" evoke the personal Jerusalem of Israel's poet laureate, Yehuda Amichai.[22]

But whereas the poetry of Shammas, 'Araidi, and Masalha eschews nationalist symbols, it openly embraces Hebrew's cultural echo chamber. As Hebrew poets, the three Palestinian Israeli writers must contend not only with contemporary Hebrew as the language of political and cultural hegemony in Israel but with Hebrew's protracted history as the language of Jewish thought, culture, and religious praxis. Gil Hochberg's analysis of *Arabesques* dwells on the troubled metaphor of possession, suggesting that "the fact that [Hebrew] has always been used by Jews does not make it an exclusively 'Jewish language'"; indeed, following Derrida, she asserts

18 Shammas, *Shetaḥ hefker*, 6.

19 See Shammas, *Krikha kasha*, 9–13. *Sha'ar*, "gate" in Hebrew, is a homograph of the Arabic word for poem, *sh'ir*, creating an interlingual pun. Bilingually, then, the title can be read as either "Five Gates of Jerusalem" or "Five Poems to Jerusalem."

20 Masalha, *Eḥad mi-kan*, 7, 53.

21 See "Hi hayta bi-rushalayim" ("She was in Jerusalem"), *Ulay zo ahava*, 32–33. 'Araidi's oeuvre contains numerous Jerusalem poems; see also 'Araidi, "Yesh li tḥusha bi-rushalayim" ("I Have a Feeling in Jerusalem"), in *Ulay zo ahava*, 34; idem, "Ahuvati yerushalayim" ("Jerusalem My Love"), in *Ḥazarti el ha-kfar*, 22, and idem, "Yerushalayim 2000," in *Mash'ir et ha-ka'as*, 45. 'Araidi's most political poem about Jerusalem is "Pesaḥ ve-ramadan bi-rushalayim, 1994" ("Passover and Ramadan in Jerusalem"), in *Mash'ir et ha-ka'as*, 7.

22 See Amichai, *Shirey yerushalayim*.

that language "does not belong to anybody and it cannot be possessed. As a cultural space that is always open to 'intrusions,' language can only possess."[23] Her comment brings to mind Yasemin Yildiz's distinction between different critiques of the monolingual premise that construes language as the property of a community. The first critical approach, the model of language appropriation, "suggests that a language can be an identitarian site for multiple communities at the same time." Alternatively, the model of language depropriation focuses on the idea of language as property and "offers an ethical injunction to transcend proprietary thinking vis-à-vis language." Yildiz argues that these must be taken together to deconstruct monolingualism and understand multilingual practices.[24] Yet even as we move away from restrictive notions of linguistic possession, language as discourse remains entrenched within the matrix of its historic legacy. For most of its history, Hebrew was not simply "used by Jews" for quotidian purposes, but rather cultivated as a distinctly religious and cultural medium and as a lingua franca for world Jewry.[25] This centuries-old semantic system of cultural and religious associations still reverberates within Modern Hebrew writing.[26] Literary Hebrew, and especially Hebrew poetry, is an intensely allusive idiom that draws widely and deeply from the Jewish canon, a vast body of scriptural and liturgical texts and commentary extending back to the Hebrew Bible.[27] As Ruth Kartun-Blum puts

23 Hochberg, "Dispossession of Hebrew," 64.

24 Yildiz, *Beyond the Mother Tongue*, 42.

25 Yonatan Ratosh (founder of the Canaanite movement; see chapter 1) reminds us of the historic production of Hebrew literature by non-Jews, recalling that in the Middle Ages, Hebrew was one of the "general languages of science," not only a Jewish language. Ratosh demonstrates that while there is an obvious overlap between "Israeli" and "Jewish" literatures, neither can exclusively "contain" the other; he concludes that "the very uniqueness of Israeli literature lies in the fact that it is not *Jewish*." However, concerning Jewish versus Israeli literature, he admits, "It may be difficult even to determine where Jewish literature ends and this new, national literature begins" (Ratosh, "Israeli or Jewish Literature?," 89–90). See also Anidjar, *Semites*, 81 and related discussion in chapter 2 of this book.

26 Israeli Hebrew literature privileges the biblical layers of Hebrew over the rabbinic; more on this will follow. For Ruth Kartun-Blum, modern Israeli literature's "intimate and quarrelsome dialogue with the Hebrew Bible" is due to the specificity of Hebrew, in that "modern Hebrew words can be used in both the contemporary and the ancient registers and so burden even the so-called colloquial register with various associations and connotations of three thousand years of semantic history." Furthermore, as the Bible is still taught in Israeli schools, educated readers can be expected to pick up on these "multilayered" uses of language (Kartun-Blum, *Profane Scriptures*, 7).

27 We may understand this to include the Hebrew Bible, the rabbinic corpus (Talmud and midrashic literatures), liturgical and ceremonial texts, prayers, *piyyut* (devotional poetry), and even certain well-known secular compositions by medieval Hebrew writers. (How much of the multilayered Jewish textual past remains accessible and relevant to the contemporary Israeli reader,

it, for the Modern Hebrew writer, to engage in dialogue with the Bible "is not an option but a must; the choices are of an existential magnitude."[28] The role of the Hebrew poet, moreover, is invested with prophetic authority. "How then," asks Michael Gluzman, "can an Israeli Arab writer participate in a Jewish literary tradition that perceives the writer as a biblical prophet, a 'watchman unto the house of Israel?'"[29] Gluzman's question begets yet another question: how would this Palestinian writer, participating in a "Jewish literary tradition," contend with its *Jewishness*?

Reuven Snir, a leading Israeli scholar of Arabic literature, attributes Shammas's and 'Araidi's use of Hebrew primarily to a "conscious aesthetic preference."[30] In his view, this aesthetic preference for Hebrew requires absorption of "Jewish cultural and religious heritage," so that "despite their efforts for the 'un-Jewing' of Hebrew language and literature, Jewish heritage is evident in their works, although these works cannot be labeled as Jewish heritage."[31] Having forfeited their original cultural identity, "they do not enter the gates of Hebrew literature as proud Arab-Palestinians" but "as lost and lonely people, slowly losing their connection with their roots and caught in an acute identity crisis."[32] Snir also observes that "the obsessive preoccupation of Shammas and 'Arayidi with their cultural identity" dominates their work to the exclusion of other themes.[33] It is true that the precariousness of being a Palestinian Arab writer of Hebrew pervades this body of writing, and that their poetry is preoccupied with reflections on identity. But even this predicament is shifting and unstable. In their poetry, there is no unified "Arab" subject addressing a unified "Jewish" reader (in a unified Hebrew language). Instead, we find different "you"s and just as many different "I"s, poetic subjects appropriating not only different idioms but different identities. While in broad strokes the three writers in question do cultivate a position of difference vis-à-vis their readers, this trait is much more pronounced

or whether Modern literary Hebrew is not still too linguistically and allusively "inflated," is a separate issue.)

28 Kartun-Blum, *Profane Scriptures*, 3.

29 Gluzman, "Politics of Intertextuality," 323.

30 Snir writes early in the article that "[Shammas] justifies writing in Hebrew as a mission, since 'as an Arab it is important to say what I want to say to the Jews,' although it *seems more likely that it is best attributed to a conscious aesthetic preference*" ("Hebrew as the Language of Grace," 167, my emphasis). The rest of the article presents the "conscious aesthetic preference" as point of fact. The phrase appears in the article repeatedly (167, 172, 173, 175) and also as "conscious aesthetic cultural choice" (176).

31 Ibid., 175.

32 Ibid., 174–175. See also Levy, "Borderline Writers," 77–78, for a lengthier discussion of Snir's remarks.

33 Snir, "Hebrew as the Language of Grace," 169.

in some poems than others; it could be argued with equal conviction that in all these poems speaker and reader are bound together in a shared community, unified by a common symbolic language and sense of place. This tension between difference and sameness is salient in the works of all three poets. Masalha, for instance, writes numerous poems accentuating his difference yet in other poems appears eminently comfortable in an idiom of Israeliness that inscribes his speaker within the collective shared by his reader. Each poem, constituting its own moment, its own self-contained world, makes us privy to another possible relation between speaker and language, speaker and place, and so forth.

On the other hand, that loneliness and alienation permeate their poems is indisputable; nor can one downplay the fact that the poems' most persistent theme is the experience of being caught between two cultural spaces. The border becomes an existential condition: the poems express a sense of bifurcation, even representing one half of the self being pitted against the other. Such sensations echo resoundingly throughout Shammas's poetic oeuvre. In poems in both Arabic and Hebrew, Shammas's speaker compares himself to the squeezed-out half shell of a juiced orange.[34] The condition of living and writing in an impossible situation becomes marked in space and on the body. In the Arabic and Hebrew poems of the three writers, it is spatialized as a junction, a no-man's-land, open doors, a treacherous road, a map, various portals of exile; it becomes internalized as possession by an alien language, as a fold of the body, as a crucifixion. At other times, it is a transcendent unification of worlds, cultures, or selves, achieved through the sublimity of nature, through erotic love, and sometimes through the space of the city, especially of Jerusalem. But does all this imply that Palestinians writing in Hebrew are any less "Palestinian," or does it merely reflect their fractured subjectivity? Ought we to expect Palestinians in Israel, severed as they have been from the larger Palestinian collective, to wave the banner of Palestinian Arab identity or of the Palestinian struggle in their work? If the identity of Palestinians in Israel—let alone those writing in Hebrew—is rife with fragmentation and internal contradictions, then it should come as no surprise to find those demons haunting the space of the text.

34 E.g., in Arabic, Shammas writes, "Sleep is an orange / like an unexpected phone ring that stops when you get up / that's how the fragrance of oranges comes to you / from the grove. And sleep is a bird / that catches your attention when it flies from the sill. No / sleep is an orange. I'm / its squeezed half" (*Asir yaqzati wa-nawmi*, 56). Compare with the Hebrew: "On your walls, with a wandering brush / I paint passwords: your charm / will fall in a voice of curses. / I lean on the wall / as the half of an orange / the juicers of domes above me" (*Krikha kasha*, 10). Compare also his images of doors in *Asir yaqzati wa-nawmi*, 83 and *Shetaḥ hefker*, 5.

The claim that Shammas's and ʻAraidi's use of Hebrew is the result of a conscious aesthetic preference is conjectural, especially in light of ʻAraidi's prolific Arabic activity, which more or less parallels his creative output in Hebrew; indeed, in one of his poems, ʻAraidi refers to himself as "the intermittent Arabic-Hebrew Hebrew-Arabic poet."[35] Masalha, who emerged on the Hebrew literary scene a few decades later, has published six collections of poetry in Arabic and only one in Hebrew.[36] Thus the choice would seem to rest as much with the author's objectives; certainly a work like *Arabesques*, written to engage the very dilemmas under discussion here, could not have been created in a language other than Hebrew.[37]

For decades now, Shammas's critics have read his novel, and more broadly the phenomenon of Palestinian writing in Hebrew, against his oft-quoted statement: "What I'm trying to do—mulishly, it seems—is to un-Jew the Hebrew language . . . to make it more Israeli and less Jewish, thus bringing it back to its semitic origins, to its place." Hebrew, argues Shammas, is "the language of those who speak it," Jews and non-Jews alike.[38] As long as the ethos of the State of Israel is based on the Right of Return, which makes any person of Jewish descent an automatic candidate for Israeli citizenship, nationality and citizenship cannot be untangled from religion. For Shammas, "deterritorialization" of Hebrew

35 In fact, ʻAraidi's published poetry is about equally divided between the two languages; his only novel, *Tvila katlanit* (Fatal baptism, 1992), appeared in Hebrew. As to the question of language choice, ʻAraidi writes, "Just as I wanted to prove to my [Jewish] teachers and parents that I could meet their expectations [of mastering Hebrew], so I wanted to prove to my people that I could also write in Arabic. And so I can, but the way I write in Hebrew is very different from the way I write in Arabic. . . . I am not sure if the Jewish people in Israel are aware of what I think of the Hebrew language, and this does not concern me. It is not for them that I write in Hebrew, but because of them. As to the question of whether or not I am a Hebrew poet, the answer is very simple; a Hebrew poet, yes, but not a Jewish poet, just as I am too a Druze and an Arab poet" ("Dreams, Ideas and Realities," 210).

36 Masalha's Arabic-language publications include *Maghnat ta'ir al-khudr* (1979), *Ka-l-ankabut bi-la khuyut* (1989), *Maqamat sharqiyya* (1991), *Rish al-bahr* (1999), *Khana farigha* (2002), and *Lughat umm* (2006).

37 Similarly, Francophone author Tahar Ben Jalloun argued in 1985 that the two novels he had published to date "could only have been written in French, his second language, which allows the transgressions he makes on his Arabo-Islamic culture. According to him, it would have been impossible to do the same thing in Arabic, a double sacred language: at once the language of the Koran and that of his parents" (Mehrez, "Translation and the Postcolonial Experience," 131).

38 Snir, "Hebrew as the Language of Grace," 165, reprinted from the periodical *Kol ha-ʻir* (Jerusalem), February 27, 1987, 58. See also Levy, "Borderline Writers," 70. Moreover, in a 1985 essay, Shammas claims that while there is "a Hebrew, Jewish literature," it is "doubtful if one can speak of an Israeli literature" (with the possible exceptions of Mizraḥi writers such as Sami Michael and Shimon Ballas, presumably because they arrived at Hebrew as a second language from a secular cosmopolitan orientation); see Shammas, "Ha-mifgash she-haya," 31.

as the Jewish language and its "reterritorialization" as the language of Israelis—the agenda he espoused throughout the 1980s and early 1990s—had explicitly political dimensions linked to his concept of an absolutely democratic Israel that would define itself not as "the Jewish state," but as the state of *all* its citizens.[39] In this vein, Shammas's literary project is still read as "a critique of the Jewishness of Hebrew literature."[40] Taking Shammas at his word (and assuming it applies to 'Araidi as well), Snir reads their poetry as a failed, misguided effort to separate Hebrew from Jewishness and to effect a transformation of Israeli culture.[41] By contrast, Gil Hochberg reads *Arabesques* not only as an effective act of "un-Jewing the Hebrew language" but also "as an attempt to undermine the disjunction between 'Arab' and 'Jew' that is prescribed by the very representation of Hebrew as both an 'Israeli' and a 'Jewish' language."[42]

Turning the tables on this debate, I want to suggest that if the writings of Shammas et al. have invited a reconsideration of the Jewishness

39 This was a position Shammas advocated throughout the 1980s in his weekly column in *Kol ha-'ir* (The City Voice, a local Jerusalem newspaper), a project Yael Feldman refers to as a "one-man campaign" ("Postcolonial Memory," 385n6). In more recent years Shammas has not actively supported this position, having seemingly abandoned the Israeli political and cultural field. "Deterritorialization," as coined by Gilles Deleuze and Félix Guattari, is the first condition in their tripartite definition of "minor literature"—i.e., minority writing in the majority language. If language acquires its "territoriality" by becoming materially inflated with a culturally specific system of meaning—an "allegory"—then "deterritorialization" is the displacement of language from that allegory. The process may be accompanied by a simultaneous process of reterritorialization (resignification), which some critics writing about Shammas have read as the deterritorialization of Hebrew as the language of Jewishness and Zionism and its reterritorialization as the language of all its speakers (inclusive of Palestinian Israelis). For Deleuze and Guattari, Hebrew is "reterritorialized" when it is transformed from a mythic to a quotidian language (with "vernacular," "vehicular," and "referential" functions). See Deleuze and Guattari, "What Is a Minor Literature?" and Hever, "Hebrew in an Israeli Arab Hand."

40 Gluzman, "Politics of Intertextuality," 323.

41 Snir, "Hebrew as the Language of Grace," 174. Although Snir assumes or infers that 'Araidi shares this goal, I have found no evidence that 'Araidi ever referred to the separation of Judaism from Hebrew as part of his own literary agenda. Invoking the Lebanese poet Sa'id 'Aql, advocate of the "Phoenician" ideology, Snir adds, "Like 'Aql, who tries to sever the link between Arabic culture and Islam, Shammas strives to purify Hebrew literature of its Jewish features and relics" (ibid., 174). Nor do I find evidence of this program in Shammas's writing, which, to the contrary, makes extensive, strategic use of Jewish features. Snir concludes that the "hope to expand the boundaries of Hebrew literature and to create a new Israeli cultural identity is nothing but a daydream" (ibid., 174). Hannan Hever espouses the opposite view in his publications from the late 1980s and early 1990s. The boundaries of Hebrew literature have in fact expanded to include Mizraḥi voices and, in the past decade, an additional Palestinian voice (Sayed Kashua). There is arguably no "new Israeli cultural identity," but then cultural identity cannot be divorced from the broader political context, which since the 1990s has moved to the far right.

42 Hochberg, *In Spite of Partition*, 79.

of Hebrew and its implications for Israeli national identity, inversely (and perhaps counterintuitively), they should also prompt us to reconsider the meaning and boundaries of *Jewishness* as a "cultural space" that is open to appropriations and intrusions in much the same way as Hebrew. The trouble with the hermeneutic suggested by the "un-Jewing" of Hebrew" is that Palestinian, Israeli, Jewish, and Arab identities are not univalent, nor are they fixed quantities locked together in a zero-sum game. Rather, in context, they are more like interdependent and constantly shifting layers, some but not all of which will be thrown into relief at any given moment. Nor, for that matter, are "Jewishness" and "Israeliness" antinomies, so that making Hebrew more "Israeli" would necessarily make it that much less "Jewish."[43] Shammas's statement thus creates a trap into which his critics fall by endeavoring to affirm or to refute that his literary project has realized what is, in any case, a paradoxical objective—inadvertently illustrating the dangers of utilizing authors' extraliterary statements as hermeneutic tools.[44] This is not to deny that Shammas's literary and journalistic writings generated debate about the nature of Israeliness, most (in)famously through the heated exchange with A. B. Yehoshua, and opened up new discursive possibilities for Israeli Hebrew culture—not least of all for younger Palestinian Israeli writers, such as Sayed Kashua and Ayman Sikseck. Nor is it to downplay the general importance of Palestinian Hebrew authorship for challenging assumptions surrounding the terms "Israeli," "Hebrew," and "Jewish" in relation to "literature" and in relation to each other. But it is to question whether, rather than divesting Hebrew of its Jewishness, Shammas and his colleagues may be *appropriating* that Jewishness (and not just Hebrew) toward new ends. How do Palestinian writers negotiate Jewish textual culture and deploy it in their Hebrew work? How do Jewish allusions contribute to the in-betweenness of their writing? How does Jewishness, when tapped by a Palestinian

43 Ratosh, for example, concludes, "And perhaps this is the real question: not *Israeli* or universally Jewish literature, an illusory opposition that a little reflection reveals to be without foundation, but *Jewish* or *non-Jewish* literature, *Jewish* literature or *national* literature" ("Israeli or Jewish Literature?," 90, emphasis in original).

44 For example, Hochberg writes, "Fortifying the static image of Hebrew literature as a Jewish literature and of Israeli culture as Jewish culture, Snir ascribes the 'identity crisis' to non-Jewish writers of Hebrew (Shammas and 'Araidi), denying the 'identity crises' of Israeli-Hebrew culture. He thus overlooks the productive effects of non-Jewish writings in Hebrew, which as Shammas describes it, 'Un-Jews the Hebrew language, making it more Israeli,' and thus 'bringing it back to its semantic origins—back to its place'" ("Dispossession of Hebrew," 56). Although Hochberg begins by taking her argument in a new and interesting direction, that of the internal identity crisis in Israeli Hebrew culture, she shorts it by returning to the same mode of thought in which Hebrew itself is caught in a tug-of-war between "Jewish" (i.e., ethnocentric, exclusive) or "Israeli" (pluralistic, inclusive).

writer, acquire new meaning—how does a canonical Jewish intertext gain a new afterlife, becoming a "Palestinian midrash," as it were?[45]

"Midrash" refers both to a body of literature (the Midrash, books of biblical exegesis written by rabbis in antiquity) and to the form of reading practiced within it, which Daniel Boyarin describes as an "inherently intertextual hermeneutic act."[46] The term is used in its more contemporary sense to denote a creative interpretative reading of traditional Jewish texts.[47] As this chapter demonstrates, Palestinian poets do indeed engage the Jewishness of Hebrew literature, transforming it from *within*: not through "separation" but through subversion, not by denuding Hebrew of its traditional cultural content, but by reworking canonical Jewish associations. They reinterpret *both* Hebrew *and* Jewishness from their unique vantage point between two languages. Furthermore, although their poetry relies on this repurposing of Jewish heritage, it sporadically incorporates traces of Christian and Islamic heritage (and references to secular Arabic culture) as well; some Jewish cultural references, particularly to biblical stories and figures, are shared with other traditions, and remain multicultural even when embedded in a Hebrew context.[48] By examining their creative uses of intertextuality for the translation of

45 My question builds on Walter Benjamin's understanding of translation as a process that imparts new life to the source text: "For in its afterlife—which could not be called that if it were not a transformation and a renewal of something living—the original undergoes a change"; in a good translation, the original language is "powerfully affected by the foreign tongue" (Benjamin, "Task of the Translator," 76, 81). See also the introduction to this book.

46 It can be described as a nonliteral, creative reading, often in narrative form, often employing parable or allegory, that seeks to explain or to elucidate a biblical passage or narrative or explain a Jewish law. See Boyarin, *Intertextuality and the Reading of Midrash*, 15.

47 See, for instance, Jacobson, *Modern Midrash.*

48 ʻAraidi is Druze, while Shammas (though nonpracticing) was born Catholic, and Masalha is Muslim. Non-Jewish references scarcely appear in Shammas's Hebrew verse. One finds no Arabic words or references, but there are a few subtle hints of his Catholic background, such as the crucifixion and Last Supper in the poem "I Feel the Crease" (*Krikha kasha*, 30) analyzed later in this chapter; the father, son, and spirit in the first poem of *Shetaḥ hefker* (5); and Talita (from *talita kumi*; see *Shetaḥ hefker*, 23). By contrast, ʻAraidi and Masalha refer explicitly to their own Arab(ic) identity and to themes of Hebrew and Arabic, Jews and Arabs, in their verse. ʻAraidi's poetry returns periodically to his village and his family; for a few examples, see "Aba ima" ("Father Mother"), where he represents his parents and tensions between Arabic and Hebrew (*Ulay zo ahava*, 49) as well as "Imi" ("My Mother"; *Mash'ir et ha-kaʻas la-aḥerim*, 10); or a poem about Mount Lebanon with many references to Arab figures and cultural context (*Ḥazarti el ha-kfar*, 17). His 2006 collection features two poems representing Joseph as a seer of dreams, a figure shared by the Hebrew Bible and the Qur'an; see *Mash'ir et ha-kaʻas*, 31, 44). Throughout his Hebrew collection *Eḥad mi-kan*, Masalha makes more varied usage of Arabic and Islamic heritage, referring, inter alia, to the mosque of his childhood village (21), bilingual Hebrew-Arabic wordplay on the Arabic word *marhaba* (26), references to pre-Islamic Arabic poetry (56–57), and references to Baghdad and the *Thousand and One Nights* (59, 61).

cultural difference, I aim to move beyond the reductive framing of "*either* Israeli *or* Jewish" toward a more open-ended understanding of Hebrew as a language and a cultural symbol whose meaning is multiple, variable, and contingent.

PALESTINIAN MIDRASH

In a poem titled "'Al ḥet" ("For the Sin"), 'Araidi writes,

> For the sin I committed against myself and my beloved
> on the way to Jerusalem approaching Bethel
> From the desert I took the fullness of my love
> until Abraham laughed and Ishmael cried.[49]

The poem is modeled on the long *vidui*, the confession of sins in the Yom Kippur (Day of Atonement) liturgy, when worshipers collectively seek forgiveness of God; subsequent stanzas of 'Araidi's poem repeat the liturgical refrain *'al ḥet she-ḥatati* (for the sin I committed), in reference to the speaker's beloved, parents, and son. The poem alludes to Bethel, a biblical place of worship, as well as Abraham and his sons Ishmael and Isaac through the phrase *yitsḥak Avraham*, punning on the etymology of "Isaac" (in Hebrew *Yitsḥak*, which literally means "he laughs")—thus also evoking the metahistory of "Jews" and "Arabs" that the mythological half-brothers Isaac and Ishmael have come to represent. For a poem about love and belonging, then, 'Araidi adopts the language of Jewish liturgy and employs biblical allusion; as we will see, in their own verse, his colleagues Masalha and Shammas do the same.

To overlook or deny that the three writers do use the Jewish canon extensively—and, more to the point, use it *creatively*—is to dilute the richness of their Hebrew poetry. It is also to miss the subversive potential of allusion. And here is where the author's position relative to the interpretive community, and not just the question of language choice, really matters.[50] All allusions are part of an intertextual system in which both readers and writers participate as members of the same interpretive community. In some cases, as Jeremy Dauber notes, "writers can and do employ this [intertextual] system not merely to establish group solidarity . . . but to subvert and to manipulate the system, simultaneously weakening and undermining communal bonds." These writers, he continues, either "become

49 *'Al ḥet she-ḥatati le-'atsmi ve-la-ahuvati / be-derekh li-rushalayim bo'akha beyt el / natalti min ha-midbar et melo ahavati / 'ad she-yitsḥak Avraham ve-yivke Yishma'el* ('Araidi, "'Al ḥet," in *Ḥazarti el ha-kfar*, 25–26).

50 On interpretive communities, see Fish, *Is There a Text in This Class?*, esp. 161–173.

'self-consuming'" or create a minor literature within the interpretive community.[51] Furthermore, as Gerard Genette argues, knowledge of the author's identity and biography functions as a paratext influencing our reading, particularly when the text relates to events in the author's life.[52] Indeed, the strategic intertextuality evinced by Shammas, 'Araidi, and Masalha depends directly on the reader's recognition not only of the intertext, but of the author's relationship to the entire intertextual system.

Palestinian Hebrew poetry adopts an oppositional stance that moves referentially between a majority and a minority perspective. Minor literature, says Caren Kaplan, "travels, moves between centers and margins. . . . The value of this conception lies in the *paradoxical movement between minor and major*—a refusal to admit either position as final or static."[53] That the movement is "paradoxical" is important for understanding how different poems by the same writer may reflect markedly different subject positions in relation to the Israeli center, as is the case for the writers discussed here. It is this movement between center and margins, the "refusal to admit either position as final," that endows their work with the character of *in-betweenness.* Irony softens the edges of protest; subtle humor hints at the pain hidden between the lines; playful overliterality draws attention to the dichotomies and conflicts within the language. Such characteristics are thrown into sharp relief by 'Araidi's rewriting of the famous Four Questions from the Haggada, the ceremonial text read by Jewish families at the annual Passover *seder* to recount the story of the Exodus from Egypt—in Western civilization, the definitive story of liberation from bondage. 'Araidi was interned in an Israeli prison for six months in 1972–1973.[54] A few years later, he published a group of "prison poems," one of which reads,

> Answer me, guard
> What makes this night different
> from all other nights

51 Dauber, "Allusion in a Jewish Key," 56–57. How intriguing that Dauber's description of the *maskilic* use of canonical Jewish texts—intensely subversive in its own context, aimed at a Jewish readership in Europe—would resonate so loudly with the Palestinian use of the same canon over a century later.

52 Genette makes this point in relation to Proust, arguing that knowledge of Proust's part-Jewish ancestry and homosexuality "inevitably serves as a paratext to the pages of Proust's work that deal with those two subjects. I am not saying that people must know those facts; I am saying only that people who do know them read Proust's work differently than people who do not and that anyone who denies the difference is pulling our leg" (*Paratexts*, 8).

53 Kaplan, "Deterritorializations," 358, my emphasis.

54 According to David Grossman, 'Araidi "spent six months in jail in the 1970s because he knew about but did not report the Syrian spy ring led by Israeli [Jewish] radical Udi Adiv" (*Sleeping on a Wire*, 286).

What makes this night different
that all the nights
pass slowly
and this night passes slowly
Answer me, guard.[55]

During the *seder*, the four reasons why Passover is "different from all other nights" are ritually enumerated. While reproducing the question verbatim, 'Araidi's poem inverts its meaning: it turns the Haggada's *literal* question into a *rhetorical* one, for this night is in fact no different from the others, as all nights in prison pass slowly.[56] Moreover, it powerfully countermands the intertext's original associations, as the Haggada recounts the story of Israel's liberation from bondage in Egypt. Finally, the poem reverses the interrogation process: here it is the Palestinian Arab prisoner who questions the Israeli Jewish guard, a situation that recalls Mahmoud Darwish's iconic poem "Identity Card," in which the speaker, a Palestinian detained for questioning by an Israeli official, defiantly repeats, "Sajjil! Ana 'arabi" ("Write it down! I am an Arab"), reclaiming his existence as an Arab and a Palestinian against a politics of erasure.[57] As a restaging of both the Four Questions and Darwish's "Identity Card," 'Araidi's poem speaks to Samia Mehrez's analysis of "radical bilingualism" as a "subversive poetics" seeking to forge a new literary space for the bilingual, postcolonial writer. "It is a space that subverts hierarchies, whether linguistic or cultural; where *separate systems of signification and different symbolic worlds* are brought together in a relation of *perpetual interference, interdependence, and intersignification*."[58] We also see how 'Araidi depends on the reader's recognition of his speaker's subject position as a Palestinian and non-Jew in order to invest these allusions and cultural references

55 The original Hebrew reads, *'Ane li shoter / ma nishtana ha-layla ha-ze / mi-kol ha-leylot / ma nishtana ha-layla ha-ze / she-kol ha-leylot le'at 'ovrim / ve-ha-layla ha-ze le'at 'over / 'ane li shoter*. The repetition of *ma nishtana ha-layla ha-ze*, the refrain of the Four Questions, immediately triggers the intertext. This poem, labeled "C, 'Ir'on. January 1973," is from a group of four poems collectively titled "Mi-shirey batey ha-ma'atsar" ("From the Prison Poems"), each identified by date and place; see *Ḥemla va-faḥad*, 28–29.

56 In many (primarily Ashkenazic) traditions, the Four Questions (and their answers) are chanted by the youngest able participant. Reading this custom into 'Araidi's poem further enhances the ironic disjunction between the poem's very political context and the rhetorical posture of innocence associated with the intertext.

57 Darwish, *Diwan Mahmud Darwish*, 1:121–127; the poem was originally published in *Awraq al-zaytun* (*Leaves of Olives*, 1964). For an English translation, see Darwish, *Mahmoud Darwish: Selected Poems*, 24.

58 Samia Mehrez, "Subversive Poetics," 260, cited in Dingwaney and Maier, *Between Languages and Cultures*, 13, my emphasis.

with irony, to give them that double edge. ʻAraidi's strategic use of Jewish heritage in this poem hardly projects the image of "a lost and lonely person . . . slowly losing his connection with his roots."[59] Rather, it is an instantiation of the cultural "mimicry" that makes the colonial subject uncanny in the eyes of the colonizer.[60]

But after reading ʻAraidi's poem as a Palestinian rewriting of the Four Questions, how do we continue to read the Four Questions themselves? How does ʻAraidi's cultural "translation" contribute to the modern afterlife of the Haggada? Will the reader recall this one-way dialogue between prisoner and guard during his or her next Passover *seder*? Engaging Jewish tradition for the purposes of political critique, the poem exemplifies the hermeneutics of Palestinian midrash: a modern midrash that reinterprets Jewish heritage through Palestinian experience. ʻAraidi's ironic use of traditional Jewish material continues the desacralization of Hebrew enacted by Jewish writers such as Yehuda Amichai, for example in Amichai's sardonic take on the Jewish requiem for the dead, "El male raḥamim" ("God Full of Mercy"):

> God is full of mercy,
> Were God not so full of mercy
> There would be some mercy in the world
> And not just in Him.[61]

In a similar manner, ʻAraidi's reworking of the Four Questions transposes them from a traditional ritualized context to a desacralized Israeli idiom. Even so, there is a critical difference between the poetic iconoclasms of Amichai and ʻAraidi. Amichai's is a complaint with the way of the world, not directly aimed at his relationship with the state. It subsumes or naturalizes Jewish liturgy into a secular cultural idiom in order to protest the universal suffering wrought by war and political violence in a language that is emotionally resonant with his readers. ʻAraidi's poem, by contrast, is written in an oppositional voice whose Other is not a remote "Him" (God) but a present "you" (the guard); obliquely, that "you" is also the implied Jewish Israeli reader. At the same time, ʻAraidi's poem serves as

59 Snir, "Hebrew as the Language of Grace," 174–175.

60 Cf. Bhabha, *Location of Culture*, 86.

61 Barbara and Benjamin Harshav's translation reads, "*God-Full-of-Mercy*, the prayer for the dead. / If God was not full of mercy, / Mercy would have been in the world, / Not just in Him" (Amichai, *Yehuda Amichai: A Life of Poetry*, 31; for the Hebrew original, see Amichai, *Shirim: 1948-1962*). Kartun-Blum expands on the relationship of the secular Modern Hebrew writer to the biblical text, one characterized by "quotation and distorted quotation, an aspiration to the sublime and a descent to the ironic, and the mocking sanctification of the profane, which merges with the profanation of the holy" (*Profane Scriptures*, 17).

an Amichai-like naturalization of Jewishness, illustrating the movement between major and minor that characterizes Palestinian Hebrew poetry.

THE LANGUAGE OF MIRRORS

In 1985, a year before the appearance of his novel, Shammas had compared writing in Hebrew to being a "guest" in the language, "one who comes to you to dinner, and at the end of the meal you find him in the kitchen, washing dishes with an almost Harold-Pinterish enjoyment, that of someone who could unintentionally break any beautiful piece. This also means that maybe, maybe, he will stay the night."[62] Some years later he added, "And the next morning he is already starting to take over. And I said, But I will try to be well-mannered. I arrive in the house of the Hebrew language under the banner of good manners."[63]

For Emile Habiby, Hebrew was still the language of the Other, albeit an intimate other. For Shammas, 'Araidi, and Masalha, all born more or less with the loss of Palestine and creation of Israel, Hebrew is, as Shammas puts it, a "stepmother tongue,"[64] feeding the fire of an explosive self-referential and metalinguistic poetic discourse. Their Hebrew poems present themselves as mirrors, as self-portraits, as portals, and as missals.[65] Their very titles oscillate between assertions of agency and expressions of uncertainty: I apologize, I feel, I write. They question even their own use of the poetic "I," as in this poem by Shammas titled "I Apologize":

62 Shammas, "Ha-mifgash she-haya," 31.

63 Grossman, *Sleeping on a Wire*, 252.

64 Shammas has stated, "I feel an exile in Arabic, my blood language. I feel an exile in Hebrew, my stepmother tongue" (Hever, "Hebrew in an Israeli Arab Hand," 289); see also Shammas, "Diary," 29.

65 In his second collection, Shammas laments,

> One-wayness is of the rules of the game. Amichai
> comes out of Hebrew poetry and hangs a sign
> 'Be back soon.' I don't, I don't. I
> send postcards in the morning to my very dear
> friends, to notify them that I send them
> postcards in the morning. (Shammas, *Shetaḥ hefker*, 13)

The late Yehuda Amichai could enter and exit the domain of Hebrew letters freely; he engaged in a two-way dialogue with his readers marked by a cultural give and take. The Palestinian Israeli author, by contrast, occupies a tenuous position characterized both by the "one-wayness" of his relationship to his readers and by excessive self-referentiality—sending them "postcards" to notify them that he is writing to them, i.e., creating metadiscourses on his own writerly activity. Shammas asserts his difference from Amichai in an approximation of Amichai's own style: another illustration of the ambivalence and slippage that characterize postcolonial "mimicry."

It's superfluous for me to begin in first person singular:
I apologize.
I didn't know that it would take me so
long to get here.

The edge of memory, on the edge of the pool's depth,
enters the subconscious. In relative quiet,
with great assuredness.

The voice is coated in velvety down
as the horns of the wretched ram. Until the great
season of mating. Until no end.

I am a self-resident, a loyal citizen
to my loves. My loves that were,
and I touched them with my hands.

The voice is covered in velvety down, and not my hand.
My Isaac has long since decided: it's not just the voice,
and not just the hands, but that this isn't even the time.

But in the end I arrived, and here I am. And I would be happy
about this, if not for my childhood, stuck in the elevator
of memory, pressing
the alarm button.[66]

This poem begins with the speaker's questioning of his own voice ("It's superfluous for me to begin in first person singular")—apologizing for his use of the "I" in the declaration "I apologize." The apology itself is followed by a cryptic explanation of his delay, conversationally concluding, "But in the end I arrived, and here I am." Where is *here*? It is none other than the house of the Hebrew language, where he, the guest-cum-resident, is washing dishes. Shammas hands us the key with the phrase "on the edge of the pool's depth" (*ba-katse he-'omek shel ha-brekha*), an allusion to one of Ḥayim Naḥman Bialik's most famous poems, "Ha-brekha" ("The Pond" or "The Pool," 1905).[67] For Bialik, the pool is a metaphor for the introspective soul. In the *poema*, the speaker describes how he is

seated then at the border of the pool,
considering the riddle of two worlds,
twin worlds (but which one prior, to me unknown)

66 Shammas, *Shetaḥ hefker*, 6.

67 Bialik's poem is "widely considered one of the greatest *ars poetic* texts in Hebrew literature"; Gluzman, "Politics of Intertextuality," 319.

This same allusion to Bialik has been analyzed brilliantly by Michael Gluzman as a key intertext in *Arabesques*, where Shammas's "act of rewriting 'The Pool' should . . . be seen as intervening in the national discourse of contemporary Hebrew literature."[68] Gluzman also reads it in the manner of Palestinian midrash, proposing that "the allusion to Bialik affects not only the alluding text (*Arabesques*) but also our understanding of the evoked text ('The Pool' . . .)."[69] Whereas Bialik's poem is written in the spirit of universalism and humanism,

> once Shammas redeploys the language of this passage, it becomes highly politicized. Moreover, Bialik's own allusions are invested with new meanings, thereby showing us that meaning is indeed a function of context. . . . For example, the first line of this passage, "seated then at the edge of the pool," now carries a different significance, for while Bialik sits on the edge of an actual pool in his home village, Shammas finds himself *on the edge of Bialik's pool*.[70]

In other words, writing in Hebrew leads Shammas to situate his artistic consciousness at a *double remove* from the spring of selfhood: it is always a mediated relationship, in which he finds himself in a tenuous position on the edge of the "pool" representing the depths of Hebrew language and culture. By contrast, the "edge of *memory*"—the repressed presence of a primal childhood self—moves with stealth and assuredness into the speaker's subconscious.[71] This struggle between the repressed but ultimately resurgent pre-Hebrew self (childhood) and the tortured Hebrew self (adulthood) suffuses Shammas's writing, so much of which responds to the pain of moving between cultures. On another level, Shammas's reworking of Bialik's "The Pool" is but one example of how his poetry anticipated *Arabesques*. Shammas was only twenty-four when he published his first two volumes of poetry, in Hebrew and in Arabic; the novel, published twelve years later, was the product of a much more mature writer. Youth notwithstanding, his early Hebrew poems demonstrate the

68 Ibid., 320. Gluzman analyzes Shammas's extensive use of "Ha-brekha" in a section of *Arabesques*. Situating it against Shammas's famous polemic with A. B. Yehoshua, Gluzman reads this moment as "the climax of his response to Yehoshua," for Shammas's allusion to Bialik cleverly inverts the Arab mimicry of Bialik represented by Yehoshua in his novel *Ha-me'ahev* (The Lover). "In using 'The Pool' to elucidate the relationship between the Jewish and the Arab writer," writes Gluzman, "Shammas responds to Bialik's deep resonance in the echo chamber of Hebrew literature" (ibid., 327).

69 Ibid., 330.

70 Ibid., 332, my emphasis.

71 Shammas also published a poem by the title "Ha-brekha" in his first collection, yet this poem shows no obvious thematic or intertextual relationship to Bialik but for the speaker's attempt to "stick" names to objects in his room, making it a poem about language (*Krikha kasha*, 36).

same profound (and, for some Israeli critics, unsettling) mastery of the Hebrew language and canon we find later in *Arabesques*. Furthermore, not only are both his poetry and his novel highly allusive, deeply coded, and self-referential, but they share some of the same key symbols.

"I Apologize" voices Shammas's ambivalence about his Hebrew writerly enterprise—he arrived, and would be happy about it, if not for that nagging sense of self-betrayal (childhood pressing the alarm button in the elevator of memory). In addition to its rewriting of "The Pool," Shammas's poem also deploys the biblical language of prophecy and sacrifice to articulate this ambivalence. The phrases "horns of the wretched ram" and "my Isaac" (*ha-Yitsḥak sheli*) allude to the binding of Isaac (Genesis 22:1-19); the biblical intertext tells us that "[l]ooking up, Abraham saw a ram caught by its horns in a bush. Abraham took the ram and offered it . . . in place of his son."[72] In the last stanza, the phrase *ve-hiney ani kan* (and here I am) is a modern adaptation of the biblical *hineyni*, Abraham's answer to God's call. Known in Hebrew as *'akeydat Yitsḥak* (the binding of Isaac) or simply *ha-'akeyda* (the binding), the Isaac story is a primary intertext for Modern Hebrew literature. As Kartun-Blum points out, there is hardly a Modern Hebrew poet who has not made use of this most archetypal story, a foundational myth for Israeli culture and collective identity; in appropriating it (as signaled by "*my* Isaac"), Shammas positions his poem within this modern canon.[73]

In this light, the "velvety down-coated voice" could be the angel of God telling Abraham not to sacrifice his son, or perhaps the speaker's memory. The speaker's "Isaac" realized long ago that something is fishy—it's not only the sugary voice and the hands, but even the timing (*ve-lo rak ha-yadayim, ela she-ze af lo ha-zman*). Will he eventually be judged for his act of cultural transgression, the betrayal of his primal childhood self? Or conversely, for his adult act of poetic trespass, for gazing into the depths of the pool? The elevator of memory is a no-man's-land of its own, suspended between here and there, past and present, one of all too many no-man's-lands in Shammas's poetic topography.

Seven years after the publication of "I Apologize," 'Araidi published a lyric "open letter" addressed to Shammas. Invoking the same central intertexts to address the same dilemma, it reads as if in dialogue with Shammas's earlier poem:

72 Genesis 22:13-14; see *Tanakh*, 40.

73 Cf. Amir Gilboa's poem "Isaac," on the Sho'ah (Holocaust). According to Kartun-Blum, the *'akeyda* "remains indisputably the most prominent and most powerful of all these biblical topoi" in Modern Hebrew literature, and its persistence in modern Hebrew culture "borders on obsession" (*Profane Scriptures*, 18). For an extended reading of the *'akeyda* in Modern Hebrew poetry, see *Profane Scriptures*, chap. 2, 15–62; see also Jacobson, *Modern Midrash*, 1–5.

THE LANGUAGE OF MIRRORS

To Anton Shammas

What shall we say to whom
about people, about peoples,
about ourselves.
. . .

Look closely at the language of visions (*sfat ha-mar'ot*)
look far off
behold
how the ancestor's knife
sharply fixes
its eyes on our eyes.
Look how they appear from afar—
elderly, women, and children
in great anger
and in great delight
distancing the rams
from above us.

What shall say our Father who art in heaven
and our father who art on earth
if there is no miracle
and if fire does not burn?
Will we live to see
with our own eyes
the number of stars in whose multitudes
will be our descendants?

Oh, how hard the waiting is by night
and how hard it is by day!
What is the language of loneliness
of artists in the image of man?
Which is the poetry,
the art,
which is the best silence of all, that,
like Abel's cry from the blood,
will be able to truly explain
what I shall say to whom
in this most perfect of moments?[74]

74 Araidi, *Ḥazarti el ha-kfar*, 13–14, translation partially adapted from Karen Alcalay-Gut, http://karenalkalay-gut.com/Araidi.html (accessed August 20, 2013).

"What," 'Araidi asks Shammas, "shall we say about ourselves?" The line is a play on the classic Israeli Bible quiz question *mi amar le-mi u-matay* (Who said unto whom and when?). As such, 'Araidi's opening question to Shammas—how do we write about ourselves in Hebrew?—is phrased as an inside joke about Israeli culture, and moreover as one that alludes to the pedagogical apparatus of the Israeli educational system. For Israeli readers, this cultural reference thematizes biblical intertextuality; and as we will see, 'Araidi's poetic apostrophe to Shammas is replete with biblical allusions to both Genesis and Exodus.

While ostensibly an answer to a question about identity and self-representation, this poem is very much about *vision*: about the limitations of ordinary human vision, the dangers of prophetic vision, and the deception of grandiose visions. In the first line of the second stanza, the phrase *sfat ha-mar'ot* can be translated as "the language of visions," "of mirrors," or "of reflections." In Hebrew, "the language of visions"[75] is another idiom evoking Bialik's aforementioned "The Pool," in which poetic language is likened to the refraction of light upon water.[76] As noted in chapter 2, throughout his career Bialik also cultivated the trope of poet as prophet, a concept he adopted from Pushkin and infused with nationalist undertones. In 'Araidi's hand, however, the "language of visions" refers not to language in the universal sense, but specifically, to the *Hebrew* language. The poem continues,

Behold
how the ancestors' knife
sharply fixes its eyes
on our eyes

Re'e
keytsad ma'akhelet ha-avot
no'etset be-ofen ḥad
et 'eyneha be-'eyneynu

Here 'Araidi uses *ma'akhelet*, the biblical term for the knife used in ritual slaughter—indeed, the knife Abraham was to use in the sacrifice of Isaac. 'Araidi takes the fixed idiom *na'ats 'eynayim* (to set one's eyes on, to stare; literally, to stab something with one's eyes) and puns on its literal and idiomatic meanings, so that the knife may be read either as *staring* at them or *stabbing* their eyes with its own. But in so doing, this mythical

75 In Bialik, it is *lashon ha-mar'ot*. Hebrew has two words for "language," *lashon* and *safa*, *lashon* literally meaning "tongue" and *safa* "lip." See note 94 below.

76 Bialik, *Kol shirey*, 361–369.

knife seems to transfer its vision, a vision that is almost prophetic in its perspicacity: the speaker ('Araidi) and addressee (Shammas) now have a panoramic view of the people in its totality, in its anger and pleasure. It is the people, as a collective, that is responsible for "distancing the rams / from above us."

That line brings us back to the moment in the *'akeyda* when Abraham finds the ram caught in the bush; after making a burnt offering of it, "Abraham named that site Adonai-yire, whence the present saying, 'On the mount of the Lord there is vision'" (Genesis 22:14).[77] In the poem, does the "distancing" of the rams mean that no sacrifice will be made in their stead, that 'Araidi and Shammas themselves are to be sacrificed on the altar of the Hebrew language, in this place of deadly, divine vision? Because of Abraham's willingness to sacrifice his only son, God promises to make his descendants as "numerous as the stars" (Genesis 22:17). But, in his own rewriting of the story, 'Araidi doubts their poetic efforts in Hebrew will be rewarded, at least not in their lifetimes:

> Will we suffice to see
> with our own eyes
> the number of stars in whose multitudes
> will be our descendants?

'Araidi's pessimism calls to mind Shammas's own prediction that he may one day be held accountable for his Hebrew literary activities.

Ultimately, then, 'Araidi's poem tells us that when one Palestinian Israeli poet speaks to another Palestinian Israeli poet through one of Hebrew culture's primal and defining moments, he uses it as foil, rewriting the story in order to point out their shared *difference*.[78] Yet in so doing, he creates a new midrash. His dialogue with Shammas, conducted through the *'akeyda*, becomes one more layer of a story whose textual life began with the Bible, was reabsorbed through rabbinic literature and midrash, and permeated Israeli literature as an archetypal paradigm.[79] Here we

77 *Tanakh*, 40.

78 Invoking a biblical intertext in order to reject its traditional interpretation or to distance oneself from the collective is a common feature of contemporary Hebrew poetry; as Kartun-Blum states, "In Israeli culture the Bible becomes the *intimate other*" (*Profane Scriptures*, 5–7, emphasis in original). In 'Araidi's poem, the insider/outsider relationship that the poem carves out is not simply about political orientation but, much more viscerally, about the place of a non-Jewish poet within a Jewish tradition.

79 In the same collection, 'Araidi also engages in Palestinian midrash through a poem assuming the perspective of Ishmael, banished to the desert, as well as another poem that reinterprets the famous "lekh-lekha" of Genesis 12, when God sends Abram forth to Canaan. See "Nin Avraham" ("The Great-Grandson of Abraham"), *Ḥazarti el ha-kfar*, 9 and "Lekh-lekha" ("Go Forth!"), ibid., 41.

may return to Gluzman's question about how a Palestinian Israeli writer can participate in a literary tradition that views the poet as a prophet. 'Araidi's speaker initially assumes a prophetic viewpoint, only to reject it as futile. In so doing, 'Araidi implicitly refuses the Romantic nationalist trope of poet as prophet (i.e., as harbinger of national revival), as well as the use of the *'akeyda* story as a Jewish, and later Israeli, symbol of martyrdom.[80] The poem ends with the impossibility of its own articulation:

> Which is the poetry
> the art,
> which is the best silence that,
> like Abel's cry from the blood,
> will be able to truly explain
> what I shall say to whom
> in this most perfect of moments?

The silence that is likened to the cry of Abel seems to answer 'Araidi's opening question to Shammas in the first stanza:

> What shall we say to whom
> . . . about ourselves?

Thus the truest form of self-explanation for the Palestinian Arab writer of Hebrew becomes silence. Yet the poem's elaborately allusive route to this conclusion suggests a metatextual answer more akin to "We may not know what to say to whom, but we *do* know 'their' texts by heart." Hebrew as *sfat ha-mar'ot* is thus transformed from Bialik's language of prophetic, mystical vision into a language of reflections—a "language of loneliness."

THE LANGUAGE OF LONELINESS: MAKING *KIDDUSH*

Expressions of loneliness and futility appear persistently throughout Shammas's poetic oeuvre, where often they are coded not only through inverted biblical allusions but through references to Jewish ritual practice. One such poem, "Ani margish be-kefel" ("I Feel the Crease"), weaves together symbols of both Judaism and of Christianity, enfolding them into an Israeli colloquial idiom to convey the speaker's sense of bifurcation:

80 Kartun-Blum elaborates on allegorical uses of the *'akeyda* in poems about war and national sacrifice as well as poems on the Sho'ah; see chap. 2 of *Profane Scriptures.* To be sure, there is also the Islamic version of the story, in which Ishmael figures as the Abrahamian son in question. Given the poem's numerous biblical allusions, 'Araidi does not appear to be invoking the Islamic version, but it should be reiterated that the story has a shared tradition in the Jewish and Muslim traditions.

Sanctifies all that has transpired, in a flash,
from the roof drops *tefillin*, choking. Imagine
that all the glory is learned from books
and you boast of the empty pages.
A colonnade of lonely people. I thought
I'd go. There's no need to make a fuss. In truth.
And also in error. And what I'm doing here is making *kiddush*
over the white city. At times
I feel a crease going down my body. Once
you saw one like it going down the body
of Jesus, in an old print of the Last Supper.
Big deal.[81]

The poem contains two distinctly Jewish references (*tefillin, kiddush*) discernible to any Hebrew reader, followed by an oblique reference to the crucifixion through the "crease," which is then reiterated more explicitly through the image of Jesus at the Last Supper. Rather than rereading a biblical intertext, this poem appropriates Jewish ritual practices. *Tefillin* are prayer phylacteries whose ritual use is incumbent upon Jewish men. They consist of wooden cubes containing prayers, attached to black leather straps that are wound tightly around the arm and forehead. Choking, the speaker drops them from the roof onto the city below. The poem begins with the speaker saying he "sanctifies all that has transpired" (*mekadesh 'al kol ma she-hitraḥesh*); the phrase *mekadesh 'al* (sanctifying) evokes the blessing of the Sabbath wine, known in English as "making *kiddush*." Ironically, here the dropping of *tefillin* seems part of the speaker's inverted, private ceremony of "sanctification" of his own past. The poem's second mention of sanctification refers to the city: *u-ma she-ani kan 'ose ze le-kadesh / 'al ha-'ir ha-levana* (And what I'm doing here is making *kiddush* over the white city). The "white city" is a snow-blanketed Jerusalem; a holy city purified by its white cover, it recalls the Sabbath tablecloth used during the *kiddush*.[82] The speaker drops the constricting *tefillin* from the roof while simultaneously making *kiddush*—contradictory impulses whose conjuncture imparts a sense of cognitive dissonance.

In fact, the poem has two distinct lyrical voices: the dominant voice of the *tefillin*-dropper, who stands over the white city desperate to express the depths of his loneliness and despair; and the contrapuntal voice of the

81 Shammas, *Krikha kasha*, 30.

82 The Arabic name for Jerusalem, "al-Quds," literally, "the Holy," is a cognate of the Hebrew *kadesh*; in a bilingual reading, the poem invokes the city's Arabic name as a subtext of the speaker's Hebrew sanctification of the city.

cynic who undercuts and dismisses the speaker's every attempt to tell us of his pain. The two voices are also marked by their different linguistic registers: the diction of the first voice is literary while the second voice is colloquial ("no need to make a fuss," *mi-ze lo tsrikhim le-hitragesh*; "big deal," *ma yesh*). The crease along the speaker's body may be the tortured seam of these two "I"s, an internal borderline, a corporealized psychic split. The poem strategically uses resonant Jewish symbols to place the speaker within the *kefel* (crease or fold), which is what makes his sense of schizophrenia so compelling: he longs to free himself from the metaphorical chokehold of the *tefillin*, but he performs the Jewish benediction over his past. The poem illuminates Bhabha's description of "a strategy of ambivalence in the structure of identification that occurs precisely in the elliptical *in-between*, where the shadow of the other falls upon the self."[83] The speaker thus situates himself neither inside nor outside the domain of *tefillin* and *kiddush*, but in the *in-between*, that interstitial space that becomes reterritorialized (in a paradoxical, antiterritorial manner) as the "no-man's-land."

In another poem, Shammas writes, "I walked to the end of the rain, until your name that burns within me was put out / And now, wrapped in the *tallith* of ash, your memory paces through the caverns of my mind" (*ve-'akhshav, 'atuf be-talit ha-efer, mehalekh zikhronekh bi-mḥilot moḥi*).[84] A *tallith* is a ritual prayer shawl; like *tefillin*, it is a male symbol of Jewish orthodoxy. In the previous poem, the speaker dropped *tefillin* from the roof; here, the memory of the female beloved is wrapped in the male *tallith* of ash (a metaphorical contravention of gendered ritual norms). Paradoxically, the *tallith* both enjoins and separates them. The speaker uses the *tallith* to capture her memory, but it is made of ash, forming an ephemeral enclosure; and as it is a Jewish ritual object, the speaker has no real claim upon it.[85]

THE LANGUAGE OF LONELINESS, II: JERUSALEM DREAMSCAPES

The language of loneliness follows Shammas throughout his work, from his Arabic volume into his two Hebrew collections. In his first Hebrew volume, Shammas composes a series of intimate poems that blur the boundaries between the personification of Jerusalem as a lover and the

83 Bhabha, *Location*, 60, emphasis in original. The point refers to theoretical concepts of the subaltern.

84 Shammas, *Shetaḥ hefker*, 15.

85 In 'Araidi's poem on Uri Tsvi Greenberg, he also invokes a *tallith* in the phrase "And the sea is not a *tallith* that is all blue" ('Araidi, *Ulay zo ahava*), 24. The phrase *talit she-kula tekhelet*, "a *tallith* that is all blue," is a Talmudic idiom meaning a morally flawless person, "a paragon of virtue"; it is usually used in the negative rather than the affirmative.

mythologization of the flesh-and-blood beloved. In "Snow in Jerusalem," he writes,

And I said your thighs are pine-downed.
Chills—pine-bumps. From the North
comes a bride, white
as a packaged shroud. Her passion drowned and I drowned,
in a veil of resin.

Ve-amarti plumat oranim
li-rekhayim. Ḥidudin ḥidudin. Mi-tsafon
tavo kala, levana ke-takhrikhim
be-ḥavilat mishloaḥ. Shak'a tshukata ve-shaka'ti,
be-hinumat ha-sraf.[86]

Pines trees are a favorite attribute of Jerusalem in Israeli poetry.[87] The bride "coming from the North" alludes to the Bible's most passionate book, the Song of Songs: "Come from Lebanon, my promised bride, / come from Lebanon, come on your way" (Song of Songs 4:8; the same allusion appears in Shammas's Arabic collection as "Ta'ali ya 'arus min lubnan!": Arise, O bride of Lebanon!).[88] The word *seraf*, resin, also connotes menstruation in rabbinic Hebrew. Interweaving place and passion, the phrase *hinumat ha-sraf*, a bridal veil of resin, integrates the three subjects: the biblical bride, the Jerusalem of snow and pine, and the flesh and blood lover (of the goose-bumped thighs and menstrual blood).

Another poem in the same Jerusalem series is titled "Im eshkaḥekh" ("If I Forget Thee"), a direct allusion to the famous Psalm 137 ("By the rivers of Babylon"), whose speaker passionately laments, "If I forget thee, O Jerusalem, may my right hand forget its cunning."[89] Shammas's poem depicts the speaker in a state of semiwakefulness during an early morning walk through the city, perhaps returning home from a tryst with the beloved:

I wanted to look for the city, and couldn't find a way
to disguise myself, not even the mask of a path. She said, take
King George Street. I did. And I buttoned my dreams

86 Shammas, *Krikha kasha*, 12.

87 For example, David Rokeah writes in a poem to Jerusalem, "Your stones I shall polish into a mirror / For in them is my yearning. / Pine's loftiness and their heart's resin" (Mintz, *Modern Hebrew Literature*, 276, Mintz's translation).

88 Shammas, *Asir yaqzati wa-nawmi*, 48.

89 Psalms 137:5. In the King James Version, it is construed as "may my right hand forget its cunning"; in JPS, "let my right hand wither" (see *Tanakh*, 1584).

by the public yawnoir. I will forget thee,
most likely, and sleep.
And the walls of the shopping center
are a sealed lullaby in my right hand.

Amarti le-ḥapes et ha-ʿir, ve-lo matsati derekh
le-hitḥapes ve-lo masekhat shvil. Amra telekh
be-king-jorj. Halakhti. Ve-kiftarti et ḥalomotay
mul ha-mifhaka ha-tsiborit. Eshkaḥekh, ka-nir'e, ve-ishan.
Ve-kirot ha-mashbir shir ʿeres atum bi-mini.[90]

This is a poem about being lost, perhaps also being lost in love. Here too Shammas rewrites the biblical language of longing and passion in a modern idiom, this time brimming over with wordplay. The verb *le-ḥapes*, to seek or search for, is echoed in *lehit-ḥapes* (its reflexive form), to disguise oneself; *mishtana ha-tsiborit*, the public pissoir, is reinvented as *mifhaka ha-tsiborit*, the public "yawnoir," where passersby button their dreams instead of their pants. The phrase *masekhat shvil* plays on the multiple meanings of *masekha/masekhet*. From the root *nasakh* (to weave), *masekha* is a covering or mask, while *masekhet*, a web of the loom, is also the term for a tractate of the Talmud (so named because of the weblike structure of the writing); in Modern Hebrew, it is used in idioms such as *masekhet beʿayot*, a web (tangle) of problems. *Masekhat shvil*, the "mask of a path," with a slight change in vowels, becomes the "tractate of a path," or a "web-like (meandering) path."

The poem's climax is its inversion of Psalm 137, when walking through downtown Jerusalem, the speaker declares: "I *will* forget thee, most likely, and sleep." Who is the addressee: Jerusalem (the subject of the intertext) or the lover whose bed he has just left? In another twist, the city's department store (a landmark in the downtown center) is a "lullaby" enclosed in the speaker's own right hand: thus the psalm is morphed into a lullaby, the biblical Jerusalem becomes the modern city, and the speaker's hand, rather than losing its cunning, encloses the city. The fate of the city is quite literally in the hand of the outsider, the lost figure who doesn't know his way.

Throughout his Hebrew and Arabic writings, Shammas's poetic voice inhabits not only the no-man's-land between languages but also that between sleep and wake. Shammas's sole Arabic collection, *Asir yaqzati wa-nawmi* (*Prisoner of My Wakefulness and Sleep*, 1974), published in the same year as his first Hebrew collection, expresses a similar intertwining of the desired lover and the city. Comparing "I Feel the Crease" and "If I Forget

90 Shammas, *Krikha kasha*, 11.

Thee" to two of his Arabic poems reveals differences of cultural context as well as intertextual practice:

> It's five o'clock in the morning
> and the city is a crusader in search of the City.
>
> Dawn's dew on helmets and children's shoes,
> the horse's neighs, moist with hymns,
> and dreams rising from windows like kites.
> Wakefulness clips their strings and they alight.
> (Who will clip this string from my neck?)
>
> And I fear standing, I fear
> becoming a stone filled with time's bubbles, a nail
> on the big Gate, or an inscription
> on a saber's handle.
>
> Tell the guitar player at Jaffa Gate
> all the houses of the city will tumble down if he stops.[91]

> You were two poems away from me, or
> even closer
> within my lips and my reach.
>
> But when the climbing paths wound behind me,
> toward childhood,
> the wilderness poured down on me suddenly, and my sadness
> dashed forward.
>
> So I became the minaret of emptiness.
>
> And you ebbed away like dawn's call for prayer.[92]

In the Hebrew poems, Jerusalem/the beloved is symbolized by the pines and by the Song of Songs; her memory is wrapped in a *tallith* of ash, or is "forgotten" as a direct inversion of Psalm 137's injunction to remember. In the Arabic poems, on the other hand, during another early morning walk suspended between a state of wakefulness and sleep, the speaker describes the city as a crusader in search of the City, as the guitar player

91 Shammas, *Asir yaqzati wa-nawmi*, 47, translation adapted from Ferial Ghazoul and Naomi Shihab Nye in Jayyusi, *Anthology of Modern Palestinian Literature*, 302.

92 Shammas, *Asir yaqzati wa-nawmi*, 34, translation adapted from Ferial Ghazoul and Naomi Shihab Nye in Jayyusi, *Anthology of Modern Palestinian Literature*, 303.

at the Jaffa Gate (*Bawabat al-Khalil*); then the city/beloved vanishes from the lover like the haunting strains of the Islamic call to prayer. Where is the minaret in the Hebrew, the *tallith* in the Arabic? Is the real "subject" of the poem formed not from the voice of either language but from the accumulation of silences, the "subtexts" in the inactive language of each poem? Shammas's poetic "I" is produced both in between and in excess of the Israeli and Palestinian, Jewish and Arab "domains of difference."[93]

SELF-PORTRAITS OF THE OTHER

If the experience of being caught between languages and cultures forms an ubiquitous undercurrent, it is at times a silent trickle, at others a roaring rush. The issue of language comes to the fore most explicitly in the writers' poetic self-portraiture. These poems metaphorize and anthropomorphize notions of language, relying heavily on the concepts of mother tongue and of language as an assemblage or limb. The subject's movement from Arabic to Hebrew and by extension to an acquired bilingualism is an unnerving journey that unsettles assumptions of origins and disrupts unity or homology among language, place, and self. At the same time, this journey into the unknown brings the writers new forms of knowledge and identification. The result is a body of verse that speaks of shared experiences in different voices—even within the work of the same poet.

"Dyokan" ("Portrait"), a poem by Shammas that appeared in a 1980 anthology of Hebrew poetry, is a stark and gripping depiction of assimilation into the language of the Other:

> I stand here in the azure light
> unwalled-loneliness around me, like a candle's flame.
> And in my mouth, another tongue[94]
> not of my mother, and not in my blood.
> My blood paces in the emptiness of my arteries,
> a boat without oars.
> And the spirit paces in my blood,
> it asks leave of my body in the azure light.
> My body is full of lesions of rust—

93 Bhabha, "Frontlines/Borderposts," 269.

94 *U-ve-fi safa aḥeret.* Both of Modern Hebrew's two words for "language," *safa* and *lashon*, are also names for parts of the mouth: *safa* is "lip" and *lashon* is "tongue." (Both terms have closely related Arabic cognates, *shafa* and *lisan.*) In the original Hebrew, the poem's use of *safa* connotes both language and tongue. Elsewhere throughout the poem I have translated *safa* as "language," but here I render it "tongue" to convey the poem's emphasis on corporeality.

no turtle dove will carry out a pitiful
mission for me.
And my body comes and asks leave
of another language,
with no love at all.

Another language seeps through my body,
pressing my temples from within,
leaving fine fissures,
leaving dripstones of darkness in my legs.
And I stand here in the azure light
growing in vain inside my portrait.
Sweat paces in my blood,
comes and asks leave of my limbs.
And my portrait, it keeps retreating,
addresses me in a forgotten language.
Formless words drip from my fingers.
Foreign, unfamiliar, my legs quaver.
And my body, once the iron loses its edge, comes and asks leave
of my rust
And my body has a wish to make—
May carob and a spring of water come forth.

A black rooster beating its wings. Jerusalem.[95]

This enigmatic poem describes the speaker's experience of becoming bilingual in intensely visceral, corporeal terms, as a kind of violent invasion of the body. Its themes of alienation and bifurcation gush forth with unsettling force, but beneath its surface trickles a quiet stream of intertextual references that would elude even highly literate readers. On the linguistic level, the text contains several opaque if not baffling words and phrases. These include the repeated refrain of *ba ve-nishal mi-* (literally, "comes and is asked/borrowed of"; in 1 Samuel 20:6, "asks leave of"[96]), the word *ḥaluda'ot*, which does not exist in Modern Hebrew (and which I render "lesions of rust" or simply "rust"), and the poem's closing lines,

95 Shammas, "Dyokan," in Ya'oz, Beser, and Ya'oz-Kest, *Shira tse'ira*, 258–259.

96 The biblical verse in which David is addressing Jonathan reads, *im pakod yifkadeyni avikha ve-amarta nishol nishal mimeni David la-ruts beyt-leḥem 'iro ki zevaḥ ha-yamim sham le-khol ha-mishpaḥa.* JPS renders it, "If your father notes my absence, you say, 'David asked my permission to run down to his home town, Bethlehem, for the whole family has its annual sacrifice there'" (*Tanakh*, 617). In the King James Version it reads, "If thy father at all miss me, then say, David earnestly asked leave of me that he might run to Bethlehem his city: for there is a yearly sacrifice there for all the family."

with their enigmatic image of the black rooster and the mysterious, final, one-word sentence "Jerusalem."

The untranslatable word *ḥaluda'ot* and the reference to water and carob work in tandem to invoke the Talmudic story of Rabbi Shim'on bar Yoḥay, who, with his son Rabbi Ele'azar, hid in a cave for thirteen years to escape a Roman death decree. While in hiding, the pair devoted themselves to Torah study; when they ran out of food, a spring of water and a carob tree miraculously appeared to sustain them. Confined with his son for thirteen years, with no other human company or diversions (and nothing but carob to eat), Shim'on bar Yoḥay attained mystical knowledge of the hidden (as opposed to the revealed) Torah, which as tradition has it would form the basis for the *Zohar*—the foundational text of Kabbalah, the Jewish mystical tradition. Subtly, Shammas's poem evokes the atmosphere of a cave: the blue light, the language "seeping" (*meḥalḥelet*) and words "dripping" (*notfot*) like water, and even "dripstones" (the secondary meaning of the word *zkifim* in the construct *zkifey ḥoshekh*, "sentries" or "dripstones" of darkness).[97] Yet in the poem, this cave is inside the speaker's body; before us are only the speaker, the portrait, and the blue light.

Throughout the entire Jewish canon (from the Bible on), we find the word *ḥaluda'ot* only once, in a fairly obscure midrash dealing with the aforementioned story of the cave: "R. Simeon b. Yohai and R. Eleazar, his son . . . spent time hiding in a cave during the thirteen years of the [Roman] repression, until their flesh was covered with *haluda'ot*"[98]—surmised, from the context, to be sores or lesions. The midrash is written in a difficult Aramaic idiom, and the word *ḥaluda'ot* itself is not quite Hebrew.[99] To the poem's readers, the word sounds like a corruption of the Modern Hebrew *ḥaluda* (rust); most likely, the two terms share an etymology linked to the idea of corruption or decay.[100] The word *ḥaluda'ot* appears twice in Shammas's poem, both times in connection with the body. While in the

97 The cave is part of a shared mystical, philosophical, and literary tradition dating to the roots of Western humanism. *The Cave* is the title of *Surat al-kahf*, chapter 18 of the Qur'an, in which we find a parable about *ashab al-kahf*, the Companions of the Cave: a group of youths who seek refuge from religious oppression in a cave where Allah puts them into a centuries-long slumber. The parable is thought to be based on an apocryphal story of Christian youths in the time of the Emperor Decius. Other famous caves include the parable of the cave in Plato's *Symposium* as well the cave in *Don Quixote*. See Levy, "Nation, Village, Cave."

98 Midrash Esther Rabbah, Parashah Gimmel, translation by Neusner, *Esther Rabbah I*, 88.

99 It is a kind of Aramaic-Hebrew hybrid, as is common in the language of Talmud and Midrash.

100 In biblical Hebrew, the same triliteral root connotes earthly existence and mortality. From the same root, the biblical word *ḥeled* means "the world," "human existence" (*kol-yoshvey ḥeled*, "all the people of the world," Psalms 49:2), and, by derivation, the duration of life, such that the expression *yamey ḥeldi* (literally, "the days of my *ḥeled*") idiomatically means "my mortal days."

rabbinic intertext the *ḥaluda'ot* appear *on* the skin, here the sores are (like the cave itself) internal, contained *inside* the body.

The poem's first two lines read, "I stand here in the azure light / unwalled-loneliness around me, as a candle's flame." The phrase *bdidut-prazot svivi* (unwalled-loneliness around me) is a play on the biblical Hebrew term *'ir prazot*, denoting an unwalled (and hence vulnerable, unprotected) city; Shammas splits the idiom by replacing *'ir* (city) with *bdidut* (loneliness). Paradoxically, the speaker is surrounded by a barrier that affords him no protection. The simile *ke-shalhevet ha-ner*, "as a candle's flame,"[101] completes the sentence with a complex and beautiful analogy: the speaker stands in the azure light and is surrounded by his loneliness, like the blue inner part of a flame, which is surrounded (but unprotected) by the permeable outer border. The idea of penetration is central to the poem, which describes how the speaker's body is invaded by a foreign language. The phrase "not of my mother, and not in my blood" (*lo me-imi, ve-lo be-dami*) alludes to Uri Tsvi Greenberg's line "and the Hebrew tongue was not my mother tongue, but my blood tongue" (*u-sfat 'ever lo hayta sfat-imi, ela sfat dami*), but refutes it: for the speaker, Hebrew is neither.[102] Without the nourishing protection of his mother tongue, which has ceased to flow in his veins, the speaker is vulnerable to the violent possession of his body by another language; in possessing him, it is slowly breaking his body down. Earlier in this chapter, we saw Shammas compare himself to a meddlesome guest in the house of the Hebrew language. Meditating on this same guest-host relationship of language, the Moroccan literary critic Abdelfattah Kilito muses,

> I do not recall who said . . . that we are the guests of language. . . . Of course, during our residence in its realm, that is, throughout our lives, we assume the respectful manners required of guests toward their host. However, sometimes it seems to me that the speaker is the host and that language is the guest—a quarrelsome and stubborn guest who arrives uninvited and who takes possession of the host and inhabits him against his will. *We are inhabited, or haunted, by language as though by a supernatural force.*[103]

Shammas's poem seems to corroborate Kilito's view of the guest-host relationship between speaker and language more than his *own* view. Inverting the metaphor of linguistic possession discussed earlier in this

101 Literally, "as the flame of the candle."
102 Uri Tsvi Greenberg, *Ba-'emtsa ha-'olam*, 101–102. Elsewhere, Shammas has played on this line by calling Arabic his "blood tongue" and Hebrew his "stepmother tongue"; see note 64 above.
103 Kilito, *Thou Shalt Not Speak*, 86, my emphasis. Kilito is most likely referring to Derrida; for Derrida's thoughts on hospitality and language, see his *Monolingualism of the Other*, esp. 22–25, 57.

chapter, the question explored by his poem is not what it means to *possess* a language, but rather what it means to *be* possessed by one.[104] In a recent study, Wendy Belcher presents an alternative model of "discursive possession." Departing from the model that views language or culture as property, Belcher sees the author entering another culture as being taken over by an external "spirit" or force, becoming an "energumen"—a body through which others speak. This, she argues, offers a "useful paradigm of agency" for understanding transcultural intertextuality.[105] "Portrait" beautifully instantiates Belcher's theory by presenting a speaker who has been taken over, in this case against his will, by the language and discourse of the Other.

The poem depicts the problem of identity through the relation of the speaker to his portrait, an idea expressed both spatially and in terms of agency. The word *dyokan* (portrait), the poem's title, appears twice within the body of the poem. In the first instance, the speaker is still inside the portrait, saying he "grows in vain" *within* it; but two lines later, we find the portrait retreating ever further *away* from him, speaking to him in a "forgotten language." The speaker's traumatic confusion of self and other turns into physical paralysis: he stands rooted in place, and every action in the poem is enacted upon his helpless body. He does not speak; instead, it is his image in the portrait that speaks to him, in his original (now forgotten) language. Shammas's poetic vision of the fractured self reverses Lacan's mirror theory: here the portrait, in the role of the mirror image, *is* the real, primary, and original self, while the subject outside the mirror/portrait becomes its Other.[106] The portrait ultimately abandons its paralyzed and wordless subject. In a *mise en abyme*, the poem is a "portrait" of a portrait, with a kind of infinite regress in which the subject simply disappears. This eerie play on self and image recalls 'Araidi's "language of mirrors." Both poems suggest that in the experience of being a Palestinian writer of Hebrew, identity becomes not only unstable but un*real*: a reflection without a fixed or tangible source, an uncanny simulacrum of a subject.

It is hard to know what to make of the poem's cryptic final lines, which leave both speaker and portrait behind altogether, juxtaposing allusions to the cave story (the "carob and a spring of water") with the seemingly unrelated image of the black rooster and the final closing mention of Jerusalem. The rooster would make most Hebrew readers think of *kapporot*,

104 Hochberg suggests a similar inversion of the possession metaphor at the close of her chapter on *Arabesques*, where she writes, "[Language] cannot be possessed, but it can surely possess: it can possess one's childhood memories, secret love, and hidden dreams" (*In Spite of Partition*, 93).

105 Belcher, *Abyssinia's Samuel Johnson*, 8–9.

106 Lacan, "The Mirror Stage."

the ritual practiced by some Orthodox Jews before the Day of Atonement in which a live fowl is swung around the head as the devotee recites a prayer for expiation of sins, but in that ritual the rooster is white.[107] At the time of writing, Shammas lived in Jerusalem; perhaps the poem's ending weaves the realm of biographical experience into the realm of metaphor. (Intriguingly, the linkage between the rooster and the cave reappears in *Arabesques*, in which a legendary rooster known as al-Rasad guards the hidden entrance to a deep cave beneath the narrator's village.[108]) But as for the carob and spring of water, why would Shammas gravitate toward this obscure rabbinic intertext? Why would this poem, whose very subject is the pain of assimilating a foreign language and culture (which happen to be Hebrew), invoke a Jewish text par excellence, let alone one as obscure as the Aramaic midrash containing the word *ḥaluda'ot*? Israeli culture is suffused with references to the Hebrew Bible, which was construed as a "national" narrative imbued with a pre-Diasporic consciousness and used as a source text for the national-literary project. As explained in chapter 1, the Bible was recoded as the more "Hebrew" (i.e., "Caananite," "semitic") and less "Jewish" part of the canon. Rabbinic texts (Talmud and Midrash, written in a mishmash of Aramaic and rabbinic Hebrew) were seen as emblematic of an effete Diasporic ethos and consequently rejected by Israeli literature; Shammas's contemporaries have not usually tapped them as a resource for their poetry. Why, then, would Shammas? The deliberate manner in which Shammas interpolates rabbinic language into this poem hardly implies that literary Hebrew needs to be deflated from its intensive textual allusiveness, to become "thinner," to be brought closer to a spoken, truly secular idiom (à la the "un-Jewing" of Hebrew). While a more consistent use of rabbinic language might be read as a rejection of the Zionist territorialization of biblical Hebrew, throughout his Hebrew poetry (and prose) Shammas also draws upon the Bible, as we have seen above. His particular way of writing Hebrew neither shirks its Jewishness nor seeks it; his is an idiosyncratic relationship to the sources.

107 The prayer's words are, "This is my substitute, this is my exchange, this is my atonement. This fowl goes to death and I shall enter a long, happy and peaceful life." (Roosters are used for men and hens for women.) The chicken is then slaughtered and it (or its cash value) is given to the poor. In Christianity, the rooster represents Peter's denial of the Christ and subsequent repentance, but this connotation seems unrelated to the poem. It has also been suggested to me that the black rooster may be an apocalyptic image.

108 Shammas, *'Arabeskot*, 17, 174, 238. But whereas in the poem we have simply the intimation of a cave, in the novel the cave is brought into full relief. In the poem, the cave is a highly individual, even hermetic site of isolation and loneliness, of sores and pain; in the novel it is a locus of the villagers' collective memory and identity.

We find a strikingly different relationship between self and language in the poetic self-portraits of Salman Masalha. A scholar of classical Arabic literature and a translator, Masalha published five volumes of poetry in Arabic before producing a volume in Hebrew (reversing the trend set by Shammas and 'Araidi). His Hebrew collection, *Eḥad mi-kan* (literally, "one from here"; English title given as *In Place*)[109] appeared in 2004—three decades after the entry of Shammas and 'Araidi into the Hebrew literary arena. The collection's title is not trivial. In the same year (2004), Masalha described his relationship to Hebrew as an evolution from a foreign language imposed on him in school, to a perceived language of otherness as he developed a political consciousness, to a language that turned out to be "my own possession," defying the intentions of those who imposed it on him. "By means of the Hebrew language," he concludes, ". . . not only [do] I gain ownership, I also strengthen *my ownership of the place*."[110] Likewise, Masalha's poetic idiom approximates a stripped-down, layerless, and self-contained "Israeli" Hebrew. Yet Masalha's "simplicity" is highly deceptive; his poetic idiom is replete with ambiguities, double meanings, and elisions. Nor does he forgo the sources; instead, he weaves them into his poems with subtlety and understatement, and complements them with references (usually ironic) to Israeli popular culture. For instance, a poem deceptively titled "Balada 'aravit'" ("Arabic Ballad") turns out to be a singsong pastiche of phrases from classic Israeli popular songs,[111] interwoven with a nod or two to Arabic culture, such as *alfey leylot safar* (he counted one thousand nights).[112] Another poem, "'Al shlosha shkarim" ("On Three Lies"), about romantic love, parodies the famous Talmudic aphorism *'al shelosha devarim* (On three things), which identifies the three pillars of faith that support earthly existence.[113] In a love poem to a vanished and vanquished Baghdad, the phrase *'al-gadat libi yashva* (she sat on the banks of my heart) softly echoes Psalm 137, *'al naharot bavel sham yashavnu* (By the rivers of Babylon, there we sat);[114] but here, rather than the exiled Jew lamenting Jerusalem in Babylon, the speaker (in Jerusalem) remembers

109 The title idiomatically suggests "someone local," "one of us."

110 *Mi-safa le-safa*, cited in Shohamy, *Language Policy*, 167–169, her translation, my emphasis.

111 E.g., *bi-tokh 'atsmo hu-shar* (from "Adam bi-tokh 'atsmo" by Shalom Ḥanokh) and *sovev lo sovev* (from "Ha-finjan" by Ḥaim Ḥefer).

112 Masalha, *Eḥad mi-kan*, 17.

113 In full: *'al shelosha devarim ha-'olam 'omed: 'al ha-tora ve-'al ha-'avoda ve-'al gemilut ḥasidim* (The world rests [literally, stands] on three things: Torah, worship, and good deeds; *Pirkey Avot* 1:2). Masalha transforms it into *'al shlosha shkarim ha-ahava 'omedet* (Love rests on three lies). See Masalha, *Eḥad mi-kan*, 54.

114 *Tanakh*, 1584.

the lost Baghdad sitting upon the banks of his heart.[115] Another poem, "'Al ha-bri'a" ("On Creation") is a classic modern midrash, wryly rewriting the story of God's plan for the creation of humanity, while also incorporating liturgical language from the *sliḥot* (repentance) prayers of the Days of Awe (*hu raḥum, hu ḥanun, ve-raḥman*) and the Kaddish, the Jewish ritual prayer for the dead (*yit'ale, yithadar, yitromem*).[116]

At least four poems in Masalha's collection are "portraits" of different kinds. The first, "Oto-portret" ("Self-Portrait"), is a striking and imagistically lovely "self-portrait" of—to the reader's surprise—an elderly alcoholic.[117] The two poems that come closest to being genuine "self-portraits" are, of course, not titled as such (although both do contain the word "I" in the title). Printed side by side in the volume, their titles read "Ani meshorer 'aravi" ("I Am an Arab Poet") and "Ani kotev 'ivrit" ("I Write Hebrew").[118] The first poem serves as another rewriting of Darwish's aforementioned "Identity Card" (Masalha translated Darwish's *Memory for Forgetfulness* into Hebrew in 1989). While the poem never explicitly refers to Hebrew, this obvious elision cannot but draw our attention to the unspoken subtext (i.e., "I am an Arab poet who writes in *Hebrew*"), making the *absence* of the word "Hebrew" conspicuous and charged, and thus highly present in its absence. The presence of Hebrew is also asserted prosodically: the poem's regular rhythm is based on anapestic trimeter with a few deviations, and alternate lines rhyme (ABAB, CDCD).[119] Anapest is the natural spoken rhythm of Modern (Israeli) Hebrew, which shifted Hebrew's stress pattern from the penultimate to the ultimate syllable. As such, the poem becomes a prosodic thematization of the language itself, a representation *through* language of the missing word "Hebrew."[120]

I am an Arab poet
Who paints everything in black.

115 "Baghdad," dedicated to "'Abd al-Qadr al-Janabbi in Paris." The entire phrase reads *'al gadat libi yashva, / heshita kokhavim le-'ever ha-midbar* (Masalha, *Eḥad mi-kan*, 61).

116 Masalha, *Eḥad mi-kan*, 38–39. *El raḥum ve-ḥanun* is a reference to the thirteen measures of mercy found in Exodus 34:6-7, incorporated into the liturgy for the Days of Awe. In a double pun, the phrase appears in the *piyyut* as *El melekh yoshev 'al-kise raḥamim* (To God sitting on the throne of mercy), while Masalha's poem portrays God sitting on his throne planning how to create humanity. See also "Ze bishvil ha-tanakh" ("It's for the Bible"), where the speaker describes his practice of reading the Bible "backward" (Masalha, *Eḥad mi-kan*, 32).

117 Ibid., 9.

118 Both appeared first in the Israeli cultural journal *Ḥadarim* 12 (1996): 147–148, and were reprinted in Masalha, *Eḥad mi-kan*, 14–16.

119 Anapestic trimeter is two unstressed followed by one stressed syllable, three stressed syllables per foot. For instance, the first stanza reads, *a-ni* ***hu*** *me-sho-****rer*** *'a-ra-****vi*** */ she-tso-ve-'a ha-****kol*** *be-sha-****ḥor*** */ ef-****taḥ*** *et segor li-****bi*** */ la-'o-****lam*** *she-so-****vev*** *le-a-****ḥor***.

120 I thank Chana Kronfeld for this observation.

I will open the latch of my heart
To a world that is spinning back.

A poet composes his rhymes
About brother dwelling with brother.
In his artifice he went just too far—
His father be cursed, and his mother.

And the sun will rise in the east
Upon an earth that is captive to dust
Blisters will blossom on hands, and al-
so the village girls must.[121]

To cherish his dreams the child
Wanted well before his betrayal.
When he was born, he found his hand
Clutching the spoon of Sheol.[122]

I am an Arab poet,
The word will suffer it all.
Letters sprouted in my heart
My leg, a peg to dance at the ball.[123]

From its very first stanza ("paints everything in black"; "world . . . spinning back"), this poem is suffused with dark undertones. The poem's strong cadences and regular rhythm and rhyme foster a deceptive sense of simplicity or naïveté that it then shatters with its startling images and jarring language, so that a sustained tension between sound and imagery pervades the entire poem.

The second stanza, beginning with "a poet composes his rhymes / about brother dwelling with brother" (*meshorer yikhtov ḥaruzim / 'al shevet aḥ ve-aḥiv*) plays on the popular Hebrew folk song "Hiney ma tov u-ma na'im / shevet aḥim gam yaḥad" ("How Good and How Pleasant It Is / That Brothers Dwell Together"), itself drawn from verse 1 of Psalm 133.[124] The poem continues, "In his artifice he went just too far—/ his father be cursed, and his mother" (*ba-kazav hu me'at higzim / imo tekulal ve-aviv*). The Hebrew word *kazav* (fib or lie) is a cognate of the Arabic *kadhib* (lie), a term that in medieval Arabic poetics was at the center of a polemic about poetry's aesthetic value versus truth value. The same concept in medieval

121 The sentence is incomplete in the original.
122 Sheol: the underworld.
123 Masalha, *Eḥad mi-kan*, 14.
124 *Tanakh*, 1580. The King James version renders it, "Behold, how good and how pleasant [it is] for brethren to dwell together in unity!"

Hebrew poetics refers to poetic *form* as an artifice, as in the expression *meytav ha-shir kzavo*, "the best part of the poem is its *kazav* [lie]." Here Masalha is poking fun at his own overuse of the poetic form (with the strong anapest meter and regular rhyme scheme), while simultaneously alluding to the common poetic roots of Hebrew and Arabic versification. I translated *kazav* as "artifice" to convey the idea of poetry as deceit. But the specific poetic artifice for which the poet's parents will be cursed is the "lie" of brothers dwelling together—perhaps because, in the reality of Israel/Palestine, "brothers" on opposite sides of the solidus are more likely to shoot missiles at one another than to congregate in mellifluous harmony.

The idea of the false or phony returns in the poem's last and most enigmatic line, *ragli totevet le-maḥol*, literally "my leg is prosthetic to dance" or "my leg is prosthetic for danc[ing]." The line's syntax, which sounds just as bizarre in Hebrew as in translation, leaves the poem's ending open to interpretation. The adjective *totevet* (prosthetic) is syntactically employed here as though it were a verb (for instance, *ragli rokedet* would be "my leg is dancing," hence *ragli totevet* sounds to the Hebrew reader like "my leg is prostheticizing"). Read in context, in which the speaker declares himself an Arab poet—and especially given the preceding lines of the last stanza—the "prostheticizing" leg is the Hebrew language: an artificial limb, a borrowed or adopted body part that enables the speaker to "dance" the dance of Hebrew poetry. (This, perhaps, is the bilingual answer to Derrida's characterization of his anomalous "monolingulism" as "the prosthesis of origin"; more on this in chapter 6.)[125] Masalha's poem subtly equates the false leg with false language (the *kazav* or fib) and false "friends."

The connection between the dysfunctional or aberrant body and the speaker's experience of language echoes the coupling of body and language that threads through Shammas's poems. Similarly, in another poem-portrait, "Mazal 'akrav" ("Sign of Scorpio"), Masalha depicts his bilingualism as a snake's forked tongue (an idea that resonates curiously with Bhabha's personification of the discourse of English colonialism as one that "speaks in a tongue that is forked, not false"[126]):

> . . .
> And over the years I also learned
> to slough off my own skin.
> Like a snake that was caught
> between scissors and paper.

125 See Derrida, *The Monolingualism of the Other*.
126 Bhabha, *Location of Culture*, 85.

Thus my fate was sealed
in words cut from the roots
of pain. With a tongue forked
in two. One, Arabic—
to mother's memory entrust.[127] Second,
Hebrew—on a winter's night
to love.[128]

Here Masalha thematizes the experience of bilingualism. In the phrase "in words cut from the roots of pain" (*be-milim nigzarot mi-shorshey / ha-makh'ov*), the words *nigzar* (cut, as in cut from a pattern) and *shorashim* (roots) have a double meaning: in Hebrew, *shoresh* (root) is also a grammatical term for the triliteral root stem that forms the morphological basis of each lexeme. In this context, *nigzar* refers to the grammatical declension of words from the triliteral root. This line, then, plays with the technical language of Hebrew grammar, and in a sense, with the work of the poet: words are "declined" from the (linguistic) "roots" of pain or heartache. Yet at the same time it should also be read as a statement about Hebrew-Arabic bilingualism; Arabic, like Hebrew, is a root-based language. Indeed, the lines that follow explicitly metaphorize the speaker's bilingualism, suggesting that here Masalha is talking about writing in both Arabic *and* Hebrew, which are linked through their common origin in "the roots of pain." Finally, the word *nigzar* is derived from the same root as *gzeyra*, "sentence" or "decree" (usually in a negative sense), thereby echoing the previous line ("thus my fate was sealed").

"Ani kotev 'ivrit'" ("I Write Hebrew"), the second poem of the pair, offers a far more optimistic take on the experience of being an Arab poet in Hebrew. Here, by contrast, Hebrew forms not the poem's subtext, but its explicit subject. Moreover, while this poem also maps language onto the body, it does so in an entirely different manner:

I write in the Hebrew language,
that is not my mother tongue,
to get lost in the world.
Whoever doesn't get lost won't

127 *Zekher ima la-'arov* (literally, "to guarantee the memory of mother"): the verb *la-'arov* (to guarantee, be a guarantor for) is declined from the root *'a-r-v*, also the basis for "Arab," "Arabic," etc., thus punning on the shared root to emphasize the idea of Arabic as "mother tongue."

128 Masalha, *Eḥad mi-kan*, 12, translation adapted from Vivian Eden's. Of this poem, Hannan Hever writes, "In 'Sign of Scorpio,' a self-portrait, poetic diction grows like a bifurcated tongue in the presence of this profound awareness of disaster. . . . The writing of poetry is like the snake's reaction to the danger it encounters. . . . The snake sheds its skin—and the response is a tongue which is bifurcated like a snake's" (Hever, "Not My Mother Tongue.")

find the whole. Because everyone
has the same toes on their feet.
And the same big toe,
walking side by side with the heel.

And Hebrew, sometimes, I write
to cool the blood that streams without
pause from the heart. There are plenty
of chambers in the palace I built inside
my chest. And yet,[129] the colors
of the night that is spread on bare walls
are peeling off without knowing
what all this wonder is.

And I write Hebrew in order to lose
my way in my words. And also
to find a little interest
for my footsteps.
My strides are not over yet.
How many are the paths that I have furrowed.
Carved in my hands. I will yet carry
my legs in my hands
and will meet many
people. And make them all my friends.
Who is a stranger? Who is far and near?
There is nothing strange in the vanities of this world.
Because strangeness, for the most part,
is found in the heart.[130]

The poem connects the act of writing in Hebrew ("not my mother tongue") with two parts of the body: the heart and the feet. In the poem's first and third sections, Hebrew is a path that leads the speaker into new vistas; in the second section, writing in Hebrew leads us into the palace of the speaker's heart. This section plays on the idiom "chamber of the heart." In Hebrew, "chest" (the body part) is *beyt he-ḥaze*—literally, the "house of the chest"—so the speaker has built his "palace" within his own body-house: *ḥadarim yesh / be-shef'a ba-armon she-baniti be-tokh / beyt he-ḥaze* (There are plenty / of chambers in the palace I built inside / my chest).[131] Thus

129 The word *ulam*, which I have translated as "yet," also means "hall," so that the sentence could be rendered, "And a hall, the colors of the night . . ."; it is a play on words enhancing the stanza's architectural metaphor of the house and heart.

130 Masalha, *Eḥad mi-kan*, 15.

131 In a 2004 interview, Masalha expands on this metaphor, describing his sense of belonging as something "not contained within a set of delineated political borders." Rather, it is "an

Hebrew takes the speaker both outward, to paths leading to eagerly anticipated unknowns, and inward, to the palace-in-the-heart, itself located within the house-of-the-chest.[132] Writing in Hebrew, in other words, is a journey of both extroversion and introspection. Either way, the emphasis is on losing one's way. In Hannan Hever's reading, the "loss of orientation . . . is depicted in the poem as the only orientation possible in a world that is replete with violence."[133] At the same time, "I Write Hebrew" is a poem that insists on sameness rather than difference: everyone has the same feet, strangers are potential friends. In this aspect, it contrasts "I Am an Arab Poet," in which the poet's family is cursed because of the lies he composes about brotherly solidarity. It is also more optimistic than 'Araidi's apostrophe to Shammas, and quite the opposite extreme of Shammas's "Portrait" in which the speaker stands paralyzed, in total isolation, watching himself slowly ebb away. Read together, Masalha's two poems on writing in Hebrew express an ambivalent view of bilingualism as a condition in which one gains as much as one loses.

If Masalha writes Hebrew in order "to get lost in the world," 'Araidi writes Hebrew in order to create that world anew. 'Araidi's most recent iteration of the question, titled "'Al ha-she'ela madu'a ani kotev be-'ivrit" ("An Answer to the Question of Why I Write in Hebrew"), takes the form of a midrash on the creation story in Genesis:

In order to create the world anew
for things to be different, really
different, and to see that it is good.
. . .

And in order to write poems on an unwritten poem
and lamentations not on death, just on what
slipped away in the recreation, and not to create
man first, ladies always first.[134]

Kdey li-vro et ha-'olam me-ḥadash
she-yihyu ha-dvarim aḥeret, mamash
aḥeret, ve-lir'ot ki tov.

emotional sense of allegiance to certain landscapes and sensations, and to both Hebrew and Arabic languages. My heart is full of chambers—not just four or five like those described in anatomy books, but an entire palace in which each open door leads to a new discovery." He also discusses the creative process in terms of "getting lost" in the act of artistic creation as "part of the quest for an existential and poetic truth." See Halkin, "A Sense of Place."

132 The word *nigar*, from the verb *le-nager* (to pour or flow from), in the phrase *ha-dam she-nigar le-lo / heref min ha-lev*, shares the root of *nagar*, "carpenter," further extending the stanza's architectural metaphor (also in the double meaning of *ulam*; see note 129 above).

133 Hever, "Not My Mother Tongue," unsigned translation of text.

134 'Araidi, *Mash'ir et ha-ka'as*, 24.

. . .

U-khdey li-khtov shirim ʻal shir she-lo nikhtav
ve-kinot lo ʻal mavet, rak ʻal ha-haḥmatsa
shel ha-bri'a ha-ḥadasha ve-lo li-vro
et ha-gever rishon, tamid rishona ha-isha.

In other words, writing in Hebrew, the language of the Bible and of creation, enables the poet to assume the task of (re-)creator: to get it right this time, and see, as did God, that it is good (*ki tov*). Perhaps not coincidentally, many years earlier, ʻAraidi also evoked the creation story in his most cogent "self-portrait." His oeuvre contains numerous self-reflections on being the "intermittent Arabic-Hebrew Hebrew-Arabic poet," but the most striking of them (titled "Naʻim ʻAraidi") is also the briefest:

In all of these scores of poems
There is but only one small spark—
Your being
Alone.[135]

The phrase *heyotkha levad*, "your being alone," echoes God's words in Genesis 2:18, *lo tov heyot ha-adam levado* (It is not good that the man should be alone), whence the Lord decides to create woman. Here too, ʻAraidi inverts the original meaning of his biblical intertext: his solitude is perhaps the only grace that this poetic journey has afforded him.

ALLUSION AND ILLUSION: TRANSLATING CULTURAL DIFFERENCE

We have seen how, writing in Hebrew, the three Palestinian poets rework Jewish canonical intertexts as well as elements of Jewish ritual practice. In their poetic "self-portraits of the Other," allusion is double-edged, a means of describing the self and situating it in a world shared by the reader, but also of asserting their difference by inverting familiar cultural associations. Allusion is treated much like a magician's tool kit, producing a vision that is real and unreal, familiar and unfamiliar, assonant and dissonant. Allusion, in this way, quickly becomes linked to *illusion*: a self-portrait retreating from its subject, a self-portrait of someone else, a self-portrait about solitude in the language of the biblical story about the invention of partnership. Allusion, in other words, enables these writers to reveal the underbelly of a reality that is itself paradoxical, unstable, and rather unreal. It is the tool through which they rewrite the idea of Hebrew from an insider-outsider perspective. Although these poems are

135 ʻAraidi, *Ulay zo ahava*, 29.

written not just in the dictionary lexicon of Hebrew but in the Jewish Israeli reader's cultural and symbolic idiom, they express a reality overlapping only in part with that of the reader—one that may be unfolding in the same time and place (as Masalha cogently lets us understand, with his emphasis on the *kan* or "here" of his collection's title), but which also faces other experiences and memories, other associations of place. If the poetry of Shammas, 'Araidi, and Masalha does not empty the Hebrew language of its Jewishness, it *does* invert or transform its associations, translating the meaning of the source text—a process I have called Palestinian midrash.

My reading of Palestinian Israeli poetry has attempted to transpose the hermeneutic framework from a question of "which" ("which one," "either/or") to a question of "how": from a politics of *claiming* to an aesthetic of *being*. This means asking not "Israeli or Palestinian?," "Hebrew or Arabic?," "Israeli or Jewish?" but rather asking what it means to *be* in between "Palestinian-ness" and "Jewishness," or in between Hebrew and Arabic. It means asking *how* Palestinian authors remake Hebrew culture through the symbolic domains of both Jewishness and Palestinian-ness. The *in-between*, in short, is the space of the translation of difference. How do we find this fraught and yet productive crossing of experience expressed within the language of being?

By way of an answer, I leave the final word with Masalha, who (split-tongue in cheek) pens "A Final Answer to the Question: How Do You Define Yourself?":

> I was born to legs of dust,
> never sprouted roots.
> I grew up with the blue horizon.
> The place [*ha-makom*] my eyes fell upon
> was a homeland for everyone.
> Thus I learned to distinguish
> between sacred and profane [*ma-hu kodesh, ma-hu ḥol*].
> And so, if you will it, I will say:
> I am an Arab poet
> from before Islam spread its wings
> toward the desert.
>
> And I was a Jew, before Jesus
> went to float on the Sea of Galilee.
> And I was an Arab crucified in the sun
> on the date palm's watch. Nailed down
> to the voice calling out, that the wind
> had spun dizzy in the remnants of love.

. . .

And I was the cliff of rock, I was
the olive tree that stayed.
The whole land became a home,
and I, a stranger made.

And I was a Muslim in the land
of Jesus, and a Catholic in the desert.
Not that any of this changed anything
in my making my way toward ashes and dust, just
that I haven't forgotten that I was born
in the sands. And that I wandered
with the light, until I landed in the shadow
of the terrible tree of knowledge
and I tasted of its fruit.

And my sentence was decreed—exile,
with no return, like the waters that flowed
and never returned to the river.

Epilogue:
Idol worship is a marvel
in the poet's soul.
It has fire and water,
soil and also air.
But more than all of those,
it has poetry in there.[136]

136 Masalha, *Eḥad mi-kan*, 56–57.

Part 3

Afterlives of Language

CHAPTER 5

"Along Came the Knife of Hebrew and Cut Us in Two"

Language in Mizraḥi Fiction, 1964–2010

What is it to be authentic,
to run through the middle of Tel Aviv's streets
and shout in Moroccan Jewish Arabic:
"Ana min-el maghreb, ana min el-maghreb"
(I'm from the Atlas Mountains, I'm from the Atlas Mountains).

—EREZ BITTON[1]

Sometimes I wonder whether this unknown language is not
my favorite language. The first of my favorite languages.

—JACQUES DERRIDA[2]

Why write in a language you don't know? Or use the one you know to imagine another, "lost" language? Or reinvent your language, perhaps as a secret language no one else understands? In his *Monolingualism of the Other*, Jacques Derrida provocatively declares, "I only have one language; it is not mine." That language, his *only* language, is "the language of the other," one he sets out to define and redefine in conflicting terms of inhabitation and alienation.[3] Derrida traces his paradoxical experience of language and resulting disorder of identity to the anomalous historical situation of Algerian Jews, to whom French citizenship was granted, revoked, and restored. In his telling, Algerian Jews were "interdicted" from Arabic and Berber, from French, and finally ("or to begin with," he says) from Hebrew. This also cut them off from "Jewish memory," from the "history and language

1 Bitton, "Taktsir siḥa" ("Summary of a Conversation"), *Sefer ha-na'na'*, 64.
2 Derrida, *Monolingualism of the Other*, 40–41.
3 Ibid., 1, 25.

that one must presume to be their own, but which, at a certain point, no longer was."[4] As an ethnic minority within a colonized nation, Algerian Jews were doubly removed from the homology of language and identity at the core of modern nationalisms. In principle, their experience of language should be diametrically opposed to that of Hebrew-speaking Jews in Israel, who are the ethnic and linguistic majority in their own sovereign nation. How then could Israeli Hebrew be construed by *any* of its contemporary Jewish speakers as a language "not their own"?

For Mizraḥi Jews in Israel, many of them descendants of Arabic-speaking Jews, Modern (Israeli) Hebrew is no more the language of "Jewish memory" than is French for Derrida. Derrida's proclamation thus finds an ironic inversion in recent literature by young Mizraḥi writers, for whom his phrase "the history and language that one must presume to be their own, but which, at a certain point, no longer was" encapsulates their feelings about *Arabic*. Arabic, the language of the recent and almost-tangible Arab Jewish past, is a minefield of contradictions. It is at once intimate and forbidden, known and unknown, remembered and forgotten. It is consciously rejected, even disparaged, by some; nostalgically romanticized and at times "Orientalized" by others. Apart from the dwindling remnant who reached maturity in Arab countries, Jews no longer have access to Arabic in an unmediated, unselfconscious way. To speak it, or to speak of it, is to have a position on it.

As we shall see, however, the Mizraḥi relationship to language is not only a dyadic question of Hebrew versus Arabic, any more than *mizraḥiyut* (Mizraḥiness) is a simple question of Ashkenazim versus "Sephardim."[5] *Mizraḥiyut* encompasses highbrow *and* lowbrow culture, radical *and* reactionary politics, Arabic *and* Hebrew (and other languages). It has taken the form of secular cultural and political movements, a vibrant popular musical industry, and a significant place in the Israeli literary arena. *Mizraḥiyut* itself is a thoroughly hybridized cultural identity. From the start, as Ella Shohat explains, Zionism "obliged Arab Jews to redefine themselves in relation to new ideological polarities . . . out of the massive encounter that has taken place between Jews from such widely separated regions as the Maghreb and Yemen emerged a new overarching umbrella identity, what came to be called 'the Mizraḥim.'"[6] In the 1950s, a recent arrival

4 Ibid., 55.

5 For the editors of *Mizraḥim be-yisra'el* (Mizraḥim in Israel), Mizraḥi identity contains both a political-economic component and cultural characteristics. "Above all," they write, "Mizraḥiness [*mizraḥiyut*] is not defined in opposition to 'Ashkenaziness,'" but rather, incorporates it "through strategies of inclusion and exclusion, mimicry and assimilation" (17).

6 Shohat, "Invention of the Mizrahim," 13.

from Baghdad or Cairo could be a politicized Marxist, an urban professional who kept only major Jewish holidays, or a strictly observant rabbi. Regardless, all were typecast in Israeli society as "traditional" and "pre-modern," and most shared in the misery of the *ma'abarot* (transit camps), the squalid camps of tin shacks and tents where immigrants began their new lives. Decades later, controversy persists in Israel as to the reality of the "ethnic question." The dominant narrative proclaims it a thing of the past, remediated through Ashkenazi-Sephardi "intermarriage" and structural changes in Israeli society. Others passionately counter that economic, social, and cultural discriminations persist, pointing to the negligible numbers of Mizraḥim occupying leadership positions in all public spheres and the absence of Mizraḥim from national symbols such as bank notes and street names.[7] But regardless of where one stands on the "ethnic question," it is clear that the violence of the *kur ha-hitukh*—the so-called smelting pot of "absorption" into Israeli society, which affected *all* immigrants, among them Holocaust survivors—lives on in Mizraḥi collective memory. Some five decades on, Mizraḥi writers and artists continue to explode Israel's foundational mythologies, from immigration as an ideologically motivated "return" to Israeli Hebrew as a single, unifying language.

This final section of the book follows strategies of linguistic representation across fifty years of Mizraḥi literature. Mizraḥi authors reclaim the languages of the Arab Jewish past while also reappropriating "other Hebrews." Some explore the possibilities of "low"-register immigrant Hebrew while others utilize "high"-register liturgical Hebrew, and even biblical Aramaic; often their writing moves between registers and sociolects, exploiting the latent possibilities of code-mixing and code-switching. Other techniques of differentiation in Mizraḥi literature include creolization, in-text translation, translation in footnotes, and thematizations of language. Collectively, Mizraḥi writers use all these approaches to reimagine Israeli Hebrew and to cultivate a *poetics of otherness*, one that gives voice to the suppressed memories and experiences of Mizraḥi families both before and after immigration to Israel.

"Mizraḥi literature" is not an entirely transparent category within the broader construct called "Israeli literature."[8] Nor is it universally embraced; for example, Ronit Matalon, one of Israel's leading authors, resists labels such as "Mizraḥi writer" or even "woman writer," which

7 In August 2013, a four-part documentary, "True Face: The Ethnic Demon," by journalist Amnon Levy renewed the public debate. See Klein, "Who's Israel's Real Ethnic Demon?" and Rolef, "Think about It: The Ethnic Demon."

8 See Mishani, "Lama tsrikhim ha-mizraḥim la-ḥazor el ha-'ma'abara.'"

tend to influence and restrict reader reception.[9] In this chapter I treat "Mizraḥi literature" not as a fixed category defined exclusively by the authors' ethnic origins or subject matter (such as *sifrut ha-ma'abara* or "transit camp literature"),[10] but as an open-ended body of writing that places both Israeliness and the Hebrew language in a dialectical relationship with other places, other languages, and other memories drawn from the wider Mediterranean and Islamic worlds. *Memory* is not to be confused with *nostalgia*: the authors discussed here hardly present life in Egypt, Iraq, and Morocco through rose-tinted lenses, nor do they subscribe to the "lachrymose" narrative that afflicts much historiography of Jews in the Arab world.[11] Instead, the works in question use memory to probe the limits and meaning of Israeli identity while revisiting it from a transnational perspective, one that goes beyond the geographic and temporal boundaries of Israel.[12] Ultimately, I am less interested in determining whether a particular work ought to be labeled "Mizraḥi literature" or pondering the label's implications than in exploring the following questions: How does this dialectical relationship foment the rewriting of Hebrew as a Middle Eastern language, and how does it recreate Israeliness as an experience constituted *doubly* by the pre- and post-immigration moments, relived by first-, second-, and even third-generation writers?

With these questions in mind, I investigate how Mizraḥi writers spanning three generations have explored the multivalent and highly contingent meanings of Arabic and of Hebrew in their work. The present chapter examines literary negotiations of Arabic, *'ivrit tiknit*, and "immigrant Hebrew" in first- and second-generation fiction; chapter 6 examines "weird language"[13] in poetry, prose, and art by second- and third-generation Mizraḥim. My analysis dwells on particularly creative and innovative uses of language, but embeds them within an argument about linguistic strategies in Mizraḥi literature more broadly. This discussion

9 See Lee, "Lama eyn lanu soferet ba-mishbetset shel Amos Oz."

10 See Shimony, *'Al saf ha-ge'ula*. Shimony identifies *sifrut ha-ma'abara* as a "subgenre" of Israeli literature (10).

11 See Cohen, *Under Crescent and Cross*, chap. 1; and Beinin, *Dispersion of Egyptian Jewry*, 14–17.

12 In some ways this argument relates to Hever's "Lo banu mi-ha-yam." However, Hever is interested in Mizraḥi representations of the *process* of immigration and its implications for the construction of Mizraḥi subjectivity within Israeli literature and culture, as an intervention into the hegemonic discourse. Here I am emphasizing not the moment of *passage* to Israel but the entire experience of the pre-Israeli past, which Hever alludes to only very briefly: "All these are [writers] whose self-representation is 'Mizrahi,' and whose involvement in the field of Israeli literature and dialogue with it almost always include *their Mizrahi antecedents* and their encounters with the non-Mizrahi Israeli experience" ("Lo banu mi-ha-yam," 181; "We Have Not Arrived from the Sea," 32, my emphasis).

13 See Ch'ien, *Weird English*.

inevitably expands to include other regional languages as well as the European languages of the colonial past. Historically, Arabic and Hebrew interacted as part of a dynamic multilingual nexus that encompassed Jewish dialects of Arabic and Aramaic, which played specific, well-defined roles in Jewish life in the Arab world before becoming relegated to a shadowy existence in Israel. All these repressed languages, but especially Arabic, resurface in contemporary Hebrew literature by Mizraḥi authors. In addition, Mizraḥim are not the only Israeli authors to interrogate the idea of a single, unified Hebrew. For example, novelists Yossel Birstein and Yoel Hoffman deploy German and Yiddish within their Hebrew prose in ways that could be productively compared to uses of colloquial Arabic in Mizraḥi novels. This struggle over language, however, has been one of the central, defining features of Mizraḥi writing ever since its genesis in the 1960s. From the first generation's narratives of immigration through the poems and essays of the third generation, Mizraḥi literature has presented a persistent, ongoing dual challenge to the idea of "standard Hebrew" and the enforced separation of Hebrew from Arabic. Furthermore, we now find third-generation Mizraḥi writers consciously positioning their work in relation to first- and second-generation writers. This inter-referential gesture consolidates the idea of "Mizraḥi literature" as an eclectic, diffuse body of work with an identifiable history and internal trajectory distinct from the mainstream Israeli canon.

Though little known outside Israel, Mizraḥi literature is a part of the global body of postcolonial and minority writing. This type of writing is usually identified with "minor" literature written in "major" languages, such as the borderlands literature of Chicano authors, the French-Arabic bilingualisms of Abdelkebir Khatibi and Taher ben Jalloun, the creolized Englishes of Salman Rushdie, Amitav Ghosh, and Gabriel Okara, and the poetic iconoclasms of Paul Celan. The strategies of linguistic differentiation and multilingualism employed by such writers have been discussed extensively in studies of minor literature and minority writing, postcolonial literature, and world literature. What often eludes the scholarly conversation, on the other hand, is the productive collision of linguistic and literary strategies in the "lesser studied" (read: non-Western, non-metropolitan) languages, of which Hebrew is one.

In part, the emphasis on metropolitan languages can be traced to two vestiges of Eurocentrism: first, an aesthetic preference for modernism and postmodernism, both of which privilege interiority and shun overtly ideological narrative forms, over the social realism and allegorical forms that tend to be more prevalent in non-metropolitan literatures, and, second, the fact that relatively few leading critics on the international scene read non-European languages. Critics from Frederic Jameson to Gilles

Deleuze and Félix Guattari to Pascale Casanova all tread more or less the same theoretical terrain of the literary and linguistic strategies adopted by minority and (post)colonial writers. Indeed, questions of language choice as it relates to discursive authority, to identitarian matters, and to political determination form the central concern of both (post)colonial and minority literary theory. These theoretical discussions of language and literature tend to veer off descriptive pathways into proscriptive approaches that either recast language choice and linguistic strategies as an ethical prerogative or argue for the political efficacy of one strategy over another. Thus Deleuze and Guattari famously claim in their essay on Kafka that "[t]here is nothing that is major or revolutionary except the minor,"[14] by which they mean the minority writer's subversive appropriation of the dominant language—a conclusion reiterated (albeit with fewer theatrics) by Casanova throughout her book *The World Republic of Letters*, where she argues that "dominated" writers can forge an innovative aesthetics and achieve international recognition only by writing in a "great literary language."[15] This perspective is passionately refuted by the Kenyan writer and critic Ngũgĩ wa Thiong'o, who maintains that as part of a revolutionary auto-decolonization, African literature must be written in languages of African origin that are accessible to working-class readers and, moreover, that literature written in European languages cannot be considered "African literature."[16] Similarly, writing on Chicano discourse, Alfred Arteaga asserts that the only means for the bilingual colonized/minority writer to resist internal colonization and assert a voice is by mixing languages; he does not see this potential within the minor appropriation of the "major."[17]

In their influential book *The Empire Writes Back*, Ashcroft, Griffiths, and Tiffin endorse the "minor literature" viewpoint, arguing that "[t]he crucial function of language as a medium of power *demands that post-colonial writing define itself by seizing the language of the center* and re-placing it in a discourse fully adapted to a colonized place." In their analysis, this process takes the form of two distinct but complementary approaches, "abrogation" and "appropriation." Abrogation refuses the colonial center's "*illusory standard of normative or 'correct' usage*, and its assumption of a traditional and 'fixed' meaning." Appropriation, by contrast, reshapes the language for new uses, using it as a tool for expressing cultural experiences that distinguish it from the "site of colonial privilege."[18] However, in

14 Deleuze and Guattari, "What Is a Minor Literature?," 26.
15 Casanova, *World Republic of Letters*, 284, also throughout the book.
16 Thiong'o, "Language of African Literature."
17 Arteaga, "An Other Tongue."
18 Ashcroft, Griffiths, and Tiffin, *Empire Writes Back*, 37–38, my emphases.

their view, abrogation alone is ineffective and possibly even detrimental as it lends itself to "culturally determinist" views of language that essentialize authenticity (here, their stance becomes diametrically opposed to Ngũgĩ's).[19]

They further identity three distinct types of postcolonial linguistic groups: "monoglossic" societies in settled colonies, "diglossic" societies characterized by bilingualism or multilingualism, and "polyglossic" communities in which "a multitude of dialects interweave," as in the Caribbean.[20] This last case, which the authors dub "the Creole continuum," exemplifies the combination of abrogation and appropriation, often carried out through "highly developed strategies of code-switching and vernacular transcription" as writers move back and forth along the spectrum of the linguistic culture.[21] Their argument runs into trouble when, in a reading of Okara, they imply that creolized language can operate as a kind of neutral space in which "the creative potential of intersecting languages" operates without regard to the relative distance of each language from the center of power.[22] However, their description of the "illusory standard of . . . 'correct' usage" and their theorization of a "continuum" of modes of speaking both prove directly relevant to Mizraḥi writing.

Indeed, while theorized in relation to postcolonial discourse, the "Creole continuum" is adaptable to any heteroglossic and/or polyglossic minority discourse responding to the social dynamics of language as power. For example, Casanova discusses literary uses of oral languages (including accents, regional idioms, and creoles) as a means of linguistic differentiation ("dissimilation") in a variety of North and South American contexts.[23] Joshua Miller notes that "[a]mong the linguistic trends that emerged in nineteenth-century African-American cultures were Frederick Douglassian rhetorical mastery of acrolects, *stigmatized and resistant vernacular Englishes containing resonances of lost African languages*, and *tactical withdrawals into silence* or non-English languages"—two strategies with strikingly close parallels in Mizraḥi writing, especially of the second

19 Ibid., 41–43.
20 Ibid., 38–89.
21 Ibid., 45.
22 Ibid., 42.
23 Casanova, *World Republic of Letters*, 282–302. She also identifies a "continuum" of linguistic strategies and approaches but questionably casts these as "uncertain and difficult, sometimes tragic, responses to their [the writers'] predicament." Apart from their tone, her observations are germane to my own purposes in this chapter. She further writes, "In the absence of an alternative language, writers are forced to devise a new idiom within their own language; subverting established usages and the rules of grammatical and literary correctness, they affirm the specificity of a popular language" (ibid., 282), and similarly, "The *littérarisation* of the oral language makes it possible not only to manifest a distinctive identity but also to challenge the standards of literary and linguistic correctness" (ibid., 293).

and third generations.[24] In *Weird English*, Evelyn Nien-Ming Ch'ien investigates the "barely intelligible and sometimes unrecognizable English" created through processes of hybridization in minority and postcolonial writing.[25] Tying these various arguments together, I suggest that in "minor" appropriations of "major" or official languages, the breaking point between co-optation and subversion is where literature begins to lose its comprehensibility to the mainstream reader through "weirding" or resistant non-translation.[26] The "weirding" of language, however, presumes the prior existence of a linguistic "norm"—which, in the case of Hebrew, is a complex historical problem.

'IVRIT TIKNIT, *'IVRIT 'ILEGET*, AND ARABIC: AUTHORIZING LANGUAGE

Throughout its history, Hebrew was a highly porous, richly multilayered language brimming with lexical, orthographical, and grammatical variation. As discussed earlier, its modernization and standardization were ideological processes driven by nationalism. Zionist Hebrew developed as a secularized Jewish language while suppressing the memory of the Jewish linguistic past. This entailed a thinning of the language, which was largely purged of rabbinic Hebrew and Aramaic elements, as well as the introduction of structural changes replicating Indo-European languages. In *After Jews and Arabs*, Ammiel Alcalay points to the linkage between the erasure of Arabic and the imposition of this secularized and Europeanized Hebrew on newly arrived Arab Jews:

> There can be little doubt that the most shortsighted and devastating effect of the socialization process undergone by the Arab Jews following their mass exodus was "de-Arabization." This was most acutely felt in the loss of Arabic as a native tongue, forced as the new immigrants were to conform to the non-Semitic structure, syntax, and pronunciation of "new Hebrew." The repulsion for things Arabic projected by the prevailing ideology was thus *inscribed phonetically within the very deepest recesses of the personal psyche, within language itself.*[27]

The far-reaching effects of this rupture with the "old" Hebrew are also eloquently revisited by Dror Mishani and Almog Behar. For Mishani,

24 Miller, *Accented America*, 192, my emphasis.
25 Ch'ien, *Weird English*, 3–4.
26 I adapt this phrase from Ch'ien; see chapter 6, note 22 below.
27 Alcalay, *After Jews and Arabs*, 51, my emphasis.

> Hebrew was never completely "white," and Jews from Arab countries and North Africa read Hebrew, prayed in Hebrew, and wrote poems of love and longing in Hebrew.
>
> But when those Jews came to Israel, they also came to a Hebrew that was already different: a Hebrew that had been renewed in Warsaw and in Tel Aviv, in Jerusalem and Odessa, in Rishon le-Tsiyon and in Berlin; a Hebrew that was crystalized in literary journals and in the institutions of the Zionist leadership. The Hebrew of Bialik and of Brenner, but also of Berl Katznelson and David Ben-Gurion.
>
> A different Hebrew [*'ivrit aḥeret*]: A Hebrew that had parted ways from the language of the Talmud and the Mishna, and that had fashioned for itself grammatical rules and paradigms, a Hebrew that already had a standard, a norm. A Hebrew that from this point onward was the pillage and the property of the European Zionist movement, well before it also conquered the land for itself.[28]

As Mishani indicates, the Mizraḥi relationship to language in Israel is deeply complicated by Modern Hebrew's ambivalent relations with the theological dimensions of Hebrew. Modern Hebrew was created, to paraphrase Bakhtin, as a centralized, unitary language accompanied by ideological unification.[29] Moreover, it was cultivated with an emphatically secular and masculine disposition. The pressure to conform both to lexical or grammatical changes and to the new ideological outlook had profound psychological implications not only for Mizraḥim, but for all Hebrew writers who did not fit the dominant mold of the "new" Hebrew subject.

Behar emphasizes that when one takes the long view of Hebrew's history, it is the "standard," rule-driven Hebrew that is in fact the aberration:

> The majority of Hebrew writing was historically "other," because Hebrew never had a uniform, standard version. But in Zionist [Modern] Hebrew, which became the quotidian spoken language for millions of people, a quintessentially modernist experiment was undertaken to create a system of rules that would create a normative center for the language (which in turn would define its margins). And even though almost no meaningful literary work was written in this standard of

28 Dror Mishani, "Ha-mizraḥi ke-hafra'a leshonit" ("The Mizraḥi as a Linguistic Disturbance"), 86–87. As the essay's title suggests, Mishani reads Mizraḥi subjectivity as largely in relation to language, and the performance of *mizraḥiyut* as a "disruption" in the presumed "norms" of *'ivrit tiknit*.

29 Bakhtin, "Discourse in the Novel," 270–271.

"non-other" Hebrew, an obsession with modern, "scientific," dictionary Hebrew sprang up in the new Israeli culture.[30]

The obsession with "dictionary Hebrew" and its rules became far more than a linguistic matter. In Israel, mastery of Hebrew is the badge of admission into the national community. Sociologist Dan Lefkowitz situates Israeli discussions of language between two poles: *'ivrit tiknit* and *'ivrit 'ileget*. Whereas *'ivrit tiknit* is the "correct," "proper," "standard" Hebrew of the establishment, *'ivrit 'ileget* literally means "stammering" or "inarticulate" Hebrew; idiomatically, it is "broken" Hebrew, that of immigrants, the uneducated, the underclass.[31] To adopt Pierre Bourdieu's economic metaphors, in the Israeli linguistic market, *'ivrit tiknit* enjoys high social capital and prestige, while all forms of colloquial or "nonstandard" Hebrew are devalued.[32] Consecrated by the educational system and media, but actualized fully only in official news broadcasts and in print, *'ivrit tiknit* is virtually a moral calling: to speak "correct Hebrew" is to fulfill a civil or patriotic duty. This ideal emanated from the same center of authority that repressed the lingering presence of Diasporic languages and relegated Mizraḥim to the societal margins. Building on Ferdinand de Saussure's concepts of *langue* and *parole*, Bourdieu theorized the reciprocal, mutually reinforcing relationship between "official" language and political authority in the context of the nation.[33] When Bourdieu writes that "the legitimate language is a semi-artificial language which has to be sustained by a permanent effort of correction, a task which falls both to institutions . . . and to individual speakers,"[34] he may as well be referring directly to the Mizraḥi characters of Sara Shilo's 2005 novel *Shum gamadim lo yavo'u* (*No Elves Are Coming*), who reminisce, "They brought us all here as new immigrants. Mixed us a bit and poured us onto the baking sheet. We hadn't even cooled off from the oven, along came the knife of Hebrew and cut us in two pieces: one that corrects how we speak, and one that gets corrected."[35]

Adding to the polysemy of "Mizraḥi" and "Hebrew," "Arabic" and "generation" are multivalent terms. Depending on the context, "Arabic" may

30 Behar, "Ba'a ha-sakin shel ha-'ivrit."

31 For Lefkowitz, *'ivrit tiknit* "refers to the rules established—and constantly updated, revised, and revisited—by the Israeli language academy for official Hebrew." Although Israelis "honor the academy's rules most by their breach, the idea that a correct form exists is widely accepted" (*Words and Stones*, 137).

32 Bourdieu, *Language and Symbolic Power*, 60.

33 Ibid., 48, 45.

34 Ibid., 60. He also notes that "correct language . . . acquires force of law in and through the educational system" (ibid., 49).

35 Shilo, *Shum gamadim*, 43, translation adapted from *Falafel King*, 33.

connote classical Arabic (*fusha*), colloquial dialects, or Judeo-Arabic, a form of written Arabic in Hebrew characters.[36] As for "generation," I employ the term loosely, as a means of understanding patterns in Mizraḥi writing vis-à-vis authors' relationships to Hebrew (and corresponding distance from Arabic) rather than their age or place of birth. While not intended as a perfectly neat or categorical distinction, my generational schema lends conceptual coherence to the diachronic analysis of Mizraḥi literature. "First-generation" writers are native speakers of Arabic who arrived in Israel as adolescents and young adults. For them, Arabic filled multiple functions as a literary language (especially in the case of Iraqi Jews), as the public language of quotidian experience, and as the private language of family. Influences from their formal Arabic education as well as Arabic popular culture inform their work. "Second-generation" writers are those who were educated in Israel, are native speakers of Hebrew, and usually know some colloquial Arabic, but are cut off from literary Arabic. Their experience of spoken language is bifurcated between Hebrew as a public language and Arabic as the intimate language of the home. The "third generation" includes functionally monolingual Hebrew speakers; their knowledge of Arabic, if any, is fragmentary. Often, school instruction or military service has served as their main source of exposure to the language.

Although writers' relationships to language are always individuated and idiosyncratic, in broad strokes, linguistic strategies in Mizraḥi literature can be mapped onto the experience of immigration and its aftermath. Over the course of these three generations, in tandem with the growing temporal distance from the lived experience of Arabic, the role of Arabic in Mizraḥi writing evolved from a *language of presence* into a *language of absence*. From an "instrumental" language deployed in Hebrew through transliteration and translation, it was gradually transformed into a "symbolic" language: one written *about* but not actually *used*. In this symbolic mode, realized by third-generation Mizraḥi writers, Arabic doubles as a metaphor for the fragmentation of identity and the loss of origins.

LITERARY TRANSPOSITIONS: WRITING ARABIC FICTION IN HEBREW

The literary encounter of Modern Hebrew and Arabic began with a small group of Palestinian Jews, native speakers of Arabic who wrote Hebrew fiction in the late 1920s and 1930s. The novels and stories of Yitzḥak Shami, Yehuda Burla, and Shoshana Shababo provide a fascinating account of Arabic-Hebrew interculturality in the decades before statehood; some

36 Throughout this book, I use "Judeo-Arabic" to refer to the traditional written language of Arabic-speaking Jews as opposed to Jewish dialects of colloquial Arabic. See chapter 1, note 77.

of their work reads like Arabic fiction written in Hebrew, in which Arabic stylistic and linguistic conventions are given a Hebrew polish. Yet as these writers predated the existence of the state, they also predated the "invention of the Mizraḥim," and so I consider them precursors rather than exemplars of "Mizraḥi" literature. The representation of Mizraḥi voices in Israeli literature began primarily with the work of recent immigrants from Iraq. Contemporaries Shimon Ballas (b. 1930) and Sami Michael (b. 1926) began publishing Hebrew-language fiction in the 1960s and early 1970s; they were joined later by Eli Amir (b. 1937), whose first novel appeared in 1983.[37] All are native speakers of Arabic who were educated in Baghdad, which in the 1940s was a quickly modernizing, urban milieu. Other important first-generation Mizraḥi writers who began publishing in the late 1970s or early 1980s include Syrian-born Amnon Shamosh (b. 1929), Egyptian-born Yitzḥak Gormezano Goren (b. 1941), founder of the theater company Bimat Kedem and author of three novels, and Jerusalem-born Dan-Benaya Seri (b. 1935), whose sophisticated first novel *'Ugiyot ha-melaḥ shel savta Sultana* (*Grandmother Sultana's Salty Biscuits*, 1980) remains a major landmark in the development of Mizraḥi fiction.[38]

Given the convergence of their backgrounds, Ballas, Michael, and Amir present a unique opportunity for comparing linguistic strategies in Hebrew writing by first-generation Mizraḥim.[39] All three were born to families in Baghdad's emerging professional middle class; all attended secular Jewish educational institutions, where their formative reading experiences were in Arabic and European languages. Likewise, all three were drawn from a young age to Arabic literature and to political ideologies (communism in the case of Michael and Ballas, Zionism in the case of Amir).[40] In Israel, the three writers published multiple novels on themes of Iraqi immigrants (beginning with novels about the transit camp), as well as on Jewish life in Baghdad before the mass emigration of

37 They were joined also by Shalom Darwish (b. 1912) who had established himself as an Arabic writer in Iraq in the 1930s and 1940s and who produced one novella in Hebrew in 1986. For more on Darwish, see Berg, *Exile from Exile*, 36–37.

38 Shamosh has been publishing fiction since the late 1970s. Gormezano Goren's works include four novels, *Kayits aleksandroni* (1978); *Blansh* (1986); *Miklat be-bavli* (1998); and *Ba-derekh la-itztadyon* (2003). On Gormezano Goren, see Alcalay, *Keys to the Garden*, 161–167; and Starr, *Remembering Cosmopolitan Egypt*, chap. 7, 122–133. Seri is the author of seven novels; see Alcalay, *Keys to the Garden*, 141. Unlike most other first-generation Mizraḥi writers, he was born in Palestine.

39 For a comparison of the thematics of these three writers' respective first novels, see Berg, *Exile from Exile*, 71–105.

40 This is a profile shared by a number of other figures who became active as poets, novelists, or scholars of Arabic literature in Israel, such as Sasson Somekh and the late David Tsemaḥ (not to be confused with the subject of chap. 2). For more on this type of personal and educational profile, see Somekh, *Baghdad, Yesterday*.

1950–1951.[41] Moreover, Michael and Ballas set some of their novels in post-1951 Baghdad, imagining life in the city decades after their own departures. In novels portraying Jewish and Muslim exiles in Paris, Jewish public figures in Ba'athist Iraq, or contemporary Iraqi society under Saddam Hussein, Michael and Ballas attempt to draw the Israeli reader into even more foreign and challenging cultural terrain.[42]

As young writers in Israel, the first question they faced was that of language choice. Michael and Ballas had begun publishing in Arabic in Iraq; after immigrating to Israel, both continued publishing in Arabic, primarily in journals associated with the Israeli Communist Party. However, within a few years, both concluded that it was necessary to learn Hebrew in order to reach the Israeli audience.[43] Ballas, who arrived in Israel at age twenty-one, wrote his first draft of his novel *Ha-ma'abara* (*The Transit Camp*) in Arabic, but then started over in Hebrew; it appeared in 1964.[44] Michael describes the process of changing his language from Arabic to Hebrew as "more difficult than changing one's sex."[45] His first novel, *Shavim ve-shavim yoter* (*Some Are More Equal Than Others*) appeared a full decade after Ballas's first novel—over two decades after Michael's arrival in Israel.[46] The slightly younger Amir, who was twelve when he immigrated to Israel, has published in Hebrew only. As such, he provides a direct counterpoint to Samir Naqqash (discussed in chapter 3), who, although he arrived in Israel at the same age as Amir, chose to write exclusively in Arabic.[47]

Both Michael and Ballas explain their decision to write in Hebrew as a matter of exigency, but insist that their Hebrew writing does not conform to the cultural expectations and norms developed by their Ashkenazi

41 See Berg, *Exile from Exile*; idem, *More and More Equal*; and Shimony, *'Al saf ha-ge'ula.*

42 See, for example, Ballas, *Ve-hu aḥer* (in English, *Outcast*) and Ballas's *Ḥoref aḥaron* on Jewish and Arab exiles in Paris (see Alcalay, *After Jews and Arabs*, 241). See also Michael, *'A'ida* on a Jewish television personality living in Baghdad under Saddam Hussein who offers shelter to a mute Kurdish woman.

43 See Berg, *Exile from Exile*, 56–59, and Berg, *More and More Equal*, 46–47. The issue was debated by Michael, Ballas, and other recent Iraqi Jewish immigrants in their club, Friends of Progressive Arabic Literature. As Berg writes, the proceedings of the meeting in question were summarized in the Israeli Communist Party's cultural supplement, *al-Jadid* (Berg, *Exile from Exile*, 57); see *al-Jadid* 3:1 (November 1954).

44 On his writing the first draft in Arabic, see Berg, *Exile from Exile*, 71; and Snir, "Ma'agalim niḥtakhim," 184, 202.

45 Berg, *More and More Equal*, 47.

46 Reuven Snir discusses the origins of *Some Are More Equal Than Others* in an Arabic story Michael published in *al-Jadid* under the name Samir Murad in 1954; see Snir, "Ma'agalim niḥtakhim," 179–182.

47 These questions are explored by Berg in *Exile from Exile*, especially chap. 4.

predecessors. Ballas also states that his work attempts to bring Hebrew closer to Arabic;[48] even after switching over to Hebrew, Ballas says he still feels that he "belongs to Arabic culture."[49] However, in the works of both writers, Hebrew is employed as a transparent literary medium that does not call attention to itself on either a linguistic or thematic level. As members of a generation that had to struggle simply to acquire the language and produce in it, they did not have the luxury of manipulating or deconstructing Hebrew. As a result, while their Hebrew prose is serviceable and correct, it is enlivened primarily by the presence of colloquial Arabic sprinkled in the dialogue. Some critics have noted the contrast between the flatness of Michael's formal Hebrew narrating prose and the richness of his mimetic language in the reported speech of characters, particularly when representing Arabic dialogue in Hebrew translation.[50]

As a minority discourse in Israel, Mizraḥi literature was inaugurated by Ballas's *The Transit Camp*. This novel was radical not in its use of language or its aesthetics but in its content and ideology. As Batya Shimony notes, the book was the first novel about new immigrants in Israel actually written *by* a recent immigrant. Invoking Bakhtin, she reads *The Transit Camp* as a "dialogical, parodic" response to an earlier novel representing the establishment's perspective on immigration.[51] In a similar vein, Hannan Hever associates Ballas's narrative strategies with Homi Bhabha's theories of mimicry.[52]

The novel depicts recent immigrants from Iraq who are assigned to a fictional transit camp called "Oriya."[53] Following the preventable death of a newborn infant, a number of youths attempt to organize the camp's residents to state their demands before the authorities. Their efforts to organize are repeatedly thwarted by the establishment, whose tactics include sabotage and incitement. Nearing its conclusion, the novel describes a violent clash with police who are trying to forcibly remove "unau-

48 Interview with Shimon Ballas in Alcalay, *Keys to the Garden*, 66.

49 *Maariv*, April 25, 1989, 9B, quoted in Snir, "Maʿagalim niḥtakhim," 184.

50 Berg, *More and More Equal*, 142.

51 The other novel is Bartov, *Shesh knafayim le-eḥad*; see Shimony, *'Al saf ha-ge'ula*, 50. In theorizing linguistic stratification in the novel, Bakhtin describes a parodic heteroglossia "aimed sharply and polemically" against "official languages" ("Discourse in the Novel," 271–272). More on this will follow.

52 Hever, *Producing the Modern Hebrew Canon*, 166, 168; on mimicry, see Bhabha, "Of Mimicry and Man." Alcalay reads Ballas's novel as a "resistance narrative" (*After Jews and Arabs*, 239). See also Berg's reading of the novel in *Exile from Exile*, 76–78; Berg focuses on the parallel between adolescence as a transitional state and the transit camp as a transitional space, both as metaphors for the liminal quality of exile.

53 The name probably alludes to Or Yehuda, a transit camp on the southwest outskirts of Tel Aviv populated mainly by Iraqi Jews.

thorized" residents from the camp. At the novel's end, the frustrated organizers, their efforts having led to naught, sit in a café full of hashish smoke, conducting a meaningless conversation.[54] As Hever writes, not only does the circular plot structure return the reader to the narrative's point of origin—the problem of life in the transit camp—but the protagonists' struggles also "fail to bring about the constitution of a clear new identity" for the immigrants in Israel.[55]

Shimony cogently discusses the role of language in conveying ideological perspectives in transit camp fiction, arguing that Ballas attempts to forge the basis of an alternative cultural identity by interpolating Arabic words and expressions into the characters' speech.[56] Shimony also observes, however, that this correlation between language and ideology is not maintained consistently throughout all transit camp literature. For example, Michael's *Some Are More Equal Than Others* initially reads as a complete repudiation of the Zionist narrative. Yet Michael uses Hebrew as the dominant language of the text not only in the narration but also in conversations between characters; as opposed to other "transit camp" novels, here Arabic appears only to a minor degree.[57] In short, in their early novels set in Israel, Michael and Ballas use Arabic—albeit in somewhat different ways—to depict the experience of immigration, the characters' alienation from their surroundings, and the Arab cultural and linguistic identity of the recent immigrants from Iraq. These observations are also pertinent to Eli Amir's first novel, the bildungsroman *Tarnigol kaporot* (*Scapegoat*), which has been adapted for use in the Israeli educational system. In their later narratives set in Iraq, by contrast, both Hebrew and Arabic must be used to convey a holistic Arabic-language world, posing a different set of challenges.

54 See also Shimony, *'Al saf ha-ge'ula*, 60–61.

55 Hever, *Producing the Modern Hebrew Canon*, 166.

56 Shimony, *'Al saf ha-ge'ula*, 27–28. Nancy Berg notes that *The Transit Camp* opens with the Arabic words *maqha al-nasr li-sahbihi Shlomo Khamra* (Café Victory—Shlomo Khamra, Proprietor), translated into Hebrew in a footnote; she adds that the original version of the novel contained entire Arabic poems with Hebrew translations, "but these were omitted by the editor as unacceptable to the Hebrew reader" (*Exile from Exile*, 60). See also Hever, "Lo banu mi-ha-yam," 45.

57 Berg states that Arabic influence permeates his writing in the novel through the prenominal "Umm" and "Abu," formulaic greetings and exclamations, and Hebrew replications of common Arabic idioms (*More and More Equal*, 50–51). Berg also notes that in later novels, Michael uses language differently. In his 1977 novel *Ḥasut* (Refuge), which depicts Jewish and Palestinian communists in Israel, the texture of the Hebrew "manages to convey the difference between the Hebrew of the Jewish characters and the Arabic of the Arab characters" (ibid., 51). See also *Exile from Exile*, 60–61, for a brief analysis of the Arabic used in other novels by Michael and Ballas.

BAGHDAD, REMEMBERED

Ballas's exquisite novella "Iya" (1992) takes up intertwined issues of language, space, identity, and community to offer a poignant meditation upon questions of belonging.[58] This semi-autobiographical story portrays a Baghdadi Jewish family on the eve of its departure for Israel, but—in an unusual twist—as witnessed by a Muslim character. The story unfurls from the perspective of Zakiyya (affectionately known as "Iya"), the family's longtime nanny and housekeeper, who lives in their home. The narrative frame occupies a single day, following Zakiyya's consciousness as it zigzags between flashbacks to her past history, her present thoughts and conversations, and her anxieties about her future without her Jewish family. In weaving the narrative around a Muslim woman who has created her home in a Jewish space, Ballas reverses the dominant paradigm of Jews living as minorities in a larger Muslim space, a paradigm that, implicitly or explicitly, informs virtually all works about Jews in Muslim lands. This move allows us to view the Jewish family with sympathy but also with an unusual degree of detachment, and to understand the tragedy of the mass emigration of Baghdad's Jews not only from the point of view of those leaving but also from the standpoint of those left behind.

Zakiyya moves between Jewish and Muslim space on a daily basis, speaking the Jewish dialect at home and with members of the family's community, and reverting back to Muslim dialect when visiting with her blood relations. Occasionally these border crossings betray her: "And when, in conversations with Naima, she was caught using words and phrases in a Jewish accent, she would laugh contentedly. 'You are more Jewish than Muslim,' Muhyi would chide her jokingly. Yes, more Jewish than Muslim and a Muslim among Jews."[59] The novel's ending perfectly captures the story's intercultural character. On the eve of departure, Ephraim (modeled on Ballas)—a young communist, the baby of the family, and the favored child of Zakiyya—hastily disposes of his books and papers, and Zakiyya absorbs the shock of her impending separation from the family. As she sits in the dim kitchen in a stupor, Ephraim appears from the shadows to give her his Qur'an.[60] The significance of Ephraim, the communist and

58 For a more extensive reading of the story and discussion of ethnic dialogues in Baghdad, see Levy, "Self and the City"; see also Snir, "Ma'agalim niḥtakhim." Snir reads the novella insightfully in the context of the full collection, whose other stories describe Jewish and Arab protagonists in Paris and Tel Aviv.

59 Ballas, "Iya," in *Otot stav*, 38–39; and "Iya," in *Keys to the Garden*, 91, Einbinder's translation. Such references to Jewish, Muslim, and Christian dialects are made frequently throughout the novels of Ballas, Michael, Amir, and Naqqash set in Iraq. See also Berg, *Exile from Exile*, 144.

60 Ballas, "Iya," in *Otot stav*, 49–50.

the Jew, giving Zakiyya his Qur'an as a parting gift cannot be overstated. If Zakiyya, the Muslim housemaid, speaks the Jewish dialect like a member of the community, then Ephraim, the budding intellectual, speaks the cultural dialect of his native country, acculturated as he is into a society where the Qur'an is not just a scriptural text but a cultural and linguistic cornerstone. But in giving her his Qur'an, Ephraim seems to be reinforcing the newly prescriptive boundaries of identity, divesting himself of all that is represented by this symbolic text while signaling to Zakiyya that she must carry on with her life as a Muslim in Muslim society and divorce her identity from that of the Jewish family.

Yet surprisingly, all this subtle cultural intimation is achieved with a minimum of Arabic. Aside from Arabic names and a tiny handful of Arabic words (*'arak, walla*) or translated expressions (*elohim gadol*—God is great; *elohim yiten lo bri'ut*—God grant him health),[61] both the narration and dialogue are written in a smooth, uniform Hebrew. There is more Arabic in *The Transit Camp*, which is set in Israel, than in "Iya," set in Baghdad. In "Iya," Ballas's linguistic strategy is one of *cultural* translation, of writing an Arabic world in Hebrew rather than representing Arabic *language* in Hebrew. Similar observations can be made of Ballas's 1991 novel *Ve-hu aḥer* (*The Other One*), which depicts the life of the Iraqi historian Ahmad Susa, a Jewish convert to Islam; there too Arabic is employed almost exclusively in proper names, place-names, and titles of books.

When we turn to the "Baghdad novels" of Michael and Amir, however, we encounter strikingly different linguistic strategies as well as worldviews. In this regard, the differences between Michael and Amir, on the one hand, and Ballas, on the other, become more pronounced. In *Viktorya* (*Victoria*, 1993), Michael's best known and most highly regarded novel, the author follows the life of a Jewish family in Baghdad from the end of Ottoman rule through the 1930s.[62] The novel was a best seller in Israel, but its largely unflattering depiction of Jewish life in Iraq generated controversy, particularly among Iraqi Jewish readers. As his magnum opus about Iraq, *Victoria* is paradoxically the high point of Michael's transformation into an *Israeli* writer.[63] It is a novel whose content, narrative

61 Ibid., 37, 40.

62 Berg notes that the writing of *Victoria* presented Michael with his greatest challenge yet, as "the world created is the most foreign to the reader of Hebrew literature and the story covers the greatest range of situations and cultures"; in her reading, the novel's credibility is due largely to the author's control over language (*More and More Equal*, 188).

63 Snir argues that Michael pandered to the preconceptions of the Israeli cultural elite, providing a "Mizraḥi folklore" in place of a substantive engagement with Arabic culture ("Ma'agalim niḥtakhim," 205), and as such *Victoria*'s success is not indicative of a cultural transformation in Israel (205). I believe Snir overstates the case somewhat, but agree that Ballas's Baghdad writings

tone, and language reflect the negotiation between two homes: Baghdad and Israel. Baghdad is the home of the characters, Israel the home of the implied reader. The story is mediated on the thematic level by a narrator who guides us through unfamiliar historical events and cultural behaviors ("In the condemning silence Victoria said: 'Then I'll light the *quraya.*' The *quraya* was a glass dish full of water and a layer of oil"[64]); it is mediated on the linguistic level by the translation, transliteration, and other adaptations of Arabic in the Hebrew text. The language of the prose oscillates between mimetic and translational impulses, between the demands of verisimilitude and of legibility.

In the interests of the former and to enliven the dialogue, Michael peppers his characters' speech with Arabic idioms, many of them characteristic of the Jewish Baghdadi dialect. But what complicates his task is that his characters' linguistic experience would include the Jewish and Muslim colloquial dialects, classical (literary) Arabic, liturgical Hebrew, and written Judeo-Arabic forms. In attempting to reproduce this dynamic heteroglossia within a Modern Hebrew framework, Michael either implicitly represents or explicitly refers to all these dialects and registers. For example, the narrator occasionally alludes to the Muslim Baghdadi dialect, as in an amusing scene in which a Jewish youth tips off his naïve cousin about an impending event of pubescent interest:

> Ezra explained in the Arabic of Muslims, "It's *layl ha-nitch* tonight [*leyl na-nitch ha-layla*]."
>
> "Aha," said Murad knowingly. . . . Later he accosted his Uncle Dahud: "'Ezra's carrying on about some *leyl ha-nitch*. What's that?"
>
> "The night of screwing, my son" [*layl ha-ziyunim, bni*], said Dahud bluntly.[65]

The episode is meant to demonstrate Murad's extreme naïveté, as he lacks familiarity with not only the word but also the concept behind it. The fact that *layl al-nitch* (semi-Hebraicized as *layl ha-nitch*) is Muslim dialect would be obvious to Arabic speakers, but would be lost on the Israeli

---

and even some of Michael's earlier works challenge the Israeli reader's expectations and sensibilities more deeply. Furthermore, as others have also noticed, *Victoria* skips over the critical period of the family's transition to Israel, disconcertingly moving back and forth from the bustle of life in Baghdad to glimpses of the protagonists as pensioners in a suburb of Tel Aviv.

64 In Hebrew, *Bi-dumiyat ha-ginu'i amra Viktorya: "Ani adlik et ha-kuraya." Ha-kuraya hayta kli shel zekhukhit male mayim ve-shikhvat shemen* (Michael, *Viktorya*, 82 and *Victoria*, 86, Bilu's translation).

65 Michael, *Vitktorya*, 90 and *Victoria*, 95, translation adapted from Bilu's. In the novel, the family's married men are all in hiding to avoid conscription into the Ottoman army when the family's matriarch decrees that they will emerge for one night to fulfill the commandment of procreation.

reader if not for the narrator's clarification.[66] Here, Ezra's use of lewd language from the Muslim dialect (*nitch*) heightens the sense of mystery and suspense surrounding the anticipated occasion.

In addition to both the Jewish and Muslim variants of colloquial Arabic, Michael also represents written Judeo-Arabic, as when Victoria and her mischievous female cousins find a paper airplane on their roof and take it to their local rabbi/folk healer for deciphering. To his chagrin, upon reading it aloud to the illiterate girls, the rabbi finds that it is a snippet of philosophical argumentation equating the practice of the healer with that of the prostitute.[67] The novel includes the original Judeo-Arabic text in its entirety, and then follows it with a translation into Modern Hebrew. Because Judeo-Arabic is written in Hebrew characters, the novel's reader can sound out the Arabic-language text, but cannot understand it. Its translation into actual Hebrew functions as a moment of "doubling": on the diegetic level it represents the rabbi's reading of the text to his illiterate audience, while on the extradiegetic level it serves as Michael's decoding of an incomprehensible Arabic-language passage into the Modern Hebrew of his readers. This moment of doubling reveals an interesting paradox: whereas the novel's Israeli readership can *read* the original Judeo-Arabic text but not understand it, in the world of the narrative the female characters can *understand* the original text but cannot read it. By placing the Hebrew translation in the mouth of the rabbi, where the Hebrew stands in for the Judeo-Arabic that is read aloud, Michael simultaneously disrupts and preserves the fiction of the text. Even knowing that his readers would not understand the Arabic words nor grasp the subtleties of the Hebrew translation, Michael chose to insert this short Judeo-Arabic text into his Hebrew narrative, this time privileging verisimilitude over legibility.

Several other scenes in the novel demonstrate how the dialogue, which is written mainly in a semiformal Hebrew, is nonetheless subtly molded by Arabic and Islamic culture. In the scene below, two of Victoria's elder relations, Dahud and 'Aziza, are discussing Toya, Dahud's child bride. Dahud makes a living by playing the zither (*qanun*) at celebrations:

66 The word *nitch* is marked as "Muslim Arabic" by the pronunciation of the final *-ik* (*kaf* preceded by a long *ya*) as *-itch*, as distinct from the Jewish dialect, which preserves the hard *k*. As it appears in Michael's text, the phrase *layl ha-nitch* is a grammatical hybrid where the definite article *al* in the compound construction *al-nitch* is replaced by the Hebrew *ha*, even though the word that follows, *nitch*, is in Arabic. Given that Ezra uses the term *nitch* because of the lack of an equivalent term in the Jewish dialect, Uncle Dahud would not actually have translated it into the Modern Hebrew equivalent *ziyunim*. This is a concession to the Israeli reader.

67 Michael, *Viktorya*, 67.

Dahood wisely brought the conversation to an end before it got out of hand. "Children and zithers bring happiness to the world [*ha-yalda ve-ha-qanun mevi'im simḥa la-'olam*], and I thank God every day for his gift of them."

"At least a zither can't get pregnant. It won't turn your old age into a nightmare of crying and baby shit."

"God is great" [*Elohim gadol*], said Dahud with a flourish of piety that was meant to draw a last laugh. When it didn't, he asked with genuine concern: "Umm Ezra, what is going on with you?"[68]

The Arabic word *qanun* (zither) is simply transliterated into the Hebrew, as is Umm Ezra (Mother of Ezra), an Arabicism the Israeli reader is expected to recognize. The phrase *elohim gadol* exists in spoken Hebrew, but is deployed here as a translation of the Arabic *Allahu akbar* or *Allah kebir*, which may be used in Arabic to convey awe or appreciation; Dahud uses it here with sarcastic intent. Even a Hebrew sentence or phrase that shows no specific lexical or syntactical sign of Arabic may have origins in Arabic culture. Dahud's statement that children and the zither bring happiness to the world echoes the well-known Arabic saying *al-mal wa-l-banun zinat al-hayat al-dunya* (wealth and children are the adornment of the life of this world), which originates in the Qur'an.[69] Dahud's adaptation of this phrase is evinced by the echo of *qanun* in *banun* and by the parallel between the material item and the child that bring joy into the world. While Michael would not expect his Israeli readers to pick up on such subtle Islamic and Arabic influences in his characters' speech, this example illustrates the process of cultural translation that takes place as Michael, imagining his characters discoursing in Arabic, transposes their dialogue into Hebrew.

The idea of Modern Hebrew intrudes into the story in a memorable scene in which the family hosts a Zionist emissary from Palestine in their courtyard. When the emissary explains in his own "foreign Hebrew" that he has come to instruct the Jews of Baghdad in Hebrew, his hosts protest that the men of Baghdad already know Hebrew very well. The emissary clarifies that he means "living Hebrew" (*'ivrit ḥaya*), that is, Modern Hebrew: "a Hebrew you can talk in, read a newspaper in, write a letter in." Dahud retorts in Arabic,

"We should learn to do all that in our mother tongue first," said Dahud. "All of a sudden I feel like an idiot. Rafael and Ezra read the newspapers, even my son Sa'id leafs through books, and I stand and stare like an ass."

68 Michael, *Viktorya*, 41 and *Victoria*, 39, translation adapted from Bilu's.

69 See verse 46 of *Surat al-kahf* (*The Cave*), where, read in its entirety, it indicates the opposite intention: "Wealth and children are only the gloss of this world, but good deeds that abide are better with your Lord for recompense, and better for expectation" (Ali, *Al-Qur'an*, 254).

> The emissary didn't understand a word and 'Izuri translated the gist of it for him. The emissary's eyes lit up. "That's the point," he said to Dahud. "You're a foreigner here, like Jews are everywhere in the diaspora. By teaching you Hebrew I'll be preparing you for immigration to Palestine."
>
> Dahud couldn't believe his ears.

Dahud then asks the emissary what harm they had done him such that he would want to send them to a land of want, when he has just finished licking the plates of the bountiful food they have served him. None of the men of the courtyard, however, are willing to translate the question into Hebrew for fear of offending their guest.[70]

All in all, Michael's use of Arabic and representation of heteroglossia do not threaten the linguistic integrity of the Hebrew narrative prose. The interpolation of Arabic terms serves as an interruption in the Hebrew prose, as a reminder of the Arabic-language world the Hebrew represents. Michael's Hebrew is not dialogically hybridized as much as *embellished* with Arabic; the languages remain ideationally distinct. Arabic is the intimate language of the characters, Hebrew is the external language of the omniscient narrator and the implied reader, and the narrator is a translator, interpreter, and authoritative native informant who mediates between them.

When compared to *Victoria*, Eli Amir's novel *Mafriaḥ ha-yonim* (*The Dove Flyer*), published just one year earlier, in 1992, contains a surprising amount of Jewish Baghdadi Arabic, much of which is untranslated. Amir's novel depicts characters in the Zionist underground in Baghdad, and by and large does not dispute the Zionist narrative, despite its criticism of the absorption of Iraqi immigrants. Nonetheless, Amir uses Arabic more liberally than his counterparts Michael and Ballas, as, for instance, in the transliterated but untranslated sentence in Muslim Baghdadi dialect: "Kabi, i-sar bitch el-yom ya khuya?" (Kabi, what happened to you today, my brother?).[71] Here, the narrator does *not* identify the utterance as "Muslim Arabic," and as such only the rare reader with the requisite background can recognize the markers of non-Jewish speech. As for the sentence's meaning, the reader must depend on context and the surrounding (Hebrew) sentences to decode it. Amir also deploys Arabic at length in his 2005 novel *Yasmin* (*Jasmine*), which opens with the 1967 war, when the commander of the Jordanian Legion, mistaking the approaching Israeli soldiers for Iraqi reinforcements, addresses them in Arabic. A Jewish Israeli soldier finally puts his confusion to rest by explaining in a

70 Michael, *Viktorya*, 214–215, and *Victoria*, 240–241, translation adapted from Bilu's.

71 Amir, *Mafriaḥ ha-yonim*, 23.

mixture of Arabic and Hebrew: "Ihna yahud, min hon, anaḥnu yehudim, mi-yisra'el" (We are Jews, from here, from Israel).[72] Here, as in examples from *Victoria*, the bilingual statement operates doubly on the diegetic and metatextual levels. Thematically, it functions as a reversal of expectations (somewhat reminiscent of the inverted norms of language and identity in "Iya"); at the same time, the repetition of the soldier's statement in Hebrew serves as a necessary in-text translation for the Hebrew reader.

Their virtuosic deployment of Arabic language and their translation of Iraqi culture demonstrate that this first generation of Mizraḥi writers is at home with Arabic in all its variants—classical, colloquial, Muslim, Jewish—with no mystery surrounding the language. They have an innate sense of linguistic identity grounded in Arabic, and a desire to communicate it in Hebrew. Their challenge is the transposition of their characters' linguistically stratified, culturally nuanced Arabic milieus into Israeli Hebrew. Their struggle is not with the metaphysics of language but rather with its mechanics. Even when their texts communicate the crises of immigration and identity, the idea of language itself is not thrown into crisis. This clarity surrounding linguistic possession breaks down in the writings of their younger counterparts, who grew up in bilingual households where Hebrew and Arabic were spoken, sometimes accompanied by a third language (such as Judeo-Berber or French). It is in the writing of the second generation that the *idea* of linguistic representation as well as resistance to the hegemony of *'ivrit tiknit* both come to the fore.

DISRUPTING/REWRITING *'IVRIT TIKNIT*: THE DIALOGISM OF "MIZRAḤI HEBREW"

> To make use of the polylingualism of one's own language, to make a minor or intensive use of it, to oppose the oppressed quality of this language to its oppressive quality . . . an animal enters into things, an assemblage comes into play.
>
> —Gilles Deleuze and Félix Guattari[73]

> After all, one's language is never a single language—in it there are always survivals of the past and a potential for other-languagedness that is more or less sharply perceived by the working literary and language consciousness.
>
> —Mikhail Bakhtin[74]

72 Amir, *Yasmin*, 13.

73 Deleuze and Guattari, "What Is a Minor Literature?" 26–27.

74 Bakhtin, "From the Prehistory of Novelistic Discourse," 66.

The transformation of literary Hebrew, conducted through a dialogue with colloquial Arabic, commences with second-generation Mizraḥi writers. While many are familiar with Arabic music and film, they lack the connection to classical Arabic that shaped first-generation writers, particularly those from Iraq (twentieth-century North African and Egyptian Jews were largely Francophone in their reading and writing habits).[75] In general, Mizraḥim educated in Israel in the 1950s and 1960s disassociated themselves from Arabic, yet numerous second-generation Mizraḥi writers present an incisive critique of this trend. The experience of immigration created a rift between parents and children, or between children and mainstream (Ashkenazi-dominated) Israeli society—both of which become archetypal story lines in Mizraḥi fiction. It is no coincidence that some of the best novels by Mizraḥim are semi-autobiographical narratives featuring adolescent and young adult protagonists: Albert Swissa's extraordinary *'Akud* (*Bound*, 1990), Ronit Matalon's interrelated *Ze 'im ha-panim eleynu* (*The One Facing Us*, 1995) and *Kol tse'adeynu* (*The Sound of Our Steps*, 2008), as well as Eli Amir's aforementioned *Scapegoat*. Second-generation Mizraḥi poets include the Algerian-born Erez Bitton (b. 1942), the Iraqi-born writers Roni Someck (b. 1951) and Amira Hess (b. 1943), and the Moroccan-born Sami Shalom Chetrit (b. 1960), all of whom write verse expressing oppositional cultural and political perspectives.

One of Erez Bitton's well-known poems ends with the words,

At dusk
I pack my things
in the shop on Dizengoff[76]
to head back to the outskirts
and another Hebrew [*la-'ivrit ha-aḥeret*].[77]

What is this "other Hebrew" that Bitton speaks of? It is any one of the variations of "immigrant Hebrew"—Moroccan Hebrew, Egyptian Hebrew, "Mizraḥi" Hebrew. Moreover, it is also the liturgical Hebrew of the Sephardi religious tradition, which bridges Ladino and Arabic-speaking Jews: the languages of *piyyut* (devotional poetry), of Kabbalah (Jewish mysticism), and of other genres of rabbinic writing. All these are "other" to *'ivrit tiknit*, and as we shall see, they all find their way into the poetry and prose of Mizraḥi writers.

75 As Matalon writes of the mother in her novel *Kol tse'adeynu*, "What did she read? Mostly detective novels, only in French. She spoke Arabic, but could barely decipher the letters: women of her class and ethnicity in Cairo didn't read or write Arabic, only men—and not all of them, either" (*Kol tse'adeynu*, 76).

76 Dizengoff is one of the main streets in central Tel Aviv, known for its fashionable shops.

77 "Shir kniya be-dizengov" ("A Poem on Shopping on Dizengoff)," in Bitton, *Tsipor beyn yabashot*, 38, translation by Alcalay, *After Jews and Arabs*, 250.

As we saw earlier, when Michael or Amir interpolated Arabic words into Hebrew prose, it indicated not a momentary or fragmentary appearance of Arabic, but a full Arabic dialogue. They use the formal register of *'ivrit tiknit* to stand in for Arabic in a one-to-one substitution. By contrast, the language of dialogue (and sometimes narration) in second-generation Mizraḥi writing is a vernacular transcription of the characters' "immigrant" or creolized Hebrew, interspersed with other languages (usually colloquial Arabic and French). This type of linguistic representation does not ask the reader to imagine a foreign language behind the Hebrew facade, but challenges the reader in another way, by presenting a different and unfamiliar kind of Hebrew literature. Initially, critics did not respond positively to the challenge.

Albert Swissa's *Bound* was a forerunner of the dialogized Mizraḥi novel. Set in a slum neighborhood of Jerusalem populated by North African immigrants, the narrative focuses on the lives of teenage residents. As Ramon Stern writes, upon its appearance, the novel "broke with many norms in Israeli fiction, unsettling the divide between the sacred and the profane while advancing a disturbing, unstable brand of ethnic and class politics." It was also highly exceptional in its social setting, which was composed largely of the Mizraḥi urban underclass; in the characters' complex cultural identity; and in its graphic exploration of gender and sexuality in the lives of the adolescent protagonists. Finally, and perhaps most important, was Swissa's unique Hebrew style, which "defies categorization."[78] With phrases in Moroccan Jewish Arabic and Judeo-Berber dialect, *Bound* is a challenging read even for native Hebrew speakers; yet as Gil Hochberg reveals, what raised the ire of Israeli critics was that Swissa mixes colloquial Israeli Hebrew not only with biblical and rabbinic Hebrew but with elements of Moroccan Jewish liturgical and mystical literature, which were alien to the corpus and the mentality of Israeli fiction.[79]

In fact, these religious-literary genres never ceased to be produced and consumed by Mizraḥim, albeit entirely under the radar of the Israeli cultural establishment. Devotional poetry and rabbinic writing, still major facets of Mizraḥi linguistic and cultural experience, are perceived

78 Stern, "Aqud: A Reading."

79 In their view, the dissonance between the often elevated, archaic, even embellished language and the hideous reality it represents is incongruous, resulting in a failure of representation. Hochberg points out that what the critics fail to read is how Swissa's "mad language" acts as a form of political resistance, "a redirection of racist violence transcribed into a new and 'foreign' kind of Hebrew text." In this manner, "blinded and dazed by Swissa's dense, overwhelming, and misplaced language, we find no defined meaning, but rather the very collapse of meaning" (*In Spite of Partition*, 108).

as foreign to the modernist and secular ethos of mainstream Hebrew literature. Similarly, contemporary *piyyut* remained one of the most popular literary genres among Mizraḥim during the first decades of statehood but is overlooked by scholarship on Israeli literature. Almog Behar discusses an important composer of *piyyut*, Rabbi David Buzaglo, who wrote bilingually in Hebrew, in Arabic, and in a special genre integrating the two languages, known as *al-matruz* (Arabic for "the interwoven"). In 1965 Buzaglo emigrated from Morocco to Israel, where he continued writing in both languages until his death ten years later. During this time, although virtually unknown outside Moroccan communities, he was, according to Behar, "one of the most widely read poets in Israel, if not *the* most read."[80]

In its radical uses of language, *Bound* was ahead of its time. The novel paved the way for the most important trend in recent Mizraḥi fiction: the rewriting of literary Hebrew. Scholars have already discussed the centrality of *space* to Mizraḥi fiction, which, beginning with the early novels of the late 1960s and 1970s, was centered on subaltern sites such as the transit camp, development towns, and urban slums.[81] But if earlier Mizraḥi prose fetishized space and identity, later works by second- and third-generation authors seem also to fetishize *language*. In fiction of the past decade, notably that of younger writers such as Sami Berdugo (b. 1970), Shimon Adaf (b. 1972), and Almog Behar (b. 1978), in addition to recent works by Sara Shilo, Ronit Matalon, and Dudu Busi,[82] one sees evidence of a "linguistic turn" in Mizraḥi literature.[83]

Three novels published within a five-year period, Sara Shilo's *Shum gamadim lo yavo'u* (*No Elves Are Coming*, 2005), Ronit Matalon's *Kol tse'adeynu* (*The Sound of Our Steps*, 2008), and Sami Berdugo's *Ze ha-dvarim* (*That Is to Say*, 2010), offer a particularly illuminating comparison of this linguistic turn. All three novels deal with the psychological nexus of language, immigration, and family, while approaching the interiority of this experience in markedly different ways. While the three novels' similarities might tell us something about the typology of second-generation Mizraḥi writing, their differences tell us even more about their individual authors' personalities, professional backgrounds, and stylistic orientations. Matalon

80 Behar, "Shivat ha-'aravit."

81 Cf. Hever, "Lo banu mi-ha-yam"; Shimony, *'Al saf ha-ge'ula*, esp. chap. 2; Peled, "Mizraḥiyut, ashkenaziyut, ve-merḥav"; Grumberg, *Place and Ideology*; and Oppenheimer, "Representation of Space in Mizraḥi Fiction."

82 For Busi, see, for instance, *Ima mitga'ga'at le-milim*.

83 Limitations of space preclude discussion of Busi and Adaf in this chapter. Adaf's work is notable for its use of medieval Hebrew and of Latin, with many erudite references to literature and philosophy; his work defies categorization as Mizraḥi, Hebrew, or European humanist.

is an established and highly respected Israeli writer, an "intensely cerebral author . . . [d]eeply reflective and exceedingly self-aware," who is well versed in literary and cultural theory.[84] Shilo is an educator whose surprisingly accomplished debut novel won critical acclaim. Berdugo is author of two novels and three story collections. Matalon and Shilo are close contemporaries, both born in Israel within a year of one another, Shilo to Iraqi Jewish parents in 1958, Matalon to Egyptian Jewish parents in 1959. Born in 1970, Berdugo is a decade younger but shares a similar profile, as the son of Moroccan immigrants.

All three novels are centered on relationships between mothers and children, and depict the Mizraḥi families assigned to subsidized housing in the so-called peripheries: poor towns, populated largely by Mizraḥim, that are geographically and culturally removed from the more prosperous urban centers. Notably, all three novels are also about abandoned or widowed mothers. Matalon's and Shilo's novels foreground the burden born by the single mother, the family's efforts to cope with the absence of the father, and the struggles of the second generation, who attempt to navigate not only a path to adulthood but a way out of the margins of Israeli society. Berdugo's novel dwells not on the absence of the father, but rather on the tension between "immigrant" and "Israeli" identity, using the broken mother-son relationship as the basis of a power struggle over memory, language, and the right to narrate. Above all, the three novels give voice to the intensely psychological place of language in the characters' lives. At their core, these narratives are very much about voice and what it means to have or lack one; the immigration experience provides the frame for this exploration. Yet the novels are dramatically different in style and in spirit, in their approaches to the meaning and to the representation of language.

MIMICRY AND HYPERCORRECTION: THE POETICS OF THE "STAMMER"

> It is no longer the character who stutters in speech; it is the writer who becomes a stutterer in language. He makes the language as such stutter: an affective and intensive language, and no longer an affectation of the one who speaks.
>
> —GILLES DELEUZE[85]

84 Grumberg, *Place and Ideology*, 202. See also Hess, "Mediterranean Mayflower?"
85 Deleuze, "He Stuttered," 108.

No Elves Are Coming unfolds in four chapters, each one of which is a long monologue narrated by members of the Dadon family. The story hinges on the death of the father, proprietor of the town's most popular falafel shop, some six years earlier—a catastrophic event for the family. Each character's story is thus narrated as a "before" and "after" demarcated by the father's death. The bereaved family lives in an impoverished town on the Lebanese border during the mid to late 1980s, when Israel and Lebanon continue intermittent cross-border fighting, and the town is subjected to retaliatory rocket attacks. The frame story occupies a single day in the present when the expectation (and eventual occurrence) of a rocket attack forces the town's inhabitants into bomb shelters and halts their everyday activity, also preventing the family from holding its annual commemoration of the father's death. The anticipation of the rocket attack sets up the time-space of the frame story as a chronotope, creating a platform for the characters' internal monologues and remembrances, ostensibly recounted throughout the long wait.

The book's setting in a remote northern border town is determinative to the story. The characters live in the self-contained world of their provincial town, cut off from the Israeli metropolis. They speak a language that has no relevance in the cultural or political life of the country—indeed, that is not even viewed as proper "Hebrew." The novel itself is written entirely in a Hebrew immigrant patois lightly laced with the colloquial Arabic dialect of Moroccan Jews, referred to in the text as *moroka'it* (in contradistinction to *'aravit*, "Arabic"). In the narrative, *moroka'it* is alluded to more often than it is directly represented; for example, we are told that Simona, the mother, is blessed repeatedly and in different forms by her mother-in-law, "all in *moroka'it*."[86] Only once does Shilo directly show us the code-switching that characterizes local speech patterns, when neighbors argue over the identity of a man rumored to be injured in the bombing:

"Amsalem from the hardware shop?"
"No, not him."
"You mean Meir from Housing? With the wife called Susie?"
"Susie? *Shkun huwwa abuha?*" [Who is her father?]
"*Bint Elyahu 'Amar?*" [Eliyahu 'Amar's daughter?]
"*Aywa!*" [Yes!]
"Why didn't you just say it was Eliyahu's daughter?"[87]

86 Shilo, *Shum gamadim*, 26.
87 Ibid., 206, translation adapted from *Falafel King*, 187.

Moroka'it exemplifies the sense of cohesion and belonging that binds the members of the town's majority Moroccan community, while marking its otherness vis-à-vis the Israeli center. It also marks their speech as a relic of the pre-Israeli or Diasporic past. As Almog Behar writes, it is inside "that battleground of language of past and present" that the book takes place.[88]

Throughout the novel, both *moroka'it* and *'ivrit 'ileget* are placed in dialectical tension with *'ivrit tiknit*. Shilo represents the idea of *'ivrit tiknit* as a social corrective through her characters, such as the Ashkenazi director of the town's daycare who scolds her Mizraḥi employees:

> Her mouth is full of Sylvie's peanut cookies, and what is she doing? Correcting her Hebrew: "It's 'apron' not 'aprin,' and I don't want to hear you saying 'I could of' instead of 'I could have' again. Little children are *tabula rasa*, blank slates, and they absorb everything they hear. Don't forget it's our responsibility to teach them to speak correct Hebrew. You say 'I could have,' not 'I could of,' Sylvie. And I don't want to hear a word of Moroccan in my nursery. Levana, too—tell her to keep her Moroccan for her husband, at night."[89]

Even in referring to *moroka'it*, the director chooses the slightly more correct-sounding variant *morokanit*. This passage illustrates the popular perception of Arabic (in any variety) as a language fit for the kitchen or for pillow talk but unfit for the public sphere, let alone an educational setting.

For the novel's characters, *'ivrit tiknit* symbolizes entry into mainstream Israeli society. Etti, the sole daughter in the family of six children, is a teenager who finds reading difficult, yet earnestly listens to radio broadcasts, hoping to absorb a Hebrew imbued with the aura of success and prestige: "[E]very time I pressed the radio to my ear, I'd tell myself that the radio-woman was patiently waiting for me to finish school and learn how to speak Hebrew just like her, with all the beautiful words she said, words that sounded as though they came from faraway lands. Without embarrassment, I kept repeating them until I understood them."[90] Etti also internalizes the injunction to correct ungrammatical Hebrew, attempting to improve the speech of her younger brothers.[91]

As opposed to the novel's earlier sections written entirely in nonstandard colloquial Hebrew, Etti's section includes sentences in hypercorrect

88 Behar, "Ba'a ha-sakin shel ha-'ivrit."
89 Shilo, *Shum gamadim*, 42–43, translation adapted from Shilo, *Falafel King*, 32–33.
90 Shilo, *Shum gamadim*, 228, translation adapted from Shilo, *Falafel King*, 208.
91 In Hebrew, "Omrim shesh yadayim, lo shisha" (Shilo, *Shum gamadim*, 239).

'ivrit tiknit. As Dror Burstein observes, whereas in the book's first three chapters the "attack" on *'ivrit tiknit* comes from "below," that is, from a "lower" linguistic register, in the fourth chapter the author does a strategic about-face. Here the attack comes subversively from "above," via an intentionally exaggerated and overblown literary register. Although Etti is just an ordinary high school student, her monologue sounds like "a refined parody of the language of the Israeli literary center," the language of leading Israeli writers Amos Oz and David Grossman.[92] The juxtaposition of the two approaches, Burstein argues, transforms the language of the first three chapters from mere imitation of a minority's speech patterns into a calculated literary style. His observations bring to mind Bakhtin's view of the novel as a dialogical system in which the meaning of any given voice or style is dependent on its relation to the others.[93] Through its exaggerated affect, hypercorrection parodically transforms the language of the narration from "direct" to "indirect" discourse, turning Etti's words into an "image" of language that, in turn, draws our attention to the artificiality of *'ivrit tiknit* itself.[94]

The unconventional language of the novel attracted the notice of critics, who applauded its originality and realism (though Burstein's enthusiastic review also recycles old platitudes, calling the language of the novel a "mutation").[95] Another critic compares the novel's *moroka'it* to the Yiddish of Jewish-American writing, a thought-provoking though perhaps not entirely straightforward comparison.[96] In Behar's estimation, "against the dominant trend of looking outward at *mizraḥiyut* as a form

92 Burstein, "Kir'u ve-yeraḥev levavkhem."

93 Bakhtin, "Discourse in the Novel," 262, my emphasis.

94 Bakhtin, "From the Prehistory of Novelistic Discourse," 60–61.

95 The full passage, bizarrely self-contradictory in its approach to the politics of language in the novel (and in Israel in general), reads, "Until the last chapter, not a single sentence in the novel is written in *'ivrit tiknit.* The book tramples on the academic standard with a virtuosic delight. Until the last chapter the standard, correct register of the language [*ha-roved ha-tikni shel ha-lashon*] is completely erased. In other words, anti-normative language becomes the only valid norm. This is wonderful. In fact, the book is not written in official Hebrew but in provincial spoken Hebrew, which is a mutation of the Hebrew in which, for instance, this column is written, as is this entire newspaper. Therefore it is impossible to translate the novel, because *first of all one would need to translate it into Hebrew* [*mipne she-reshit yihye tsorekh le-targemo le-'ivrit*], a task which itself is impossible to carry out without ruining the novel" (Burstein, "Kir'u ve-yeraḥev levavkhem," my emphasis).

96 The critic decreed the novel "a story of brokenness told in a broken language" and its language "the language of poverty," comparing it to Pier Paolo Pasolini's *A Violent Life*. "*Moroka'it*, like Yiddish—which survives beneath the vocabulary and syntax of Hebrew—brings home the experience of immigration . . . [t]he traumatic experience of immigration is the first and fundamental break between the characters and their environment"; see Feldman, "Eyn zo agada." Feldman also describes the novel's "low" language as "the kind of language we are used to

of inarticulateness [*ha-mizraḥiyut ke-'ilegut*]," *No Elves Are Coming* poses "an internal Mizraḥi attempt to describe or create a Mizraḥi Hebrew that could become an alternative to the reigning Hebrew in Israel." But, Behar pointedly asks, "How can one represent the Mizraḥi story in a language that does not surrender to the standard, modernist Hebrew, but that also doesn't replicate the view of itself as ridiculous, as stammering [*ke-'ilegut nil'eget*]?"[97] I argue that Shilo does precisely this by defamiliarizing the language of the Israeli center so that it momentarily becomes more "ridiculous" than the Mizraḥi Hebrew it "corrects." What the book shows is that it is not the characters' language that is ridiculous, but pretense and mimicry—the aftereffects of core ideas of "correctness" in language.[98] Following Deleuze, we might say that in writing unconventional Hebrew, Shilo makes not her characters but the idea of Hebrew itself draw back into itself and "stutter."[99]

In the characters' self-perception, *moroka'it* is clearly differentiated from "Arabic" (*'aravit*): "God's name would come to me along with a curse, in a single package. I would curse Him in Hebrew, I would curse Him in Arabic, in Moroccan, I'd come up with custom curses just for Him."[100] While *moroka'it* is the language of family and community, "Arabic" is the language of the "enemy," of "terrorists"; if *moroka'it* is the opposite of *'ivrit tiknit*, then *'aravit* is simply the other of Hebrew, period. When two adolescent brothers discuss how they would scare terrorists away ("You've got to say it in Arabic. I can't think like I'm a terrorist in Hebrew"), the other brother promptly supplies him with the requisite vocabulary: "Ahlan wa-sahlan, tfaddalu, Allahu akbar! Allahu akbar! Ruh min hon! Itbah al-yahud!" (Welcome, be our guest, God is Great! God is Great! Get out of here! Slaughter the Jews!).[101] This stream of Arabic is a mélange of unrelated idioms ranging from innocuous greetings to bombastic slogans associated with terrorism and violence, interspersed with the phrase *ruh min hon* (go away, get out of here) more typically directed by Israeli Jews

hearing in satirical television shows, but Shilo knows well that in a literary text the language acquires a new validity and a different meaning."

97 Behar, "Ba'a ha-sakin shel ha-'ivrit."

98 Her stilted language corroborates the Moroccan literary critic Abdelfatah Kilito's reading of the mimic as a tragicomic figure marked by his or her effort. In this light, it is closer to Kilito's conception of mimicry in "Dog Words" than to the theory of mimicry developed by Homi Bhabha ("Of Mimicry and Man"). See also Levy, "Exchanging Words."

99 Deleuze, "He Stuttered."

100 In Hebrew, "Ha-shem shel elohim haya ba li maka eḥat 'im klala. Hayiti mekalel oto be-'ivrit, hayiti mekalel oto be-'aravit, be-moroka'it, hayiti gam mamtsi lo klalot speshal" (Shilo, *Shum gamadim*, 84).

101 Ibid., 89.

at Palestinians than vice versa. In this darkly humorous passage, Shilo captures the essence of most Israeli Jews' limited and skewed familiarity with Arabic, not to mention an adolescent boy's fantasy of "thinking like a terrorist." For the reader familiar with the social context, this short linguistic performance functions implicitly as metacommentary on Jewish Israeli perceptions of Arabic and Arabs.

Elsewhere, in one of the book's most psychologically riveting sections, Shilo portrays Jewish-Arab relations in a multicolored light, capturing their complexities and nuances: the oscillation between trust and distrust, the sense of individual affinity weighed against an ingrained fear of the Other, the inevitable second-guessing that trails after interpersonal transactions. In this chapter, Kobi, the family's eldest son, who works as a factory director's assistant, seeks out Jamil, his Palestinian Israeli colleague, a bookkeeper to whom he has entrusted his savings for safekeeping. Although it is unusual for a Jewish Israeli to venture alone into an Arab village, Kobi makes his way there and asks to be taken to his coworker's home:

> Then they take me to him, all of them together. First they run ahead, but then they see how I can hardly move, so they walk slowly, all around me, and they don't stop talking to each other in Arabic. What are they talking about, why are they laughing like that?
>
> I catch a word here and there, but I can't make out what they're saying, the words don't come together for me. It's not the Moroccan of our old folks [*ze lo ha-moroka'it shel ha-zkanim shelanu*].[102]

"Arabic" is foreign, alienating, and disconcerting, not despite but especially *because* of its proximity to *moroka'it*, which makes it all the more uncanny in Kobi's ears. The fact that he is the outsider in the Arabic-speaking group raises his suspicions and arouses his fear, even as he recognizes a basic kinship between the two languages as two different forms of spoken Arabic. By complicating the representation of *both* Hebrew and Arabic, Shilo reaches the heart of the troubled Mizraḥi relationship to language.

IMMIGRATION AS TRANSLATION: THE POETICS OF UNSTABLE LANGUAGE

The problem of navigating *'ivrit tiknit* and *'ivrit 'ileget* leads Ronit Matalon to an entirely different literary solution. Matalon brings what she would call a "Levantine" cultural perspective into her Hebrew prose, reflecting the lingering memory of the hybrid, cosmopolitan cultural milieu of

102 Ibid., 189–190.

colonial Cairo, with its mix of Arab, Mediterranean, and European influences.[103] *The One Facing Us* and *The Sound of Our Steps*, her first and third novels, both portray an Egyptian Jewish family through the perspective of a young female protagonist (named "Esther" in the first novel, "Toni" in the later one). In the two works, Matalon transcribes the dialogue of her characters in a mixture of Hebrew, Egyptian Arabic, and French, which imparts the text with "an almost vocal dimension."[104] Tamar Hess calls this language a "unique 'formula' or *nusaḥ* that mimics not only Levantine linguistic blends but also the spoken language of immigrants and second-generation, Israeli-born speakers."[105] *The One Facing Us* addresses this multilingual Levantine past and its ambivalent relationship to the Israeli, Hebrew-language present. In the novel, the Cairene past appears in photographs in the book, some of which are provocatively labeled as "missing" and represented only as blanks, visually marking the *presence of absence.*[106] The idea of the presence of absence will return time and again in art, literature, and essays by third-generation Mizraḥim, as elaborated in chapter 6. *The Sound of Our Steps*, however, focuses on life in Israel; the narrative presents fewer forays into the Cairene past, and apart from the centrality of the father's absence, it does not indulge the trope of absence as a means of thematizing either language or identity.

If *No Elves Are Coming* presents a coherent narrative about the disintegration of a family, Matalon's *The Sound of Our Steps* offers a succession of self-contained episodes, each describing a particular moment or memory; the novel is constructed as a series of very short chapters with minimal narrative continuity and no chronological order. As Riki Traum observes, the narrative "enacts the unsystematic and selective functioning of memory"; as such, the relation between chapters is purely associative.[107] More significant than questions of narrative structure and temporal perspective, however, is the marked difference in the two authors' respective approaches to language and representation: whereas Shilo depicts the tension between immigrant Hebrew and *'ivrit tiknit* thematically and mimetically, through the speech of her characters, Matalon problematizes language as representation altogether. As Hess notes, throughout

103 For more on Levantinism in the context of Israel and Hebrew literature, including Matalon, see Hochberg, *In Spite of Partition*, 50–56, and Starr and Somekh, *Mongrels or Marvels*, xii–xxviii.
104 Traum, "From the Wildness We Feared"; I thank Traum for allowing me to cite her paper.
105 Hess, "Mediterranean Mayflower?," 295.
106 Others are even forgeries as they are actually photos of other sites, such as a photo of two figures, supposedly at a railway station on the Nile River in Cairo, that was actually taken in Warsaw; see Hochberg, *In Spite of Partition*, 56, and Hess, "Mediterranean Mayflower?," 294.
107 Traum, "From the Wildness We Feared."

Matalon's work, language is conceived as limited in its representational capacity; specificity and detail are emphasized.[108]

The language of *The Sound of Our Steps* is a polyphonic free-for-all of languages and linguistic registers—including immigrant Hebrew, *'ivrit tiknit*, Egyptian colloquial Arabic, spoken and written French, and the idioms of political pamphlets and garden manuals—all thrown into a kind of internecine struggle. Yet on another level, the entire text is a metalinguistic discourse contained and controlled by the narrator's voice. Here Bakhtin's theories of novelistic discourse are highly germane to my reading. Bakhtin argues that language in the novel breaks down into "images of languages," each of which becomes the *object* of representation while simultaneously doing the work of representing. As such, the novel is a "system of languages that mutually and ideologically interanimate each other," all intersecting through the author (although Bakhtin seems to shift agency from the author to the languages themselves).[109] In *The Sound of Our Steps*, not only are the different languages, registers, and styles "interanimated" by one another, but a convergence—if not a reconciliation—takes place at the level of the author; for in the novel, the narrator (implicitly identified with the author) represents and interprets each of the novel's different voices in turn.

"Language" in the Bakhtinian sense corresponds more closely to "voice" or "idiolect" than to national languages (e.g., "English," "French," "Arabic"). In the novel, the mother and grandmother both speak the sociolect of Mizraḥi immigrants: ungrammatical Hebrew laced with other languages, in this case mainly Egyptian Arabic and French.[110] In this sense, Matalon is not actually representing *different* languages so much as an overarching state of heteroglossia, with characters drawing on words and expressions from Hebrew, Arabic, French, Italian, and English, all contained within a colloquial Hebrew frame. In *The Sound of Our Steps*, the narrator constantly "translates" fragments of the mother's discourse into the standard Hebrew implicitly shared with the reader. This impulse of translation and explanation becomes the narrative's center of gravity.

The question the novel tries to resolve, anticipated in *The One Facing Us*, is that of the relationship between home and language. The literary criticism on Matalon has elucidated her destabilization of "home" as the node

108 Hess, "Mediterranean Mayflower?," 295.

109 Bakhtin, "From the Prehistory of Novelistic Discourse," 47–49.

110 E.g., *hi yoshenet* rather than *yeshana*; *ha-laḥats dam* rather than *laḥats ha-dam*. One can often hear the colloquial Egyptian Arabic through the Hebrew. For example, in the mother's statement "Anaḥnu mi-livorno ha-motsa shelanu" (roughly, "Us, our family goes back to Livorno"), through the superfluous *anaḥnu* (we, us) and the nonstandard syntax, one hears the Arabic *ihna asasna min livorno*. Ibid., 46.

of identity and her valorization of movement and mobility, ideas that run counter to Zionist ideology.[111] Yet Matalon herself emphasizes the writer's need to be rooted in a language *and* a place. In a collection of essays, she writes, "The fact that I am the daughter of immigrants but not an immigrant myself must not be obscured—that is to say: I am already someone who acts by force of a sense of place and of Hebrew, someone who is already a native inhabitant—or at least partly one . . . literature, especially prose, requires a home."[112] Gil Hochberg also notes that in an earlier essay on "Language and Home," Matalon "points to the fact that within Israeli literature, the master of language is also the master of home. He or she is the native, the rooted Israeli who has successfully made Hebrew his or her language and Israel his or her homeland" and who speaks for the immigrant, who lacks a language.[113] In *The Sound of Our Steps*, Matalon further develops this triangulation of home, language, and immigration, and considers their implications for identity by destabilizing not only the meaning of home, but also the meaning of language: the idea of language itself is broken down into fragments and supplanted by that of *voice*.

Compare the two passages below, the first describing the errant father's arbitrary and unannounced visit, the second the family home (in the father's absence):

> It was from there that he [the father] went in, weak and crooked. His weakness was that of the voice, the voices coming from the kitchen, that seemed really sick like the light, and then recovered, arose reinvigorated and then fell ill again, dissolved into the limpness that was the girl's hands wrapped around a book, her feet limp beneath the blanket, like the light, like the voices.[114]

> They were three in the shack: the older brother the older sister and the girl. The mother wasn't another someone, she was the shack that had no man and that became a man. She spoke to them in her different languages, each time in another language, each one in turn collapsing into a void where it simply went out, little by little, making room for

111 See, for example, Hochberg, *In Spite of Partition*, 56–66; Grumberg, *Place and Ideology*, 203–221, and Tsal, "He Is Missing." Hever's reading of the novel focuses less on movement than on the visual mediation represented by the use of photography, but also in relation to alternative or oppositional modes of identity formation. See Hever, *Ha-sipur ve-ha-le'om*, 329–336.

112 Matalon, "Mi-ḥuts la-makom, be-tokh ha-zman," 48, cited in Tsal, "He Is Missing," 305–306, Tsal's translation.

113 Matalon, "Ha-lashon ve-ha-bayit"; see Hochberg, *In Spite of Partition*, 63–64.

114 Matalon, *Kol tse'adeynu*, 82.

> another language that would continue it, not succeed it. That was just it—that there were no successors, neither actual nor symbolic ones, and the things that were languages, and even the languages that were only languages, never completely disappeared, didn't vacate their place, were just hidden for a while, coming back and bursting forth in a different pattern, a different arrangement, like a face that changed its features around.[115]

These passages highlight the centrality of *voice* and *language* in the book. These are given away by the book's title, *Kol tse'adeynu* (*kol* literally means "voice") alongside the title of the first chapter, "Kol." Voice in the novel is a quality or attribute of strength or weakness of character; language is its vehicle. The mother is indeed obsessed with movement and instability, incessantly rearranging the house, even making structural changes; yet for the mother, language too is inherently in flux. In *No Elves Are Coming*, the family's shared language constitutes the family as a whole entity, a unit. By contrast, in *The Sound of Our Steps*, each member of the family has a distinct idiolect or voice, all of which collectively contribute to the narrator's developing subjectivity. The most dominant voice in the novel is the mother's, albeit as mediated by the narrator. The daughter Toni is mostly silent; she is referred to throughout the novel not by name but as *ha-yalda*, "the girl." Yet she is implicitly identified with the adult narrative voice—that which interprets and explains the family's different "languages" to the reader.

In Traum's view, Matalon's use of foreign languages in the novel is meant to represent untranslatability. To illustrate, Traum analyzes a scene in which the narrator describes a visit to New York City with her ailing mother. In that passage, the narrator recalls how she and her mother try to pinpoint the "precise Hebrew translation of the French phrase that becomes a leitmotif in the story: '*a mon seul desir.*' The daughter, presumably Matalon herself, translates the phrase in response to her mother's request: 'to my only desire, or maybe, to the one I desire the most.' 'Do you know what it means?' her mother asks. 'I don't understand,' the daughter replies."[116]

Traum relates "this existential miscommunication" to the narrative's grammatical complexity; the latter is derived from Matalon's act of tracing and representing memory, given memory's elasticity and relational quality as well as its high propensity for revision. For Traum, the novel's central project is the destabilization of the distinction between past and

115 Ibid., 116.
116 Traum, "From the Wildness We Feared"; see Matalon, *Kol tse'adeynu*, 215.

present, a project also represented in terms of sound or voice. This "deliberate confusion between the authentic sound of the past and its echo in the present" is emphasized in the first chapter, with the narrator's slippage between past and present tense: "We *feared* the wildness, we [still] *dread* the paleness" (*me-ha-pra'ut paḥadnu, me-ha-ḥivaron anaḥnu yere'im).*[117]

While it is true that the narrative highlights the temporal and spatial effects of memory, it then counterbalances them with the tight linguistic control exercised by the narrator. The text is filled by the presence of the narrator as the arbiter of memory; the voices of her family members are represented *within* and *through* her own memories. The dominance of the narrator's voice, and her role as curator and interpreter of linguistic artifacts from the family's past, can be sharply contrasted with Shilo's extended monologues in her *characters'* voices. Whereas the artistry of Shilo's novel is its effect of unmediated presence, in Matalon's novel it is the *mediation* itself that is the artistry. And here is the crucial point: where the voices of the other characters are all represented in their polyphonous "immigrant" Hebrew, Matalon's narrator translates them into her own erudite, rarified, perfect Hebrew. For example, consider her disquisition on the mother's use of the word *basis* (pronounced ba-*sees*), a Hebrew calque from "basis," meaning "base" or "foundation":

> What, in [the mother's] opinion, made an impression on people was not the European or the Mizraḥi [ethnic background] but rather "*ha-motsa shelanu*" [our family origins]. The very fact that we had origins, lineage, "*basis.*" The *basis* occupied her thoughts. She would say:
>
> "Him, he has a good *basis.*"
>
> "When the *basis* is rotten—then everything else is rotten." (The implied addressee was usually Morris.)
>
> or
>
> "Don't clean from the top, you start from the *basis.*"
>
> or
>
> "How did you expect us to turn out? We didn't have what they call a *basis.*"
>
> The "*basis*" aroused her not only as an existential proverb, but in the main as a tangible reality. Concrete to her bones, she hated the dim, the hazy and especially the convoluted like black death. . . . The hut had no *basis*, not really.[118]

Note the sudden movement from the mother's earthy speech to the narrator's elevated language of thought: "existential proverb" (*mashal kiyumi*),

117 Traum, "From the Wildness We Feared"; Matalon, *Kol tse'adeynu*, 15, my emphasis.
118 Matalon, *Kol tse'adeynu*, 46–47.

"tangible reality" (*metsi'ut muḥeshet*), "the dim, the hazy, . . . the convoluted" (*ha-'amum, ha-me'urpal, . . . ha-mefutal*). Elsewhere, the narrator discusses how the mother uses the Hebrew word *ḥaser* (to be missing) rather than the verb *le-hitga'age'a* (to miss or yearn for someone);[119] in another extended commentary, she discusses the Egyptian Arabic word *yimkin* (maybe, it could be).[120] Throughout the course of the narrative, the first time Matalon presents a character's idiosyncratic use of an Arabic word or idiom, such as *al-bini adam* (people) or *al-'alam* (the world), she places it in quotation marks and glosses it in Hebrew, after which the untranslated term appears seamlessly in the dialogue, as part of a shared lexicon of the characters, narrator, and reader. The novel as a whole is replete with metalinguistic representations and discussions of words or phrases from Hebrew, Arabic, and French. All this is a form of in-text translation in which the *process* of translation itself is highly aestheticized, consciously foregrounded rather than hidden. If the narrator (presumably Matalon) refuses to complete the translation of *a mon seul désir*, she has no hesitation translating from one Hebrew to another Hebrew, from her mother's voice to her own.

In his review of the novel, Yitzhak Laor criticizes Matalon for privileging *'ivrit tiknit* by translating the characters' voices into a "higher" Hebrew rather than allowing them to speak at length in their own voices:

> It is not that the others are silent. Everyone talks in this narrative; however, they are quoted only sparingly. . . . There are also no monologues from any of the book's characters. Instead, there is a translation into the narrator's language. This, of course, is the problem of mimesis or realism: The "low" characters are always left out of the language of both the readers and the narrator. In fact, this is the problem of the Ashkenazi collective, or at least, of its "aesthetics patrol" (*mishmeret ha-astetika shelo*). Perhaps the reading collective has no patience for any other language. And Matalon does not say "no" to this collective, if I am not mistaken. Perhaps her "no" is, in fact, directed toward the "politics of identity." Perhaps her liberty has been preserved thanks to this caution, not to [her] knowledge of the "impossible" language.[121]

In other words, Laor faults Matalon for preserving her liberty—as an Israeli writer rather than as an "ethnic" Mizraḥi writer—by choosing to identify her authorial voice with that of the cultural elite. Following Laor, one might even read *No Elves Are Coming* as espousing the more radical

119 Ibid., 12.
120 Ibid., 206.
121 Laor, "Ha-yalda ve-ha-'lo.'"

politics of language, given that it takes the unprecedented step of dispensing entirely with *'ivrit tiknit,* and utilizes "low" characters as narrators. But in Matalon's novel, the narrator's commentary on the characters' language never reads as *correction.* Far from being condescending, it evinces understated empathy, tenderness, and humor, as in the two examples below:

> At some point they shut down the public library in Ramleh, and brought the books to the "Central Study House" where she [the mother] worked. She brought the girl into a room on the top floor that she called "the storeroom." The books rested in stacks, in towers that reached almost to the ceiling. "Choose some and we'll take them later," she said to the girl, locked her in there for a few hours, so that "*ha-ele*" [them, those] wouldn't know. ("*Ha-ele*" or "*ha-ele sham*" [those there]: the authorities, those responsible, those in charge. Even a junior clerk in the municipality whose name she didn't know was "*ha-ele.*")[122]

> "You'll see," she [the grandmother] whispered gloomily . . . "you'll see yet that she'll be buried, that one, with the hoe in her hand, in the garden, *fi al-ganeyna,*" she said, spitting *fi al-ganeyna* out of her mouth with disgust, like a rotten pistachio.[123]

The fact that *ha-ele* (those [people]) is Hebrew while *fi al-ganeyna* (in the garden) is Arabic is inconsequential to their representation. The narrator treats all the characters' distinctive idioms and phrases as unique linguistic artifacts, without trying to locate them within a taxonomy of the local or the foreign. Rather than flattening the language or stripping it of its character, the narrator's translations and representations highlight the speakers' eccentricities and bring the reader into the psychology of each speaker.

As for the wayward father, his voice is represented mainly through excerpts of his political writings on the Mizraḥi issue (themselves marked by a disjunction between style and content). Yet his spoken voice is the polar opposite of the mother's, and a source of contention between the other characters:

> There was no measure to the burning of his narrow brown eyes, nor to the sweetness of his language; no one, ever, could speak like Morris could. And no one ever swooned from the sweetness of his language

122 Matalon, *Kol tse'adeynu*, 96.
123 Ibid., 61.

> like Nona. "*El-lisan el-hilwa*," she sighed longingly every day, with that veiling of her sky-blue eyes: "That sweet tongue."
>
> . . . The mother detested *el-lisan el-hilwa*, saw it as a pact made against her, as a many-armed octopus. "What are you going on about, around and around, just say what you want to say already, just say it!"—the grandmother drove her crazy.[124]

Matalon's *el-lisan el-hilwa* is a corruption of the Egyptian Arabic idiom *al-kalam al-hilu*, connoting clever riffs on stock phrases of politeness and flattery.[125] Israeli culture values simplicity and directness, even bluntness; it privileges action over words. For the pragmatic mother and her elder daughter, Corinne, the father's smooth-talking style epitomizes his infuriating charlatanism. His "sweet language" is not a preamble for meaningful contribution to the family's circumstances; in this sense, Morris is "all talk."

In this novel about voice, then, each character has not only a voice but a style of language. Neither Matalon nor her characters employ distinctions such as *'ivrit tiknit*, "Hebrew" or "Arabic." Rather, language is presented as *character*. It is *strong* rather than *correct* language that matters: language imbued with a sense of self, a sense of place, and the integrity that comes of its fulfillment in deed. Through her emphasis on voice, Matalon demonstrates that meaning in language is not stable; her characters subject language to a continuous process of resignification, investing words with their own personal meanings.

WORDS VERSUS THINGS: THE DOUBLE POETICS OF *DVARIM*

Berdugo's second novel, *Ze ha-dvarim* (*That Is to Say*), brings together the major themes examined in this chapter: representations of Arabic, of *'ivrit tiknit*, of *'ivrit 'ileget*, of the pre-Israeli Arab Jewish past, and of *mizraḥiyut* in conflict with Israeli national identity. Although somewhat uneven in execution, it is a highly ambitious novel that exemplifies the linguistic turn in Mizraḥi fiction. The narrative is modeled on the archetypal clash-of-generations story, revolving around the emotional conflict between immigrant parents and acculturated children who reject their parents' "old world" ways. But Berdugo throws a wrench into this familiar script

124 Ibid., 125; see also 407.

125 *Lisan* in Arabic is masculine, so the expression cannot exist as Matalon writes it. Most likely, Matalon had heard *al-kalam al-hilu* in her youth but recalled it incorrectly due to Hebrew interference, since the Hebrew cognate *lashon* is feminine.

by deepening the intergenerational conflict into a philosophical question about the primacy of *structure* versus *meaning* in language.

The plot is deceptively simple. A single man takes a week off from his work as a librarian and collects his illiterate, ailing mother from her old age home. He brings her back to the empty, dilapidated house they once shared, where the mother, widowed young, had raised him. Inside await a blank whiteboard, dry erase pens in three colors, paper, and pencils. His plan: to teach the mother to read and write Hebrew letters, to compel her to enter the world of *'ivrit tiknit* after her many years of an immigrant existence in Israel. The son narrates the story, and the narrative follows the structure of his lesson plan. The novel is divided into three sections titled *ma'arekhet* ("Class Schedule"), *mo'ed bet* ("Makeup Exams"), and *gmar* ("Finals"); the individual chapters are titled "lessons" ("Lesson One," "Lesson Two").

The mother, however, turns out to be an unruly student. Rather than meekly copying letters, she wrests the lesson time away from her son, bursting into lengthy unprompted monologues. These gush forth in profoundly broken Hebrew interspersed with Moroccan Arabic and a considerable amount of French. In her fragmented but vibrant language, the mother tells the story of Maha, a young girl in Morocco who is shuttled between relatives, denied a stable home and family, and thwarted in her desire for schooling. The son resists his mother's repeated injunctions to listen to her story, insisting that they are there for the sole purpose of learning to read and write correct Hebrew; for her part, the mother resists his attempts to forcibly "educate" her, and demands his attention. They strike a deal: they will alternate between the Hebrew lessons and the mother's story by turns. Reluctantly, the son is drawn into his mother's tale, which is implicitly revealed as her own. (Here the novel pushes the limits of plausibility, for he does not begin to consciously identify "Maha" with his mother until the novel's end.) There is no resolution, no catharsis, no emotional reconciliation between mother and son, but there is development. In the last section, the mother's story overpowers the lesson plans; likewise, her character overpowers his. The son, who remains unnamed in the novel, is revealed as weak, emotionally stifled, and sexually confused. By contrast, Maha perseveres throughout a never-ending series of setbacks.

The narrative moves back and forth between three stories: Maha's life, set in North Africa; the frame story; and the son's own life story, consisting of his disjointed thoughts and recollections about his childhood, his mother, his work at the library, and his frustrated love life. While Maha's story wanders dramatically throughout the whole of Morocco and even into Algeria, the frame story is confined almost entirely to the house, and has the quality of a stage backdrop for a two-person drama. Passages of time and shifts in voice are marked by light and shadow. This leitmotif underscores the novel's reliance on antithesis: literacy versus orality; the son's coldly analytical and at times strikingly opaque language versus the ungrammatical, transparent, emotionally perceptive style of the mother; the "here and now" of the literacy lessons versus the "there and then" of the mother's story. In both content and style, the novel "creates conflicting systems of consciousness and of language."[126]

Paradoxically, the conflict between mother and son is rooted in their mutual desire to close the emotional gap as their time is running out. Each wants to bring the other into his or her world and identity; he by means of teaching her correct Hebrew, she by means of imparting her life history. His attempt to fix her broken language is a thinly veiled metaphor for his misdirected desire to correct their broken relationship, not by understanding or accepting her but by forcibly transforming her. His thoughts reveal the colonizer's mentality of "benevolent" domination, verging on outright cruelty: "I see her opposition. . . . I hadn't thought about this kind of thing, this disguised opposition. I'll give her this night to rest one last time, and tomorrow we'll deal with her" (*ve-maḥar kvar netapel ba*).[127] In order to teach her, he must (quite literally) silence her. For the son, correct grammar is not just rule of language but rule of law separating the civilized from the natives. In short, the narrator embodies the story of second-generation Mizraḥim who experienced their parents' broken Hebrew as a shameful failure. For this group, the parents' perceived failure to become proper national subjects unleashes a deep insecurity about their *own* national identities.

Although the son narrates the frame story, his power over the narrative is subverted formally, linguistically, and thematically by the mother's extended monologues. By the novel's midpoint it is her voice that dominates the text; it is her meandering story rather than his structured lessons that opens new vistas for the reader. As the novel progresses, it becomes evident that above and beyond their struggle over the right to narrate and to control the flow of time, the true subject of the novel is *language*. The mother's language is naked, unmediated, and powerful. Devoid of complicated metaphors or any literary pretense, the rawness of her language exceeds even that of *No Elves Are Coming*. It reads as though transcribed word for word from a live recording. As one reviewer writes, "Aside from the story itself, what Berdugo does here mainly is to infuse the language with life, struggle with it, push its limits, and use it to reach

126 See also Herzog, "Ze ha-dvarim shel Sami Berdugo."
127 Berdugo, *Ze ha-dvarim*, 79.

the fiber of truth in the inner experience."[128] Were the novel's aspirations to end there, the book's major achievement would be this bare-bones retelling of the mother's life story in her own language; its second achievement is the recreation of her peripatetic life in colonial Morocco in astonishingly extensive and convincing detail.

Berdugo aspires, however, to infuse the text with a deeper layer of meaning that would link the two stories of mother and son. Beginning with its title, *Ze ha dvarim* (lit., This is the words), the novel's lynchpin is the word *davar* (plural *dvarim*). This is reinforced by the conspicuous and dense repetition of *davar* and *dvarim* on virtually every page of the text. *Dvarim* means not only "words," but also "things"; in context, it can also mean "matters" or "events." The double meaning of *davar* has a substantial history in Hebrew thought and literature as well as in Israeli literature and culture.[129] In the novel, this double meaning symbolizes the dual nature of language either as structure and form (embodied in the idea of "rules"), or as essence and meaning. At the beginning of the novel, bringing his mother back into their old home, the narrator informs her, "There inside the things (*dvarim*) are waiting for us."[130] The narrator is referring to the accoutrements of his lessons, but against the philosophical backdrop of the novel his declaration is an obvious wordplay: there, inside, await the *words*.

Reflecting on his life with his mother, the narrator reveals that going into his twenties he realized that "[i]n fact we were two people without the stuff of letters, and because of that we did not truly exist."[131] Representing the opposing view, the mother repeatedly asserts that her story is about the *be-emet* (the "really"; that is, the truth): "That's right, that's the truth" (*ze nakhon, ze emet*).[132] The mother insists that people understand her Hebrew perfectly well. More than once, she challenges her son, averring that the essence of her story supersedes formal correctness:

> This ain't the way I oughtta talk, that's what ya think, ain't it? That's what ya want—that I don't talk like this. You think those letters are supposed to help me, if I read I mean, like how ya said over there at my place there's that newspapers and stuff, and then I'll know some new things, do some progress. But if all this things I'm tellin ya ain't over,

128 Gabbai, "Dvarim she-ratsiti lomar."

129 One of Israel's first major daily newspapers was called *Davar*; the Israeli poet Yona Wollach's first collection of poetry was titled *Dvarim* (1966).

130 Berdugo, *Ze ha-dvarim*, 10.

131 In Hebrew, *Hayinu be-'etsem shnayim bli ḥomer ha-otiyot, u-veglal ze lo be-emet hayinu* (ibid., 15).

132 Ibid., 161; "ze kakha ze, ha-emet shel ha-dvarim shel kol ha sipurim, lo shel ha-sipurim, she ma she-kore be-emet ba-ḥayim shel benadam" (that's how it is, that's the truth of things in all the stories—not of the stories, of what happens really truly in the person's life; ibid., 162).

then how can I do some progress? [*Aval im kol ze ha-dvarim she-ani omeret le-kha 'od lo nigmar, az eykh ata ḥoshev ani yekhola mitkademet?*][133]

The title phrase *ze ha-dvarim* is one of the mother's repeated pronouncements, which she uses both to emphasize elements of her story and to complete a section: "That's it. That's the things" (*Zehu. Ze ha-dvarim*).[134] Although *dvarim* is plural, the mother uses it idiosyncratically with the singular *ze* (that) instead of *ele* (those). In her usage, it connotes one's lot in life, the "way things were," the nature of things: "That's the way it is when someone doesn't have a knowledge of things" (*ze kakha mi she-eyn lo et ha-yedi'a shel ha-dvarim*).[135] The mother also frequently repeats variations of the phrase *ze lo nigmar* (it's not over), insisting that the *dvarim* are without end. Even the son echoes her use of *dvarim* in the sense of an event that crosses over from past to present: "These too were our things" (*gam ele hayu ha-dvarim shelanu*).[136]

"THESE ARE THE WORDS THAT MOSES SPOKE": WORDS AND LAWS

In fact, *ze ha-dvarim* is a grammatically corrupted echo of "Ele ha-devarim asher diber Moshe" (These are the words that Moses spoke), the opening phrase of the Book of Deuteronomy, known in Hebrew as "Devarim."[137] Deuteronomy reports the contents of Moses's address to the Israelites as they stand poised to enter the Land of Israel after their long sojourn in the desert wilderness. Through a few subtle but persistent hints and keywords, Berdugo links his narrator to the biblical Moses. Early in the novel, the son reveals that his ambition of becoming a teacher was thwarted by his "weak throat" (*garon ḥalash*)—a chronic inflammation that returns during his attempts to teach his mother.[138] Elsewhere the son says he was "exposed" by his "weak voice."[139] The coercive teaching program he

133 Ibid., 80.

134 Ibid., 94, 222; also, "Ata kvar mavin [sic] et ze ha dvarim" (119); "Ata mavin et ha-dvarim she-hem lo beseder? Ze-ze ha-dvarim" (128).

135 Ibid., 181.

136 Ibid., 260.

137 The full phrase reads, *Ele ha-devarim asher diber Moshe el-kol yisra'el be-'ever ha-yarden* (These are the words that Moses addressed to all Israel on the other side of the Jordan); see Deuteronomy 1:1 (*Tanakh*, 373). (Throughout this book, my transliterations from Hebrew omit the *shva na'*, e.g., *dvarim* rather than *devarim*, but the biblical Hebrew must include the *shva*, hence *devarim*.)

138 In Hebrew, *Az kvar yad'ati she-lo ochal li-hiyot mor'e be-yisra'el. Vitarti 'al ha-ma'amad be-'ikar beglal ha-garon ha-ḥalash sheli* (Berdugo, *Ze ha-dvarim*, 73).

139 Ibid., 112. Esti Adivi Shoshan reads the "weak throat" as an "expression of the weakness of the narrator's male identity; as the son of an illiterate female immigrant, and as the possessor

imposes on his mother is an obvious sublimation of his unfulfilled desire. Ironically, the mother's deep childhood desire for schooling and literacy was also thwarted by circumstances beyond her control, but as she is well aware, the damage is hardly reversible by a chimerical plan thrust upon her in the twilight of her life.

The would-be teacher is an inversion of Moses, the reluctant prophet and lawgiver. In Exodus 4:10, Moses implores God to relieve him of the burden of being His prophet: "Please, O Lord, I have never been a man of words . . . I am heavy of mouth and heavy of tongue" (*Bi adoni lo ish devarim anokhi . . . ki kavad pe u-khavad lashon anokhi*).[140] The rabbinic tradition interprets this passage to mean that Moses had a speech impediment. Where the narrator is "weak of throat," Moses is "heavy of tongue." Where Moses gave Israel the law of Judaism, the son wants to give his mother the rules of language; in Hebrew both "rule" and "law" are denoted by the same word, *ḥok* (pl. *ḥukim*). Moreover, Moses gave Israel the initial set of laws at Mount Sinai on *luḥot ha-brit*, the stone tablets with the famous Ten Commandments. The word *lu'aḥ* (pl. *luḥot*) is also the Modern Hebrew word for "board" or "blackboard."

Second only to *davar*, the word *lu'aḥ* appears persistently in the novel, where it refers to the whiteboard the son uses for the lessons; the phrase *luḥot ha-brit* appears once.[141] Appropriating the role of Moses vis-à-vis the unruly Israel, the son "civilizes" his mother through his instruction from the *lu'aḥ*.[142] The *lu'aḥ* is an imposing presence, almost a third figure in the house—a possibility strongly intimated in a few passages, as when the mother rebukes the son: "You left the *lu'aḥ* out here in the middle [of the room at night], why didn't you move it? You scared me, for a second there I thought it was a person."[143] Elsewhere the narrator narrowly avoids breaking it, hinting at the iconic image of Moses breaking the tablets.[144] Near the novel's end, the mother's spiritual victory is conveyed through the *lu'aḥ* when the son sees it leaning on the wall and notes that now it appears "smaller, neither exalted nor majestic";[145] shortly afterward, in one of the novel's most symbolic moments, mother and son cooperate in wiping it clean.[146] The key-

of a conflicted Israeli male identity, he lacks the 'voice' of the teacher" ("Yesh mishehu le-daber ito"). I fully agree with her interpretation but see it as secondary to the intertextual evocation of Moses, which she and other critics overlook.

140 *Tanakh*, 119.

141 Berdugo, *Ze ha-dvarim*, 219.

142 Ibid., 116–117.

143 Ibid., 99.

144 Ibid., 243.

145 Ibid., 261.

146 Ibid., 292.

words *davar/dvarim* and *lu'aḥ* thus work in tandem to convey the novel's conflict between form and meaning in language.

"THE POWER OF EXCLUSIVE HEBREW": NATIONAL IDENTITY, SEXUAL IDENTITY, AND LANGUAGE

The question of language spills over into every aspect of the narrator's subjectivity. For the narrator, national identity is an unfulfilled aspiration. He frequently uses "Israeli" as a descriptive term; at one point he even refers to Hebrew letters as "Israeli" letters.[147] By contrast, he sees *mizraḥiyut* as a deficiency, practically a pathology, inherited from his mother. Awareness of his status as a Mizraḥi male (*gever mizraḥi*) troubles both his national and sexual identities. This connection becomes more pronounced in the second half of the novel, when we learn of his romantic involvement with the son of a deceased journalist from Tel Aviv whose writing he had once fetishized as an icon of perfect Hebrew and of ideal Israeliness. For the narrator, Israeli identity is directly equated with correct Hebrew. If his mother's multilingualism is the mark of the despised "weak" Diasporic identity, he embraces monolingualism as the sign of a "strong" national identity: "I was already internally convinced of the power of exclusive Hebrew" (*koḥa shel 'ivrit bila'dit*).[148] He attributes his mother's faulty Hebrew not only to her lack of formal instruction but with the interference of French and Arabic; when she uses the Arabic *al-wad* for wadi, he forcibly translates her: "*Vadi*. Say *vadi*. That's in Hebrew. You mean *vadi*, that's how it's said, that's how you'll say it."[149] He describes her as "weak and an immigrant, still a foreign Israeli" (*'adayin yisra'elit zara*)[150] and believes she failed in her most important duty: to be the proper Hebrew-speaking Israeli mother he deserved.

He thus attempts to free himself of the burden of the Diasporic past represented by his mother. In his work as a librarian, he is asked to sort and catalogue a large donation of old books from a French Jew of North African heritage. Printed in Hebrew, Arabic, and French, the books mirror the languages of the mother's story while providing the narrator with a tangible alternative to the monolingual model of Israeli book culture. In other words, they break the binary of creolized, ungrammatical Hebrew orality and Hebrew literacy, offering a third option of *multilingual* literacy, in which Hebrew is only one piece of a triad. Yet here too the narrator

147 Ibid., 176.
148 Ibid., 151.
149 Ibid., 182.
150 Ibid., 210.

finds almost nothing of interest in the project or in the books, stating that he is "nearly convinced" that the project is a waste of time, "because I too prefer to occupy myself with other things [*dvarim aḥerim*]. Only the near future interests me."[151] Later he even states, "I became annoyed at the incongruous quality of the books, which were not connected to the time or place of Haifa."[152] Halfway into the novel we learn of a break-in at the library and the disappearance of some of the crates of books; the narrator, for reasons unexplained, suspects his lover, the son of the journalist, but this thread remains unresolved.

Although the mother is characterized by her son as linguistically impoverished and deficient, in fact she is highly attuned to the roles of different languages in her life. In telling her story, she tacitly expresses how linguistic experience informs her identity, for instance by noting her sense of linguistic disassociation when she crosses the border from Morocco to Algeria, with the sudden overwhelming dominance of French and an unfamiliar Arabic.[153] Throughout the novel she searches for words in Hebrew, at times correcting herself, and prefaces idiomatic Hebrew expressions with "as you say here in Israel." French and Arabic permeate her direct discourse, and her Hebrew is fully hybridized, with French terms freely integrated into Hebrew structures, as in *ha-le-shoz ha-ze* ("that *le chose*").[154] In the section of her story set in Algiers, the reported dialogue is all in French and is mostly untranslated; the untranslated French and Arabic of her story compel the reader to enter her linguistic and cultural world.

This is more work than the narrator is willing to do. His desire to impose his Hebrew-centric, rule-ordered world upon his mother leads him to repeatedly dismiss her story as trivial and incorrectly articulated.[155] Yet at the same time, the narrator understands (or at least admits) that his plan to teach the mother Hebrew is one not of giving, but of taking; one of forcibly erasing her Diasporic past in order to actualize *his* identity as a monolingual, present-tense Israeli. This awareness is expressed in an astonishing passage that brings the novel's interwoven issues of language, place, and identity to the fore:

> I don't give her extra time. The permission [to speak] is mine alone. She scatters her words and allows me to think only for brief moments

151 Ibid., 96.
152 Ibid., 258.
153 Ibid., 93, 104–107.
154 Ibid., 158.
155 Ibid., 150.

> about the girl's travails, . . . Algiers and North Africa are in our house now, but she doesn't notice that she is killing their language and place. In my head the Arab towns and cities are joining Israel in a way that is so strange, so illogical, of neither here nor there. . . .
>
> Once I was an eternal *tsabar* [Israeli native]. I smelled of the mixed character of this home and this place. I felt pure also when she spoke to me. I pretended to be listening to her, but her sentences always registered within me as weak, as having no ring to them, despite the melody of the French words; despite the residue of the Arabic letters, which, if I encountered them in writing, I always saw as being too black, too wide and rolling, too curly, trying to give the eyes of the beholder the wonder of a fairy tale that did not correspond to any period [of life in] our community and in the country whose sympathy I expected. . . .
>
> Why is she choosing to make for us a partitioned space [*makom shel ḥayits*], a no-man's-land [*shetaḥ hefker*], an isolated region lacking columns and devoid of a totality [*mikhlol*] that would pass between them? Now I have come here also to destroy this void, this vacuum, I came here to see if the foundations were perhaps here after all. I must check quickly, must eliminate her words, her language, her sayings, her stories [*le-ḥasel et divrata, et sfata, et amiroteyha, et ha-sipurim shela*]. And all this in order to preserve myself, as I am, as I've succeeded until now.[156]

The passage is remarkable for its concentration of images and metaphors: the blackness and curliness of the Arabic letters, connoting an unwanted presence, is directly contrasted by the "partition," "no-man's-land," and "isolation" of the home life created by his mother, which is correspondingly devoid of the kind of Israeliness the narrator desires. Paradoxically, to fill the void, he wishes to erase her yet further. About halfway through the novel, the narrator dimly understands his mother is dying; yet at the very end, even as her death is imminent, he is still thinking about the future of their Hebrew lessons.[157] The novel ends with his futile attempt to recollect the words of a book as the light (metaphorically, of his mother's life) fades out.[158] The mother ends her own story with the unfinished sentence "And no one knows when all this [*kol ha-ze*] will end—."[159] Both the sentiment and the grammatical lack of closure symbolize the intrusion of past into present—a sign of the permanent liminality of the eternal immigrant.

156 Ibid., 128–129.
157 Ibid., 317.
158 Ibid., 322.
159 Ibid., 321.

CONCLUSION: FROM HEBRAICIZING ARABIC TO FOREIGNIZING HEBREW

Through their representations of "immigrant Hebrew," Shilo, Matalon, and Berdugo recreate the language of the Hebrew novel. Their representations of language and their metalinguistic discourse transfigure literary Hebrew into a multiform language. Bakhtin writes of heteroglossia in the novel that "[t]hese dialects, on entering the literary language and preserving within it their own dialectological elasticity, their other-languagedness, have the effect of deforming the literary language; *it, too, ceases to be that which it had been, a closed socio-linguistic system*."[160] If this is true of novelistic discourse generally, it is borne out emphatically in cases where authors use vernacular languages to explode the "verbal-ideological worldview" of the unitary literary language. In encountering the "otherworldliness" of Mizraḥi discourse, *'ivrit tiknit* itself becomes an image; Hebrew is dialogized.

For Bakhtin, dialogization is at its most powerful when "individual differences and contradictions are enriched by social heteroglossia" and "the dialogue of voices arises directly out of a social dialogue of 'languages.'"[161] Although the three novels demonstrate this interplay of individual voice and sociolect, and all three depict a dialogue of voices, each offers a different take on the *meaning* of voice. For Shilo, voice is not strongly differentiated from language. Both are related primarily to community and belonging—to notions of inclusion and exclusion, when *how* one speaks becomes a defining line. On the other hand, both Berdugo and Matalon are intensely interested in the question of voice and its relation to character. Matalon's novel represents contrasting pairings of voice and character through the dominant voice of the mother, the sleek but ineffective voice of the father, the silent voice of the child, and the translational voice of the narrator. For Berdugo, the narrator's "weak throat" and insecure personality, coupled with his obsession with "legitimate" language, are directly opposed to the vitality and emotive power of the mother's voice. Similarly, the three authors' negotiations of *'ivrit tiknit* differ subtly. Shilo and Berdugo not only challenge the authority of *'ivrit tiknit* by writing in an Arabic-inflected Hebrew creole but also explicitly thematize *'ivrit tiknit* in order to interrogate it as a symbol of status and authority. In Matalon's novel, *'ivrit tiknit* frames the narrative and contains the characters' idiosyncratic, immigrant patois, while its authority is not directly contested or undermined. Yet Matalon's prose shatters

160 Bakhtin, "Discourse in the Novel," 294, my emphasis.
161 Ibid., 284–285.

the presumed unity of "Hebrew" and challenges the distinction between "Hebrew" and "Arabic" as separate languages by recreating the idea of a language not as a collective lexicon but as an idiosyncratic style. Every person, every speaker, speaks his or her own "language."

Whether set in Baghdad of the 1940s, the transit camps of the 1950s, or the development towns and public housing projects of the 1960s and beyond, Mizraḥi fiction has presented its authors with the challenge of representation—of space, of culture, of identity, and of language. Mizraḥi authors translate cultural difference, writing against entrenched preconceptions of *mizraḥiyut*, Arabness and Arabic, and "Levantinism." Their writing depicts experiences that are alien to many Hebrew readers while also resisting total translation of language; their work seeks not to domesticate *mizraḥiyut*, but to foreignize Israeli Hebrew.[162] In the novels of both first- and second-generation Mizraḥi authors, Arabic is an incisive tool for redefining the cultural orientation and linguistic limits of Hebrew. But along with the transition from writing in Hebrew as a second language to writing in Hebrew as a mother tongue, the representation of language is transformed. Over the course of five decades, Mizraḥi authors have shifted between strategies of abnegation and appropriation in relation to *'ivrit tiknit*. The novels of first-generation Mizraḥim are characterized by diglossia rather than polyglossia, and by the appropriation of *'ivrit tiknit*. Their writing moves referentially between cultural systems, mediating and explaining, doing the work of transposing the world of the characters into the language of the readers. Second-generation Mizraḥi literature boldly unsettles the linguistic foundations of the national "home"—paradoxically, the creative prerogative of those who are at home in their language. Now language itself takes center stage in the inner world of the narrative, lending the Mizraḥi novel psychological tension and aesthetic grit. In such works, Mizraḥi Hebrew is transfigured from *'ivrit 'ileget*—a "broken," "stammering" Hebrew—into a poetics of otherness: a language that speaks its own truth.

162 On "domesticizing" and "foreignizing" translations, see Venuti, *Scandals of Translation.*

CHAPTER 6

"So You Won't Understand a Word"

Secret Languages, Pseudo-languages, and the Presence of Absence

I've forgotten Eve's garden at the entry to eternity
I've forgotten the use of my small organs
I've forgotten how to breathe with my lungs
I've forgotten speech
I'm scared for my language
Leave the rest and just bring back my language!
My nurse says: you were shivering violently and screaming
I don't want to return to anyone
I don't want to return to any land
After this long absence
I only want to return to my language
deep in the cooing of a dove

—MAHMOUD DARWISH[1]

I write bilingual poetry
in Hebrew and in my silence
and before sleep, peruse the map of the world
plotting my escape routes.
I write poetry outside of language
in signs resembling letters that light up
Under the blanket, embarrassed, I repeat by rote,
Hu tsel hu tselem hu matslema
Hu dam hu adam hu adama
Hu el hu tsel hu hatsala.
(He is shadow, he is image, he is a camera
He is blood, he is man, he is earth,
He is God, he is shadow, he is salvation.)

—ALMOG BEHAR[2]

1 Darwish, *Mural*, 36.

2 Almog Behar, *Tsim'on be'erot*, 142. In his novel, *Tchaḥla ve-Ḥezkel* (Rachel and Ezekiel), the protagonist also begins writing bilingual poetry "in Hebrew and in silence" (46).

LANGUAGE TROUBLE: THE POSTMONOLINGUAL AND THE MELANCHOLIC

In her study of multilingualism in German literature, Yasemin Yildiz defines the "postmonolingual" condition as a "field of tension" between the monolingual paradigm of nation-states and the persistence or resurgence of multilingual practices.[3] Taking Kafka as a primary example of this condition, Yildiz explores how his language has inspired "competing models of linguistic affiliation."[4] Interpretations of Kafka's language vary wildly, with critics claiming that his writing is "Hebrew in German words," or that his entire corpus can be read as translated from Yiddish; that he is the exemplar of "minor literature," or that he embodies a deep affinity for the German canonical tradition.[5] Yildiz attributes these contradictory interpretations to Kafka's writing itself, which explores the monolingual paradigm "in a concentrated manner as a part of his very aesthetics." In her view, Kafka's multilingualism could not but leave its mark on his "monolingual" German writing; the need to reflect on his own relationship to language catalyzed his celebrated "aesthetics of negativity."[6]

Yildiz's keen observations notwithstanding, much ink will yet be spilled over the question of "what language" Kafka was "really" writing in when he was producing modernist masterpieces in his mother tongue, German. Was he writing Yiddish in German, Hebrew in German, or simply a "different German" in German? Due to his exceptional status as a canonical minority author, Kafka and his language problems offer us a seemingly limitless buffet for critical thought. At the same time, that a Prague Jew writing in German during the heyday of Yiddish modernism should strike us as weird is not, after all, that weird or surprising in itself. Much weirder, I suggest, is the "language trouble" of the second- or third-generation Jewish Israeli writer of Hebrew, who by all counts ought to embody the very essence of the "homology between native language and ethno-cultural identity" that defines the monolingual paradigm of the modern nation-state.[7]

3 Yildiz, *Beyond the Mother Tongue*, 5.

4 Ibid., 33.

5 Ibid., 33–34; for the first position, see Suchoff, "Kafka's Canon"; for the second, see Casanova, *World Republic of Letters*, 269; for the third, see Guattari, *Kafka*; for the last, see Corngold, *Lambent Traces*. Yildiz also notes that Kafka uses German to write *about* Yiddish (*Mother Tongue*, 35). See also Kronfeld, *On the Margins of Modernism*, whose introduction rebuts Deleuze and Guattari's reading of Kafka.

6 Yildiz, *Mother Tongue*, 34.

7 Ibid., 34.

If Derrida dubs his own linguistic situation the "monolingualism of the other," Kafka's might be the "multilingualism of the other," a multilingualism trapped in a monolingual case and yearning for escape. This concluding chapter examines poetry and prose by Mizraḥi writers working in and between those two paradigms: the suppressed multilingualism of Kafka and the destabilized monolingualism of Derrida. Their texts, written in hyperlanguage, are performative repudiations of Israeli Hebrew. In the poems and stories below, we find authors writing "Ashdodian" in Hebrew, writing pseudo-Aramaic in Hebrew, writing Jewish Baghdadi Arabic in Hebrew, and simply writing a different Hebrew in Hebrew. In different yet interrelated ways, they all return to the seat of trauma: the rupture with Jewish multilingualism, and especially with Arabic, that took place during the implementation of nationalist monolingualism.

As noted in chapter 5, many Mizraḥim experienced the radical transformation of Hebrew as a psychological shock that only compounded the painful delegitimization of Arabic. In writing by second- and especially third-generation Mizraḥim, these language troubles become a site of melancholia. Their works are heavily thematized through metaphors of absence and traces, ghosts and hauntings, reality and unreality. Such themes are not uncommon in exilic and postcolonial writing, when language is associated with a place fixed in the receding past. "Melancholy," sagely observes Dorris Sommer, "haunts minority lives, doubled between an undead particular identity and the 'new' person. . . . If a home culture stays ghostlike in a new context, it can overshadow and undo new relationships."[8] Similarly, Evelyn Ch'ien muses,

> For my parents, China is fixed in 1949. The development of this relationship to China continues internally, privileging interiority and memory over the physical world. This dreamlike, hallucinatory quality associated with interiority pervades the works of the authors discussed here. . . . For all these writers, their English is interpolated by a language of the past and reworked into their literature; their imagined communities invoke a ghosted language. The past is like a shadow that detaches itself from the body and clings to the new linguistic body to sustain itself.[9]

The same sentences may well have been written of post-1948 Palestinian writers, or of Jewish Iraqi authors writing about Baghdad. Moreover, Ch'ien postulates that in the wake of physical displacement and the disembodiment of language, "the subject material of such writers is not simply

8 Sommer, *Bilingual Aesthetics*, 8–9.
9 Ch'ien, *Weird English*, 16–17.

a narrative but an effort to reembody language: its historical residue, its syntax, its grammar, its tone, and its sentiment. . . . *The shadow quality of a former culture manifests itself concretely in language.*"[10] In this regard, Mizraḥi literature complements the roster of well-known "weird English" writers studied by Ch'ien. Indeed, Mizraḥi fiction is deeply "interpolated by a language of the past," and the texts analyzed in this chapter are heavily invested with "this dreamlike, hallucinatory quality associated with interiority." In interpolating the landscape of the present with a dreamscape of the past, Mizraḥi discourse—both fiction and criticism—frequently utilizes the trope of the *presence of absence*. Moreover, as I will elaborate below, this trope is a shared leitmotif of recent Palestinian and Mizraḥi writing in Israel. Whereas in Palestinian writing it alludes to traces of the obscured, often concealed Palestinian past, in Mizraḥi writing it relates to the repressed language, culture, and memories of the Arab Jewish past.

As Ch'ien further observes of the "weird-language authors" she studies, those who "move in and out of the [interpretive] community," alternately enticing and resisting their readers, may "experience some madness, perhaps, in the process"[11]—a supposition certainly supported by the poems and stories we will encounter. In this chapter, we see where the psychic life of language in the Hebrew-Arabic no-man's-land reaches its (il)logical conclusion, with literature voiced in imaginary languages, in secret languages, and in the hallucinations of language experienced by a disconnected narrator traversing the line between speech and silence. The intense anxiety surrounding language that pervades these texts brings us back to Anton Shammas's hair-raising lines quoted in this book's introduction:

> I do not know.
> A language beyond this,
> and a language beyond this.
> And I hallucinate in the no-man's-land.[12]

"AN OTHER HEBREW," PART 1: *ASHDODIT*

If the novelists we read in the previous chapter challenged the discursive hegemony of *'ivrit tiknit* by means of polyglossia and creolized Hebrew, second- and third-generation Mizraḥi poets are even more audacious in

10 Ibid., 18, my emphasis.

11 Ch'ien, *Weird English*, 25.

12 Shammas, "Yud-gimel drakhim le-histakel be-ze," *Shetaḥ hefker*, 46; see notes 6 and 9 of the introduction.

their challenges to the *idea* of Hebrew. This chapter presents a group of works that not only dialogize Hebrew but fundamentally challenge the presumption that the language we are reading is something that can or *ought* to be called "Hebrew." Here, the authorial impulse is entirely one of abnegation. This impulse shouts out from the very title of Sami Shalom Chetrit's *Shirim be-ashdodit* (*Poems in Ashdodian*, 2003). Chetrit, a Moroccan-born Israeli activist, academic, and poet, frequently interpolates lines of Moroccan colloquial Arabic in his Hebrew poems (following the lead of Erez Bitton, who began publishing a decade earlier). The title poem of Chetrit's collection reads,

> I write you poems
> In the Ashdodian language [*be-lashon ashdodit*]
> . . . so you won't understand a word.[13]

Who is the "you" the speaker is addressing, and what is the Ashdodian language the speaker claims to write? Why does he not want his readers to understand?

Until leaving Israel in the early 2000s, Chetrit had lived in Ashdod, a working-class port city south of Tel Aviv once populated mainly by Mizraḥim (now also by newer immigrants from the former Soviet Union and Ethiopia).[14] The fact that most of the poem is written not in *'ivrit tiknit* but in an admixture of Hebrew and Arabic slang suggests that Chetrit's term *ashdodit* ("Ashdodian") is meant to denote the colloquial Hebrew of Ashdod. The speaker writes in this other language not only at the expense of his readers' comprehension but expressly *so that* they won't understand. "Ashdodian" is a declaration of refusal, one that explicitly rejects *'ivrit tiknit* in favor of *'ivrit aḥeret*, an "other" Hebrew; virtually every line of the poem critiques some aspect of language in Israeli society.

As discussed in chapter 1, Israeli colloquial Hebrew absorbed Arabic words primarily in a few low-register semantic areas such as food, greetings, and (most notably) obscenities. In Chetrit's poem, in a kind of linguistic revenge, Arabic obscenities boomerang back to the Hebrew reader. After the speaker's declaration that he writes in Ashdodian, the poem continues in a mélange of mixed Hebrew and Arabic curses and slang, volleying insults at the reader:

13 Chetrit, *Shirim be-ashdodit*, 7. From *Shirim be-ashdodit* (Poems in Ashdodian), Tel Aviv: Andalus, 2003. Reprinted with permission.

14 For more on Ashdod as a multicultural city and as a forum for debates on ethno-national politics, see Yacoby and Tzfadia, "Multiculturalism, Nationalism, and the Politics of the Israeli City."

שלא תבינו מילה

אֲנִי כּוֹתֵב לָכֶם שִׁירִים
בְּלָשׁוֹן אַשְׁדּוֹדִית
כּוּס אֶם אֶם אֶמְכֵּם,
כְּלָה דַאר בּוּכֵּם,
שֶׁלֹּא תָּבִינוּ מִלָּה.
לָמָּה מָה ?
לָמָּה מִי ?
מִי שָׂם עֲלֵיכֶם,
וּוּלָאד אלְחְרָם
אֶחָד אֶחָד,
לָמָּה מָתַי שַׂמְתֶּם
אַתֶּם שֶׁכָּזֶה
אַתֶּם שֶׁכְּאִלּוּ
אַתֶּם שֶׁאַחְלָה.

אֲנִי כּוֹתֵב לָכֶם שִׁירִים
בְּלָשׁוֹן אַשְׁדּוֹדִית
שֶׁלֹּא תָּבִינוּ מִלָּה.

SHE-LO TAVINU MILA

Ani kotev la-khem shirim
be-lashon ashdodit
kus em em emkum,
khlla dar bukum,
she-lo tavinu mila.
Lama ma?
Lama mi?
Mi sam ‘aleykhem,
wulad al-hram
eḥad eḥad,
lama matay samtem
atem she-ka-ze
atem she-ke’ilu
atem she-aḥla.

Ani kotev la-khem shirim
be-lashon ashdodit
she-lo-tavinu mila.

So You Won't Understand a Word

I write you poems
in Ashdodian—
fuck your mother's cunt,
wreck your father's house—
so you won't understand a word.
What gives, how come?
Who gives a fuck about you,
you sons of bitches,
each and every one.
Why, since when did you give a damn
you [people who say] "kind of," "like," "awesome."
I write you poems
in Ashdodian
so you won't understand a word.

The language of the poem is hardly the pinnacle of lyricism, but that is exactly the point: to reject "high" literary Hebrew. That said, *'ivrit tiknit* is not the only sociolect the speaker confronts, recalling Bakhtin's postulations about the struggle between different sociolinguistic points of view. Chetrit's poem is thoroughly dialogized in that each line of the poem serves as "a rejoinder in a given dialogue whose style is determined by its interrelationship with other rejoinders in the same dialogue."[15] The speaker begins with the slang or "dialect" of Ashdod, proceeds to roundly curse his addressee, and then finally identifies his addressee as "you who [say] *ka-ze*, *ke-ilu*, and *aḥla*"—Hebrew slang words similar to "kind of," "like," and "awesome" in American English (the last term, *aḥla*, being another loanword from Arabic). These idioms are the mark of another Israeli "dialect": that of the snobby environs of North Tel Aviv. In fact, the Hebrew literally reads "you who are kind of, you who are like, you who are awesome"—eliding the word "say." The implication is that you *are* what you speak; your language determines your identity. Furthermore, not all the Arabic curses in the poem are equally familiar to the reader. For instance, whereas *kus emkum* (your mother's cunt) is a universally recognized insult in Israeli street slang, the Moroccan Arabic curse *khlla dar bukum* (May your fathers' houses be destroyed) and *wulad al-hram* (from the classical Arabic *wilad al-haram*: children of sin, bastards) are unintelligible to most of the poem's readers, but legible to the speaker's social group. This type of differentiation recalls Henry Louis Gates's conception of the "mask" in African American literature

15 Bakhtin, "Discourse in the Novel," 274.

in which the embedded use of locutions and cultural referents that evoke African American experience signals an address to the linguistic community of the poet.[16] "Ashdodian" thus becomes a "dialect" marked *doubly* by its low-register Hebrew and its incorporation of Arabic; it represents ethno- and sociolinguistic stratification *within* Israeli Hebrew, rather than signifying a division between Hebrew and Arabic. Through its use of "masks" and by separating the poem's speaker from the reader as speakers of different languages, "Ashdodian" and Israeli Hebrew, the poem "shatters two myths": that of a single Israeli people and that of a single Israeli language.[17]

Yet *ashdodit* also conceals another critical layer of meaning. Although Chetrit reappropriates the word as a metonym for Mizraḥi Hebrew, in the Bible *ashdodit* was the language of the Philistines, the biblical enemies of the Jews, who lived where else but in the ancient city of Ashdod. Thus, in biblical antiquity, Ashdodian was Hebrew's "Other." In the words of the Prophet Neḥemiah,

> Also at that time, I saw that the Jews had married Ashdodite, Ammonite, and Moabite women; a good number of their children spoke Ashdodian and the language of these various peoples, and did not know how to speak Judean [*u-veneyhem ḥetsi medaber ashdodit ve-eynam makirim le-daber yehudit ve-kilshon 'am va-'am*]. And I censured them, cursed them, flogged them, tore out their hair, and adjured them by God.[18]

The biblical intertext tells us that Jews are supposed to speak a certain language ("Judean," the biblical equivalent of Hebrew), and that deviators must be punished.[19] In Chetrit's poem, the angry speaker appropriates the prophetic voice but reverses the message. Unlike the biblical prophet, the poem's speaker identifies not with the Judean-speaking Jews (the equivalent of proper Hebrew-speaking Israelis), but rather with the

16 Gates, "Dis and Dat," 92–94, cited in Bell, "In the Shadow of the Father Tongue," 60–61; my summary of Gates follows Bell's reading of him.

17 Bakhtin, "From the Prehistory of Novelistic Discourse," 68. In an interview, Chetrit described "Ashdodian" as "the Hebrew of today," adding that "Ashdodi[an], according to the [authoritiative] Even-Shoshan dictionary, is 'foreign language, language intermingled with foreign elements. Dialect.'" When asked about the different linguistic registers employed in the poem, Chetrit explained, "Today I try to write from within all those registers at once, as though I were drawing from one large amalgam, or reservoir, without determining if the language is poetic (that is, elevated), biblical, or of the street. I used to choose registers of speech very consciously—today it just flows" (Chetrit, *I'm an Arab Jew*, 105–106).

18 Neḥemiah 13:23-25 (*Tanakh*, 1888).

19 The word *'ivrit* (Hebrew) is never mentioned in the Bible; it (or its closest equivalent) is referred to variously as *sfat kna'an* (the language of Canaan) and as *yehudit* (Judean), the dialect of the tribe of Judea.

Ashdodian-speaking half-breeds, who represent the kind of ethnic and cultural hybridity found in contemporary Ashdod. Rather than censuring, cursing, flogging, and tearing the hair of the speakers of Ashdodian, the poem's speaker censures, curses, and flogs the elitist speakers of Hebrew.

But ultimately, although the speaker claims to write a poem in Ashdodian so that his readers "won't understand a word," he does not literally make it incomprehensible. Despite the presence of a few unfamiliar Arabic words, the poem is still legible to any reader of Hebrew. When queried about his motivation for writing in "Ashdodian," Chetrit responded,

> This is a call from the Mizraḥi margins toward the hegemonic Ashkenazi center; actually, I'm declaring that in order to understand this language you'll have to learn it; that I'm beyond your control and your understanding. You'll have to move closer to "Ashdod" in every way, culturally, socially, and religiously. And Ashdod here involves an entire world. So in fact it becomes an invitation, an opening of a door, despite the [Moroccan and Arabic] curses that play an interactive role in the poem.[20]

This type of "resistant" writing by minority authors is discussed by Sommer: "By marking off an impassable distance between reader and text, and thereby raising questions of access or welcome, resistant authors intend to produce constraints that more reading will not overcome." Their strategic incorporation of foreign languages or sociolinguistic codes produces "the rhetoric of selective, socially differentiated understanding."[21] Sommer productively questions our assumptions concerning the mastery of reading, locating the limits of interpretation at the threshold placed by the author. Yet Chetrit describes his own gesture of resistance not as the closing of a door, but as the opening of another door; as an "invitation" to the reader.[22] Like a pseudo-translation, a work that claims to be a translation when it is not, this poem lays claim to an imaginary language and pretends to be incomprehensible when it is not. Its claims before the reader are a smoke screen, its strategy one of reverse psychology: "So you won't understand a word" means "so you have to work to understand me," turning the staging of linguistic difference into a principled power play.

20 Chetrit, *I'm an Arab Jew*, 105.

21 Sommer, "Rhetoric of Particularism," 8. The phrase "strategic incorporation of foreign languages or sociolinguistic codes" is adapted from a source whose reference was obliterated by my computer. I apologize to the unidentified author.

22 Ch'ien critiques Sommer's position on similar grounds, claiming that in "weird English" literature, "appeals for community are embedded in the writing" (*Weird English*, 25). Elsewhere, in a chapter on unintelligible language, Ch'ien explores the potential of "assertive nontranslation" (ibid., 234), writing, "Narratives contain this potential for linguistic unintelligibility and illuminate the social impenetrability between communities, illustrated by garbled, jargon-like, or hybrid languages" (ibid., 201–202). So, clearly, do poems.

"AN OTHER HEBREW," PART 2: *ARAMIT*

If Chetrit invents "Ashdodian" as an escape from *'ivrit tiknit*, Amira Hess's wildly inventive, iconoclastic poetry respects no boundaries, taking heteroglossia and polyphonic language to new levels. Amira Hess (nee Barzani), who was born in Baghdad and immigrated to Israel as a child, published six collections of poetry from 1984 to 2007. Her writing moves fluidly along the historical continuum of the Hebrew language, drawing from biblical, rabbinic, and Modern Hebrew, from the lowest to the highest linguistic registers, with the occasional neologism thrown into the mix. In the same poem, street slang may abut the arcane vocabulary of the Jewish mystical tradition.[23] Often Hess's shifts in register intensify or complicate the semantic level of the text. She tends to indulge multiple semantic possibilities whose meanings hinge upon ingenious puns, wordplays, and homonyms. Furthermore, her Hebrew is studded with words and even entire sentences in Arabic, Yiddish, and English (distantly recalling Avot Yeshurun, who mixed Yiddish and Arabic expressions into his Hebrew poetry). At times Hess conjoins two languages within a single word, creating bilingual neologisms or provocative hybrid forms; in the poem "Ho imi" ("Oh Mother"), she takes "Auschwitz" and adds the Aramaic plural suffix *-in* while also changing the first vowel from "au" to "u," to form *ushvitsin*, a German-Aramaic "Auschwitzes."[24] Hess's writing is also experimental in its disregard for gender norms. This unique *nusaḥ* or literary idiom weaves extraordinarily rich language with a vast range of literary and extraliterary materials drawing on biographical, historical, cultural, and mythological sources. The proliferation of references to Jewish, Near Eastern, and world religious and textual traditions, to geographies and histories from the ancient world to the present, is immense; the code that combines them, enigmatic and opaque. These are woven together and recast in her distinctive tone, a blend of parody and prophetic lyricism. While her adroit use of language is a source of beauty and richness, it also poses a challenge. To the reader, this is poetry that often seems private to the extreme, introverted, and inaccessible.

Through her lyric voice, Hess identifies herself explicitly with Iraqi Jews, the descendants of biblical-era Babylonian Jewry. She makes frequent references to the modern Baghdadi past as well as the ancient

23 For example, *ḥarakot* (the screech of tires), *le-hizdayen* (to fuck), *sefuna* (ensconced), and *zikat ha-ru'aḥ* (the spark of the soul) all appear in "Ani basar ve-dam" ("I'm Flesh and Blood"), in Hess, *Bole'a ha-informatsya*, 36–39.

24 *Mi-tokh ke'ev ha-ushvitsin* (Hess, *Ve-yare'aḥ notef shiga'on*, 26). This invented word, *ushvitsin*, sounds much like the Aramaic word *ushpetsin* (guests), which many readers would identify due to its association with the Sukkoth holiday.

Babylonian Jewish heritage, using the terms "Bavel" (Babylon) and "Baghdad" almost interchangeably. She is keenly aware of her lineage as a scion of the Kurdish-Jewish Barzani family, which produced Kabbalists and poets including the seventeenth-century poetess Asenath Barzani.[25] Hess notes that her relationship with Hebrew began "with the *shirey shevaḥot* in my father's house.[26] . . . In Baghdad we still treated the Hebrew word as holy. You see a scrap of paper with the word *zona* [whore] written on it, you pick it up and kiss it, because it's written in Hebrew."[27] Although she was a girl of eight when she left Iraq, she mentions clear memories of life in Baghdad and visits to Bahrain, where her family had relatives in the pearl trade.[28]

Thus it is perhaps no surprise that Arabic is featured prominently throughout Hess's oeuvre. At times the influence of Arabic bears directly upon the Hebrew word. In a poem quoting her father's Hebrew, Hess not only portrays a common lexical error and the unidiomatic mix of formal and informal registers characteristic of immigrant speech, but also mimetically transcribes his accent, replicating his pronunciation of the Hebrew letter *tsadi* as the Arabic *sad*: *Sakh-ha-kol ata gus / ḥasi parsufkha mekhuse mishkafayim / lovesh kova' minimali / lekh hal'a / tilbash kova' maksimali* (All in all you're a midget / half your face covered by spectacles / wearing a minimal hat / Go forth / wear a maximal hat). Here, orthographic variation (replacing *tsadi* with *samekh*) aurally and visually highlights the father's alienation from his new surroundings, yet not without a touch of humor.[29]

If Hess's use of Arabic, her first language, in her Hebrew poetry makes her a "postmonolingual" writer, then what of her bizarre use of Aramaic? Hess's 1987 collection *Shney susim al kav ha-or* (*Two Horses on a Beam of Light*) features an intriguing untitled poem beginning "Kolot mesaprim" ("Voices Tell"). This poem is written almost entirely in Aramaic, with a smattering of Hebrew, at least one word in Arabic, and some Hebrew-Aramaic hybrids. It begins with three lines in Hebrew, then metamorphoses into a kind of pseudo-Aramaic or Aramaicized Hebrew that does not quite follow Aramaic syntax. Aramaic has a long and complex historical relationship with Hebrew; for millennia, it superseded Hebrew as the language of Jewish continuity. In Israeli Hebrew, however, it is an archaic and formal register used primarily for legal writing; Aramaic expressions in Hebrew are akin to Latin expressions in English. No one in Israel writes

25 Levy and Mu'alem, "Eykh ata shlemut'," 68.

26 "Songs of praise"; hymns sung on the Sabbath and holidays.

27 Levy and Mu'alem, "Eykh ata shlemut'," 74.

28 Ibid., 71.

29 Hess, *Ve-yare'aḥ notef shiga'on*, 38. Hess also mentions the incident that inspired these lines (Levy and Mu'alem, "Eykh ata shlemut," 74).

(or even pretends to write) in Aramaic, which is considered an ancient language. Most non-Orthodox Jews would associate Aramaic with liturgical texts such as the Kaddish (the ritual prayer for the dead) and the *kol nidre* service on Yom Kippur, while Orthodox Jews associate Aramaic primarily with the Talmud. Hess's composition of a poem in Aramaic is thus a highly anomalous if not altogether unique act in Modern Hebrew poetics. Virtually incomprehensible to the vast majority of the Israeli readership, most of whom have not been educated in the Aramaic of biblical or rabbinic literature, the poem is recondite even for the reader who can understand the literal meaning of the words.[30]

קוֹלוֹת מְסַפְּרִים צֶבַע הַשָּׁמַיִם אָדֹם
צֶבַע הַלְּבָנוֹן שְׁקִיעַת בֵּין עַרְבַּיִם.
וִירוּשָׁלַיִם אָדֹם-חַכְלִילִית.
כִּי בְּעַנְפּוֹהִי יִשְׁרֵי בְּהָלַיָּא
דִּין שְׁמַיָּא, אִילָנַיָּא וְרוּמֵהּ אוּרְנַיָּא
נִפְלוּ גְּזֵרַת עִירִין, מִשְּׁמַיָּא נַחַת דִּין,
בִּטְעֵים לוּחֲמַיָּא נְפַל אוֹמְרִין הָאֲרָזִים וִיהוֹנָתָן.

אַנְתָּא הוּא אֱלֹהִים דִּי יַהוּד
דִּי אֱלֹהִים בְּךָ וּשְׂכַלְתָּנוּ?
וּפְשַׁר מַעֲשֶׂיךָ אַרְגְּוָנָא לָבְשָׁה עִיר וּשְׁמַיָּא,
אֶקְרָא לְמַלְכָּא וּפִשְׁרֵהּ,
אֲקִים אוֹתָם מֵעָפָר
וְאַחֲוָיַת אֲחִידָן עֲשֵׂה בָּעוֹלָם וְנַהִירוּ
וְיָאִירוּ דִּי כָּתְבָה לְהָבִיא אַחֲרִית יָמִים
כָּל כַּבְלֵי דִּי רוּחַ הַתֵּרָה כְּאֵבוּן
שַׁלִּיט דְּמַלְכוּתָא, שִׁנְתֵה נַדַּת יָמֵינוּ,
כִּי שָׁוְעָה.
הִוֵּת כֹּחֲךָ עוֹשֶׂה יְרוֹמְמֶנְהוּ מִכָּל רַע
יַרְחִיקֶנְהוּ מִשְּׁאוֹל.

שִׁמְשָׁא הֲוָה מִשְׁתַּדַּר לְהַצָּלוּתֵהּ
אֶת הָעִיר הַזֹּאת.

Kolot mesaprim tseva' ha-shamayim adom
tseva' ha-levanon shki'at beyn 'arbayim.
Vi-rushalayim adom-ḥakhlilit.
Ki be-'anapohi yishrey behalaya

30 Hess, *Shney susim*, 15; I am indebted to Azzan Yadin for his help with the translation and annotation of the poem and to Shamma Boyarin for his contributions to its interpretation.

din shamaya, ilanaya ve-rume urnaya[31]
niflu gezerat ʿirin, mi-shamaya naḥat din,[32]
bi-teʿim luḥamaya nafal omrin ha-arazim vi-honatan.

Anta hu elohim di yahud
di elohim be-kha u-shekhaltanu?
U-fshar maʿasekha argevana[33] *lavsha ʿir u-shmaya,*
ekra le-malka u-fishre,
akeym otam me-ʿafar
ve-aḥavayat aḥidan ʿase ba-ʿolam ve-nahiru
va-ya'iru di katva[34] *le-havi aḥarit yamim*[35]
kol kavley di ru'aḥ ha-tera ke-evun
shalit de-malkhuta, shinte nidat[36] *yameynu,*
ki shavʿa.
Hivet koḥakh ʿose yeromemenehu mi-kol raʿ
yarḥikenehu mi-she'ol.

Shimsha hava mishtader le-hatsalute[37]
et ha-ʿir ha-zot.

Voices tell of the sky being colored red
The color of the Lebanon the dusk of sunset.
And Jerusalem is scarlet red.
For in its branches dwells the fear
of the judgment of the heavens, the trees and the tops of the pines
The verdict of the angels has fallen, judgment has descended from the heavens,
On account of the warriors he fell, say the cedars and Jonathan.
You are the God of the Jews—
is God in you, as well as understanding and bereavement?
And the interpretation of your deeds, the city wore purple, and the heavens too,

31 *Rume urnaya*, the tops of the pines, may be a play on Hess's first name, "Amira," which in Hebrew connotes treetops (in Arabic it is "princess").

32 The sequence *ʿir ve-kadish min-shmaya naḥat* (holy watcher coming down from heaven) appears in Daniel 4:10; *ve-di ḥaza malka ʿir ve-kadish naḥat min-shmaya* (The holy Watcher whom the king saw descend from heaven) is in Daniel 4:20 (*Tanakh*, 1814).

33 *Argevana* is mentioned in Daniel three times, referring to Daniel being adorned before the king (5:7, 5:16, 5:29), and mirroring the story of Mordechai in the Book of Esther.

34 *Di katva* appears in Daniel 5:5 and 5:15.

35 See Daniel 10:14.

36 *Ve-shinte nadat ʿalohi*, Daniel 6:19, referring to sleep fleeing from the king.

37 *Mishtader le-hatsalute*, in Daniel 6:15, is the sole appearance of *mishtader* in the Bible. In Daniel 6:15 the king makes every effort to save Daniel until the sun goes down, and in the poem the sun itself is "saving the day."

I will summon the king and the interpretation
I will raise them from dust
and he did the explaining of riddles in the world and its
enlightenment
and they will illuminate the writing to bring forth the End of Days.
Pain has unleashed all the chains of the spirit
Ruler of the kingdom, sleep is fleeing from our days
for it is crying out.
Your might is lifting him from all evil,
keeping him away from Sheol.
The sun is attempting to save
this city.

In broad strokes, the poem seems to be an apocalyptic vision of Jerusalem; the third line, *vi-rushalayim adom-ḥakhlilit*, means "and Jerusalem is scarlet-red." Suffused with red and with an aura of doom, the poem connotes bloodshed. Its final lines, *shimsha hava mishtader le-hatsalute / et ha-'ir ha-zot*, which can be read either as "the sun is attempting to save / this city" or "the sun is attempting to pray for / this city," hint that it may be a prayer for the redemption of Jerusalem, or perhaps a prophecy.[38] The poem also mentions Lebanon and cedar trees, Lebanon's national symbol. Given the poem's publication in 1987, and considering the general mood in Israel following its disastrous 1982–1983 war in Lebanon (not to mention the slew of protest literature it generated), one suspects a linkage. Adducing a connection between Lebanon and the apocalyptic vision of Jerusalem, we might paraphrase the poem as saying "We are the ones burning, as a result of our deeds." This is supported by the double meaning of *u-shekhaltanu* in *Anta di elohim di yahud / di elohim be-kha u-shekhaltanu?* (You are the God of the Jews—/ is God in you, as well as *shekhaltanu*?), which can be read either as "understanding" or "bereavement."[39] Read as "bereavement," *shekhaltanu* seems to admonish God that if he loses his children, the Jews, he will be an *av shakul*, a "bereaved father." In such a reading, the poem is a modern rendition of the warning of *ḥurban yerushalayim*, the destruction of Jerusalem; it recalls the writing on the wall foreseeing the fall of the Babylonian kingdom in Daniel 5, whose language the poem revives.[40] Indeed, Hess draws

38 In Hebrew, *le-halutsey* is "to save"; in Aramaic, *tsaluta* with an alef at the end is "to pray." In the full Kaddish, in Sephardic *minhag*, one finds the variants *tsalotana* (our prayer) and *tsalotahon* (prayers).

39 The almost identical word *sakhaltanu* appears three times in Daniel (5:11, 5:12, 5:14), as a noun translated as "understanding." In light of the poem's subject of war and death, however, this seems a clear wordplay, which can be read in Hess's poem as "you have bereaved us."

40 "The king addressed the wise men of Babylon, 'Whoever can read this writing and tell me its meaning shall be clothed in purple . . . and shall rule as "one of three" in the kingdom'"; Daniel 5:7; *Tanakh*, 1816).

the poem's vocabulary largely from the biblical Aramaic of Daniel and Ezra, which tell the story of the Jewish captives in Babylon; the poem's intertextual references follow a progressive sequence drawing from Daniel 4–6.

Yet however one interprets this poem, its opaque thematic content is quickly overtaken by its spectacularly strange hermeneutics of language. Although the poem does not thematize language, its cipher-like Aramaic code, an extreme case of hyperlanguage, cannot but be understood as anything *but* a statement about language. As with Chetrit's poem, Hess's poem problematizes communication between author and reader, but here a suitable preface might read, "I write you a poem in Aramaic, so that you *really* won't understand a word." Writing in biblical Aramaic instead of Modern Hebrew, Hess demonstrates the kind of authorial impulse Ch'ien describes as the "pathology of creating versions of English that are not entirely translatable, that are on some level intensely individualistic, hyper-stylistic, and resistant to a stable production of meaning."[41] At the same time, the poem's *sound* would not be entirely foreign to the Hebrew reader, as its cadences are reminiscent of the Kaddish, the ritual prayer for the dead.[42] Furthermore, some of Hess's Aramaicized Hebrew words such as *behalaya* (fear, from *behala*) and *urnaya* (trees, from *oranim*) impart a sense of familiarity with the Aramaic forms even as they defamiliarize the Hebrew words. These hybridized Hebrew-Aramaic words elicit a vague, uncanny sense of recognition coupled with (at least momentary) incomprehension on the part of the reader. Notably, the sole Arabic word to appear in the poem is none other than *yahud*, Jews (the Aramaic form is *yehud*, as it appears in Daniel 2:23); it appears in a sentence combining Hebrew, Aramaic, and Arabic, "Anta hu elohim di-yahud" (You are he, the God of the Jews).

In what linguistic or cultural context ought we to situate this poem: is it a Hebrew poem, an Aramaic poem, an Israeli poem, an exilic poem? If it is supposed to be a protest poem, why write it in a language nobody can understand? Moreover, what does it mean that Hess chooses to write about Jerusalem, that most canonical and symbolic topos of Modern Hebrew poetry, in a thoroughly hybrid mishmash of Hebrew and Aramaic (with one word in Arabic)?[43] While both poet and poem carefully guard the secret, when read as metalinguistic discourse the poem offers a legible statement of cultural irredentism. In addition to broadening

41 Ch'ien, *Weird English*, 25.

42 The resemblance to the prosody of the Kaddish is most pronounced in the musicality of these lines: *Ki be-'anpohi yishrey behelaya / din shamaya, ilanaya ve-rume urnaya / niflu gezerat 'irin, mi-shamaya naḥat din / bi-te'im luḥmaya nafal omrin ha-arazim vi-honatan.*

43 When queried on this point, Hess enigmatically answered, "Don't ask me why I wrote in Aramaic, I just felt that I needed to express this subject in that language" (Gutkind, "Hess—Ha-shira").

the Hebrew-Arabic dyad, Hess's Aramaic poem takes us not into a lower register of street Hebrew but into the lexicon of the high biblical past—from *ashdodit* to *aramit*. This move is an obvious reappropriation of the Hebrew-Aramaic past and a total abnegation of Modern Hebrew. Rather than appropriating the dominant idiom to distance it from the political or ideological center, this type of writing embraces the unreadable and untranslatable as a form of resistance. If Chetrit's poem functions as an explosive declaration of *mizraḥiyut* asserted through "Ashdodian" as the *symbol* or *idea* of an incomprehensible language, then Hess's Aramaic poem is a more subtle assertion of Diasporic identity performed by writing in a *literally* incomprehensible language.[44] Both poems seek to decenter Israeli Hebrew and to unsettle the relationship between author and reader; the difference is that Chetrit declares his intention of subverting this relationship without actually *doing* it, whereas Hess does it through poetic praxis without explicitly *declaring* it.

"AN OTHER HEBREW," PART 3: *BAGDADIT*

Hess's experiment with writing Aramaic was undertaken in 1987, early in her literary career. It was not so much a *return* to language as a dream about linguistic possession; from the place of not knowing the language, Hess imagined it, concocting a contemporary Hebrew speaker's fantasy of Aramaic. It was not until two decades later, at an Israeli poetry festival in 2007, that Hess returned to her actual mother tongue, reciting a bilingual Hebrew-Arabic poem that she had written using colloquial Jewish Baghdadi Arabic. This was her first work in that language.[45] For a Jewish writer to publicly recite an Arabic poem at a Hebrew poetry festival in Israel is the height of performativity, an "act of identity."[46] Hess's decision to use her native dialect of colloquial Arabic in the poem can be read in two different lights. Although it is a resounding affirmation of her Iraqi Jewish identity, it is also indicative of her inability to write poetry in literary Arabic.[47] Immigration to Israel, which effectively severed the Mizraḥi relationship with literary Arabic, thus also breaks down the distinction

44 The poem is written in the style of the "high" Aramaic of the Bible (*aramit mamlakhtit*) rather than the "middle register" of rabbinic writing (*lashon ḥazal*). Nonetheless, both forms of Aramaic are of special significance to Iraqi Jews; the Bavli (Babylonian) tradition is epitomized by the writing of the Babylonian Talmud in Judeo-Aramaic or in a Hebrew-Aramaic fusion.

45 Notably, at the same festival, another poet, Shimon Chelouche, declaimed his own poem in Moroccan Jewish Arabic. See Behar, "Amira Hess ve-ha-shiva le-'aravit"; I thank Almog Behar for referring me to the poem and to his analysis.

46 Le Page and Tabouret-Keller, *Acts of Identity.*

47 Although there is a long-standing tradition of colloquial Arabic poetry, Hess's poem is positioned in relation to a different politics of language.

between "high" and "low" Arabic that strongly influences reception patterns for native Arabic speakers—paradoxically opening up new spaces for writing in the vernacular.[48] Alternating between the Jewish Baghdadi dialect and its Modern Hebrew translation, the poem calls to mind the work of Samir Naqqash discussed in chapter 3.

Five years after its performance, the poem appeared under Almog Behar's stewardship in the inaugural issue of *La-roḥav/Maqtaʻ ʻardi* (*Crosswise/Wide Crossing*), a bilingual Hebrew-Arabic literary journal published online by the activist group Gerila Tarbut (Cultural Guerrilla).[49] The poem's title, "Kentu be-ghayr deni" ("I Was in Another World"), is taken from its opening line, written in Baghdadi Jewish dialect. The poem continues,

כנתו בריר דני. בלקט בדני מלכם.	הָיִיתִי בְּעוֹלָם אַחֵר. אוּלַי בְּעוֹלָמְכֶם
כנתו בריר אמכאן	הָיִיתִי בְּמָקוֹם אַחֵר
בלכאת בלמכאן מלכם	אוּלַי בַּמָּקוֹם שֶׁלָּכֶם
כנתו קעדי מא בינתכם	הָיִיתִי יוֹשֶׁבֶת לֹא בֵּינֵיכֶם
כנתו בריר נשמה	הָיִיתִי בִּנְשָׁמָה אַחֶרֶת
מא בנשמתי.	לֹא בְּנִשְׁמָתִי.
סר ביי שק	נִהְיָה בִּי חוֹר
סר ביי בכה	נִהְיָה בִּי בְּכִי
סרת ביי כופה.	נִהְיָה בִּי פַּחַד
מא ערפתו אש אסווי	לֹא יָדַעְתִּי מָה אֶעֱשֶׂה
מתו. מא תם מני שיין.	מַתִּי. לֹא נִשְׁאַר מִמֶּנִּי כְּלוּם.

balkat be-deni malkem.
Kentu be-ghayr emkan
balkat bil-mekan malkem
kentu qeʻdi ma benatkem
kentu be-ghayr neshama
Ma binishameti.

Sar bi shaqq
sar bi baka

48 See also Behar, "Amira Hess ve-ha-shiva le-ʻaravit," 127.

49 Gerila Tarbut is a grassroots Jewish/Palestinian cultural-social action group founded in 2007 that stages bilingual Hebrew-Arabic poetry readings at politically sensitive or symbolic sites. In keeping with the disposition of linguistic melancholia discussed at the opening of this chapter, the journal's first volume was suggestively titled with the Hebrew and Arabic cognates *Ḥurban/Kharab*. The title bilingually denotes destruction, ruination, or a ruined building; in Hebrew, the term is reminiscent of *ḥurban ha-bayit*, the traditional name for the destruction of the Temple in Jerusalem, and the title also evokes the destroyed Palestinian villages and ruins of Palestinian houses in Israel. See also chapter 1, note 155.

saret bi khofa.
Ma 'aghaftu ash asawwi[50]
Mettu. Ma tamm minni shen.[51]

Perhaps in your world,
or in a place not yours.
I was sitting not among you
I was in a different soul,
not my own.

Within me formed a gap, a rent,
weeping and fear.
I knew not what to do—
I died. Nothing was left of me.[52]

The poem repeats these stanzas in Hebrew, and then continues alternating between Arabic and Hebrew; most (but not all) of the material appears in both languages, with a handful of lines in just one language. Following the Judeo-Arabic tradition, Hebrew characters are used for the text in both Arabic and Hebrew; the Arabic words, however, are not vocalized.

A return to traumatic childhood memories of immigration, the poem is a bold indictment of the speaker's spiritual death by the social imperative to extinguish her original language and identity. Although the theme of language and identity infuses Hess's oeuvre from its inception, in more ways than one this poem reads as the culmination of her poetic trajectory—not least of all because it is written bilingually, *recovering* the lost language of her childhood rather than merely lamenting its loss. The stanza below appears first in Arabic and then in Hebrew:

Now I want to speak in my language that I had forgotten
I don't want to forget it
I don't want to forget my mother and my father
I don't want to forget them, *ya hayati*, oh my life
that I didn't live, and that I know
would have been wondrous.

50 In Jewish Baghdadi dialect, *ray* is pronounced as *ghayn*; I have replicated this in my transliteration. See also chapter 3, note 100.
51 The sections in Jewish Baghdadi dialect were not vocalized in the Hebrew text. I have tried to transliterate them as phonetically as possible; I thank Sasson Somekh for his assistance. I have substituted *e* for *u* or *a* in several places (*malkem, kentu, mettu*) as Jewish Baghdadi dialect utilizes a vowel that is somewhere between the English *e* and *u* but closer to *e* (Somekh, personal communication, July 8, 2013).
52 Hess, "Kentu be-ghayr dini," 119.

The following stanza appears only in Hebrew:

> The river left them
> memory left them
> the scent left them
> the streets left
> we left them, until now
> and from here on out we will walk in the emptiness
> until our death.

In Behar's reading, Hess depicts the "emptiness of her life only in Hebrew . . . ; life without the original language, Arabic, and without the original place, Baghdad, are not life, they are death in life, and are walking in a vacuum."[53] Throughout the poem, Hess plays with the idea of exile from language as a kind of death; the speaker declares that she died, for she became "something else" (*davar aḥer*) because that is what she believed was expected of her. Yet, "Despite it all, I didn't also lose my death / for I was among the most vital dead one could imagine."[54] Perhaps, she muses in both Arabic and Hebrew, she never left at all;

> In my soul Amira was perhaps in Bahrain
> perhaps in Basra
> perhaps in the salon of her father's house
> she stays there
> but comes here . . .
> Perhaps Amira stayed inside the bus
> that took that world away.

Once in Israel, she recalls,

> I ride the bus and carry my corpse from place to place
> from Jerusalem to Or Yehuda
> and from Or Yehuda to Jerusalem

53 Behar, "Amira Hess ve-ha-shiva le-'aravit," 129.

54 Hess, "Kentu bi-ghayr dini," 121. Hess discussed this psychological experience in a 1998 interview with Ahuva Mu'alem and myself:

> **Ahuva:** You use the word *nispeti* ["I perished"; in Israeli Hebrew the verb *nispa* is strongly associated with the Holocaust] in one of your poems.
>
> **Amira:** I feel that I died and that I am not a living person. I see many Ashkenazim who were lost thirty years ago, and now they look young and happy. They feel that here [in Israel] they struck roots. And we who had roots, they didn't let us grow them here. Nor even our children. One is afraid even to say this. It's a kind of paranoia that you are betraying the country, the establishment (Levy and Mu'alem, "Eykh ata shlemut," 74–75).

I discovered that in Or Yehuda there is a great light[55]
there are words in another language
words in my unspoken language
in the language of my soul
my soul in Or Yehuda
runs from store to store to buy itself a cover
to make a garment for its body.

But ultimately, "no garment fits me"; the speaker is unable to find a new form, a new language, to accompany her in the world of the living. In short, "assimilation" is not a new beginning; it is an ending, it is cultural extinction. The last part of the poem is written mostly in Hebrew. For the speaker, Jewish Baghdadi Arabic is "another language," "my unspoken language," "the language of my soul," "the language of my father's house"; but it is frozen in time, belonging to the past.[56] The poem, in short, is a journey between Hebrew as a "foreign" language (*safa zara*) and Jewish Baghdadi Arabic as an "other" language (*safa aḥeret*), and "the movement between them is one of memory and forgetting, of repression and regret."[57]

Nearing its conclusion, the poem gathers force for its coup de grâce, a sacrilege against one of Israel's most cherished national myths:

Would you like me to say: "It is good to die for our country" [*tov la-mut be'ad artsenu*]?
I know that you'll want to beat me with sixty shoes
you'll want to spit in my face
you'll want to say, "Why, had you stayed in Baghdad,
would you have had it any better?"
Perhaps it would have been better
if I had died for her.
But the reason for dying is not very clear to me
she is known to me yet she is not lucid before me
within me there is no Nehardea[58] to know all this killing

55 In the Hebrew, this is a pun, as *or* (the first part of Or Yehuda) means "light." Now a town outside Tel Aviv, Or Yehuda was the site of a large transit camp housing mostly Iraqi Jewish immigrants in the 1950s; see also chapter 5, note 53.

56 Behar, "Amira Hess ve-ha-shiva le-'aravit," 130.

57 Ibid., 131.

58 Nehardea, from the Aramaic *nher-da'a* ("river of knowledge"), was a town in ancient Babylon situated on the Euphrates River that housed one of the earliest centers of Babylonian Jewish learning. The line puns on the idea of knowledge embedded in its name: *eyn bi naharde'a la-da'at et kol ha-mita ha-zot.*

As the Iraqi proverb says,
Ana b-idi jerhit idi
u-sammoni jerhit al-id
ba'd al-nadam ma yafid

With my one hand I wounded the other
and they called me "gimpy hand."
Now regret is of no use.[59]

At the poem's close, Hess invokes the Israeli national hero Joseph Trumpeldor's famous statement *tov la-mut be-'ad artsenu* (It is good to die for our country), which he declared while dying of wounds sustained in the 1920 Battle of Tel Hai. Anticipating her audience's rage, Hess deflects his words through the Iraqi proverb, implying that she is both the agent and the victim of her own wound.[60] The poem thus ends by rejecting the Hebrew narrative of sacrifice for the good of the state in favor of a much more ambiguous idea of the wound, a move that expresses her honest perplexity in the face of history. She knows very well that the Iraq she left as a child no longer exists, and admits that she cannot fathom the morass of violence and killing that plagues the Iraq of the present. Nonetheless, she says, if it is good to die for one's homeland, perhaps that homeland should have been the one she left behind.[61] The speaker's direct challenge to the reader, almost daring the reader to strike out at her, recalls the speaker of Chetrit's poem, who curses his readers in both Hebrew and Arabic.

In this, her first and so far only bilingual Arabic-Hebrew poem, Hess thematizes her linguistic dilemma. She reaches no equilibrium or solution; the speaker merely oscillates between two different experiences of linguistic alienation. Behar's analysis of the poem emphasizes that bilingualism is the historic norm in Jewish textual culture, much of which rested on the principle of an original and translation (from Hebrew to another Jewish language) and which became "unnatural" only in Israel; in his reading, the poem's othering of both Hebrew and Arabic is counterbalanced by its restoration of bilingualism and translation.[62] Traditionally, however, a clear sense of order was maintained between the Hebrew source text and its translation (for Arab Jews, the *sharḥ*); by beginning the poem in Arabic and *then* translating into Hebrew, Hess's

59 Hess, "Kentu bi-ghayr dini," 123–124.
60 Behar, "Amira Hess ve-ha-shiva le-'aravit," 131.
61 When asked how she would have been different if she had remained in Baghdad, she replied, "It's hard to know. Maybe in Baghdad I would have been a less insecure artist" (Levy and Mu'alem, "Eykh ata shlemut," 72).
62 Behar, "Amira Hess ve-ha-shiva le-'aravit," 131.

poem confuses this order. As a poem that is clearly and explicitly directed at its monolingual Hebrew-speaking audience, its use of bilingualism may perhaps gesture at traditional Jewish multilingualism, but it is used more assertively to disorient the Israeli listener/reader, bringing the reader into the speaker's experience of alienation.

Each of the three poems analyzed here is a performance of "language and its Other"—Ashdodian and its Hebrew Other, Aramaic and its Hebrew Other, Jewish Baghdadi Arabic and its Hebrew Other. Each poem strives to reverse the Zionist dictum "Yehudi, daber 'ivrit!" (Jew, speak Hebrew!) by foreignizing the idea of Israeli Hebrew, whether through explicit declaration (Chetrit's "I write in Ashdodian"), implicit representation (Hess's use of Aramaic), or a combination of the two strategies (Hess's bilingual poem). Moreover, in their othering of Israeli Hebrew, all three poems utilize linguistic sources that resituate their readers within a larger Middle Eastern context. Chetrit invokes the Bible not as a source of "authentic" Hebrew national culture, but conversely as a social document reflecting linguistic differentiation and ethnic pluralism. In her 1987 poem, Hess turns to the Aramaic language and to the Babylonian context of the Book of Daniel; two decades later, she uses both Arabic and Hebrew to ask her Israeli reader to imagine *Iraq*, not Israel, as a homeland that one could live in and even die for.

THE THIRD GENERATION: MOTHER TONGUES, MUTENESS, AND THE PRESENCE OF ABSENCE

In 2007, a group of young Mizraḥi activists announced their arrival in an anthology called *Tehudot zehut: ha-dor ha-shlishi kotev mizraḥit* (*Echoing Identities: The Third Generation Writes Mizraḥish*).[63] The title replaces *'ivrit*, Hebrew, with *mizraḥit*, "Mizraḥish," suggesting that the discourse on *mizraḥiyut* has taken on an identity of its own. Its contributors, born between

63 The title also plays on the collocation *te'udot zehut* (identity cards), replacing *te'udot* (documents) with *tehudot* (echoes). In his review of the collection, Yitzhak Laor lambastes it as whiny and narcissistic, faulting the contributors for leaning on trendy postcolonial terms such as "hybridity" rather than engaging with the ideas of major Mizraḥi activists and intellectuals, or even pushing their own narratives past the suffering of their parents and the fetishization of their own identity. As he pointedly asks, "What difference is there between those graduates of the interdisciplinary program [an elite accelerated program] at Tel Aviv University whose origins are 'completely Ashkenazi' and those who are 'half Mizraḥi'? Is it only the pain and affront of the [Mizraḥi] father?" (Laor, "Between Family and Postcolonial Earth"). I am inclined to agree with him, but find the collection to be of interest as a social text about recent developments in the intellectual discourse on *mizraḥiyut*. Many of the volume's contributors are in fact of mixed ethnicity, with one Mizraḥi parent. This fact in itself reveals that *mizraḥiyut* is becoming an active form of *self*-affiliation and identification rather than simply an ethnic label.

the late 1960s and the early 1980s, embody the realization of Israel's systematic drive to Hebraicize its Jewish population. Not only do members of this "third generation" (by and large) speak no Arabic, but they have no firsthand experience of life in the Arab world or of Arabic culture. Third-generation Mizraḥi writers thus face quite a different linguistic dilemma than that of fully bilingual writers such as Michael and Ballas, or of partially bilingual writers such as Matalon, who can write only in Hebrew, but who has access to French and Arabic. Notwithstanding their overtures to Arabic or the idea of Arab Jewish identity, in reality "post-Arabic" third-generation Mizraḥi writers have no language other than Hebrew. To return to Derrida, what happens to the writer trapped in the "monolingualism of the other"? As we already know from the German Jewish poet Paul Celan and the Francophone Algerian writer Assia Djebar, these conflicted monolinguals—functionally (or deliberately) monolingual authors who do not fit the monolingual paradigm—will find ways to rewrite their own language from within.

With this, we return to the *presence of absence*, a shared trope of Palestinian and Israeli writing in both Arabic and Hebrew. As noted in chapter 1, the phrase can be traced back to Israel's Absentee Property Law of 1950, which created the absurd category of "present absentees" (*nifkadim nokheḥim*): Palestinians who left their property during the 1948 war but remained within the borders of Israel, becoming internal refugees with no legal claim to their lands. Awareness of this issue permeated Jewish Israeli consciousness largely through David Grossman's 1992 book *Nokheḥim nifkadim* (*Absent Presentees*), a collection of interviews with Palestinians in Israel also published in English as *Sleeping on a Wire*. The *presence of absence* pervades Israeli and Palestinian discourses and appears in critical writings on Israeli legal history, sociology, literature, art, and archaeology.[64] In literary works in both Arabic and Hebrew, it connotes reality and unreality, memory and forgetting, recognition and denial, and the permeable border between them.

We have already seen how second-generation Mizraḥi poets such as Bitton, Chetrit, Hess, and Someck represented the loss of language. In the 1990s, Orly Castel-Bloom, a contemporary of Matalon also born to Francophone Egyptian Jewish parents, best known for her iconoclastic, bitingly satirical novels about Israeli urban life, broke with the reining norms of Hebrew fiction through her liberal use of English and French, even interpolating foreign words in Latinate script into her Hebrew; like

64 For sociology, see for example Handelman and Handelman, "The Presence of Absence," and Handelman, *Nationalism and the Israeli State*, 144–170. Handelman uses it to discuss Israeli national memorialism, especially as pertaining to military casualties.

the work of Swissa, Matalon, and the Ashkenazi Israeli writer Yoel Hoffman, her writing also explodes Hebrew monolingualism.[65] Because of her eclectic subject matter, Castel-Bloom is not discussed in Hebrew criticism as a "Mizraḥi writer." Yet she published two stories, "Jo, ish kahir" ("Cairo Joe," 1989) and "Ummi fi shughl" (Arabic for "My Mother Is at Work," 1993), that directly addressed the questions of language and memory at the heart of Mizraḥi literary discourse, just before the burst of Mizraḥi fiction on these topics in the following decade.[66]

In "Ummi fi shughl," an Israeli woman sits on a park bench when a sharp prick on her leg draws her attention to a derelict elderly woman hiding beneath it. The woman repeatedly claims to be her mother, sparking an unforgettable exchange. After much back and forth, the old woman asks the narrator, "What are you writing about now?" (suggesting the narrator is Castel-Bloom). Dodging the question, the narrator asks the elderly woman if she is a ghost, to which she unexpectedly replies in Arabic, "I told you already—*ana ummik* [I am you mother]!" Even more remarkably, the narrator then switches to Arabic as well. The bizarre dialogue continues in Arabic, alternating between the older woman's assertion that she is the narrator's mother or sister and the narrator's retort that her mother (or sister) is at work (*fi shughl*). Finally the elderly woman asks the narrator, in Hebrew, to take her home and look after her; when the narrator refuses, she slips back under the bench, back out of sight. The story reads as a thinly veiled allegory for the presence of absence: the absence of Arabic, of the mother tongue, among Mizraḥi Jews in Israel. In this story, however, even while the memory of the neglected or repressed mother tongue haunts the author, it fails to persuade her to bring it back "home."[67]

65 On Castel-Bloom's linguistic poetics, see Starr, "Reterritorializing the Dream," 224–225 and Grumberg, "Ricki Lake in Tel Aviv."

66 "Jo, ish kahir" ("Cairo Joe") depicts a Jewish family in Cairo during Egyptian-Israeli hostilities in the 1948 war. As Deborah Starr argues, a vision of spirits and visit to an exorcism ritual serve as a prolepsis of the "expulsion of Jews from the body politic of the Egyptian nation" (Starr, *Remembering Cosmopolitan Egypt*, 108).

67 See also Starr, "Reterritorializing the Dream"; Grumberg, "Ricki Lake in Tel Aviv"; and Hochberg, *In Spite of Partition*, 1–2. Hochberg reads the story differently, as an allegory about the repressed memory of "the proximity, indeed familial ties, between Hebrew and Arabic, the Arab and the Jew" (*In Spite of Partition*, 2). Hochberg's reading assumes that the ghostly figure is an "old Arab woman," an interpretation not supported by the text, which if anything indicates that she is a Mizraḥi Jew, given that she initially addresses the narrator in fluent Hebrew and that her first question concerns the narrator's ethnic origin (*me-eyfo ani, klomar me-ezu 'eda ani*; Castel-Bloom, "Ummi fi shughl," 10)—a question highly characteristic of an elderly Jewish Israeli woman. I concur with Hochberg that what is at stake is a haunting, but it is the haunting of Arabic as a *Jewish* language, the language of the author/narrator's *own* familial past.

If the ghostly idea of the presence of absence was intimated in these Hebrew texts of the 1990s, by the mid-2000s the concept was overtly named and circulated widely in both Palestinian and Mizraḥi discourses. For example, Mahmoud Darwish's last major work was a poetic autobiography called *Fi hadrat al-ghiyab* (2006), translated into English as *In the Presence of Absence.* The book elegiacally recapitulates all the leitmotifs of his lifetime of writing—language, poetry, exile, Palestine, memory and forgetting—with references to the presence of absence threading throughout his haunting meditations.[68] While alluding to Darwish's own mortality, the play on presence and absence also connotes the existential condition of Palestine. Three examples from different places in the text illustrate how the presence of absence glides across metaphorical domains:

> Alone . . . you try to find your own line in this white thicket that stretches between writing and speech. You no longer ask: What will I write, but rather how will I write? You call upon a dream, but it flees from the image; you seek a meaning, but the rhythm resists. You think you have crossed the threshold that separates the horizon from the abyss and are ably trained to open up metaphor to an absence that is present and a presence that is absent in a seemingly responsive spontaneity.[69]

> The homeland was born in exile. Paradise was born from the hell of absence.[70]

> What can I say to you, my friend, in the presence of this pure absence, now that you have dictated this fragmented farewell address.[71]

While the first passage relates to the process of writing poetry, of creating and expressing meaning—between absence and presence—the second refers to Palestine, and the third to the death of the poet's friend (most likely Emile Habiby, whose death Darwish discusses in a previous section). The common thread of the *presence of absence* in relation to writing, to Palestine, and to mortality unifies those three themes, which, in Darwish's poetics, are never very far apart.

68 See, for example, Darwish, *In the Presence of Absence*, 25, 35, 45, 52, 90, 124, 135–136, and 149.
69 Ibid., 90.
70 Ibid., 124.
71 Ibid., 149.

Around the same time, the presence of absence also becomes a recurring theme in writing by Mizraḥim, where it relates to the absence of *Arabic*. Its transformation is an inversion of the ideas of the early *yishuv*, when Zionist settlers symbolically became present in the land through the prototype of the Arabic-speaking Palestinian. In this recent turn, however, Mizraḥim are not objectifying Palestinians as figures of envy, fear, or disdain, but are imagining themselves as post-Arabic subjects, often in solidarity with Palestinian narratives of loss. In such works, Arabic hovers beneath the surface as a trace or a ghostly presence. Their authors cultivate the effect of a modern Israeli Hebrew literature written over the incomplete erasure of Arabic language and culture: a palimpsestic textual formation with obvious structural correspondences to the spatial realities of Israel, much of which was literally built over the ruins of the Palestinian past.

In 2002, a major Mizraḥi art exhibit and film festival called *Sfat em/ Lughat umm* (*Mother Tongue*) was convened. In the exhibit, twenty-two artists dealt with questions and representations of Mizraḥi identity. Two years later, a lengthy volume titled *Hazut mizraḥit-Hove ha-na' ba-svakh 'avaro ha-'aravi* (*Eastern Appearances: A Present Moving in the Thicket of Its Arab Past*) merged a catalogue of the art exhibit with a collection of essays on issues of language and identity, Hebrew, Arabic, and Judeo-Arabic, presence and absence. In her introduction to the catalogue (published trilingually in English, Hebrew, and Arabic), Tal Ben Zvi, the exhibit's curator, focuses on language as a theme in Mizraḥi visual art. Her essay seamlessly combines the two central tropes of Mizraḥi writing, the idea of absence and the family allegory, folding them into one another through a discussion of language:

> Arabic . . . was and is a mother tongue for many Israelis, including second generation Mizrahi Jews. Some of the artists participating in the exhibition have spoken Arabic since childhood, as it was the language spoken at home. But for most of the artists, Arabic is like a present absence that informs their biographies and lingers in their memories on the familial and communal levels. The tension between mother tongue (exercised in the private spheres of home, neighborhood, and synagogue) and father tongue (public speak or the language of the state, the law, the canon) defines and reinforces the deferral of the mother tongue. She is marginalized in both space and time, exiled to the provinces of reminiscence and dream. Father tongue pushes mother tongue aside, imposing inconsistencies in their freedom of speech.

This distinction between Arabic as (private) "mother tongue" and Hebrew as (public) "father tongue" is further complicated by Judeo-Arabic dialects, which, Ben Zvi says, moved from the status of "father tongue" in the Arab world to "mother tongue" in Israel.[72] In fact, historically speaking, Judeo-Arabic dialects were always intimate languages spoken at home and within the Jewish community; in the presence of non-Jews, speakers would code-switch into the majority dialect. Ben Zvi's gendering of the linguistic division of labor is thus less useful as a heuristic device than as an example of the psychological tension projected onto questions of language in recent Mizraḥi discourse. It also demonstrates the power that the "mother tongue" metaphor wields over *any* discussion of language and community in the national context. In critiquing the "division between 'mother tongue' and 'father tongue' [as] the product of post-migration and nationalization in the Israeli-Zionist context,"[73] Ben Zvi unwittingly reifies the gendered stereotypes underlying the idea of "mother tongue," which arose to consecrate the imagined linkages between language and nation in the formative period of modern European nationalism. Yasemin Yildiz describes the "mother tongue" as the "affective knot at the center of the monolingual paradigm," arguing that it "constitutes a condensed *narrative* about origin and identity" in which only one socially sanctioned language is the "locus of affect and attachment."[74] Ben Zvi sidesteps this paradigm without surpassing it, assigning traditional gender roles to Hebrew, Arabic, and Judeo-Arabic while setting them in struggle, instead of envisioning a multilingual paradigm in which multiple languages (just like multiple parents) can serve as the locus of affect and attachment.

One year after the *Mother Tongue* exhibit, in 2003, the journal *Ha-kivun mizraḥ* (*Eastward Bound*) produced a bilingual Hebrew-Arabic issue titled *al-Adab bayn lughatayn/Ha-sifrut beyn shtey safot*, Arabic and Hebrew respectively for *Literature between Two Languages*. The cover image, an abstract representation of a man and a woman (identified by their moustache and lips) in embrace, over which the Hebrew and Arabic titles are superimposed, suggests a passionate bilingual entanglement (see Figure 8). In fact, the image is a graphic representation of an iconic still in which the Jewish Egyptian actress and singer Layla Murad (1918–1995), the diva of Egypt's cinematic golden age, gazes into the eyes of her costar (and briefly, husband) Anwar Wagdi.[75]

The journal opens with a poem printed bilingually in Hebrew and Arabic, whose title, "Calling Card," alludes to Mahmoud Darwish's poem

72 Ben Zvi, "Deferring Language," 182 in English, 109 in Hebrew.

73 Ibid., 182 in English, 109 in Hebrew.

74 Yildiz, *Beyond the Mother Tongue*, 10–13.

75 See *Ha-kivun mizraḥ* 7 (Fall 2003), 87 (film still) and cover.

Figure 8. Estina Lavy Chernyavski, "Layla Murad and Anwar Wagdi" (graphic adaptation); front cover for "Literature between Two Languages," *Ha-kivun mizraḥ* 7 (Fall 2003). Courtesy of Bimat Kedem Publishing.

"Identity Card" discussed in chapter 4.[76] Like Darwish's poem, it begins with the speaker's assertion of his identity:

כרטיס ביקור

אֲנִי מִן הַמִּזְרָח
כָּל הַשֶּׁמֶשׁ נִקְוְתָה בְּעֵינַי
וְרַגְלַי הוֹלְכוֹת וּמַעֲרִיבוֹת

שְׂפַת אִמִּי עַרְבִית
וּשְׂפַת אֵם אִמִּי קַוִּים עַל כַּף הַיָּד
וְעִבְרִית אֵלֶם אָבִי
כְּתוּבוֹת עַל הַקִּיר

بطاقة زيارة

أنا من الشرق
كل الشمس تجمعت فى عيني
وقدماي تتجهان غربا

لغة أمي عربية
ولغة أم أمي خطوط على كف اليد
وعبرية أبي الخرساء
عناوين على الجدار

CALLING CARD

I am from the East [*ani min ha-mizraḥ/ana min al-sharq*]
all the sun is collected in my eyes
and my feet are going West

My mother tongue is Arabic [*sfat-imi ʻarvit/lughat ummi ʻarabiyya*]
and my mother's mother's tongue is lines on the palm of the hand
[*u-sfat em-imi kavim ʻal kaf ha-yad/wa-lughat umm ummi khutut ʻala kaff al-yad*]
Hebrew is my father's muteness [*ve-ʻivrit eylem avi/wa-ʻibriyyat abi al-khursa'*],[77]
Writings on the wall [. . .]

Both the poem's author, Yo'av Ḥayyik, and translator, Jacqueline Sha'shu'a, are Iraqi-Israelis.[78] The issue's contents are devoted largely to the little known Arabic literature of Iraqi Jewish writers, including Samir Naqqash; the texts included are printed in Arabic with a side-by-side Hebrew translation on every page, an unusual and visually striking format that in and of itself recuperates or (re)normalizes Arabic-Hebrew bilingualism. The last section of the journal, also printed bilingually, is devoted to poetry and prose by Palestinian writers. The editors' decision to include Palestinian writing in the volume as well as the crossover of influence between

76 Ḥayyik, "Kartis bikur," 3.

77 The Arabic translation changes the meaning to "my father's Hebrew is mute" or "my father's Hebrew is muteness"; there is some confusion as *khursa'* is the feminine form of "mute" (so the adjective here, modifying *ʻibriyya*, should not receive the definite *al-*) whereas "muteness" should be *al-kharas.*

78 The topic is also introduced with essays by Reuven Snir and Sasson Somekh.

Palestinian and Mizraḥi writing indicated by Ḥayyik's nod to Darwish in the journal's opening poem represent the aspiration for a convergence of Palestinian and Mizraḥi voices in the Hebrew-Arabic no-man's-land.

The journal's back cover displays a picture of a red tapestry emblazoned with a dark green, almost black triangle (see Figure 9). Filling the space of the triangle are the Arabic words "Ana yahudi" (I am a Jew), which leap out at the viewer from the dark background. This work by Israeli artist Haim Maor was originally exhibited in a Tel Aviv gallery in 1990. The image is simultaneously evocative of multiple pasts: the tapestry's fringes hint (perhaps not without irony) at an Oriental carpet, which in one context may connote a lost home and in another, Oriental kitsch; at the same time, the sewn-on emblem inscribed with "Jew" cannot but allude to darker memories from the collective Jewish past. Yet it is also an inversion and reclamation of the forced badge of identity, as the *ana* (I) turns *yahudi* (Jew) into an affirmative statement rather than a pejorative label. As pronouncing oneself a Jew in Arabic is oxymoronic if not taboo in Israel, this work distills the anti-normative project of Arab Jewish identity.[79] Moreover, insofar as most Jewish viewers would not be able to read the Arabic letters, the orthography itself does the work of reminding the viewer of the absence of Arabic as a Jewish language. In a review of the issue of *Ha-kivun mizraḥ*, Dror Mishani discusses how recovery of the Arab Jewish cultural past (literature, music, and cinema) plays a crucial role in the development of "a Mizraḥi language in Hebrew" (*lashon mizraḥit be-'ivrit*). This return to the past enriches not only "Mizraḥi language," but Israeli Hebrew and culture; "It reminds [Israeli] Hebrew of all the opportunities it missed, of all the possible Hebrews that it put to sleep inside itself, that it forgot, and that resurface now to speak."[80] All these themes—the resurgence of the past, muteness and silence, the possibility of speaking "another Hebrew"—come to the fore in the Mizraḥi fiction of the new millennium, a fiction that collectively develops this Mizraḥi language or *lashon mizraḥit*.

THIRD-GENERATION LIMINALITY: GHOSTS OF THE PALESTINIAN AND ARAB JEWISH PASTS

> To inherit is to reaffirm through transformation, change, and displacement.
>
> —Jacques Derrida[81]

79 It is worth noting that the artist, Haim Maor, is not himself of Arab Jewish descent.

80 Mishani, "Leshonot mi-mizraḥ."

81 Derrida, "Language Is Never Owned," 104.

Figure 9. Haim Maor, *Ana yahudi* (*I Am a Jew* in Arabic), 1990, embroidery, application of satin and velvet, 140 × 190 cm, artist's collection. Courtesy of the artist.

It was in 2005, when a then-unknown student by the name of Almog Behar won the annual short story contest sponsored by *Haaretz*, Israel's highbrow daily newspaper, that the absence of Arabic became present with a vengeance. Of mixed Iraqi, Turkish, and German Jewish descent, Behar was raised in a traditional but not religiously observant family, in a monolingual Hebrew environment; yet his literary project revives the language and spirit of traditional Sephardi Judaism. His winning story, which launched his literary career, was titled "Ana min al-yahud," Arabic for "I Am of the Jews." As noted in chapter 1, the story was translated into Arabic and reprinted in *al-Hilal*, a major Egyptian cultural journal.[82] Both the Hebrew original and the Arabic translation were also reprinted in Behar's first short story collection (2008) by the same title—here too, the striking image of the final Hebrew page abutting the first page of the Arabic translation makes a strong graphical statement.

More than any previous literary work, "Ana min al-yahud" confronted Israel's erasure of Arabic as a Jewish language and explored the inheritance of linguistic memory. Its intricately wrought language complements the thematic layer of the story, creating a parallel metanarrative. Like Chetrit's poem in Ashdodian and Hess's bilingual Arabic-Hebrew poem, Behar's story explicitly addresses the dispossession of language. While this is a more challenging topic to sustain at length in prose narrative, the story is driven less by plot than by language. The poetic and prosodic qualities of the text render it a transgeneric piece between prose poem and story; as we will see shortly, Behar repeats some of the story's language verbatim in a poem on the same theme. The text's crossover from story to prose poem is accentuated by the unusual choice to fully vocalize the accompanying Arabic translation in the story collection (as with Hebrew, Arabic prose is usually unvocalized except in cases of grammatical ambiguity, whereas poetry in both languages is typically vocalized). I read the story as belonging to the same metaphysical mode of "language and its Others" as the poems discussed above.

Behar's surreal, Borgesian tale begins with the outbreak of a mysterious virus that causes young native Israelis to revert to the Diasporic accents of their immigrant grandparents—in the narrator's case, the Iraqi Arabic accent of his deceased grandfather. Although the pathogen initially affects Mizraḥim, it eventually spreads to the Ashkenazi population, at which point the narrator declares, "this *dybbuk* is now haunting the Ashkenazim too."[83] The reference to the *dybbuk*, in Ashkenazi folklore a disembodied spirit that possesses living bodies, cleverly makes this a story about Israel's dispossession of *all* Diasporic languages, including Yiddish. Yet the *dybbuk* possessing Israeli Hebrew speech does not actually restore Diasporic *languages*; it only brings back Diasporic *accents*. The narrator searches in vain for a return to Arabic; indeed, the story's only Arabic statement is the titular "Ana min al-yahud." The *accent*, a middle

82 'Abud, "Shazaya al-qahr al-thaqafi."

83 Behar, "Ana min al-yahud," 60; all translations of the text that follow below are adapted from "Ana min al yahoud—I'm One of the Jews," Eden's translation.

ground between foreignness and nativity, works in the story to reverse the multigenerational process of linguistic naturalization, symbolically transforming native speakers back into immigrants (and thus reversing the Zionist narrative). Behar then further complicates this tale of linguistic dispossession by writing it in an anachronistic, quasi-rabbinic Hebrew vaguely reminiscent of the language of S. Y. Agnon. This "weird Hebrew" contributes to the reader's sense of disorientation while following the narrator's disjointed, almost delirious recounting of his affliction.

Behar continued the cultivation of his unique style throughout his story collection as well as his first novel, *Tchaḥla ve-Ḥezkel* (*Rachel and Ezekiel*, 2010). His idiosyncratic language rebels against both the loss of Arabic and the flattening of Modern Hebrew; Behar compensates for these losses through linguistic excess, creating the very antithesis of the *'ivrit raza* or "thin Hebrew" associated with the work of Etgar Keret and the aforementioned Orly Castel-Bloom, two of the leading Israeli writers of the 1990s. His novel garnered mixed reviews. One critic lauded the "varied and beautiful uses of the language,"[84] while another called the language "infuriating," claiming that Behar uses this dense, "thick" language as "camouflage" to hide the fact that "there is no novel there." For this second reviewer, Behar's attempt to utilize the rabbinic stratum of Hebrew in contemporary prose rings false, in contradistinction to the language of Haim Sabato, a religious writer of Syrian Jewish descent whose style has been compared favorably to Agnon's.[85] A third reviewer expressed bafflement, noting that "of course this is not the accepted literary style [of Hebrew], neither biblical nor rabbinic language even though Bible and Talmud reverberate in it. It sounded to me almost unidentifiable and yet nonetheless familiar."[86] This reviewer expresses the uncanniness of confronting the distantly familiar unknown, a sensation that accompanies all types of hauntings. Indeed, Behar's double-pronged destabilization of Israeli Hebrew through the weirding of Hebrew and through the present-absenting of Arabic brings us back to Kafka. As Yildiz explains, for Kafka, "nonnative languages such as Yiddish and French play a crucial identity- and affect-producing role, even if they never enter the [German] texts themselves. Thus, what looks like a monolingual text may, in fact, suggest the contours of a multilingual paradigm," so that Behar, like Kafka before him, "rearticulates the mother tongue as uncanny rather than familiar."[87] In Behar's story, Arabic does not supplant Hebrew; rather, Hebrew

84 Schweimer, "Alkhimiya shel ha-mila ha-ktuva."

85 Glasner, "'Al Tchaḥla ve-Ḥezkel, shel Almog Behar."

86 Lahman, "Tchaḥla ve-Ḥezkel/Almog Behar."

87 Yildiz, *Beyond the Mother Tongue*, 35. Yildiz explains further that "Freud defines the uncanny as a special case of anxiety—namely, one in which the familiar and unfamiliar slide disturbingly

becomes uncanny via its close encounter with Arabic.[88] Creating a monolingual text with a bilingual consciousness, Behar effectively breaks down these distinctions and renders language itself "uncountable," to use Derrida's term.[89]

A number of reviewers noted that the novel's unusually thick linguistic texture is partly explained by its dedication, which I suggest reading as a paratext. Behar dedicates the book to an odd couple the likes of which no one else could have placed on the same flyleaf: Ovadia Yosef, the now-legendary spiritual leader of the *Shas* (*Shomrey sefarad* or Sephardic Guardians) movement, an Orthodox Sephardi political party and social phenomenon; and Sasson Somekh, an important writer, translator, and Israeli professor emeritus of Arabic literature, author of several books including a memoir pertaining to Arab Jewish identity, who happens to be an avowed secularist. Aside from the fact that both figures are Iraqi Jews and were public figures in Israel (Yosef died in 2013), they have nothing in common, and their juxtaposition would strike most readers as highly ironic, if not downright comic. Behar chooses to frame his text this way for a reason. His novel, and indeed his entire literary project, can be viewed as an attempt to reconcile their radically different approaches to Mizraḥi cultural identity. The first (Yosef's), which aims to revive the traditional, multilayered, polyphonic Hebrew of the liturgical, poetic, and mystical traditions of Sepharad, is utilized by writers such as Swissa, Sabato, Hess, and the poet Ḥaviva Pedaya; the other (Somekh's), which draws on the cosmopolitan, secular, and often multilingual Arab Jewish or Levantine experience (epitomized by Jewish involvement in Arab cinema, music, and modern Arabic literature), is represented in the novels of Ballas, Michael, Gormezano Goren, and Matalon. Behar positions himself at the junction of these two roads, yearning equally for the Arabic of Somekh and the Hebrew of Yosef. Indeed, in a highly inter-referential moment in his novel, the protagonist Ḥezkel ponders this very dilemma while ruminating on Somekh's memoir, *Baghdad, Yesterday*: "In the end he decided that the book by Somekh had a holy quality, and he placed it on top of a book that discusses Jewish law."[90] At the same time, Behar openly acknowledges Amira Hess's influence on his work, conducting academic research on her poetry and even writing a novella-length story about her, which appears in the same collection as

---

into each other"; as such, she reasons, "not a 'foreign' language but a 'familiar' one becomes a potential site of the uncanny" (ibid., 53–54).

88 Furthermore, "Instead of appropriating Yiddish, Kafka's interest in Yiddish leads to a depropriation of German"—again, a process paralleled in Behar's depropriation of Israeli Hebrew; ibid., 44.

89 Derrida, *Monolingualism of the Other*, 29.

90 See Alon, "Hebrew Fiction/Old-New Hymns" and Somekh, *Baghdad, Yesterday.*

"Ana min al-yahud."[91] The linguistic hyperawareness as well as the prophetic tonality of "Ana min al-yahud" invite comparisons with Hess's poetry and read as an adaptation of her style to prose narrative.

But if the language of "Ana min al-yahud" links the text to other Hebrews, its thematic perspective hones in directly on the absence of Arabic. The presence of Arabic as an absent language, or the *presence* of its *absence*, is the story's thematic polestar. The story eloquently protests the hegemony of Hebrew that silenced the narrator's grandfather and led his parents to transform themselves into model Hebrew-speaking Israelis. Mentally addressing his Iraqi-born parents, who had once struggled to purge their acquired Hebrew of all traces of Arabic influence, the narrator muses, "I write poems of opposition to Hebrew in Hebrew . . . because I have no other language to write in, for out of shame, you did not bequeath me a thing."[92] "Ana min al-yahud" thus represents not only a third-generation Israeli's cry against the theft of his linguistic and cultural inheritance, but his confrontation of the second generation's complicity. He continues, "And the language that has become my language commands me to pour my soul in it, to be an empty flute [*ḥalil*] for its gusts of air, until together we produce a sound, and together we become a hoarse *nay* [Arabic flute]—*we will be disguised as a different language, an absent language* [*nitḥaze safa aḥeret, ne'ederet*]."[93] This union between the Arabic language and the narrator seemingly transforms him as an instrument of language from the Hebrew flute (*ḥalil*) into the Arabic flute (*nay*). Yet it is not a genuine transformation as much as a disguise, for the narrator says that both he and the *nay* wear the costume of an "absent language."

Written in an almost prophetic idiom, in first-person narration without a straightforward plot, "Ana min al-yahud" reads like a meditation on the dispossession of language and the return of the repressed. But it offers no resolution. It is not a story about recovery, either in the literal sense of recovering from an illness (symbolized here as the "language plague") or in the figurative sense of recovering a lost language or identity, for the narrator achieves neither. Rather, it is a story about anamnesis, as through his illness, the narrator seems to access and reawaken knowledge from his grandfather's life. Alternatively, one can also read it through Wendy Belcher's theory of discursive possession, in which case the narrator becomes an energumen (a body through which others

91 See Behar, "Amira bat Salima." The longest single piece in the book, it begins with the opening lines of the first poem in Hess's first collection.

92 Behar, "Ana min al-yahud," 63.

93 Ibid., 63, my emphasis.

speak).[94] Throughout the story, the narrator holds an internal dialogue with his dead Iraqi grandfather, whose accent he has suddenly acquired. The grandfather speaks to the narrator through the narrator's own voice, advising him to take refuge in silence: "And my grandfather would speak to me, asking me in my voice whether there is any end to this story, and why is this history of mine mixed up with yours, how have I come to disrupt your life, I am the generation of the desert [*ani dor midbar*] and how have you arisen to renew me." The grandfather's monologue concludes, "I did not meet my death in Jerusalem, nor in the land of my birth, but rather in the desert between them, a great desert of silence [*harbe midbar shtika*]."[95]

In the Hebrew, the juxtaposition of *midbar* (desert) and *shtika* (silence) is evocative, as *midbar* is a homograph of *medaber* (speaking). This semantic connection is deeply resonant in the Jewish tradition, which construes the desert both as a wasteland and as a site of prophecy. The idiom *dor midbar* (the generation of the desert) denotes the generation of Israelites who went out of Egypt but were prohibited from entering the Land of Israel, either as divine retribution for their waywardness and lack of faith (cf. Numbers 14) or, as aggadic tradition has it, because their slave mentality left them unprepared for life as a free people in their own land. Doomed to die in the desert, they became known as *metey midbar* (the desert dead), whose bid for freedom would be realized only by their progeny. In Israel, the "generation of the desert" became an epithet for all those who did not conform to the Zionist ideal of the New Jew. In the early decades of statehood, the Ashkenazi Labor-led establishment dismissed first-generation Mizraḥi immigrants as a *dor midbar* hopelessly mired in their Diasporic mentality, as a liability to be written off, whereas their children might still be redeemable.[96] Behar's invocation of the phrase alludes to this paternalistic attitude but also doubles as a reappropriation of the "desert dead" from Bialik's 1902 poema "Metey midbar" ("The Desert Dead"), one of Bialik's major works. In the poem, the "desert dead" awaken from their slumber and rebel against God and their fate; Bialik portrays these rebels as heroes.[97] In an ironic repetition/reversal of Bialik's heroic mode,

94 Belcher writes, "Discourse, like a virus or a spirit, can slip into a host. . . . Through intimate contact, these agents of the other spread, momentarily taking over or possessing their hosts. Under the influence, the host then produces objects . . . that are partially animated by this other"; the process reminds us that authors are not "entirely aware of their own processes of creation or in control of the objects they create" (*Abyssinia's Samuel Johnson*, 8).

95 Ibid., 62.

96 See, for example, Ram, *The Changing Agenda of Israeli Sociology*, 101, and Shimony, *'Al saf ha-ge'ula*, 21, 28.

97 Bialik, *Shirim*, 349. A historical poema composed of three distinct episodes, it is based on the Talmudic legend that the desert generation of the Exodus, which mutinied and was therefore

Behar's antiheroes, the *dor midbar* of first-generation immigrants, also rise from the dead to rebel against their enforced silence, in this case by possessing the speech of their progeny. Eventually, everyone is infected by the language plague except for the narrator's parents, who represent the second-generation Mizraḥim that had repressed their cultural identities and successfully assimilated. Distraught by their son's silence, they beg him to speak in any language at all—just to speak. The story ends with the narrator telling his parents he will share his stories with them, so that they will recognize them as their own.

The story is unabashedly political in its integration of the Arabic language, Arabic Jewish identity, and the Palestinian past, a triad that could be described as the soft underbelly of the collective Israeli psyche. Early in the story, in the course of his wanderings through the streets of Jerusalem, the narrator is detained by the police, who mistake him for a Palestinian suicide bomber. The narrator tries to explain to the police that he is Jewish, but the words come to him only in Arabic; what's more, he is unable to voice them aloud. Furthermore, his response is not "Ana yahudi," Arabic for "I am Jewish" or "I am a Jew," but rather "Ana min al-yahud": "I am of the Jews" or "I am one of the Jews" or even "I am from the Jews"—a more ambiguous, less direct, and somewhat less idiomatic response. This unvoiced statement is poignantly multivalent in other ways. It is the story's only full sentence in Arabic and also its only explicit statement of identity, but again it is never sounded *out loud*, only internally; the narrator's inability to articulate it locks him in silence, and alludes to the impossibility of being both Arab and Jewish in the State of Israel.

Not knowing what to make of him, the police subject him to a strip search. In what is doubtless the story's most provocative moment, the narrator describes how this mistreatment stokes the embers of a growing rage:

> And then they'd check me slowly, rummaging in my clothes, going over my body with metal detectors, stripping me of words and thoughts in their thorough silence, searching deep in the layers of my skin for a grudge, seeking an explosive belt, an explosive belt in my heart, eager to defuse any suspicious object. And when the policemen presented themselves to me in pairs, a few minutes into their examination one would tell the other, look, he's circumcised, this Arab really is a Jew, and then the other one would say, an Arab is also circumcised, and explosive belts don't care about circumcision,[98] and they would continue

prevented from entering the Land of Israel, did not perish but merely fell into an eternal sleep in the wilderness. See Alter, "Haim Nahman Bialik: Superimposed Worlds."

98 Alternatively, "they don't care about the word" (*ve-ḥagurot ha-nefets eynan me-ʻinyan ha-mila*); Behar, "Ana min al-yahud," 57.

> their search. And really, during the time when I left my body to them, explosive belts began to be born on my heart, swelling and refusing to be defused, thundering and thundering. But as they were not made of steel or gunpowder they succeeded in evading the metal detectors.[99]

In treating him as a terrorist, the policemen sow the emotional seeds of terrorism within him. Through the metaphor of the explosive belt, the narrator intimates identification with the psychology of suicide bombers—a daring and dangerous stance for a Jewish Israeli writer (although it is critical to note that he rationalizes only the *rage*, not the action). The narrator also flirts with Palestinian historical experience, seeking acceptance into an imagined alternative community. Here, he invokes Palestinian neighborhoods in West Jerusalem, befittingly ghostly places that have retained the architectural traces of the Palestinian presence and are still known by their original Arabic names. He imagines what these neighborhoods might still look like had history taken a different path, and even attempts to "converse" with the ghosts of their erstwhile residents, but is ultimately unable to bridge the gaps of language and history:

> And I would start to walk the streets of Katamon and the streets of Talbiyyeh and the streets of Baqa' and instead of seeing the wealthy Jerusalemites who had gathered there in the spacious homes . . . I'd once again see the wealthy Palestinians [*ashirey falastin*], and they were the way they had been before the 1948 war, as if there had never been a 1948 war. I see them and they are strolling in the yards among the fruit trees and picking fruit as though the newspapers had not told them that the trees would wither, that the land would be filled with refugees. And it was as though time had gone through another history, a different history. . . .
>
> And I would walk through the wealthy Palestinians' streets, and I thought that perhaps they would speak to me respectfully, not like the policemen. . . . I do not succeed in commingling with them because all I have at my disposal is Hebrew with an Arabic accent, and my Arabic, which doesn't come from my home but from the army, is suddenly mute, choked in my throat, cursing itself without uttering a word, hanging in the suffocating air of the refuges of my soul, hiding from family members behind the shutters of Hebrew. And all the time, when I tried to speak to them in the small, halting vocabulary of the Arabic I knew, what came out was Hebrew with an Arabic accent, until they thought that I was ridiculing them, and had my accent not been so Iraqi, had it not been for that, they would have been certain that I was making fun of them.

99 Ibid., 56–57.

> But like that, with the accent, they were confused, they thought I was making fun of the Iraqis, the Saddam Husseins, or maybe some old Iraqi who had kept his accent but forgotten his language. And I didn't make friends there even though I wanted to. . . . I had lost their language and they didn't know my language and between us remained the distance of the police forces and the generations.[100]

Here the narrator identifies an alternative language community and unsuccessfully attempts to interpolate himself into it; he remains outside both the Hebrew and Arabic speech communities. The language of this section is also worked into a poem called "Ha-'aravit sheli 'ilemet" ("My Arabic Is Mute") that appeared in Behar's first volume of poetry, published only months before the short story collection. Like the story, the poem is also printed in Hebrew alongside an Arabic translation:

My Arabic is mute
choked from the throat
cursing itself
without getting out a word
sleeping in the stifling air
of the shelters of my soul
hiding
from the rest of the family
behind Hebrew shutters.
And my Hebrew storms
dashing from room to room and the neighbors' porches
making its voice heard to many
prophesizing the coming of God and
bulldozers
then she takes her place in the living room
putting on airs
openly on the lip of her skin
concealed between the pages of her flesh[101]
naked one moment and clothed the next
she shrinks into the armchair
asking the forgiveness of her heart.

My Arabic is frightened
quietly poses as Hebrew

100 Ibid., 57–59.

101 *Geluyot geluyot 'al sfat 'ora / kesuyot kesuyot beyn dapey besrara*: the phrase *'al sfat 'ora* puns on the triple meaning of *safa* as edge, lip, and language, so the line might be translated as "on her skin's language." The two lines also play with the notion of revealment and concealment in language (*gilui ve-khisui be-lashon*) (Behar, *Tsim'on be'erot*, 15).

with every knock at her gates
whispers to friends:
Ahlan ahlan [Welcome].
And for every policeman she passes
in the street
she pulls out her papers
pointing out the protective clause:
Ana min al-yahud, ana min al-yahud.
And my Hebrew is deaf
sometimes so very deaf.[102]

The poem is a distillation of the story; both express the struggle of Arabic to make itself heard. Yet in the poem the speaker is absent, and the protagonists are the languages themselves, personified.

EXILE AND MUTENESS

The connection between exile and muteness, or exile and incomprehensible language, is well established in world literature; think for example of Conrad's Yanko in "Amy Foster," Nabokov's Professor Pnin, or Rushdie's tongue-tied porter in "The Courter."[103] In Modern Hebrew literature, however, the trope of muteness is a politically charged topic often associated with the silencing of Palestinians and Israel's erasure of the Palestinian past. Critics have previously addressed this theme through A. B. Yehoshua's 1963 story "Mul ha-ye'arot" ("Facing the Forests"), which portrays a failed Jewish doctoral student-cum-forest fire scout, who is assigned to an Israeli forest planted over the remains of a destroyed Palestinian village. He is assisted only by a groundskeeper, a Palestinian Arab who is completely mute, his tongue having been cut out in unspecified circumstances. Much has been made by literary critics of the Arab's muteness. The Lebanese novelist and critic Elias Khoury reads it in terms of the larger problem of the muteness of the Palestinian in Israeli literature, an issue he pursues as a connecting thread through readings of Benjamin Tammuz, Amos Oz, and Anton Shammas. In his view, "The question of muteness is not only a literary problem; it is an integral part of a literary paradigm."[104] Intriguingly, Khoury connects this thread to muteness in Palestinian literature, most famously in Ghassan Kanafani's highly influential novella *Rijal fi al-shams* (*Men in the Sun*), which was published the same year as "Facing the Forests." Khoury tries to define this notion of muteness, asking, "What is the

102 Ibid., 15–16, Arabic translation by Rima Abu Jaber, 17.
103 See Conrad, "Amy Foster"; Nabokov, *Pnin*; and Rushdie, "The Courter."
104 Khoury, "Rethinking the *Nakba*," 251.

meaning of a literature written without a tongue?" Ultimately, for Khoury muteness is about the status of the post-1948 Palestinian: "The muteness of literature is part of the muteness of history or, in other words, part of the inability of the victim to write the story."[105]

For Behar, muteness means something different, demonstrating once more how themes and tropes cross borders between Hebrew and Arabic literature in Israel/Palestine, acquiring different (but not unrelated) valences in their different discursive contexts. As Behar's story unfolds, the narrator finds that he has become a linguistic pariah who can speak in an acceptable way neither to Israelis nor to Palestinians; his Hebrew is too Arabic, his Arabic is too mute. He is the epitome of Derrida's monolingual writer, an "aphasic" who is thrown into a state of "absolute translation":

> Because he is therefore deprived of *all* language, and no longer has any other recourse—neither Arabic, nor Berber, nor Hebrew, nor any languages his ancestors would have spoken—because this monolingual is in a way aphasic (perhaps he writes because he is an aphasic), he is thrown into absolute translation, a translation without a pole of reference, without an originary language, and without a source language.[106]

In the story, the narrator is also in a disorienting state of absolute translation, in which there are no source languages, only imagined target languages, and the indeterminacy of the movement between linguistic states; his identity breaks down into total confusion. However, the narrator's inability to speak to Palestinians is not only a metaphor about his own linguistic impotence as he weighs his desire for the lost Arabic past against the reality of his Hebrew monolingualism. It is also a tacit recognition of the affective limits of empathy, its inability to undo history and bridge the terrible rift of "the police forces and the generations" (*ha-mishtarot ve-ha-dorot*). Even in his own fictitious recreation of the counterfactual, the narrator is stymied—a pessimism that belies the formative arguments of radical Mizraḥi intellectuals who theorized Arab Jewish identity in the Israeli context. Their discourse called for solidarity between Mizraḥim and Palestinians based in part on their mutual dispossession by Zionism, which sought to erase both Palestinian national identity and the Arab identity of Mizraḥi Jews. Behar's narrator seems to want to say, "I tried to rekindle my Arab identity through the nearest accessible model of Arabness—the Palestinians—but history stood between us as an unassailable barrier." Again, we have come full circle since the Hebrew Bedouin; if a hundred years ago European Jews looked

105 Ibid., 254.
106 Derrida, *Monolingualism of the Other*, 60–61.

to the Palestinian native when imagining an "authentic" Hebrew self, now a third-generation Mizraḥi Israeli turns to the ghosts of the Palestinian past in imagining his escape from Hebrew and the Zionist ethos.

With its *dybbuks* and hauntings, Behar's story brings to mind two other recent works of Hebrew fiction that address similar themes from very different perspectives. The first of these might described as Behar's ideological antithesis, the second as his analog. A. B. Yehoshua, a leading Israeli novelist who is of Sephardi-Mizraḥi heritage but is rarely if ever discussed as a "Mizraḥi writer," has represented questions of language and identity for decades, often as a matter of Palestinian-Israeli relations, but without penetrating the psychology of the linguistic encounter from the perspective of Arab Jews or Mizraḥim.[107] One scene from his 2001 novel *Ha-kala ha-meshaḥreret* (*The Liberated Bride*) is simultaneously one of the most provocative and most problematic episodes in the history of Modern Hebrew fiction's engagement with Arabic.[108] In the section in question, the protagonist Rivlin, an Ashkenazi Israeli scholar of classical Arabic and a self-styled "Orientalist" (*mizraḥan*), attends a staging of the central scene from *The Dybbuk*, an iconic early twentieth-century Jewish play and cornerstone of Zionist culture memory.[109] The performance depicts the exorcism of a *dybbuk* from the living body of his intended bride. This is no ordinary show, but rather a Hebrew-Arabic rendition performed in the West Bank city of Ramallah by Rivlin's student, who is a Palestinian Israeli, along with her cousins. In the novel, *The Dybbuk*'s famous exorcism scene, in which a rabbi converses with the *dybbuk* and orders it to depart the maiden's body, is played out bilingually, recited in Hebrew and echoed in Arabic; the Arabic lines are transliterated into Hebrew in the text. With its underlying metaphors of occupation and forced expulsion, Yehoshua's *dybbuk*-in-Palestine is so overdetermined that its exegesis could take up its own chapter in this book. In general, *The Liberated Bride* seems to reinforce the assumptions of Israeli *mizraḥanut* even as it parodies its practitioners in the academy: while the Jewish Israeli characters celebrate the beauty of classical Arabic poetry, they are always cognizant of Arabic as an instrument of control.

107 For a brilliant critique of A. B. Yehoshua's conflicted treatment of Sephardi/Mizraḥi identity vis-à-vis Israeli identity, see Laor, "'Mihu ashkenazi?': Ḥor be-idyologya shel A. B. Yehoshua." See also the related discussion of Yehoshua and Shammas in chapter 4 of this book, and Halpern, "Overstepping Boundaries," on Yehoshua and Kashua.

108 Its title means "The liberating bride," but it was published in English as *The Liberated Bride*.

109 See Morahg, "Perils of Hybridity"; I paraphrase from 370, in which Morahg cites Dorit Yerushalmi. *The Dybbuk* or *Between Two Worlds* is a 1914 Yiddish play by the Russian ethnographer and writer S. An-sky; it was translated into Hebrew by Bialik and performed in Israel, where it played a major role in the development of a national theater. The scene in question appears in Yehoshua, *Ha-kala*, 420–424.

For our immediate purposes, however, I turn to the characters' appropriation of the Hebrew play as a vehicle for the Palestinian political narrative, and inversely, to the interpolation of Arabic into the Hebrew text. In Gilead Morahg's insightful reading, Yehoshua intends the scene as a critique of Palestinian insistence on the Right of Return. As for the *presence of absence*, far from privileging it as a generative concept, the novel critiques it on ideological grounds. This critique is carried out through a structural parallel between the protagonist's son, who is fixated on the lost paradise of his former marriage, and the Palestinian devotion to the lost paradise of the homeland; Yehoshua, in short, "thematizes the debilitating effects of obsessive striving to restore an unattainable past."[110] Yet, as with much of Yehoshua's writing, the novel is rife with internal contradictions, its subliminal hints and choices of metaphor often colliding with the narrative's ideological frame. Even if this Hebrew-Arabic *dybbuk* is intended by Yehoshua to represent what he takes for a pathological Palestinian fantasy, it is nonetheless the intertext chosen by the Palestinian characters to express their political aspirations and, thus, a subversive appropriation of Jewish-Israeli culture. That is to say, the *dybbuk* has migrated from its Diasporic Yiddish origins into its national Hebrew body and finally (if only in fiction) into a subversive Palestinian Arabic garb, which it wears to represent the Israeli usurper of the Palestinian bride. In this manner it is reimagined by Yehoshua as a metaphor that is shared between two national narratives, each with its conflicting memories and future aims (regardless of Yehoshua's own position on those aims). Moreover, his inclusion of the Arabic translation of the play *within* his Hebrew narrative rewrites *The Dybbuk* on the linguistic level. This reimagined *dybbuk* seems to tell us that Hebrew-Arabic cultural transfer in Israel/Palestine is, to begin with, a process that invites metaphors of possession, split selves, and hauntings. At least with that much, Anton Shammas himself would probably not disagree.

As much as Behar's story is at odds with Yehoshua's novel, it finds an ideological counterpart in *El yafo* (*To Jaffa*, 2010), a first novel by Behar's contemporary Ayman Sikseck, a Palestinian Israeli writer and journalist.[111] Although Sikseck's wry tone and realism are hardly like the calculated anachronisms and surreal style of Behar, *To Jaffa* resonates with "Ana min al-yahud" in that it is very much a "third-generation" piece. Like Behar, Sikseck studied literature at the Hebrew University of Jerusalem. His novel recounts the experiences of a Palestinian Israeli student,

110 Morahg, "Perils of Hybridity," 371.

111 Sikseck also co-edited a collection of Hebrew poetry about the *nakba*; see Hever et al., *Al tagidu be-Gat*.

a flaneur-type character who records his observations in a notebook. As in Behar's story, here too the protagonist is an unnamed male narrator. He inhabits the no-man's-land between Arabic and Hebrew in multiple ways, continually traveling between worlds: between the brash, earthy Arabic-Hebrew milieu of Jaffa and the austere Hebrew environment of his studies in Jerusalem, and between intimate entanglements with a Muslim woman who is engaged to another man and a Jewish woman who is an impossible match. Finally, as in Behar's story, the narrator's relationship to both Arabic and Hebrew is uncertain. Unlike Behar's narrator, he is fully bilingual, but he too evinces insecurity in his linguistic identity. In the first chapter he admits that he doesn't understand the "forceful, shattering Arabic" of guests who visit his home,[112] and in another chapter he is criticized by an Arabic bookseller who (wrongly) presumes he reads the major Hebrew writers but is unfamiliar with major Palestinian authors such as Ghassan Kanafani.[113] On the other hand, the narrator also demonstrates moments of political resistance through language, as we shall see below. The disassociated narrator-observer (whom one finds also in the novels of Sayed Kashua) who exhibits self-awareness of his liminality and of his linguistic limitations is part and parcel of Sikseck's literary affect. In an interview with *Haaretz*, Sikseck self-identifies as a member of the "irreverent third generation of the *nakba*" that rejects the complicity and fear of previous generations, whom he holds accountable for the silencing of Palestinian history and of the *nakba* in Israeli society.[114] In Behar and Sikseck's respective works, one senses the convergence of a "third-generation" sensibility; for Sikseck, the point zero of the generational chronology is the *nakba*, whereas for Behar and other Mizraḥi writers it is their elders' immigration to Israel.

At times, Sikseck's Jaffa reads as though it is on a symbolic continuum with Behar's Jerusalem. Through three interrelated scenes, the presence of absence intersects with the ruins of the past and the (re)possession of language.[115] In the first of these moments, the narrator hunts for written traces of the pre-1948 Palestinian past in Jaffa, such as "Palestine Fund" inscribed in Arabic and English on sewage drain covers, or a plaque with the Arabic name of a school, "al-Zahra," dated 1938. He tells an elusive addressee (understood to be Palestine) that he has found her, and records

112 Sikseck, *El yafo*, 11.

113 Ibid., 39–40.

114 In Hebrew, *ha-dor ha-shlishi la-nakba hu dor ḥatsuf*; see Ḥalutz, "Ha-biyografya shel Ayman Siksek" (English version titled "Language Is My Anchor.")

115 See also Hannan Hever's afterword to the novel, 137–142, which also ties in these three scenes with other themes in the novel.

each sighting in his notebook. In a highly symbolic moment, he decides to take a sharp rock and etch "Palestine" in Hebrew letters into the ground "so that from now on, passersby will know that you are here in Hebrew too,"[116] but before he can act, he is chased away by a suspicious resident. In the second scene, the narrator's mother spontaneously takes him to visit the ruins of her childhood home in the 'Ajami neighborhood of Jaffa; mother and son stand silently before the mounds of sand and bits of metal that offset the backside of the new luxury constructions (owned by Jewish Israelis) dotting the seascape.[117] The idea of writing "Palestine" in Hebrew letters is then inverted in another scene toward the book's end, when the narrator picks up a stick and uses it to write *alif* (the first letter of the Arabic alphabet) in a puddle of car oil.[118] This is important not only thematically but visually as in this scene, the letter *alif* is represented typographically in Arabic script, a single Arabic letter intruding into the visual unity of the Hebrew text. On the thematic level, however, as opposed to engraving a word into stone, etching a letter into oil is only a temporary act of inscription. The material presence of the *alif* in the artifact of the text counterweighs the ephemeral *alif* of the narrative. Comparing the two different scenes that entail writing on the ground, we also find more plays on presence and absence: "Palestine" in Hebrew letters was intended as a permanent reminder, but is never written; *alif* in Arabic is written, but will vanish. Whereas the sight of the mother's ruined home evokes the presence of absence in terms of the built landscape, these unfulfilled moments of linguistic resistance symbolize the elusive presence of Arabic language and Palestinian memory in Israeli society. These themes are also recapitulated by Palestinian Israeli artists and critics throughout the exhibition catalog of *Rijal fi al-shams/Gvarim ba-shemesh/Men in the Sun* (2009), another trilingual volume edited by Tal Ben Zvi (with Hanna Farah) that takes the aforementioned novella of Ghassan Kanafani for its title and inspiration. The exhibition featured contemporary art by Palestinians in Israel; the catalog juxtaposes the images and art criticism with theoretical essays, literary analysis, and poems, drawing on the work of Kanafani, Habiby, Darwish, and Taha Muhammad 'Ali. As Farah writes of seeing a photo of a broken Muslim tombstone on the renamed Kibuts Galuyot (Ingathering of the Exiles) Road, "In a single heartbeat I recall-reconstruct an entire culture that has been made to disappear: names, places, tastes, scents,

116 Sikseck, *El yafo*, 27.
117 Barbara Mann associates this scene in the book with the "presence of absence" in relation to architectural history and public memory in Tel Aviv-Jaffa (Mann, "Apartment to Remember").
118 Sikseck, *El yafo*, 98–99.

stories; a culture which bursts forth from amidst the traces of names, in the light and darkness of memory and consciousness."[119]

THE PRESENCE OF ABSENCE, REVISITED: MIZRAḤI VOICES AND THE FUTURE OF ISRAELI LITERATURE

In their literary rewritings of Hebrew, Chetrit, Hess, and Behar all appropriate the prophetic voice or style. While the conflation of poet and prophet is a convention of Hebrew poetry grounded in the Bible and tapped by canonical writers such as Bialik and Uri Tsvi Greenberg, in Mizraḥi literature the prophetic voice is closely linked to the concept of subversive language. For these second- and third-generation Mizraḥi poets, the fantasy of linguistic possession—of Ashdodian, of Aramaic, of Arabic—doubles as political and social critique. Moreover, the idea of the *accent* plays a supporting role in this critique. The imaginary "Ashdodian," heir to the language of half-breeds that incurred the prophet Neḥemiah's wrath, is code for "Mizraḥi Hebrew": an amalgamation of sociolect and accent. For Behar, while the fetishized, forbidden language is the Arabic of his silenced grandfather, the concept of subversive hybridity is also played out through Diasporic-accented Hebrew, considered unacceptable for native Israelis. As for Hess, her work utilizes every conceivable aspect of linguistic heterogeneity to challenge the doctrines of Israeli culture and identity; among them, we saw her portrayal of her father's Iraqi accent in Hebrew, which adumbrated her later return to the Jewish Baghdadi dialect in her bilingual poem.

Mizraḥi writers are not the only authors whose words dig into the surface of Modern Hebrew to excavate its subterranean vaults. Hiding inside the edifice of *'ivrit tiknit* are countless language *dybbuks.* Through these explosions of other languages into Hebrew literature, we see language resisting attempts to force it into ideological clarity. What is distinctive about Mizraḥi rewritings of Hebrew is the collective breadth and depth of their engagement with Jewish multilingualism, spanning multiple Diasporic languages as well as different registers and layers of Hebrew, sometimes even within a single text. Furthermore, Mizraḥi negotiations of Hebrew are distinguished by their continuity over three generations, by the emerging intergenerational dialogue between third-generation Mizraḥi writers and their predecessors, and by their growing collective presence within the Israeli literary arena. Finally, in this "third-generation" moment shared by younger Mizraḥi and Palestinian writers, artists, and

119 Ben Zvi and Farah, *Rijal fi al-shams/Gvarim ba-shemesh/Men in the Sun*, E/06, their translation; see also the exhibition and catalog website, http://www.men-in-the-sun.com/.

activists, we witness an intensified blurring of the boundaries between discourses, such that the language *dybbuk* seems to haunt *all* those who dare to walk in the Hebrew-Arabic no-man's-land. To be sure, Chetrit, Hess, and Behar, in addition to Sikseck and the contributors to *Rijal fi al-shams/Gvarim ba-shemesh*, are all haunted by the idea of loss.

Above all else, the texts examined in chapters 5 and 6 explode the myth of Israeli Hebrew as a single unitary language while giving powerful representation to the presence of absence. Beyond resisting nationalist monolingualism, these literary strategies reintroduce Hebrew into the multilingual regional framework whence it originated and in which it had persisted for millennia. The reclamation of Arabic both as a native language and as a Jewish language challenges its enforced separation from Hebrew. By resisting the erasure of Arabic, Aramaic, and other Diasporic languages, the texts in question renegotiate of the rules of identity and of discursive possession within the context of Israeli state and society. Their strategies of linguistic representation bring Modern Hebrew to places and histories outside the purview of the modern Hebrew canon: to the histories of Jewish literary creativity in places like Morocco, Baghdad, and Kurdistan. In other words, by inviting Arabic and Aramaic to interfere in their Hebrew language, the authors create new modes of writing in Hebrew that enable us to reimagine Modern Hebrew as a Middle Eastern language. In thinking of such writings as multilayered texts, we are also reminded of the multilayered history of the land at the heart of these stories; as Anton Shammas writes in *Arabesques*, "Our village [Fassuta] is built on the ruins of the Crusader castle of Fassove, which was built on the ruins of Mifshata, the Jewish village that had been settled after the destruction of the Second Temple by the Harim, a group of deviant priests."[120] By bringing the ruins of the Arab Jewish or Palestinian past into their Hebrew poems and stories, by intentionally allowing Arabic and Aramaic to shape their Hebrew words, these writers create a literary palimpsest in which Israeli Hebrew actually reveals, rather than covers, the traces of that which came before.

120 Shammas, *'Arabeskot*, 15; in English, *Arabesques*, 11.

CONCLUSION

Bloody Hope

The Intertextual Afterword of Salman Masalha and Saul Tchernichowsky

Indeed, it is not just that, as a fiction, the mimetic or representative character of Antigone is already put in question but that, as a figure for politics, she points somewhere else, not to politics as a question of representation but to *that political possibility that emerges when the limits to representation and representability are exposed.*

—JUDITH BUTLER[1]

In September 2006, the poet Salman Masalha declared the establishment of a new state, a story reported by *Haaretz*:[2]

> On September 11 . . . Dr. Salman Masalha stood on the balcony of Jerusalem's King David Hotel and announced the establishment of the State of Homeland [*hikhriz ha-doktor Salman Masalha 'al hakamata shel "medinat homland"*]. He titled himself the visionary of the state. The "essence of Homeland" is that "all of us—Jews, Arabs, and others—will be 'Homelanders' with equal rights and standing." . . . Not for nothing did the visionary, who writes his poems in Hebrew and Arabic, choose an English name for his country. "So there would be no burdens to start arguing over immediately," he says. "We are Homelanders, a peace-seeking people [*anu, ha-homlandim, 'am shokher shalom*]. We will go with a name everyone can identify with." . . . The language of the land, Homelandic, will be a combination of Hebrew and Arabic. It will be created on its own, the way of all languages *not born of a decision*. . . . When asked whether, at this important juncture, the visionary has not just established Israel as "a state of all its citizens," he answers in the

1 Butler, *Antigone's Claim*, 2, my emphasis.

2 As noted in chapter 4, Masalha (b. 1953) is a bilingual Palestinian-Israeli poet and scholar from the Galilean village Mghar, who has lived in Jerusalem since 1972.

> affirmative, but adds one codicil: "A state of all its proper citizens," with a strong emphasis on "proper." "We, the people of Homeland, will be a light unto the nations," he says [*Anu, bney ha-'am ha-homlandi, nihye or la-goyim*].[3]

This delectable satire is a metacommentary on the discourse of Zionism. The visionary of the State of Homeland borrows some of this discourse's most hackneyed clichés (*'am shokher shalom*, a "peace-seeking people"; *or la-goyim*, a "light unto the nations"), exposing them as discredited platitudes. Of the defining features of Masalha's utopian State of Homeland, the most exciting may be its utopian language, Homelandic, the Hebrew-Arabic hybrid that will be born naturally, organically, *not* by way of a decision.

This parodic declaration of statehood was not Masalha's first attempt to rewrite Israel's symbolic codes. His 2003 collection *Eḥad mi-kan* (*In Place*) ends with the provocatively titled poem "Ha-tikva" (literally, "The Hope")—also the title of none other than Israel's national anthem.

התקווה

בָּרְחוֹב הַחַד-סִטְרִי
הַמּוֹבִיל לְשָׂדֶה פָּתוּחַ לִרְוָחָה,
גְּוִיָּה מֻטֶּלֶת לְרוּחָהּ. בְּשׁוּלָיו
שִׁבְרֵי מַתֶּכֶת שֶׁנָּשְׁרוּ מִשְּׁמֵי
הָרוּחַ שֶׁנָּדַם. וְרוּחַ אֱלֹהִים
לֹא עַל מַיִם מְרַחֶפֶת
עַל הַדָּם.

הָעֵצִים, שֶׁיָּנְקוּ חֲלֵב אִמָּם,
כְּבָר צָמְחוּ – שִׁנֵּי תּוֹתֶבֶת
שֶׁל הָעִיר הַזְּקֵנָה.

מַה נִּפְלָא עֵץ הַתּוּת
שָׁרָשָׁיו – שִׁירֵי מוֹלֶדֶת.
עוֹד מְעַט יָקִיץ
הַסְּתָו.
הַתִּקְוָה –
עֲלֵי
שַׁלֶּכֶת.

3 Galili, "Nikhbosh et ha-'olam bli af yeri'a"; in English, "A Homeland of All Its Citizens," my emphasis.

THE HOPE

On the one-way street
leading to a wide-open field,
a corpse sprawled out to its soul. On the sides,
fragments of metal that fell from the heavens
of the spirit that fell silent. And the Spirit of God
hovers not over water;
over the blood.

The trees, which suckled their mothers' milk,
have already grown—false teeth
of the elderly city.

How wonderful is the mulberry tree
Its roots—patriotic songs.
Soon fall
will awaken.
Ha-tikva, the hope—
        falling
                leaves.[4]

In the first stanza, the speaker describes the composition of a scene: a body sprawled out in the street, framed by fragments of metal and pools of blood. Jewish Israeli readers would immediately think of a bombing. This terse description places the speaker in the position of witness to a specific, terrible event. Yet at the same time, the description has a universal quality. Nothing in it fixes the location of the scene or the victim's identity; the body could just as well belong to a Palestinian in Gaza as to an Israeli in Jerusalem. The speaker's tone is detached, almost omniscient, and the image of the narrow one-way street leading into a wide-open field suggests the passage to an afterlife. The word *ru'aḥ* (spirit or soul) appears repeatedly: *gvi'a mutelet le-ruḥa* (a corpse sprawled out to its soul), *ha-ru'aḥ she-nadam* (the spirit that fell silent; perhaps alluding doubly to the silence of God and to the moment of silence after the explosion) and *ve-ru'aḥ elohim* (and the spirit of God). Phonologically, the phrase *'al ha-dam* echoes the phrase *ha-ru'aḥ she-nadam*, so that the first stanza emphasizes the twin topoi of *spirit* and *blood.*

The second stanza pans outward to the trees and the city. In a strange image of the life cycle, the trees that had suckled their mothers' milk like toothless babes grow up to become the false teeth of that "old lady," the

4 Masalha, *Eḥad mi-kan*, 68.

city (*ha-'ir ha-zkena*). This image also adds *milk* to the blood and water of the previous stanza. The poem then concludes with four one-word lines: "Autumn. / The hope / falling / leaves" (*ha-stav. / Ha-tikva / 'aley / shalekhet*). From the immediate aftermath of destruction, then, the speaker looks beyond to show us the trees, who suckle their mothers' milk, grow old, and drop their leaves. Somehow, perhaps through the cycle of nature and renewal, the fragments of metal (*shivrey matekhet*) that fell from the sky are metaphorically transformed into falling leaves (*'aley shalekhet*). These two constructs, *shivrey matekhet* and *'aley shalekhet*, are associated through rhyme and assonance as well as image.

But if the transformation of shrapnel into autumn leaves seems to convey hope, think twice. For the idea of hope in the poem is impossibly and ineluctably double-edged, given the inescapable association of the words *ha-tikva* (the hope) with "Ha-tikva," the title of Israel's national anthem (colloquially rendered *ha-tik-va*, strong emphasis on the second syllable). Masalha's placement of the definite article before *tikva*, "hope," is a sure indication that he wants us to think of the anthem and not just of hope in the abstract. For a Palestinian Israeli poet to write a poem called "Ha-tikva" is quite a statement, especially as the anthem, along with the flag, is one of the two most important and contested symbols of Israel as a Jewish state.

The anthem's lyrics are (depending your perspective) either famously or infamously concerned with the national longings of the *nefesh yehudi*, the "Jewish soul":

As long as deep within the heart
A Jewish soul stirs,
And to the ends of the East
An eye looks toward Zion,
Our hope is not yet lost.
The hope of two thousand years,
To be a free nation in our own land,
The land of Zion and Jerusalem.[5]

Due to its exclusive address to the "Jewish soul," "Ha-tikva" is a symbolic focal point of Palestinian Israeli discontent. In 1995, in a memorial book for the assassinated Israeli leader Yitzhak Rabin, Masalha had written that "there is no hint of 'Israeliness'" in the anthem, whose tonality he reads as theological: "The combination of . . . the [Jewish] soul and the place [Zion], cannot but be mytho-religious. The Israeli national anthem is a Jewish

5 The text was adapted from a nine-stanza poem by Naftali Herz Imber; see Kabakoff, *Master of Hope* and Goldman, *Zeal for Zion*, esp. chap. 1.

religious prayer—and not Israeli."[6] Over the past decade, controversy erupted every few years when high-ranking non-Jewish officials—Israel's first Druze and Muslim cabinet members, a Maronite Christian judge in its Supreme Court—refused to sing "Ha-tikva" at public ceremonies, though in all cases they stood respectfully. When questioned, all explained that "Ha-tikva" was written as the "Jewish anthem," not the anthem of all Israelis.[7] Mizraḥi activists have also pointed out that the anthem's lyrics say the "Jewish soul" looks *eastward* to Zion (*le-fatey mizraḥ*), thereby writing out all the non-Ashkenazi Jews who happened to be looking *westward*, from countries such as Iraq, Iran, and India.

The political consciousness and self-definition of Palestinians in Israel underwent a sea change following the outbreak of the second *Intifada* and the devastating events of October 2000, when, in the midst of an unprecedented, weeklong explosion of violence between Palestinians and Jews within Israel proper, thirteen Palestinian citizens of Israel were shot dead by Israeli police.[8] Through this lens, Masalha's 2003 poem, an act of witnessing violence, reads as an ironic subversion of the Israeli anthem: a comment on the nature of life in the Jewish state (perhaps the implosion of the Zionist dream in a shower of metal?), and an implicit statement of the author's conflicted position within it. In this light, we might see the movement from the aftermath of a violent event depicted in the first stanza to the universality of nature evoked by the last stanza as a wish for escape from the suffocating context of the conflict, from the narrow one-way street to the wide-open field.

That this poem is a rejoinder to the national anthem is a powerfully seductive idea. But in fact, we can also read "Ha-tikva" *not* as the title of the anthem, but literally as *hope*. For Masalha delicately crafts a second, more complex meaning through an intertextual dialogue with the Bible and with a seemingly unlikely interlocutor: the Russian-born Saul Tchernichowsky (1874–1943), a famous Modern Hebrew poet whom Robert Alter has described as a "militant Zionist."[9] It is through this double discourse (rewriting of anthem; intertextual dialogue with Tchernichowsky) that the poem asks another, larger question: what is the role of the poet as *witness*?

6 Masalha, "Nefesh yisra'eli homiya," translation by Vivian Eden, cited in Masalha, "Anthem for the Tribe of Israel." Masalha later composed an alternative anthem and published it in *Haaretz* in December 2006.

7 Ghaleb Majadele, a former member of the Labor Party appointed minister in 2007, stated, "I fail to understand how an enlightened, sane Jew allows himself to ask a Muslim person . . . to sing an anthem that was written for Jews only" (Meranda, "Majadele Refuses to Sing National Anthem"). See also Bradley Burston, "Israel Needs a New Anthem"; on the other incidents, see "Behind the Headlines" and Bronner, "Anger and Compassion."

8 On the events of October 2000, see Ilan Pappé, "2000 Earthquake and Its Impact."

9 Alter, "To the Sun," 98.

BLOOD AND HOPE

Set in the middle of the first stanza, the poem's first intertext is one of the most famous passages in the Hebrew literary canon: "And the spirit of God was hovering over the water" (Genesis 1:2).[10] In the poem, not only is this line negated, but it is appended to another intertext that follows as a corrective: "hovering not on water, [but] on the blood" (*lo 'al mayim meraḥefet / 'al ha-dam*). In fact, the little line *'al ha-dam* ("on" or "over" the blood) invokes a complex network of intertextual associations. The original intertext is the biblical law "You shall not eat anything with blood" (*lo tokhlu 'al ha dam*).[11] In the twentieth century, the same words, *'al ha-dam*, also become the title of a famous poem by Tchernichowsky. At the head of the poem, Tchernichowsky writes a one-line epigraph, "Their unavenged blood shall be avenged" (*ve-nikeyti damam lo-nikeyti*)—the concluding line of the Book of Joel:

> Egypt shall be a desolation, and Edom shall be a desolate wasteland because of the violence done to the people of Judah, in whose land *they have shed innocent blood*. But Judah shall be inhabited forever, and Jerusalem for all generations. *Their unavenged blood shall be avenged*, and the Lord shall dwell in Zion.[12]

The line in question, literally "Thus I will treat as innocent their blood which I have not treated as innocent," is more idiomatically rendered, "I will not pardon those who shed their blood."[13] Why would Masalha begin a poem about hope with the taking of an innocent life? In the poem, *ha-tikva*, the hope, is the mirror image of violence and death. We saw how in the first stanza God's spirit hovers over not the waters of creation, but the blood of destruction (*lo 'al ha-mayim / 'al ha-dam*); in the last stanza we saw the transformation of the shards of metal into falling leaves. Masalha is working out a dialectical relationship of creation and destruction, death and birth, hope and despair; that much is obvious. What is less obvious is how we get from the *blood* to the *hope*; this is where Tchernichowsky comes in.

Saul Tchernichowsky is considered one of the two great poets of the Hebrew revival, along with Ḥayim Naḥman Bialik, whom we encountered in chapter 2. Born in Ukraine, Tchernichowsky studied medicine

10 In Hebrew, *ve-ru'aḥ elohim meraḥefet 'al-pney ha-mayim* (*Tanakh*, 1).

11 Leviticus 19:26 (*Tanakh*, 252).

12 Joel 4:19-21, translation from Moss, *Midrash and Legend*, 54, except for "Thus I will treat as innocent" (*Tanakh*, 1307–1308, my emphasis).

13 See note 12 above.

at Heidelberg and served as a Russian army doctor in the First World War and again during the Russian Civil War. He began publishing poetry in the 1890s, and immigrated to Palestine in 1931.[14] From 1919 to 1921 he composed his two famous sonnet coronas, "La-shemesh" ("To the Sun") and "'Al ha-dam" ("On the Blood"). These were written in the tumult of the years following the First World War and the Soviet Revolution, while the Russian Civil War was still raging.[15] As Robert Alter explains, the sonnet corona (known in Hebrew as *klil sonetot*) "consists of fifteen interlocked Petrarchan sonnets . . . the last line of each sonnet becomes the first line of the next one, with the fifteenth [and final] sonnet made up of all the lines in the first sequence."[16] In Alter's reading, the "ultimate impulsion of 'To the Sun' may well be Tchernichowsky's need to work out the relation between poetry and violence."[17] "On the Blood," in turn, is widely read as an expression of Tchernichowsky's profound disappointment over the implosion of the Russian Revolution and its betrayal of Russian Jewry, who continued to be persecuted following 1917.[18] "To the Sun" is suffused with metaphors of light, while "On the Blood" is filled with images of darkness and blindness, yet both coronas question the possibility and the responsibility of art in the face of wanton destruction of human life. In "The Hope," Masalha conducts an intertextual dialogue with Tchernichowsky about the witnessing of destruction and the related question of redemption through art or nature.

WITNESSING: TESTIMONY AND POETRY

In his essay "Poetics and Politics of Witnessing," Derrida takes Celan's poem "Aschenglorie" ("Ashes-Glory," 1967) as an occasion to reflect on "poetics as bearing witness."[19] Like much of Celan's work, the poem relates to the problem of representing the Holocaust. Derrida reads it to piece together the multifaceted relationship of witnessing to testimony,

14 For more on Tchernichowsky, see Arpaly, *Sha'ul Tshernihovski*.

15 Alter, "To the Sun," 92. See also Barzel, *Shirat ha-teḥiya*, 201.

16 Alter, "Saul Tchernikhovsky," 168.

17 Alter, "To the Sun," 93.

18 A year after the October revolution, "the Ukraine was a battlefield and its Jews often victims of bloody pogroms. The Bolshevik government dissolved the traditional Jewish institutions in 1918, and the Yevsektsiya had commenced its campaign against 'bourgeois' Zionist and Hebrew. . . . The situation had become so intolerable that by 1921 many of the leading Hebrew writers, led by Bialik, left Odessa for Istanbul on 21 June 1921. Tchernichowsky, both a Zionist and a Hebraist, obviously knew he had no future in the Soviet Union. He left for Istanbul in early summer 1922" (Band, "To the Sun," 89–90).

19 Derrida, "Poetics and Politics of Witnessing," 65.

of testimony to poetry, and of both testimony and poetry to truth and certainty in language. He proposes that the testimony of the witness both reveals and conceals itself, much like the language of a poem. Poetry and testimony are also linked in their resistance to translation, poems because of their multiple meanings, and testimony because it is based on a singular experience that cannot be definitively reproduced in language. The essay repeatedly returns to the last three lines of Celan's poem, "No one / bears witness for the / witness," which Derrida reads as an untranslatable "secret."[20] In testimony, the "secret" relates to an inherent uncertainty given the possibility of perjury and the unreliability of memory. In poetry, the "secret" is the limit of interpretation, where there can be no transparency of meaning. The secret, however, is not just a limitation—it is the *essential condition* of all poetic language.

In "The Hope," we don't know when or where the disaster occurred, whether it is fictitious or real, an isolated incident or an amalgam of similar incidents. This poem, then, is full of secrets; like Celan's poem, it bears witness primarily to the act of bearing witness. But then, Masalha titles it "Ha-tikva" and writes it in Hebrew, tying it directly to the politics of Israel/Palestine, and implying that the poem's reader is the Jewish Israeli. Reading the disaster as a bombing compels us to ask, what does it mean for a Palestinian Israeli to bear witness to a terror attack when a significant part of the Jewish Israeli public associates him with the perpetrators, discrediting his testimony? How does the poem serve as a form of testimony both on behalf of the victim, who cannot speak, and for the witness, who, in a political sense, cannot speak for the victim? For that matter, who *is* the victim? If the victim is Palestinian rather than Jewish, does this influence our reception of the witness's testimony? Does it make him any "more" or "less" of a witness? All these questions lead us to the central question posed by Masalha's poem: what are the conditions of being a witness, and how are they related to the politics of identity—not to mention the politics of language?

By way of an answer, we return to Tchernichowsky's sonnets. In his invocation of the poet-witness in "To the Sun" and "On the Blood," Tchernichowsky followed the precedent of Bialik's epic poem "In the City of Killing," about the 1903 Kishinev pogrom. In "To the Sun," witnessing had played a central role in a famous battlefield scene where the speaker, an army doctor, watches a wounded soldier die.[21] Its successor "On the Blood" is suffused from start to finish with metaphors of vision and blindness. Consider the opening sonnet:

20 Ibid., 67.

21 Alter, "To the Sun," 68, and Band, "To the Sun," 86.

Tired of mankind, the ages' legacy,
bearing a paltry and an emptied heart
bereft of strength or will, each man apart
we stumble like a horse that cannot see.

We drift like flotsam tossed by a stormy sea,
Or fetid addicts, dulled in every part;
each jealous of his fledgling, lest it start
to look towards the light, and to be free.

God's lightning rends the sky from side to side
piercing the clouds—but in our pretty sight
if it appears at all, it is a spark—

thus do we stare at Genesis, squint-eyed:
in webs of mystery, rotting in the dark,
our eyes are yearning for the distant light.[22]

We humans cannot face God's creation head-on, but only squinting from the side, yet our eyes are still looking high for distant hope (*le-me'orot merḥakim*)—a conflict replayed throughout the poem.[23] The poem's motifs and ideas are brought together in the fifteenth and crowning sonnet of the corona, composed of the first line of each of the preceding sonnets:

Tired of mankind, the ages' legacy,
our eyes are yearning for the distant light;
ageing, we wait for the great and wondrous sight
we rove and seek for creeds of mystery.

We turn to streams, and paths of fantasy
thirsty for words of truth, limpid and bright,
from trap to pit, from shadows to the night,
they wearied us, those seers of prophecy.

Cursed be the priests of idols and of Bel
Prophets of truth and those who give them ear
Let world-reformers rot in endless Hell!

The priests of beauty and the artists' throng
followers of poesy who hold her dear
will save the world with music and with song.

22 Tchernichowsky, "'Al ha-dam," in *Kol kitvey Sha'ul Tsherniḥovski*, 242–252; translation from Tchernichowsky, "On the Blood," in Silberschlag, *Saul Tchernichowsky*, 163–171.
23 Luz, "'Al ha-dam," 93.

"On the Blood" implicates ideology and institutional culture in the bloodbath of modernity. Salvation is unreachable (as represented by the distant lights); the poet recognizes that "humanity has failed in its greatest aspirations, and that all its prophets and reformers . . . have led it into bloodshed." The epigraph from the Book of Joel augments the motif of blood as well as the poet's disappointment in humanity's abuse of the weak.[24] Poetry offers the only hope of salvation: it is the "priests of beauty, kings of poetry," who will "redeem the world in song and melody" (*yig'alu ha-'olam be-shir u-mangina*).[25] As a statement of "witnessing," then, "On the Blood" offers not testimony about an event—the death of a soldier, the death of a terror victim—but rather a description of our *failure* to see, to understand, to empathize. On the textual level, it bears witness to the failed state of human existence. On the metatextual level, it reflects Tchernichowsky's witnessing of violence as a Jew in Russia during the upheavals of the early twentieth century. Finally, it acknowledges the limitations of language in capturing experience—that double bind in which language is at once never enough and yet all we have.[26]

THE WITNESS AND THE OBSERVER

What, then, does it means to be a "partial witness," an observer perceived by the listener as an outsider? Tchernichowsky's sonnet coronas and Masalha's poem ask not what it means to bear witness in an abstract philosophical sense: they are both about the *political* agency of witnessing trauma, about its implications for the possibility of representation. Above all, what links Masalha and Tchernichowsky is the ontological problem of being an insider/outsider while witnessing. Both are watching destruction ensue in a place to which they're intimately connected—an intimacy we see, for example, in Masalha's performance of Israeliness through the nationalistic idiom *shirey moledet*, "songs of the homeland." Yet at the same time it is a place to which they can never fully belong, a sentiment perhaps intimated in Masalha's dégagé, almost sublime description of the scene of destruction. Where the doctor in "To the Sun" is a full witness to the soldier's death, the speaker of "On the Blood" is a semidetached observer, at once inside and outside the disaster he depicts. In the progression from the earlier to the later poem, Tchernichowsky seems to

24 Barzel, *Shirat ha-teḥiya*, 201.

25 Tchernichowsky, "'Al ha-dam," in *Kol kitvey Sha'ul Tsherniḥovski*, 252.

26 See Peretz, *Literature, Disaster, and the Enigma of Power*. See also Shoshana Felman's pioneering study *Testimony*, in which she discusses witnessing in writers such as Celan and Camus.

have taken a step back, perhaps reflecting his disillusionment during the civil wars following the Revolution. As a Palestinian in Israel and as a Jew in Russia witnessing the ravages of political violence and war, Masalha and Tchernichowsky can bear witness *only* through poetic language—a language that is inherently multivalent, that contains "secrets," and whose political meaning is highly contingent on reading at the paratextual level, on knowing the author's biography.

In "To the Sun," Tchernichowsky finds redemption in nature; in "On the Blood," redemption is found in poetry. We saw how Masalha's poem begins with a violent death and ends with nature's life cycle, represented by the parallelism between *shivrey matekhet* (fragments of metal) and *'aley shalekhet* (falling leaves). But then again, this redemptive transformation is equated with falling leaves: with nature's moment of death, not rebirth. To evoke another Palestinian Israeli writer, then, this is a kind of pessoptimism. In other words, this is not quite the utopian State of Homeland, but it *is* the hope that is permissible within the parameters of the hideous reality represented by the unidentified body in the blood splattered, narrow, one-way street.

Through his dialogue with Tchernichowsky, Masalha reappropriates the title "Ha-tikva," divesting of it of what, for Palestinians in Israel, is a politics of exclusion, and reimaging it as *hope*. Read against Masalha's declaration of the State of Homeland, this may also be an act of reterritorialization, in which "the hope" is transformed into *Masalha's* hope for the actual and meaningful inclusion of Palestinians in a reenvisioned Hebrew-Arabic state. In his poem, the roots of the mulberry tree themselves are *shirey moledet*, songs or poems of the "homeland." Might we reclaim this idiom as well to imagine an anthem for a state of all its citizens—one that would fulfill Tchernichowsky's closing vision that "the world will be redeemed through poetry and song"?

Finally, Masalha's poem reminds us once more that language choice is about much more than aesthetic preference. In the literary contexts explored in this book, language choice is bound to the struggle for political representation, for social presence, for the right to narrate history. Masalha's translation of Tchernichowsky's language of witnessing into a Palestinian-Israeli counteranthem is one of the very many such translations that together form the Hebrew-Arabic no-man's-land. The authors and literary dialogues we have encountered—from Ḥayim Naḥman Bialik and Dahud Semaḥ to Emile Habiby and Samir Naqqash; from first-generation Iraqi Jewish novelists forging new pathways for Hebrew literature to third-generation Mizraḥi and Palestinian writers reclaiming the Arab Jewish and Palestinian pasts; from the Palestinian midrash of

Anton Shammas, Na'im 'Araidi, and Salman Masalha, all the way back to the poetic witnessing of Saul Tchernichowsky—do not all fit together seamlessly. Their writings speak to one another through their mutual investment in the *idea of language*, where language is at once the most ever-present and most contested site of political and cultural negotiation. Language is not a utopian space; to the contrary, as de Saussure, Foucault, and Bourdieu have taught us, its usage is governed by an infinitude of rules, spoken and unspoken, visible and hidden. Yet language is also the domain of rule bending and rule breaking, of genesis and of recreation. It is this tension between the ubiquity of rules and their constant transgression that generates the productive, creative uses of language we have encountered in this book. To seek to change the rules of language is to take ownership of it, to stake one's claim to it as an individual or in the name of a collective. The self-awareness and performativity of hyperlanguage are both the direct result of this struggle over linguistic ownership.

I began this conclusion with Salman Masalha's utopian State of Homeland and its utopian language, Homelandic; I close with another (anti) utopian gesture. In *Writing Degree Zero* (1953), his manifesto on the writer's political and ethical responsibility, Roland Barthes contemplates the meaning of the immense changes that took place in contemporary literature as writers moved away from a "universal" literary language toward a language of vernacular specificity, resulting in a "proliferation of the modes of writing." He concludes the book by declaring that the newness of these new modes of literary writing "hastens towards a dreamed-of language whose freshness, by a kind of ideal anticipation, might portray the perfection of some new Adamic world where *language would no longer be alienated*. The proliferation of modes of writing brings a new Literature into being only in order to be a project: *Literature becomes the Utopia of language*."[27] The author forges a new language, with the intent of fully reconciling language and experience. This remains an unattainable state, for like all revolutions, this new writing must borrow from the past it seeks to break with in order to reimagine the future. Thus literary writing carries within it both the "alienation of History" and the "dream of History." But in this struggle, literature becomes the "utopia of language": the free zone of projection, of imagination, and of desire. The writers we have encountered in this book attempt to liberate language from the repressive politics thrust upon it, to forge a new language that "would no longer be alienated" in a very immediate, political sense. Their efforts, too, are marked doubly by the alienation and by the dream. Their

27 Barthes, *Writing Degree Zero*, 88, my emphasis.

literary journeys are not a return to Eden; nor do they lead us out of the political quagmire and its many paradoxes of language and experience. Their journeys are the charting of the Hebrew-Arabic no-man's-land, the zone of poetic trespass, where impossibility is the essential condition of creation.

Bibliography

Abisaab, Rula. "*The Pessoptimist*: Breaching the State's *da'wa* in a Fated Narrative of Secrets." *Edebiyat* 13.1 (2003): 1–10.

'Abud, Muhammad. "Ana min al-yahud: shazaya al-qahr al-thaqafi" [I am one of the Jews: Splinters of cultural oppression]. *Majallat al-hilal* (June 2006): 115–123.

Academy of the Hebrew Language. *Collection of Documents on the History of the Language Committee and the Academy of Hebrew Language 1890–1970 and on the Revival of Hebrew Speech* [in Hebrew]. Jerusalem: Academy of the Hebrew Language, 1970.

'Ajami. Directed by Scandar Copti and Yaron Shani. DVD. Israel: Kino International, 2010.

Ajami, Mansour. *The Alchemy of Glory: The Dialectic of Truthfulness and Untruthfulness in Medieval Arabic Literary Criticism*. Washington, D.C.: Three Continents Press, 1988.

Alcalay, Ammiel. *After Jews and Arabs: Remaking Levantine Culture*. Minneapolis: University of Minnesota Press, 1993.

——, ed. *Keys to the Garden: New Israeli Writing*. San Francisco: City Lights Books, 1996.

Ali, Ahmed, trans. *Al-Qur'an: A Contemporary Translation*. Princeton, NJ: Princeton University Press, 1984.

Allen, Roger. *The Arabic Novel: An Historical and Critical Introduction*. 2nd ed. Syracuse, NY: Syracuse University Press, 1995.

Alon, Ketzia. "Hebrew Fiction/Old-New Hymns." *Haaretz*, February 17, 2011. Accessed August 28, 2013. http://www.haaretz.com/culture/books/hebrew-fiction-old-new-hymns-1.344006.

Alter, Robert. "Haim Nahman Bialik: Superimposed Worlds." In *Canon and Creativity: Modern Writing and the Authority of Scripture*, edited by Robert Alter, 97–149. New Haven, CT: Yale University Press, 2000.

——. *Hebrew and Modernity*. Bloomington: Indiana University Press, 1994.

——. *The Invention of Hebrew Prose: Modern Fiction and the Language of Realism*. Seattle: University of Washington Press, 1988.

——. "Saul Tchernikhovsky: To the Sun—A Corona of Sonnets." *Literary Imagination* 3.1 (Winter 2001): 159–179.

——. "To the Sun: Shaul Tchernichowsky." In *Reading Hebrew Literature: Critical Discussions of Six Modern Texts*, edited by Alan Mintz, 64–101. Hanover, NH: Brandeis University Press, 2003.

Amichai, Yehuda. *Shirey yerushalayim* [Jerusalem poems]. Tel Aviv: Schocken, 1987.

——. *Shirim: 1948–1962* [Poems: 1948–1962]. Tel Aviv: Schocken, 1977.

——. *Yehuda Amichai: A Life of Poetry, 1948–1994*. Translated by Barbara and Benjamin Harshav. New York: HarperCollins, 1994.

Amir, Eli. *The Dove Flyer.* Translated by Hillel Halkin. London: Halban, 2010.

——. *Mafriaḥ ha-yonim* [The dove flyer]. Tel Aviv: 'Am 'oved, 1992.

——. *Scapegoat: A Novel*. Translated by Dalya Bilu. London: Weidenfeld and Nicolson, 1987.

——. *Tarnegol kaporot* [Scapegoat]. Tel Aviv: 'Am 'oved, 1983.

——. *Yasmin* [Jasmine]. Tel Aviv: 'Am 'oved, 2005.

Amit-Kochavi, Hannah. "Hebrew Translations of Palestinian Literature—from Total Denial to Partial Recognition." *TTR: Traduction, terminologie, rédaction* 13.1 (2000): 53–80.

——. "Integrating Arab Culture into Israeli Identity through Literary Translations from Arabic into Hebrew." In *Cultural Encounters in Translation from Arabic*, edited by Said Faiq, 51–62. Clevedon, UK: Multilingual Matters, 2004.

——. "Israeli Arabic Literature in Hebrew Translation: Initiation, Dissemination and Reception." *Translator* 2.1 (1996): 27–44.

——. "Israeli Jewish Nation Building and Hebrew Translations of Arabic Literature." In *Literature and Nation in the Middle East*, edited by Yasir Suleiman and Ibrahim Muhawi, 100–109. Edinburgh: Edinburgh University Press, 2006.

——. "Performing Arabic Plays on the Israeli Hebrew Stage (1945–2006)—Some Case Studies and Reviews." *Mercurian* 1.1 (2007): 172–190.

——. "Translation from Arabic into Hebrew—An Overview." *Meta: Translators' Journal* 43.1 (1998): 79–86.

Anderson, Benedict. *Imagined Communities: Reflections on the Origin and Spread of Nationalism*. London: Verso, 2006.

Anidjar, Gil. *Semites: Race, Religion, Literature*. Stanford, CA: Stanford University Press, 2008.

Ansky, S. *The Dybbuk and Other Writings.* Edited by David G. Roskies. Translated by Golda Werman. New York: Schocken, 1992.

Anzaldúa, Gloria. *Borderlands/La Frontera: The New Mestiza.* San Francisco: Aunt Lute, 2007.

——. "How to Tame a Wild Tongue." In *Borderlands/La Frontera: The New Mestiza*, 75–86. San Francisco: Aunt Lute, 2007.

"Arabic Studies to Become Compulsory in Israeli Schools." *Haaretz*, August 24, 2010. Accessed August 27, 2013. http://www.haaretz.com/news/national/arabic-studies-to-become-compulsory-in-israeli-schools-1.309941.

'Araidi, Na'im. "Dreams, Ideas and Realities (Cultural Dialogue in the Middle East)." *Jerusalem Review* 1.1 (April 1997): 208–213.

——. *Ḥazarti el ha-kfar* [I returned to the village]. Tel Aviv: 'Am 'oved, 1986.

——. *Ḥemla va-faḥad* [Compassion and fear]. Tel Aviv: 'Akad, 1975.

——. *Kol ha-'onot: mivḥar shirim 1972–2006* [All the seasons: Selected poems, 1972–2006]. Tel Aviv: Gvanim, 2010.

——. *Mash'ir et ha-ka'as la-aḥerim* [Leaving the anger to others]. Tel Aviv: Gvanim, 2006.

——. *Ulay zo ahava* [It might be love]. Tel Aviv: Sifriyat ma'ariv, 1989.

Arpaly, Boaz, ed. *Sha'ul Tsherniḥovski: meḥkarim u-te'udot* [Saul Tchernichowsky: Studies and documents]. Jerusalem: Mosad Biyalik, 1994.

Arteaga, Alfred. "An Other Tongue." In *An Other Tongue: Nation and Ethnicity in the Linguistic Borderlands*, edited by Alfred Arteaga, 9–34. Durham, NC: Duke University Press, 1994.

——, ed. *An Other Tongue: Nation and Ethnicity in the Linguistic Borderlands*. Durham, NC: Duke University Press, 1994.

Ashcroft, Bill, Gareth Griffiths, and Helen Tiffin. *The Empire Writes Back: Theory and Practice in Post-Colonial Literature*. 2nd ed. London: Routledge, 2002.

Austin, J. L. *How to Do Things with Words*. Oxford: Clarendon, 1962.

Avineri, Shmuel. "Bialik ve-'edot ha-mizraḥ: anatomya shel 'alila ve-shel 'elbon shav" [Bialik and the Mizraḥi communities: An anatomy of false charges and baseless insult]. *Haaretz*, January 2, 2004. Accessed August 29, 2013. http://www.haaretz.co.il/misc/1.934678.

Avishur, Yitshak. "Sidud ma'arakhot sifrutiyot u-tmurot leshoniyot be-kerev yehudey 'irak ba-'et ha-ḥadasha (1750–1950)" [Change and transformation in the language and literature of Iraqi Jews in modern times, 1750–1950]. *Mi-kedem u-mi-yam* 6 (1995): 235–254.

——. *Ha-sipur ha-'amami shel yehudey 'irak: mivḥar sipurim mi-kitvey yad* [The folktales of the Jews of Iraq]. Vol. 1. Haifa: University of Haifa, 1992.

Bachi, R. "A Statistical Analysis of the Revival of Hebrew in Israel." *Scripta Hierosolymitana* 3 (1956): 179–247.

Bakhtin, Mikhail. *The Dialogic Imagination: Four Essays*. Edited by Michael Holquist. Translated by Caryl Emerson and Michael Holquist. Austin: University of Texas Press, 1982.

——. "Discourse in the Novel." In *The Dialogic Imagination: Four Essays*. Edited by Michael Holquist. Translated by Caryl Emerson and Michael Holquist, 259–331. Austin: University of Texas Press, 1982.

——. "From the Prehistory of Novelistic Discourse." In *The Dialogic Imagination: Four Essays*. Edited by Michael Holquist. Translated by Caryl Emerson and Michael Holquist, 41–83. Austin: University of Texas Press, 1982.

Ballas, Shimon. *Ḥoref aḥaron* [Last winter]. Jerusalem: Keter, 1984.

——. "Iya." In *Keys to the Garden: New Israeli Writing*, edited by Ammiel Alcalay, translated by Susan Einbinder, 69–99. San Francisco: City Lights Books, 1996.

——. "Iya." In *Otot stav* [Signs of autumn], 9–50. Tel Aviv: Zmora-Bitan, 1992.

——. *Ha-ma'abara* [The transit camp]. Tel Aviv: 'Am 'oved, 1964.

——. *Outcast*. Translated by Ammiel Alcalay and Oz Shelach. San Francisco: City Lights Books, 2007.

——, ed., trans. *Sipurim palestiniyim* [Palestinian stories]. Tel Aviv: 'Eked, 1970.

——. *Ve-hu aḥer* [The other one]. Tel-Aviv: Zmora-Bitan, 1991.

Band, Arnold J. "To the Sun: Shaul Tchernichowsky." In *Reading Hebrew Literature*, 81–91. Philadelphia: Jewish Publication Society, 2003.

Bar-Adon, Pesah. *Be-oheley midbar: mi-reshimotav shel ro'ey tson 'ivri beyn shivtey ha-bedu'in* [In the desert tents: Notes of a Hebrew shepherd among the Bedouin tribes]. Jerusalem: Kiryat Sefer, 1981 [1934].

Bardenstein, Carol. "Threads of Memory and Discourses of Rootedness: Of Trees, Oranges, and the Prickly-Pear Cactus in Israel/Palestine." *Edebiyat* 8.1 (1998): 1–36.

Bargad, Warren, and Stanley F. Chyet, eds., trans. *Israeli Poetry: A Contemporary Anthology*. Bloomington: Indiana University Press, 1988.

Barthes, Roland. *Writing Degree Zero*. Translated by Annette Lavers and Colin Smith. New York: Hill and Wang, 1968.

Bartov, Hanokh. *Shesh knafayim le-eḥad* [Everyone had six wings]. Merḥavya: Sifriyat po'alim, 1954.

Barzel, Hillel. "Klil ha-sonetot: hakpada ve-hazara" [Sonnet coronas: Strict form and defamiliarization]. *Moznayim* 61 (1987): 24–28.

———. *Meshorerey bsora* [Poets of prophecy]. Tel Aviv: Hotsa'at yaḥdav, 1983.

———. *Shirat ha-teḥiya: Sha'ul Tsherniḥovski* [Poetry of S. Tchernichowsky]. Tel Aviv: Sifriyat po'alim, 1992.

Barzilay, Isaac. "The Arab in Modern Hebrew Literature: Image and Problem." *Hebrew Studies* 18 (1977): 23–48.

Bashkin, Orit. *New Babylonians: A History of Jews in Modern Iraq*. Stanford, CA: Stanford University Press, 2012.

Behar, Almog. "Amira bat Salima" [Amira, daughter of Salima]. In *Ana min al-yahud*, 83–159. Tel Aviv: Hotsa'at bavel, 2008.

———. "Amira Hess ve-ha-shiva le-'aravit" [Amira Hess and the return to Arabic]. *La-roḥav: magazin gerila tarbut/Maqta' 'ardi: majallat 'asabat thaqafa* [Crosswise/wide crossing: The journal of Cultural Guerrilla] 1 (2012): 126–131.

———. "Ana min al yahoud—I'm One of the Jews." Translated by Vivian Eden. *Haaretz*, April 28, 2005. Accessed August 29, 2013. http://www.haaretz.com/ana-min-al-yahoud-i-m-one-of-the-jews-1.157191.

———. "Ana min al-yahud." In *Ana min al-yahud* [I am of the Jews], 65–76. Tel Aviv: Hotsa'at bavel, 2008.

———. "Ba'a ha-sakin shel ha-'ivrit, 'asta otanu shtey ḥatikhot" [Along came the knife of Hebrew and cut us in two]. *Haaretz*, May 25, 2006. Accessed August 29, 2013. http://www.haaretz.co.il/literature/1.1107888.

———. "Shivat ha-'aravit le-shira ha-mizraḥit" [The return of Arabic in Mizraḥi poetry]. Unpublished paper, 2010.

———. *Tchaḥla ve-Ḥezkel* [Rachel and Ezekiel]. Jerusalem: Keter, 2010.

———. *Tsim'on be'erot* [The thirst of wells]. Tel Aviv: 'Am 'oved, 2008.

Behar, Moshe, and Zvi Ben-Dor Benite, eds. *Modern Middle Eastern Jewish Thought: Writings on Identity, Politics, and Culture*. Hanover, NH: University Press of New England, 2013.

"Behind the Headlines: Not All Israeli Arabs Cheer Appointment of Druse Minister." *JTA*, March 6, 2001. Accessed August 29, 2013. http://www.jta.org/2001/03/06/archive/behind-the-headlines-not-all-israeli-arabs-cheer-appointment-of-druse-minister#ixzz2b0rRt0ef.

Beinin, Joel. *The Dispersion of Egyptian Jewry: Culture, Politics, and the Formation of a Modern Diaspora*. Berkeley: University of California Press, 1998.

Belcher, Wendy Laura. *Abyssinia's Samuel Johnson: Ethiopian Thought in the Making of an English Author*. New York: Oxford University Press, 2012.

Bell, Sharon Masingale. "In the Shadow of the Father Tongue: On Translating the Masks in J.-S. Alexis." In *Between Languages and Cultures: Translation and Cross-Cultural Texts*, edited by Anuradha Dingwaney and Carol Maier, 51–74. Pittsburgh, PA: University of Pittsburgh Press, 1995.

Ben-Dor, Zvi. "*'Eyb, Heshumah, Infajrat Qunbula*: Towards a History of Mizrahim and Arabic." November 23, 2005. Accessed August 29, 2013. http://www.oznik.com/toward-a-history-of-mizrahim-and-arabic.html.

———. "'Eyb, hshuma, infajarat qunbula: likrat historya shel ha-mizraḥim ve-ha-'aravit" ['Eyb, hshuma, infajarat qunbula: Toward a history of Mizraḥim and Arabic]. In *Ḥazut mizraḥit: hove ha-na' bi-svakh 'avaro ha-'aravi* [Eastern visage: A present moving in the tangle of its Arab past], edited by Yigal Nizri, 29–44. Tel Aviv: Hotasa'at bavel, 2004.

Ben-Rafael, Eliezer, Elana Shohamy, Muhammad Hasan Amara, and Nira Trumper-Hecht. "Linguistic Landscape as Symbolic Construction of the Public Space: The Case of Israel." *International Journal of Multilingualism* 3.1 (2006): 7–30.

Ben Ya'akov, Avraham, ed. *Shira u-fiyut shel yehudey bavel ba-dorot ha-aḥaronim* [Hebrew poetry of Baghdadi Jewry: Collected and selected poems]. Jerusalem: Ben Tsvi Institute, 1970.

———. *Yehudey bavel mi-sof tekufat ha-ge'onim 'ad yameynu* [Babylonian Jewry from the late Gaonic period to the present]. Jerusalem: Kiryat sefer, 1979.

Ben-Yehuda, Eliezer. *A Complete Dictionary of Ancient and Modern Hebrew*. New York: Thomas Yoseloff, 1960 [1940].

———. *He-ḥalom ve-shivro: mivḥar ketavim be-'inyene lashon* [The dream come true: Selected writings on topics of language]. Edited by Reuven Sivan. Jerusalem: Mosad Biyalik, 1986.

Ben-Yehuda, Netiva. *1948-Beyn ha-sfirot* [1948–Between calendars]. Jerusalem: Keter, 1981.

Ben Zvi, Tal. "Deferring Language as a Theme in the Work of Mizrahi Artists." In *Sfat em/Lughat Umm*, edited by Tal Ben Zvi, 154–184. Exhibition catalog for "Sfat am/Lughat Umm" (2002), curated by Tal Ben Zvi for Ein Harod Museum of Art, published in *Ḥazut mizraḥit: hove ha-na' bi-svakh 'avaro ha-'aravi* [Eastern visage: A present moving in the tangle of its Arab past], edited by Yigal Nizri. Tel Aviv: Hotasa'at bavel, 2004.

Ben Zvi, Tal, and Hannah Farah, eds. *Rijal fi al-shams/Gvarim ba-shemesh/Men in the sun*. Exhibition catalog for "Rijal fi al- shams/Gvarim ba-shemesh," curated by

Tal Ben Zvi and Hannah Farah. Herzliya: Herzliya Museum of Contemporary Art, 2009.

Benjamin, Walter. "The Task of the Translator." In *Illuminations*, edited by Hannah Arendt, translated by Harry Zohn, 69–82. New York: Schocken, 1986.

Berdugo, Sami. *Ze ha-dvarim* [That is to say]. Tel Aviv: Ha-kibuts ha-me'uḥad, 2010.

Berg, Nancy E. *Exile from Exile: Israeli Writers from Iraq*. Albany: State University of New York Press, 1996.

———. *More and More Equal: The Literary Works of Sami Michael*. Lanham, MD: Lexington Books, 2005.

Bhabha, Homi. "Frontlines/Borderposts." In *Displacements: Cultural Identities in Question*, edited by Angelika Bammer, 269–272. Bloomington: Indiana University Press, 1994.

———. *The Location of Culture*. London: Routledge, 1994.

———. "Of Mimicry and Man: The Ambivalence of Colonial Discourse." In *The Location of Culture*, 85–92. New York: Routledge, 1994.

Bialik, Ḥayim Naḥman. *Igarot Biyalik, kerekh dalet* [Letters of Bialik, vol. 4]. Tel Aviv: Dvir, 1938.

———. "Introduction." In *Shirey Shelomo ben Yehuda ibn Gabirol* [The poems of Solomon ibn Gabirol], vol. 1., edited by Ḥ. N. Bialik and Y. Ḥ. Ravinitsky, 7–16. Tel Aviv: Dvir, 1927.

———. *Kol kitvey Ḥ. N. Biyalik* [Collected writings of Bialik]. Tel Aviv: Dvir, 1964.

———. *Kol shirey Ḥ. N. Biyalik* [Collected poems of Bialik]. Tel Aviv: Dvir, 1966.

———. *Leket shirim/Mukhtar min diwan Hayim Nahman Biyalik* [Selected poems of Bialik]. Translated by Zakai Binyamin. Tel Aviv: Beyt ha-hotsa'a ha-'aravi mi-yesodo shel ha-va'ad ha-po'el shel ha-histradrut, 1964.

———. "Shirateynu ha-tse'ira" [Our young poetry]. Accessed August 30, 2013. http://benyehuda.org/bialik/article07.html.

———. "Teḥiyat ha-sfaradim" [The revival of the Sephardim]. In *Dvarim she-be-'al-pe, sefer rishon* [Collected lectures, vol. 1], 110–119. Tel Aviv: Dvir, 1935.

Bikur ha-tizmoret [The band's visit]. Directed by Eran Kolirin. Israel, 2007.

Bitton, Erez. *Sefer ha-na'na'* [The book of mint]. Tel Aviv: 'Eked, 1979.

———. *Tsipor beyn yabashot* [Bird between continents]. Tel Aviv: Ha-kibuts ha-me'uḥad, 1990.

Blanc, Haim. *Communal Dialects in Baghdad*. Cambridge, MA: Harvard University Press, Center for Middle Eastern Studies, 1964.

Bourdieu, Pierre. *The Field of Cultural Production: Essays on Art and Literature*. Edited by Randal Johnson. New York: Columbia University Press, 1993.

———. *Language and Symbolic Power*. Edited by John B. Thompson. Translated by Gino Raymond and Matthew Adamson. Cambridge, MA: Harvard University Press, 1991.

Boyarin, Daniel. *Intertextuality and the Reading of Midrash*. Bloomington: Indiana University Press, 1990.

Brann, Ross. "The Arabized Jews." In *The Literature of Al-Andalus*, edited by Maria Rosa Menocal, Raymond P. Scheindlin, and Michael Sells, 435–454. Cambridge: Cambridge University Press, 2000.

———. *The Compunctious Poet: Cultural Ambiguity and Hebrew Poetry in Muslim Spain.* Baltimore: Johns Hopkins University Press, 1991.

Brenner, Rachel Feldhay. "'Hidden Transcripts' Made Public: Israeli Arab Fiction and Its Reception." *Critical Inquiry* 26.1 (Autumn 1999): 85–108.

———. *Inextricably Bonded: Israeli Arab and Jewish Writers Revisioning Culture.* Madison: University of Wisconsin Press, 2003.

———. "The Search for Identity in Israeli Arab Fiction: Atallah Mansour, Emile Habiby, and Anton Shammas." *Israel Studies* 6.3 (2001): 91–112.

Bronner, Ethan. "Anger and Compassion for Arab Justice Who Stays Silent during Zionist Hymn." *New York Times*, March 4, 2012. Accessed August 29, 2013. http://www.nytimes.com/2012/03/05/world/middleeast/anger-and-compassion-for-justice-who-stays-silent-during-zionist-hymn.html?_r=0.

Burnshaw, Stanley, T. Carmi, Susan Glassman, Ariel Hirschfeld, and Ezra Spicehandler, eds. *The Modern Hebrew Poem Itself.* Cambridge, MA: Harvard University Press, 1989.

Burstein, Dror. "Kir'u ve-yeraḥev levavkhem: 'Shum gamadim lo yavo'u'" [Read it and weep: 'No elves will come']. *Haaretz*, December 25, 2005. Accessed August 29, 2013. http://www.haaretz.co.il/literature/elef/1.1069776.

Burston, Bradley. "Israel Needs a New Anthem, One That Arabs Can Sing." *Haaretz*, March 18, 2007. Accessed August 29, 2013. http://www.haaretz.com/print-edition/opinion/israel-needs-an-anthem-that-represents-arabs-and-jews-1.417908.

Busi, Dudu. *Ima mitga'ga'at le-milim* [Mother longs for words]. Jerusalem: Keter, 2006.

Butler, Judith. *Antigone's Claim: Kinship between Life and Death.* New York: Columbia University Press, 2000.

———. *Bodies That Matter: On the Discursive Limits of "Sex."* London: Routledge, 1993.

———. *Excitable Speech: A Politics of the Performative.* London: Routledge, 1997.

Campos, Michelle U. *Ottoman Brothers: Muslims, Christians, and Jews in Early Twentieth-Century Palestine.* Stanford, CA: Stanford University Press, 2010.

———. "A 'Shared Homeland' and Its Boundaries: Empire, Citizenship, and the Origins of Sectarianism in Late Ottoman Palestine, 1908–1913." Doctoral dissertation, Stanford University, 2003.

Casanova, Pascale. *The World Republic of Letters.* Translated by M. B. DeBevoise. Cambridge, MA: Harvard University Press, 2004.

Castel-Bloom, Orly. "Jo, ish kahir." In *Sviva oyenet* [Hostile surroundings], 93–109. Tel Aviv: Zmora-Bitan, 1989.

———. "Ummi fi shughl." In *Sipurim bilti restoniyim* [Involuntary stories], 9–11. Tel Aviv: Zmora-Bitan, 1993.

Chaver, Yael. *What Must Be Forgotten: The Survival of Yiddish in Zionist Palestine.* Syracuse, NY: Syracuse University Press, 2004.

Chetrit, Sami Shalom. *I'm an Arab Jew: Poems (1982–2008) and Conversation with Ronit Chacham*. New York: Shira, 2010.

——. *Intra-Jewish Conflict in Israel: White Jews, Black Jews*. London: Routledge, 2010.

——. "Revisiting Bialik: A Radical Mizrahi Reading of the Jewish National Poet." *Comparative Literature* 62.1 (2010): 1–21.

——. *Shirim be-ashdodit* [Poems in Ashdodian]. Tel Aviv: Andalus, 2003.

Chetrit, Sami Shalom, and Orly Eskhol-Mikhlin, eds. *Me'a shanim, me'a yotsrim: asupat yetsirot 'ivriyot ba-mizraḥ ba-me'a ha-'esrim: shira* [A century of Hebrew writing: An anthology of Modern Hebrew writing in the Middle East: Poetry]. Tel Aviv: Bimat kedem le-sifrut, 1999.

Ch'ien, Evelyn Nien-Ming. *Weird English*. Cambridge, MA: Harvard University Press, 2004.

Coffin, Edna Amir. "The Image of the Arab in Modern Hebrew Literature." *Michigan Quarterly Review* 21.2 (1982): 319–341.

Coffin, Nancy. "Reading Inside and Out: A Look at Habibi's *Pessoptimist*." *Arab Studies Journal* 8.2/9.1 (2000/2001): 25–46.

Cohen, Julia Philips, and Sarah Abrevaya Stein. "Sephardic Scholarly Worlds: Toward a Novel Geography of Modern Jewish History." *Jewish Quarterly Review* 100.3 (2010): 349–384.

Cohen, Mark. *Under Crescent and Cross: The Jews in the Middle Ages*. Rev. ed. Princeton, NJ: Princeton University Press, 2008.

Conrad, Joseph. "Amy Foster." In *The Complete Short Fiction of Joseph Conrad*, vol. 1, edited by Samuel Hynes, 181–209. New York: Ecco Press, 1991.

Corngold, Stanley. *Lambent Traces: Franz Kafka*. Princeton, NJ: Princeton University Press, 2004.

Darraj, Faysal. "Imil Habibi: tikniyyat al-hikaya wa-bina'a al-sira al-dhatiyya" [Emile Habiby: The technique of storytelling and autobiographical form]. *Majallat al-Karmel* 52 (Summer 1997).

Darwish, Mahmoud. *Awraq al-zaytun, shi'r* [Leaves of olives: Poems]. Haifa: Matba'at al-ittihad al-ta'awuniyya, 1964.

——. *Diwan Mahmud Darwish* [Collected poems]. Vol. 1. Beirut: Dar al-'awda, 1977.

——. *Fi hadrat al-ghiyab: nass* [In the presence of absence]. Beirut: Riyad al-rayyis li-l-kutub wa-l-nashr, 2006.

——. *al-Gha'ib al-hadir* [The present absentee]. Amman: Muhammad Nimr Mustafa, 2010.

——. *In the Presence of Absence*. Translated by Sinan Antoon. Brooklyn, NY: Archipelago Books, 2011.

——. *Mahmoud Darwish: Selected Poems*. Translated by Ian Wedde and Fawwaz Tuqan. Cheadle Hulme: Cheshire Carcanet Press, 1973.

——. *Mural*. Translated by Rema Hammami and John Berger. London: Verso, 2009.

Dauber, Jeremy. "Allusion in a Jewish Key: Literary Theory and the Study of Haskala Literature." In *Antonio's Devils: Writers of the Jewish Enlightenment and the Birth of Modern Hebrew and Yiddish Literature*, 32–66. Stanford, CA: Stanford University Press, 2004.

de Man, Paul. "'Conclusions': Walter Benjamin's 'The Task of the Translator.'" In *The Resistance to Theory*, 73–105. Minneapolis: University of Minnesota Press, 1986.

Deleuze, Gilles. "He Stuttered." In *Essays Critical and Clinical*, translated by Daniel W. Smith and Michael A. Greco, 107–114. Minneapolis: University of Minnesota Press, 1997.

Deleuze, Gilles, and Félix Guattari. "What Is a Minor Literature?" In *Kafka: Toward a Minor Literature*, translated by Dana Polan, 16–27. Minneapolis: University of Minnesota Press, 1986.

Derrida, Jacques. "Language Is Never Owned." In *Sovereignties in Question: The Poetics of Paul Celan*, edited by Thomas Dutoit and Outi Pasanen, 97–107. New York: Fordham University Press, 2005.

——. *The Monolingualism of the Other; or, The Prosthesis of Origin*. Translated by Patrick Mensah. Stanford, CA: Stanford University Press, 1998.

——. "Poetics and Politics of Witnessing." In *Sovereignties in Question: The Poetics of Paul Celan*, edited by Thomas Dutoit and Outi Pasanen, 65–96. New York: Fordham University Press, 2005.

Diamond, James. *Homeland or Holy Land: The "Canaanite" Critique of Israel*. Bloomington: Indiana University Press, 1986.

Dingwaney, Anuradha. "Introduction: Translating 'Third World' Cultures." In *Between Languages and Cultures: Translation and Cross-Cultural Texts*, edited by Anuradha Dingwaney and Carol Maier, 3–15. Pittsburgh, PA: Pittsburgh University Press, 1995.

Dingwaney, Anuradha, and Carol Maier, eds. *Between Languages and Cultures: Translation and Cross-Cultural Texts*. Pittsburgh, PA: University of Pittsburgh Press, 1995.

Djebar, Assia. *Fantasia: An Algerian Cavalcade*. Translated by Dorothy S. Blair. London: Quartet Books, 1985.

Drory, Rina. "The Maqama." In *The Literature of Al-Andalus*, edited by Maria Rosa Menocal, Raymond P. Scheindlin, and Michael Sells, 190–210. Cambridge: Cambridge University Press, 2000.

Edwards, John. *Language and Identity: An Introduction*. Cambridge: Cambridge University Press, 2009.

Elad-Bouskila, Ami. "Arabic and/or Hebrew: The Language of Arab Writers in Israel." In *Israeli and Palestinian Identities in History and Literature*, edited by Kamal Abdel-Malek and David Jacobson, 133–158. New York: St. Martin's, 1999.

——. *Modern Palestinian Literature and Culture*. London: Frank Cass, 1999.

Eliachar, Elie. *Living with Jews*. London: Weidenfeld and Nicholson, 1983.

Eliachar, Eliyahu. *Lihiyot 'im yehudim* [Living with Jews]. Jerusalem: Hotsa'at Y. Markus ve-shutafav, 1980.

Elkayyam, Shelley. *Mi-tokh shirat ha-arkhitekt: shirim ve-shirot* [Songs of the architect]. Tel Aviv: Zmora-Bitan, 1987.

Elmaleḥ, Abraham. *Milon 'ivri-'aravi: kolel ha-milim ha-'araviyot ha-yoter neḥutsot* [Hebrew-Arabic dictionary, including essential words]. Jerusalem: Mitspe, 1928/1929.

——, trans. *Sipurey kalila ve-dimna* [Tales of Kalila and Dimna]. Tel Aviv: Dvir, 1926.

Evans, Ruth. "Metaphor of Translation." In *Routledge Encyclopedia of Translation Studies*, edited by Mona Baker, 149–153. New York: Routledge, 1998.

Even-Shoshan, A., ed. *Ha-milon he-ḥadash* [New Dictionary]. Jerusalem: Kiriyat sefer, 1999.

Even-Zohar, Itamar. "The Emergence of a Native Hebrew Culture in Palestine, 1882–1948." *Poetics Today* 11.1 (Spring 1990): 175–191.

Eyal, Gil. *The Disenchantment of the Orient: Expertise in Arab Affairs and the Israeli State*. Stanford, CA: Stanford University Press, 2006.

"Eyn ani mevin keytsad melamdim ha-sfaradim mi-tokh sifrey limud shel ashkenazim" [I don't understand how they teach Sephardim from Ashkenazi schoolbooks]. *Haaretz*, Tarbut ve-sifrut [Literary supplement], January 2, 2004.

Feldman, Levana. "'*Ajami*, seret dover 'aravit—nora seksi . . ." ['*Ajami*, an Arabic-speaking movie—so sexy . . .]. *Marker* (Café), October 8, 2009. Accessed August 28, 2013. http://cafe.themarker.com/post/1261235.

Feldman, Maya. "Eyn zo agada" [No legend]. *Ynet*, December 28, 2005. Accessed August 29, 2013. http://www.ynet.co.il/articles/0,7340,L-3191337,00.html.

Feldman, Yael. "Postcolonial Memory, Postmodern Intertextuality: Anton Shammas's *Arabesques* Revisited." *PMLA* 114 (May 1999): 373–385.

Felman, Shoshana. *Testimony: Crises of Witnessing in Literature, Psychoanalysis, and History*. New York: Routledge, 1992.

Fish, Stanley. *Is There a Text in This Class? The Authority of Interpretive Communities*. Cambridge, MA: Harvard University Press, 1980.

Fisherman, Haya, and Joshua Fishman. "The 'Official Languages' of Israel: Their Status in Law and Police Attitudes and Knowledge Concerning Them." In *Multilingual Political Systems: Problems and Solutions*, edited by Jean-Guy Savard and Richard Vigneault, 497–535. Quebec: Les Presses de l'Université Laval, 1975.

Fishman, Joshua. *Yiddish: Turning to Life*. Amsterdam: John Benjamins, 1991.

Gabbai, Yael. "Dvarim she-ratsiti lomar" [Things I wanted to say]. *Ynet*, January 8, 2010. Accessed August 29, 2013. http://www.ynet.co.il/articles/0,7340,L-3936775,00.html.

Galili, Lily. "A Homeland of All Its Citizens." *Haaretz*, September 21, 2006. Accessed August 29, 2013. http://www.haaretz.com/a-homeland-of-all-its-citizens-1.197856.

———. "Nikhbosh et ha-'olam bli af yeri'a" [We'll conquer the world without a single shot]. *Haaretz*, September 21, 2006. Accessed August 29, 2013. http://www.haaretz.co.il/misc/1.1558533.

Gates, Henry Louis. "Dis and Dat: Dialect and the Descent." In *Afro-American Literature: The Reconstruction of Instruction*, edited by Dexter Fisher and Robert Steptoe, 88–119. New York: MLA, 1978.

Genette, Gerard. *Paratexts: Thresholds of Interpretation*. Cambridge: Cambridge University Press, 1997.

Ghanayim, Mahmud. "A Dream of Severance: Crisis of Identity in Palestinian Fiction in Israel." In *Palestinian Collective Memory and National Identity*, edited by Meir Litvak, 193–216. New York: Palgrave Macmillan, 2009.

——. "A Magic Journey: The Admission of Palestinian Fiction in Israel to the Arab World." *Arabic and Middle Eastern Literatures* 1.2 (1998): 205–222.

Glasner, Arik. "'Al Tchaḥla ve-Ḥezkel, shel Almog Behar" [On Almog Behar's Rachel and Ezekiel]. *Ma'ariv*, literary supplement, January 2011. Accessed August 29, 2013. http://arikglasner.wordpress.com/2011/01/29/.

Glass, Eytan. *Ani Simon Naḥmias* [I am Simon Naḥmias]. Tel Aviv: Ha-kibuts ha-me'uḥad, 1995.

Gluzman, Michael. *The Politics of Canonicity: Lines of Resistance in Modernist Hebrew Poetry*. Stanford, CA: Stanford University Press, 2003.

——. "The Politics of Intertextuality in Anton Shammas's *Arabesques*." *Journal of Modern Jewish Studies* 3.3 (November 2004): 319–335.

——. "The Return of the Politically Repressed: Avot Yeshurun's 'Passover on Caves.'" In *The Politics of Canonicity: Lines of Resistance in Modernist Hebrew Poetry*, 141–180. Stanford, CA: Stanford University Press, 2003.

Golan, Avirama. "Bi-zkhut 'ajami" [Thanks to *'Ajami*]. *Haaretz*, September 30, 2009. Accessed August 28, 2013. http://www.haaretz.co.il/opinions/1.1282875.

Goldberg, Harvey. "From Sephardi to Mizrahi and Back Again: Changing Meanings of 'Sephardi' in Its Social Environments." *Jewish Social Studies* 5.1 (Fall 2008): 165–188.

Goldman, Shalom. *Zeal for Zion: Christians, Jews, and the Idea of the Promised Land*. Chapel Hill: University of North Carolina Press, 2009.

Gormezano Goren, Yitzḥak. *Ba-derekh la-itztadyon* [On the way to the stadium]. Tel Aviv: Bimat kedem le-sifrut, 2003.

——. *Blansh* [Blanche]. Tel Aviv: 'Am 'oved, 1986.

——. *Kayits aleksandroni* [Alexandrian summer]. Tel Aviv: 'Am 'oved, 1978.

——. *Miklat be-bavli* [Shelter in bavli]. Tel Aviv: Bimat kedem le-sifrut, 1998.

Gottreich, Emily. "Historicizing the Concept of Arab Jews in the Maghrib." *Jewish Quarterly Review* 98.4 (2008): 433–451.

Greenberg, Uri Tsvi. *Ba-'emtsa ha-olam u-ve-'emtsa ha-zmanim: mivḥar shirim* [In the middle of the world, in the middle of time]. Tel Aviv: Ha-kibuts ha-me'uḥad, 1979.

Grossman, David. *Nokheḥim nifkadim* [Present absentees]. Tel Aviv: Ha-kibuts ha-me'uḥad, 1992.

——. *Sleeping on a Wire: Conversations with Palestinians in Israel*. Translated by Haim Watzman. New York: Farrar, Straus and Giroux, 1993.

Grumberg, Karen. *Place and Ideology in Contemporary Hebrew Literature*. Syracuse, NY: Syracuse University Press, 2011.

——. "Ricki Lake in Tel Aviv: The Alternative of Orly Castel-Bloom's Hebrew-Englishes." In *Anglophone Jewish Literatures*, edited by Axel Stahler, 234–248. New York: Routledge, 2007.

Gutkind, Nomi. "Hess—Ha-shira ke-nevu'at ha-lev" [Hess—poetry as the prophecy of the heart]. *Hatsofe* 20 (March 1987).

Habiby, Emile. *Ikhtiyya* [alternate spellings *Ikhtayyi* and *Ekhtayye*] [What a shame!]. Niqusiya, Qubrus: Mu'assasat bisan bris li-l-sihafa wa-l-nashr wa-l-tawzi, 1985.

——. *Khurafiyyat Saraya bint al-ghul* [The fable of Saraya, the ghoul's daughter]. Haifa: Dar 'arabask, 1991.

——. *Luka' ibn Luka': Thalath jalsat amam sanduq al-'ajab* [Luka', son of Luka': Three sessions before the treasure chest of wonders]. Beirut: al-Farabi, 1980.

——. *Ha-opsimist: Ha-kronika ha-mufla'a shel he'almut Sa'id Abu al-Nahs al-Mutasha'il* [The pessoptimist: The amazing chronicle of the disappearance of Sa'id Abu al-Nahs al-Mutasha'il]. Translated by Anton Shammas. Haifa: Mifras, 1984.

——. *Saraya, the Ogre's Daughter: A Palestinian Fairy Tale*. Translated by Peter Theroux. Jerusalem: Ibis Editions, 2006.

——. *The Secret Life of Saeed the Pessoptimist*. Translated by Trevor Le Gassick and Salma Khadra Jayyusi. 2nd ed. New York: Interlink Books, 2002.

——. *Sudasiyyat al-ayyam al-sitta* [The sextet of the six days (war); alternatively, Stories of the six days, 1969]. Beirut: Dar al-'awda, 1969.

——. *al-Waqa'i' al-ghariba fi ikhtifa' Sa'id Abi al-Nahs al-Mutasha'il: qissa* [The strange tale of Sa'id Abi al-Nahs al-Mutasha'il; alternatively, The strange tale of Sa'id Abi al-Nahs the ill-fated pessoptimist: A story]. Beirut: Dar ibn Khaldun, 1974.

——. *al-Waqa'i' al-ghariba fi ikhtifa' Sa'id Abi al-Nahs al-Mutasha'il: qissa* [The strange tale of Sa'id Abi al-Nahs al-Mutasha'il; alternatively, The strange tale of Sa'id Abi al-Nahs the ill-fated pessoptimist: A story]. Haifa: Dar 'arabask, 2006.

Hakak, Lev. *Nitsaney ha-yetsira ha-'ivrit ha-ḥadasha be-bavel* [The budding of Modern Hebrew creativity in Babylon]. Or Yehuda: Babylonian Jewry Heritage Center, 2004.

Halevy, Yosef. *Bat ha-mizraḥ ha-ḥadasha: 'al yetsirata shel Shoshana Shababo* [Daughter of the new Orient: The writings of Shoshana Shababo]. Ramat Gan: Bar-Ilan University, 1996.

Halkin, Talya. "A Sense of Place." *Jerusalem Post*, Arts, May 14, 2004, 34.

Halperin, Liora R. "Babel in Zion: The Politics of Language Diversity in Jewish Palestine, 1920–1948." Doctoral dissertation, University of California, Los Angeles, 2011.

——. "Orienting Language: Reflections on the Study of Arabic in the Yishuv." *Jewish Quarterly Review* 96.4 (Fall 2006): 481–489.

Halpern, Orly. "Overstepping Boundaries." *Jerusalem Post*, Books, February 18, 2005, 22.

Ḥalutz, Doron. "Ha-biyografya shel Ayman Siksek dramatit yoter me-'alilat sifro" [Ayman Sikseck's biography is more dramatic than his book's plot]. *Haaretz*, April 9, 2010. Accessed August 29, 2013. http://www.haaretz.co.il/misc/1.1197458.

——. "Language Is My Anchor." *Haaretz*, April 11, 2010. Accessed August 29, 2013. http://www.haaretz.com/weekend/magazine/language-is-my-anchor-1.284042.

Handelman, Don. *Nationalism and the Israeli State: Bureaucratic Logic In Public Events*. Oxford: Berg, 2004.

Handelman, Don, and Lea Shamgar Handelman. "The Presence of Absence: The Memorialism of National Death in Israel." In *Grasping Land: Space and Place in Contemporary Israeli Discourse and Experience*, edited by Eyal Ben-Ari and Yoram Bilu, 85–128. Albany: State University of New York Press, 1997.

Hareven, Alouph, ed. *Every Sixth Israeli: Relations Between the Jewish Majority and the Arab Minority in Israel.* Jerusalem: Van Leer Institute, 1983.

al-Ḥarizi, Yehuda. *Taḥkemoni.* Translated by Victor Emmanuel Reichert. Vol. 1. Jerusalem: Raphael Haim Cohen's Press, 1965.

———. *Taḥkemoni, o: maḥberot Heman ha-Ezraḥi.* Edited by Yosef Yahalom and Na'oya Katsumata. Jerusalem: Makhon Ben Tsvi, 2010.

Harshav, Benjamin. *Language in Time of Revolution.* Berkeley: University of California Press, 1993.

Ḥayyik, Yoav. "Kartis bikur" [Calling card]. Translated by Jacqueline Sha'shu'a. *Ha-kivun mizraḥ* 7 (2003): 3.

Ḥazan, Ephraim. *Ha-shira ha-'ivrit bi-tsfon afrika* [Hebrew poetry in North Africa]. Jerusalem: Magnes Press, 1995.

Heath, Peter. "Creativity in the Novels of Emile Habiby, with Special Reference to *Sa'id the Pessoptimist.*" In *Tradition, Modernity, and Postmodernity in Arabic Literature,* edited by Issa J. Boullata, Kamal Abdel-Malek, and Wael B. Hallaq, 158–172. Leiden: Brill, 2000.

Heller, Monica, ed. *Code-Switching: Anthropological and Sociolinguistic Perspectives.* Berlin: Walter de Gruyter, 1988.

Herzog, Omri. "Ze ha-dvarim shel Sami Berdugo" [Sami Berdugo's *Ze ha-dvarim*]. *Haaretz,* July 28, 2010. Accessed August 29, 2013. http://www.haaretz.co.il/literature/1.1214083.

Hess, Amira. *Bole'a ha-informatsya* [The information eater]. Tel Aviv: Zmora-Bitan, 1993.

———. "Kentu be-ghayr dini" [I was in another world]. *La-roḥav: magazin gerila tarbut/Maqta' 'ardi: majallat 'asabat thaqafa* [Crosswise/Wide crossing: The journal of Cultural Guerrilla] 1 (2012): 121–124.

———. *Shney susim 'al kav ha-or* [Two horses on a beam of light]. Tel Aviv: 'Am 'oved, 1987.

———. *Ve-yare'aḥ notef shiga'on* [And the moon drips madness]. Tel Aviv: 'Am 'oved, 1984.

Hess, Tamar. "A Mediterranean Mayflower?" *Prooftexts* 30.3 (Fall 2010): 293–302.

Hever, Hannan. "Hebrew in an Israeli Arab Hand: Six Miniatures on Anton Shammas's *Arabesques.*" In *The Nature and Context of Minority Discourse,* edited by Abdul R. JanMohamed and David Lloyd, 264–293. New York: Oxford University Press, 1990.

———. "Lo banu mi-ha-yam: kavim le-geyografya sifrutit mizraḥit" [We did not come by sea: Outlines of a Mizraḥi literary geography]. *Te'orya u-vikoret* 16 (Spring 2000): 181–195.

———. "Not My Mother Tongue." *Haaretz,* March 5, 2004. Accessed August 30, 2013. http://www.poetryinternationalweb.net/pi/site/cou_article/item/3148/Not-my-Mother-Tongue.

———. "Of Refugee Gals and Refugee Guys: Emil Habibi and the Hebrew Literary Canon." In *Producing the Modern Hebrew Canon: Nation Building and Minority Discourse,* 205–232. New York: New York University Press, 2002.

——. *Producing the Modern Hebrew Canon: Nation Building and Minority Discourse.* New York: New York University Press, 2002.

——. *Ha-sipur ve-ha-le'om: kri'a bikortit be-kanon ha-sifrut ha-'ivrit* [The narrative and the nation: A critical reading of the Hebrew literary canon]. Tel Aviv: Resling, 2007.

——. "We Have Not Arrived from the Sea: A Mizrahi Literary Geography." *Social Identities* 10.1 (2004): 31–51.

Hever, Hannan, Moran Banit, Ayman Sikseck, Mati Shemoelof, and Tomer Gardi, eds. *Al tagidu be-gat: ha-nakba ha-palastinit be-shira ha-'ivrit, 1948–1958* [Don't say in Gat: The Palestinian *nakba* in Hebrew poetry]. Israel: Zokhrot, Parhesya, Pardes, 2010.

Hever, Hannan, Yehouda Shenhav, and Pnina Motzafi-Haller, eds. *Mizraḥim be-yisra'el: 'iyun bikorti meḥudash* [Mizraḥim in Israel: A new critical observation]. Jerusalem: Van Leer/Ha-kibuts ha-me'uḥad, 2002.

Hill, Brad Sabin. "Hebrew Printing in Baghdad." *Report of the Oxford Centre for Hebrew and Jewish Studies* (2003–2004): 53–77.

Hillel, Hagar. *"Yisra'el" be-kahir: 'iton tsiyoni be-mitsrayim ha-le'umit, 1920–1939* ["Israel" in Cairo: A Zionist newspaper in nationalist Egypt]. Tel Aviv: 'Am 'oved, 2004.

Hochberg, Gil. "'The Dispossession of Hebrew': Anton Shammas's *Arabesques* and the Cultural Space of Language." In *Crisis and Memory: The Representation of Space in Modern Levantine Narrative*, edited by Ken Seigneurie, 52–66. Wiesbaden: Reichert Verlag Wiesbaden, 2003.

——. *In Spite of Partition: Jews, Arabs, and the Limits of Separatist Imagination.* Princeton, NJ: Princeton University Press, 2007.

——. "To Be or Not to Be an Israeli Arab: Sayed Kashua and the Prospect of Minority Speech-Acts." *Comparative Literature* 62.1 (Winter 2010): 68–88.

Hoffman, Yoel. *Sefer Yosef* [The book of Joseph]. Jerusalem: Keter, 1988.

Horn, Bernard. *Facing the Fires: Conversations with A. B. Yehoshua.* Syracuse, NY: Syracuse University Press, 1997.

ibn Gabirol, Shlomo. *Shirey Shelomo ben Yehuda ibn Gabirol* [The poems of Solomon ibn Gabirol]. Vol. 1. Edited by Ḥ. N. Bialik and Y. Ḥ. Ravinitsky. Tel Aviv: Dvir, 1927.

Ibrahim, Mohammad H. "Language and Politics in Modern Palestine." *Arab Journal for the Humanities* 1 (1981): 323–341.

al-'Id, Yumna. "Arabesques." *al-Karmel* 35 (1990): 83–84.

——. *Tikniyyat al-sard al-riwa'i fi daw' al-manhaj al-bunyawi* [Narrative techniques in fiction according to the structuralist method]. Beirut: al-Farabi, 1990.

Ilan, Shahar. "MKs: Make Hebrew the Only Official Language." *Haaretz*, May 19, 2008. Accessed August 27, 2013. http://www.haaretz.com/print-edition/news/mks-make-hebrew-the-only-official-language-1.246058.

Isaksen, Runo. *Literature and War: Conversations with Israeli and Palestinian Writers.* Translated by Kari Dickson. Northampton, MA: Olive Branch Press, 2009.

'Ivri, Yuval. Letter to the editor. *Haaretz*, Tarbut ve-sifrut [Literary supplement], January 9, 2004, H3.

Jabotinsky, Ze'ev. *Ha-mivta ha-'ivri.* Tel Aviv: Hotsa'at ha-sefer, 1930.

Jacobs, Adriana X. "From IDF to .PDF: War Poetry in the Israeli Digital Age." In *Narratives of Dissent: War in Contemporary Israeli Arts and Culture*, edited by Rachel S. Harris and Ranen Omer-Sherman, 153–166. Detroit, MI: Wayne State University Press, 2013.

Jacobson, David. *Modern Midrash: The Retelling of Traditional Jewish Narratives by Twentieth Century Jewish Writers.* Albany: State University of New York Press, 1987.

Jakobson, Roman. "Closing Statement: Linguistics and Poetics." In *The Stylistics Reader: From Roman Jakobson to the Present*, edited by Jean Jacques Weber, 10–35. London: Arnold, 1996.

——. "Linguistic Aspects of Translation." In *On Translation*, 232–239. Cambridge, MA: Harvard University Press, 1959.

Jameson, Fredric. "Third-World Literature in the Era of Multinational Capitalism." *Social Text* 15 (Autumn 1986): 65–88.

Jarrar, Mahar. "A Narration of 'Deterritorialization': Imil Habiby's *The Pessoptimist.*" *Middle Eastern Literatures* 5.1 (2002): 15–28.

Jayyusi, Salma Khadra, ed. *Anthology of Modern Palestinian Literature.* New York: Columbia University Press, 1992.

Jiryis, Sabri. *The Arabs in Israel.* New York: Monthly Review Press, 1976.

Kabakoff, Jacob. *Master of Hope: Selected Writings of Naphtali Herz Imber.* New York: Herzl Press, 1985.

Kaplan, Caren. "Deterritorializations: The Rewriting of Home and Exile in Western Feminist Discourse." In *The Nature and Context of Minority Discourse*, edited by Abdul R. JanMohamed and David Lloyd, 357–368. New York: Oxford University Press, 1990.

Kaplan, Eran. "Between East and West: Zionist Revisionism as Mediterranean Ideology." In *Orientalism and the Jews*, edited by Ivan Davidson Kalmar and Derek J. Penslar, 125–141. Waltham, MA: Brandeis University Press, 2005.

Karfel, Dalia. "Emil ve-ha-mashmitsim" [Emile and the slanderers]. *Kol ha-'ir*, May 1, 1992, 34.

Kartun-Blum, Ruth. *Profane Scriptures: Reflections on the Dialogue with the Bible in Modern Hebrew Poetry.* Cincinnati, OH: Hebrew Union College Press, 1999.

Kashua, Sayed. "Gdolim yoter mi-Bar Rafaeli" [More popular than Bar Rafaeli]. *Haaretz*, February 20, 2009. Accessed August 27, 2013. http://www.haaretz.co.il/misc/1.1246766.

Kayyal, Mahmoud. "Hebrew-Arabic Translations in the Modern Era: A General Survey." *Meta* 43.1 (1998): 1–10.

——. "Intercultural Relations Between Arabs and Israeli Jews as Reflected in Arabic Translations of Modern Hebrew Literature." *Target* 16.1 (2004): 53–68.

——. *Targum be-tsel ha-'imut: normot targum min ha-sifrut ha-'ivrit ha-ḥadasha la-safa ha-'arvit ba-shanim 1948-1990* [Translation in the shadow of confrontation: Norms in the translations of Modern Hebrew literature into Arabic between 1948–1990]. Jerusalem: Magnes Press, 2006.

Khater, Akram. "Emile Habibi: The Mirror of Irony in Palestinian Literature." *Journal of Arabic Literature* 24.1 (March 1993): 75–94.

Khatibi, Abdelkebir. *Love in Two Languages*. Translated by Richard Howard. Minneapolis: University of Minnesota Press, 1990.

Khazzoom, Aziza. "The Great Chain of Orientalism: Jewish Identity, Stigma Management, and Ethnic Exclusion in Israel." *American Sociological Review* 68.4 (August 2003): 481–510.

Khoury, Elias. "Rethinking the *Nakba*." *Critical Inquiry* 38.2 (Winter 2012): 250–266.

Kilito, Abdelfattah. *The Author and His Doubles: Essays on Classical Arabic Culture*. Translated by Michael Cooperson. Syracuse, NY: Syracuse University Press, 2001.

———. "Dog Words." In *Displacements: Cultural Identities in Question*, edited by Angelika Bammer, translated by Ziad Elmarsafy, xxi–xxxi. Bloomington: Indiana University Press, 1994.

———. *Thou Shalt Not Speak My Language*. Translated by Waïl S. Hassan. Syracuse, NY: Syracuse University Press, 2008.

Kimmerling, Barukh, and Joel Migdal. *The Palestinian People: A History*. Cambridge, MA: Harvard University Press, 2003.

Klein, Yossi. "Who's Israel's Real Ethnic Demon?" *Haaretz*, August 4, 2013. Accessed August 29, 2013. http://www.haaretz.com/weekend/.premium-1.539432.

Kramsch, Claire. *Language and Culture*. Oxford: Oxford University Press, 1998.

Kronfeld, Chana. *On the Margins of Modernism: Decentering Literary Dynamics*. Berkeley: University of California Press, 1996.

Kuzar, Ron. *Hebrew and Zionism: A Discourse Analytic Cultural Study*. Berlin: Mouton de Gruyter, 2001.

Lacan, Jacques. "The Mirror Stage as Formative of the *I* Function as Revealed in Psychoanalytic Experience." In *Ecrits: A Selection*, translated by Bruce Fink, 3–9. London: Norton, 2004.

Lahman, Dan. "Tchaḥla ve-Ḥezkel/Almog Behar." *E-mago*, January 30, 2011. Accessed August 29, 2013. http://www.e-mago.co.il/Editor/literature-3557.htm.

Landau, Jacob M. "Israël (Cairo)." In *Encyclopedia of Jews in the Islamic World*, edited by Norman A. Stillman. Leiden: Brill, 2010. http://www.brill.com/publications/online-resources/encyclopedia-jews-islamic-world-online.

Laor, Yitzhak. "A Beautiful Bildungsroman." *Haaretz*, May 2, 2008. Accessed August 29, 2013. http://www.haaretz.com/general/a-beautiful-bildungsroman-1.245067.

———. "Between Family and Postcolonial Earth." *Haaretz*, August 23, 2007. Accessed August 29, 2013. http://www.haaretz.com/weekend/week-s-end/between-family-and-postcolonial-earth-1.228017.

———. "'Mihu ashkenazi?': ḥor be-idyologya shel A. B. Yehoshua" [Who is an Ashkenazi? A hole in A. B. Yehoshua's ideology]. In *Anu kotvim otakh moledet: masot 'al sifrut yisra'elit* [We write you, homeland: Essays on Israeli literature], 105–114. Tel Aviv: Ha-kibuts ha-me'uḥad, 1995.

———. "Ha-yalda ve-ha-'lo'" [The girl and the "no"]. *Haaretz*, April 29, 2008. Accessed August 30, 2013. http://www.haaretz.co.il/literature/1.1321386.

Le Gassick, Trevor. "The Image of the Jew in Modern Arabic Fiction." *Michigan Quarterly Review* 21.2 (1982): 249–267.

Le Page, R. B., and Andrée Tabouret-Keller. *Acts of Identity: Creole-Based Approaches to Language and Ethnicity*. Cambridge: Cambridge University Press, 1985.

Lee, Benjamin. *Talking Heads: Language, Metalanguage, and the Semiotics of Subjectivity*. Durham, NC: Duke University Press, 1997.

Lee, Vered. "Lama eyn lanu soferet ba-mishbetset shel Amos Oz" [Why don't we have a woman writer in Amos Oz's spot: An interview with Ronit Matalon and Dana Olmert]. *Haaretz*, March 6, 2013. Accessed August 29, 2013. http://www.haaretz.co.il/literature/study/.premium-1.1946165.

Lefkowitz, Daniel. "Conflict and Identity in Palestinian Narratives about Arabic in Israel in the Early 1990s." Paper presented at the Middle East Studies Association, Boston, November 2009.

———. *Words and Stones: The Politics of Language and Identity in Israel.* New York: Oxford University Press, 2004.

Lerer, Yael. "The Andalus Test—Reflections on the Attempt to Publish Arabic Literature in Hebrew." *Jadaliyya*, May 16, 2012. Accessed August 27, 2013. http://www.jadaliyya.com/pages/index/5566/the-andalus-test_reflections-on-the-attempt-to-pub.

———. "De l'autre côté." *Printemps* 4 (2008): 136–145.

———. "Publishing Arabic Literature in Hebrew." *Qantara*, December 2, 2004. Accessed August 27, 2013. http://www.qantara.de/webcom/show_article.php/_c-310/_nr-134/i.html.

LeVine, Mark. *Overthrowing Geography: Jaffa, Tel Aviv, and the Struggle for Palestine, 1880–1948*. Berkeley: University of California Press, 2005.

Levy, Lital. "Borderline Writers in Arabic and Hebrew: The Poetry of Na'im 'Araidi and Anton Shammas." Bachelor's thesis, Columbia University, 1996.

———. "Exchanging Words: Thematizations of Translation in Arabic Writing from Israel." *Comparative Studies of South Asia, Africa, and the Middle East* 23.1–2 (2003): 106–127.

———. "From Baghdad to Bialik with Love: A Reappropriation of Modern Hebrew Poetry, 1933." *Comparative Literature Studies* 42.3 (2005): 125–154.

———. "Haddad, Ezra." In *Encyclopedia of Jews of the Islamic World*. Leiden: Brill, 2010. http://referenceworks.brillonline.com/entries/encyclopedia-of-jews-in-the-islamic-world/haddad-ezra-SIM_0008820?s.num=2&s.au=%22Lital+Levy%22&s.f.s2_parent_title=Encyclopedia+of+Jews+in+the+Islamic+World.

———. "Historicizing the Concept of Arab Jews in the *Mashriq*." *Jewish Quarterly Review* 98.4 (Fall 2008): 452–469.

———. "Jewish Writers in the Arab East: Literature, History, and the Politics of Enlightenment, 1863–1914." Doctoral dissertation, University of California, Berkeley, 2007.

———. "Mi-hu ha-yehudi ha-'aravi? 'Iyun mashve be-toldot ha-she'ela, 1880–2010" [Who is an Arab Jew? A comparative inquiry into the origins of the question, 1880–2008]. *Te'orya u-vikoret* 38–39 (Winter 2011): 101–135.

———. "Nation, Village, Cave: A Spatial Reading of 1948 in Three Novels of Anton Shammas, Emile Habiby, and Elias Khoury." *Jewish Social Studies* 18.3 (Spring/Summer 2012): 10–26.

———. "Reorienting Hebrew Literary History: The View from the East." *Prooftexts* 29.2 (Winter 2009): 127–172.

———. "Self and the City: Literary Representations of Jewish Baghdad." *Prooftexts* 26.1–2 (Winter/Spring 2006): 163–211.

———. "Self-Portraits of the Other: Toward a Palestinian Poetics of Hebrew Verse." In *Transforming Loss into Beauty: Essays in Honor of Magda al-Nowaihi*, edited by Marle Hammond and Dana Sajdi, 343–402. Cairo: American University in Cairo Press, 2008.

———. "Shams (Cairo), al-." In *Encyclopedia of Jews in the Islamic World.* Leiden: Brill, 2010. http://www.encquran.brill.nl/entries/encyclopedia-of-jews-in-the-islamic-world/shams-cairo-al-SIM_0001770?s.num=1.

———. "The 'Whirling Dervish' vs. 'The Universal': Discourses of Culture and Power in Israel." *Arab Studies Journal* 9.2/10.1 (Fall 2001/Spring 2002): 10–30.

Levy, Lital, and Ahuva Mu'alem. "Eykh ata shlemut'—siḥa 'im Amira Hes" [How are you, wholeness—a conversation with Amira Hess]. *'Edut mi-tsaḥ* [Testimony from "Social Justice"] (Winter 1998): 68–76.

Levy, Lital, Lena Salaymeh, and Adriana Valencia. "Poetic Structures on Contested Space: The *bayt/bayit* of Siham Daoud and Shelley Elkayam." *Critical Sense* 9.1 (Winter 2001): 9–54.

Lis, Jonathan. "Lawmakers Seek to Drop Arabic as One of Israel's Official Languages." *Haaretz*, August 4, 2011. Accessed August 27, 2013. http://www.haaretz.com/print-edition/news/lawmakers-seek-to-drop-arabic-as-one-of-israel-s-official-languages-1.376829.

Liu, Lydia, ed. *Tokens of Exchange: The Problem of Translation in Global Circulations.* Durham, NC: Duke University Press, 1999.

López-Morillas, Consuelo. "Language." In *The Literature of Al-Andalus*, edited by Maria Rosa Menocal, Raymond P. Scheindlin, and Michael Sells, 33–59. Cambridge: Cambridge University Press, 2000.

Luz, Tsvi. "'Al ha-dam: 'iyun temati ba-klil sonetot le-Tsherniḥovski" [On the blood: A thematic study of Tchernichowsky's sonnet corona]. *'Aley si'aḥ* [Literary conversations] 29–30 (1991): 91–104.

Malki, Sa'd. "Nahdat al-yahud al-safaradim; 'ala dhikr muhadarat Biyalik (2)" [The revival of the Sephardim: Regarding Bialik's lecture, part 2]. *Isra'il*, March 25, 1927, 1.

———. "Nahdat al-yahud al-safaradim; 'ala dhikr muhadarat Biyalik (3)" [The revival of the Sephardim: Regarding Bialik's lecture, part 3]. *Isra'il*, April 1, 1927, 1.

Mann, Barbara. "'An Apartment to Remember': Ayman Sikseck's *To Jaffa* (2010) and Israeli Memory Culture." Lecture delivered at National Association of Professors of Hebrew, New York, June 24, 2013.

Mansour, Atallah. *Be-or ḥadash* [In a new light]. Tel Aviv: Karni, 1966.

Masalha, Nur. "Present Absentees and Indigenous Resistance." In *The Israel/Palestine Question: A Reader*, 2nd ed., edited by Ilan Pappé, 255–284. London: Routledge, 2007.

Masalha, Salman. "Anthem for the Tribe of Israel." Translated by Vivian Eden. Accessed August 29, 2013. http://salmaghari-en.blogspot.com/2008/12/anthem-for-tribe-of-israel.html.

——. *Eḥad mi-kan* [In place]. Tel Aviv: 'Am 'oved, 2004.

——. *Ka-l-ankabut bi-la khuyut* [Like a spider without webs]. Jerusalem, 1989.

——. *Khana farigha* [Blank space]. Jerusalem: Zaman, 2002.

——. *Lughat umm* [Mother tongue]. Jerusalem: Zaman, 2006.

——. *Maghnat ta'ir al-khudr* [Green bird song]. Jerusalem: al-Katib, 1979.

——. *Maqamat sharqiyya* [Oriental scales]. Jerusalem, 1991.

——. "Nefesh yisra'eli homiya" [The Israeli soul yearning]. In *Asher ahavta et Yitsḥak* [Yitzhak, whom you love], edited by Zisi Stavi and Aliza Zeigler. Tel Aviv: Miskal, 1995.

——. *Rish al-bahr* [Sea feathers]. Jerusalem: Zaman, 1999.

Massad, Joseph. "The 'Post-Colonial' Colony: Time, Space, and Bodies in Palestine/Israel." In *The Pre-Occupation of Postcolonial Studies*, edited by Fawzia Afzal-Khan and Kalpana Seshadri-Crooks, 311–346. Durham, NC: Duke University Press, 2000.

——. "Zionism's Internal Others: Israel and the Oriental Jews." *Journal of Palestine Studies* 25.4 (Summer 1996): 53–68.

Matalon, Ronit. *Kol tse'adeynu* [The sound of our steps]. Tel Aviv: 'Am 'oved, 2008.

——. "Ha-lashon ve-ha-bayit" [Language and home]. *Mi-karov: ktav 'et le-sifrut u-le-tarbut* [Mikarov: A journal for literature and culture] 2 (1998): 169–171.

——. "Mi-ḥuts la-makom, be-tokh ha-zman" [Out of place, inside time]. In *Kero u-khetov*, 41–50. Tel Aviv: Ha-kibuts ha-me'uḥad, 2001.

——. *The One Facing Us*. Translated by Marsha Weinstein. New York: Metropolitan Books, 1999.

——. *Ze 'im ha-panim eleynu* [The one facing us]. Tel Aviv: 'Am 'oved, 1995.

May, Stephen. *Language and Minority Rights*. London: Pearson Longman, 2001.

——. *Language and Minority Rights: Ethnicity, Nationalism, and the Politics of Language*. New York: Routledge, 2008.

McCarthy, Justin. *The Population of Palestine: Population Statistics of the Late Ottoman Period and the Mandate*. New York: Columbia University Press, 1990.

Mehrez, Samia. "al-Mufaraqa 'inda Jayms Juyis wa-Imil Habibi" [Irony in Joyce's *Ulysses* and Habibi's *Pessoptimist*]. *ALIF* 4 (Spring 1984): 33–54.

——. "The Subversive Poetics of Radical Bilingualism: Postcolonial Francophone North African Literature." In *The Bounds of Race: Perspectives on Hegemony and Resistance*, edited by Dominick La Capra, 255–277. Ithaca, NY: Cornell University Press, 1991.

——. "Translation and the Postcolonial Experience: The Francophone North African Text." In *Rethinking Translation: Discourse, Subjectivity, Ideology*, edited by Lawrence Venuti, 121–138. London: Routledge, 1992.

Menaḥem, Naḥum. *Metaḥim ve-aflaya 'adatit be-yisra'el* [Ethnic tensions and discrimination in Israel]. Haifa: Aḥdut, 1983.

Mendel, Yonatan. "Arabic and Security in Israel: 1967–1973." Paper presented at the Middle East Studies Association, Boston, November 2009.

Meranda, Amnon. "Majadele Refuses to Sing National Anthem." *Ynet*, March 17, 2007. Accessed August 29, 2013. http://www.ynetnews.com/articles/0,7340,L-3377681,00.html.

Mi-safa le-safa [From language to language]. Directed by Nurith Aviv. Israel, 2004.

Michael, Sami. *'A'ida*. Or Yehuda: Kineret/Zmora-Bitan, 2008.

——. *Fiktorya: Riwaya*. Cologne: Manshurat al-jamal, 2005.

——. *Shavim ve-shavim yoter* [Some are more equal than others]. Tel Aviv: Hotsa'at bustan, 1974.

——. *Victoria*. Translated by Dalya Bilu. London: Macmillan, 1995.

——. *Viktorya*. Tel Aviv: 'Am 'oved, 1993.

Miller, Joshua. *Accented America: The Cultural Politics of Multilingual Modernism*. Oxford: Oxford University Press, 2011.

Miller, Tom, ed. *Writing on the Edge: A Borderlands Reader*. Tucson: University of Arizona Press, 2003.

Mintz, Ruth Finer. *Modern Hebrew Literature: A Bilingual Anthology*. Berkeley: University of California Press, 1996.

Miron, Dan. *From Continuity to Contiguity: Toward a New Jewish Literary Thinking*. Stanford, CA: Stanford University Press, 2010.

——. *The Prophetic Mode in Modern Hebrew Poetry*. Milford, CT: Toby Press, 2010.

Mishani, Dror. "Lama tsrikhim ha-mizraḥim la-ḥazor el ha-'ma'abara': maḥshavot 'al ha-historyografya shel 'ha-kol ha-mizraḥi' ba-sifrut ha-'ivrit" [Why do Mizraḥim need to return to the "ma'abara"? Thoughts on the historiography of the "Mizraḥi voice" in Hebrew literature]. *Mi-ta'am* 3 (2005): 91–98.

——. "Leshonot mi-mizraḥ ba'ot el ha-'ivrit le-hizakher be-tokha" [Languages of the East come to Hebrew to be remembered within it; review of *Ha-kivun mizraḥ* 7]. *Haaretz*, December 22, 2003. Accessed August 30, 2013. http://www.haaretz.co.il/misc/1.932809.

——. "Ha-mizraḥi ke-hafra'a leshonit" [The Mizraḥi as a linguistic disturbance]. In *Hazut mizraḥit: hove ha-na' ba-svakh 'avaro ha-'aravi* [Eastern appearances: A present moving in the thicket of its Arab past], edited by Yigal Nizri, 83–89. Tel Aviv: Bavel, 2004.

Morag, Ra'aya. "Koder yoter mi-'Ha-ḥayim 'al-pi Agfa'" [Gloomier than *Life According to Agfa*]. *Haaretz*, October 23, 2009. Accessed August 28, 2013. http://www.haaretz.co.il/literature/1.1286531.

Morahg, Gilead. "The Perils of Hybridity: Resisting the Postcolonial Perspective in A.B. Yehoshua's *The Liberating Bride*." *AJS Review* 33.2 (November 2009): 363–378.

Moreh, Shmuel, ed. "Oriental Literature." In *Encyclopaedia Judaica*, 2nd ed., 15 vols., edited by Michael Berenbaum and Fred Skolnik, 12:471–474. Detroit, MI: Macmillan, 2007.

———. *al-Qissa al-qasira 'inda yahud al-'iraq* [Short stories by Jewish writers from Iraq]. Jerusalem: Magnes Press, 1981.

———. "Ha-shira ve-ha-sifrut ha-yafa" [Poetry and belletristic literature]. In *'Irak: kehilot yisra'el ba-mizraḥ ba-me'ot ha-tsha' 'esre ve-ha-'esrim* [Iraq: Jewish communities in the East in the nineteenth and twentieth centuries], edited by Haim Sa'dun, 101–107. Jerusalem: Misrad ha-ḥinukh and Ben Tsvi Institute, 2002.

Moss, Joshua. *Midrash and Legend: Historical Anecdotes in the Tannaitic Midrashim.* Piscataway, NJ: Gorgias Press, 2004.

"Muhadarat Biyalik 'an nahdat al-yahud al-safaradim fi nadi halusi ha mizrah fi al-quds (1)" [Bialik's lecture on the Sephardi revival for the Organization of Mizraḥi Pioneers in Jerusalem, part 1]. *Isra'il*, March 18, 1927, 1.

Nabokov, Vladimir. *Pnin*. New York: Knopf Doubleday, 1985.

"Nahdat al-yahud al-safaradim; 'ala dhikr muhadarat Biyalik (1)" [The revival of the Sephardim: Regarding Bialik's lecture, part 1]. *Isra'il*, March 18, 1927, 3.

Naḥmias, Victor. "Al-shams: 'iton yehudi be-mitsrayim, 1934–1948" [Al-Shams: A Jewish newspaper in Egypt, 1934–1948]. *Pe'amim* 16 (1983): 128–141.

Naqqash, Samir. *Ana wa-ha'ula' wa-l-fisam: majmu'at qisas 'iraqiyya* [I, they, and the split: Iraqi stories]. Tel Aviv: Jam'iyat tashji' al-abhath wa-l-adab wa-l-funun, 1978.

———. *Awrat al-mala'ika* [The angel's genitalia]. Cologne: Manshurat al-jamal, 1991.

———. *Fi ghiyabih* [In his absence]. Shafa'umru: Dar al-mashriq, 1981.

———. *Fuwa ya dam! Nubila 'iraqiyya* [Blood for sale: an Iraqi novella]. Republished ed. Beirut: Manshurat al-jamal, 2011 [1987].

———. *Hikayat kull zaman wa-makan* [Tales of any time and place]. Tel Aviv: Jam'iyat tashji' al-abhath wa-l-adab wa-l-funun, 1978.

———. *al-Khata'* [The mistake]. Jerusalem: Makba'at al-ma'arif, 1972.

———. *Nubu'at rajul majnun fi madina mal'una: majmu'a qisasiya* [Prophecies of a madman in a cursed city: stories]. Jerusalem: Rabitat al-jami'iyin al-yahud al-nazihin min al-'iraq, 1995.

———. *Nuzulu wa-khayt al-shaytan: riwaya 'iraqiyya* [Tenants and cobwebs: an Iraqi novel]. Jerusalem: Rabitat al-jami'iyin al-yahud al-nazihin min al-'iraq, 1986.

———. *al-Rijs* [The abomination]. Israel: self-published, 1987.

———. *Shlumu al-kurdi wa-ana wa-l-zaman* [Shlomo the Kurd, myself, and time]. Cologne: Manshurat al-jamal, 2004.

———. *Yawma habilat wa-ajhadat al-dunya: qissas 'iraqiyya* [The day the world was conceived and miscarried: Iraqi stories]. Jerusalem: al-Sharq al-'arabiyya, 1980.

Neusner, Jacob. *Esther Rabbah I: An Analytical Translation*. Atlanta: Scholars Press, 1989.

Neuwirth, Angelika. "Traditions and Counter-Traditions in the Land of the Bible: Emile Habibi's De-Mythologizing of History." In *Arabic Literature: Postmodern Perspectives*, edited by Angelika Neuwirth, Andreas Pflitsch, and Barbara Winckler, 197–219. London: Saqi, 2010.

Niranjana, Tejaswini. *Siting Translation: History, Post-structuralism, and the Colonial Context*. Berkeley: University of California Press, 1992.

Nizri, Yigal, ed. *Hazut mizraḥit: hove ha-na' ba-svakh 'avaro ha-'aravi* [Eastern appearances: A present moving in the thicket of its Arab past]. Tel Aviv: Bavel, 2004.

Nocke, Alexandra. *The Place of the Mediterranean in Modern Israeli Identity.* Leiden: Brill, 2009.

Oppenheimer, Yochai. "Representation of Space in Mizraḥi Fiction." *Hebrew Studies* 52 (2012): 335–364.

Oz, Amos. *In the Land of Israel.* Translated by Maurie Goldberg-Bartura. New York: Harcourt, 1983.

——. *Po va-sham be-erets yisra'el bi-stav 1982* [Here and there in the land of Israel in autumn 1982]. Tel Aviv: 'Am 'oved, 1983.

——. *Qissa 'an al-hubb wa-l-zalam* [A tale of love and darkness]. Beirut: Manshurat al-jamal, 2010.

——. *Sipur 'al ahava ve-ḥoshekh* [A tale of love and darkness]. Jerusalem: Keter, 2002.

Oz, Kobi. *'Avaryan tsa'atsu'a* [Petty thief]. Tel Aviv: Keshet, 2002.

Pappé, Ilan. *The Forgotten Palestinians: A History of the Palestinians in Israel.* New Haven, CT: Yale University Press, 2011.

——. "The 2000 Earthquake and Its Impact." In *The Forgotten Palestinians: A History of the Palestinians in Israel*, 229–263. New Haven, CT: Yale University Press, 2011.

Paz, Octavio. "Translation: Literature and Letters." In *Theories of Translation*, edited by Rainer Schulte and John Biguenet, translated by Irene de Corral, 152–162. Chicago: University of Chicago Press, 1992.

Peled, Shimrit. "Mizraḥiyut, ashkenaziyut, ve-merḥav ba-roman ha-yisra'eli le-aḥar milḥemet 1967" [Mizraḥiness, Ashkenaziness, and space in the post-1967 Israeli novel]. *Te'orya u-vikoret* 29 (Fall 2006): 149–172.

Peleg, Yaron. *Orientalism and the Hebrew Imagination.* Ithaca, NY: Cornell University Press, 2005.

Penslar, Derek. "Broadcast Orientalism: Representations of Mizrahi Jewry in Israeli Radio, 1948–1967." In *Orientalism and the Jews*, edited by Ivan Davidson Kalmar and Derek J. Penslar, 182–200. Waltham, MA: Brandeis University Press, 2005.

——. *Israel in History; The Jewish State in Comparative Perspective.* London: Routledge, 2007.

Peretz, Eyal. *Literature, Disaster, and the Enigma of Power: A Reading of Moby Dick.* Stanford, CA: Stanford University Press, 2003.

Pinsker, Shachar M. *Literary Passports: The Making of Modernist Hebrew Fiction in Europe.* Stanford, CA: Stanford University Press, 2010.

Pinto, Moshe. *Ha-meshorer ha-le'umi: retsef sipurim* [The national poet: Stories]. Tel Aviv: 'Emda/Bitan 2002.

Piterberg, Gabriel. "Domestic Orientalism: The Representation of 'Oriental' Jews in Zionist/Israeli Historiography." *British Journal of Middle Eastern Studies* 23.2 (1996): 125–145.

Pratt, Mary Louise. *Imperial Eyes: Travel Writing and Transculturation.* London: Routledge, 1992.

Rafael, Vicente L. *Contracting Colonialism: Translation and Christian Conversion in Tagalog Society under Early Spanish Rule*. Ithaca, NY: Cornell University Press, 1988.

Raizen, Michal. "Cairo as Translation Zone." Paper presented at the National Association of Professors of Hebrew, Los Angeles, 2012.

Ram, Uri. *The Changing Agenda of Israeli Sociology: Theory, Ideology, and Identity*. Albany: State University of New York Press, 1995.

Ramras-Rauch, Gila. *The Arab in Israeli Literature*. Bloomington: Indiana University Press, 1989.

Ratosh, Yonatan. "Israeli or Jewish Literature?" In *What Is Jewish Literature?*, edited by Hana Wirth-Nesher, 88–94. Philadelphia: Jewish Publication Society, 1994.

Ravid, Barak. "Lieberman: Peace Talks Must Reassess Israeli-Arabs' Right to Citizenship." *Haaretz*, September 19, 2010. Accessed August 27, 2013. http://www.haaretz.com/news/diplomacy-defense/lieberman-peace-talks-must-reassess-israeli-arabs-right-to-citizenship-1.314596.

Rejwan, Nissim. *The Jews of Iraq: 3000 Years of History and Culture*. London: Weidenfield and Nicolson, 1985.

———. *Outsider in the Promised Land: An Iraqi Jew in Israel*. Austin: University of Texas Press, 2006.

Rifa'i, Jamal Ahmad. *Athar al-thaqafa al-'ibriyya fi al-shi'r al-filastini al-mu'asir: dirasa fi shi'r Mahmud Darwish* [Traces of Hebrew culture on contemporary Palestinian poetry: A study of Mahmoud Darwish's poetry]. Cairo: Dar al-thaqafa al-jadida, 1994.

Rivlin Y. Y. "Ha-mizraḥ bi-yetsirotav shel Biyalik" [The East in Bialik's works]. *Hed ha-mizraḥ* 3.8 (July 14, 1944): 7.

Robinson, Abraham. "Israeli Market Needs for Arabic Translations." *Meta: Translators' Journal* 43.1 (1998): 95–97.

Rolef, Susan Hattis. "Think about It: The Ethnic Demon." *Jerusalem Post*, August 12, 2013. Accessed August 29, 2013. http://www.jpost.com/Opinion/Columnists/Think-About-it-The-ethnic-demon-322838.

Rozental, Rozik. "Ha-zira ha-leshonit: ha-'aravit ha-me'orbevet shel ha-seret 'ajami" [The linguistic arena: The hybrid Arabic of *'Ajami*]. *Maariv*, November 5, 2009. Accessed August 28, 2013. http://www.nrg.co.il/online/47/ART1/962/843.html.

Rushdie, Salman. "The Courter." In *East, West*, 175–211. New York: Random House, 1994.

Safran, William. "Nationalism." In *Handbook of Language and Ethnic Identity*, edited by Joshua Fishman, 77–93. New York: Oxford University Press, 1999.

Saposnik, Arieh B. *Becoming Hebrew: The Creation of a Jewish National Culture in Ottoman Palestine*. New York: Oxford University Press, 2008.

Saulson, Scott B. *Institutionalized Language Planning: Documents and Analysis of the Revival of Hebrew*. The Hague: Mouton, 1979.

Savin, Ada. "Bilingualism and Dialogism: Another Reading of Lorna Dee Cervantes's Poetry." In *An Other Tongue: Nation and Ethnicity in the Linguistic Borderlands*, edited by Alfred Arteaga, 215–224. Durham, NC: Duke University Press, 1994.

Schachter, Allison. *Diasporic Modernisms: Hebrew and Yiddish Literature in the Twentieth Century*. New York: Oxford University Press, 2012.

Scheindlin, Raymond P. "Moses Ibn 'Ezra." In *The Literature of Al-Andalus*, edited by Maria Rosa Menocal, Raymond P. Scheindlin, and Michael Sells, 252–264. Cambridge: Cambridge University Press, 2000.

Schirmann, Jefim (Ḥayim). *Ha-shira ha-'ivrit bi-sefarad u-vi-provans* [Hebrew poetry in Spain and Provence]. 2 vols. Tel Aviv: Dvir, 1956.

——. *Toldot ha-shira ha-'ivrit bi-sefarad ha-muslemit* [The history of Hebrew literature in Muslim Spain]. Edited by Ezra Fleischer. Jerusalem: Magnes Press, 1995.

Schweimer, Yotam. "Alkhimiya shel ha-mila ha-ktuva" [The alchemy of the written word]. *Ynet*, January 3, 2011. Accessed August 29, 2013. http://www.ynet.co.il/articles/0,7340,L-4003640,00.html.

Segal, Miriam. *A New Sound in Hebrew Poetry: Poetics, Politics, Accent*. Bloomington: Indiana University Press, 2010.

Seidman, Naomi. *A Marriage Made in Heaven: The Sexual Politics of Hebrew and Yiddish.* Berkeley: University of California Press, 1997.

Sela, Maya. "Beirut Publisher Releases Translation of Amos Oz Autobiography." *Haaretz*, March 3, 2010. Accessed August 30, 2013. http://www.haaretz.com/print-edition/news/beirut-publisher-releases-arabic-translation-of-amos-oz-autobiography-1.264018.

Semaḥ, Dahud. *Amthal al-da'udiya—aqwal 'ilmiyya* [David's proverbs and learned sayings]. 4 vols. Baghdad: Matba'at Elisha' Shohet, 1926–1929.

——. *Kitab wurud al-da'udiya—malahi adabiyya* [David's blossoms and literary anecdotes]. 2 vols. Baghdad: Matba'at Elisha' Shohet, 1925–1927.

Seri, Dan-Benaya. *'Ugiyot ha-melaḥ shel savta Sultana* [Grandmother Sultana's salty biscuits]. Tel Aviv: M. Nuyman 'al yede Tserikhover motsi'im le-or, 1980.

Shammas, Anton. *'Arabeskot* [Arabesques]. Tel Aviv: 'Am 'oved, 1986.

——. *Asir yaqzati wa-nawmi: qasa'id* [Prisoner of my wakefulness and sleep: Poems]. Al-Quds: al-Sharq, 1974.

——. "At Half Mast—Myths, Symbols, and Rituals of an Emerging State: A Personal Testimony of an 'Israeli Arab.'" In *Postzionism: A Reader*, edited by Laurence J. Silberstein, 219–225. New Brunswick, NJ: Rutgers University Press, 2008.

——. "Diary." In *Every Sixth Israeli: Relations between the Jewish Majority and the Arab Minority in Israel*, edited by Alouph Hareven, 29–44. Jerusalem: Van Leer Institute, 1983.

——. *Krikha kasha* [Hardcover]. Tel Aviv: Sifriyat po'alim, 1974.

——. "Ha-mifgash she-haya, ha-mifgash she-lo yihye" [The encounter that was, the encounter that will not be]. *Moznayim* 59.3 (1985): 30–32.

——. "Mixed as in Pidgin: The Vanishing Arabic of a 'Bilingual' City." In *Mixed Communities, Trapped Towns: Historical Narratives, Spatial Dynamics, Gender Relations and Cultural Encounters in Palestinian-Israeli Towns*, edited by Daniel Monterescu and Dan Rabinowitz, 303–312. Burlington, VT: Ashgate, 2007.

——. *Shetaḥ hefker* [No-man's-land]. Tel Aviv: Ha-kibbutz ha-me'uḥad, 1979.

Shemoelof, Mati, Naphtaly Shemtov, and Nir Baram, eds. *Tehudot zehut: ha-dor ha-shlishi kotev mizraḥit* [Echoing identities: The third generation writes Mizraḥish]. Tel Aviv: 'Am 'oved, 2007.

Shenhav, Yehouda. *The Arab Jews*. Stanford, CA: Stanford University Press, 2006.

Shilo, Sara. *The Falafel King Is Dead*. London: Portobello Books, 2011.

——. *Shum gamadim lo yavo'u* [No elves are coming]. Tel Aviv: 'Am 'oved, 2005.

Shimony, Batya. *'Al saf ha-ge'ula, sipur ha-ma'abara: dor rishon ve-sheni* [On the threshold of redemption: The story of the ma'abara, first and second generations]. Or Yehuda: Zmora-Bitan/Dvir, 2008.

——. "Shaping Israeli-Arab Identity in Hebrew Words—The Case of Sayed Kashua." *Israel Studies* 18.1 (Spring 2013): 146–169.

Shira mefareket ḥoma: gerila tarbut be-abu dis/Shi'r yuhattimu al-jidar: gharila thaqafa fi abu dis [Poetry dismantling walls: Cultural Guerrilla in Abu Dis]. Israel: Kafe Masada, 2010.

Shnitzer, Meir. "Be-shkhuna shelanu: bikoret 'al 'ajami" [In our neighborhood: Criticism of '*Ajami*]. *Maariv*, September 21, 2009. Accessed August 28, 2013. http://www.nrg.co.il/online/47/ART1/944/555.html.

Shoham, Reuven. *Poetry and Prophecy: The Image of the Poet as a "Prophet," a Hero and an Artist in Modern Hebrew Poetry*. Leiden: Brill, 2003.

Shohamy, Elana. *Language Policy: Hidden Agendas and New Approaches*. London: Routledge, 2006.

Shohat, Ella. "The Invention of the Mizrahim." *Journal of Palestine Studies* 29.1 (Autumn 1999): 5–20.

——. *Israeli Cinema: East/West and the Politics of Representation*. Austin: University of Texas Press, 1989.

——. "Sephardim in Israel: Zionism from the Standpoint of its Jewish Victims." *Social Text* 19–20 (Autumn 1988): 1–35.

Shoshan, Esti Adivi. "Yesh mishehu le-daber ito" [There is someone to speak with]. *Haaretz*, July 23, 2010. Accessed August 29, 2013. www.haaretz.co.il/misc/2.444/1.1213386.

Siddiq, Muhammad. "al-Kitaba bi-l-'ibriyya al-fusha: taqaddum riwayat 'arabask wa-hiwar ma' Antun Shammas" [Writing in Hebrew *fusha:* A presentation of *Arabesques* and a conversation with Anton Shammas]. *Alif* 20 (2000): 155–167.

Sikseck, Ayman. *El yafo* [To Jaffa]. Tel Aviv: Yedi'ot aḥaronot, 2010.

Silberschlag, Eisig. *Saul Tchernichowsky, Poet of Revolt*. Ithaca, NY: Cornell University Press, 1968.

Simon, Sherry, and Paul St. Pierre, eds. *Changing the Terms: Translating in the Postcolonial Era*. Ottawa: University of Ottawa Press, 2000.

Snir, Reuven. "Arab-Jewish Culture." In *Encyclopedia of Modern Jewish Culture*, vol. 1, edited by Glenda Abramson, 29–37. London: Routledge, 2005.

——. "'Hebrew as the Language of Grace': Arab-Palestinian Writers in Hebrew." *Prooftexts* 15.2 (1995): 63–183.

——. "Ma'agalim niḥtakhim beyn ha-sifrut ha-'ivrit le-veyn ha-sifrut ha-'arvit" [Intersecting circles between Hebrew and Arabic literature]. In *Beyn 'ever la-'arav: ha-maga'im beyn ha-sifrut ha-'arvit le-veyn ha-sifrut ha-yehudit bi-mey ha-benayim u-va-zman he-ḥadash* [Between *'ever* and *'arav*: contacts between Arabic literature and Jewish literature in medieval and modern times], edited by Yosef Tobi, 177–210. Tel Aviv: 'Afikim, 1998.

——. "Tmura tarbutit bi-re'i ha-sifrut: rashit ha-sipur ha-'aravi ha-katsar me-'et yehudim be-'irak" [Cultural change as seen through literature: The origins of the Arabic short story by Jewish writers in Iraq]. *Pe'amim* 36 (1988): 108–129.

——. "'We Were Like Those Who Dream': Iraqi-Jewish Writers in Israel in the 1950s." *Prooftexts* 11.2 (1991): 153–173.

Someck, Ronny. *Gan 'eden le-orez* [Rice paradise]. Tel Aviv: Zmora-Bitan, 1996.

——. *Roni Somek: Khawaja Biyalik—10 rishumim ve-shir be-'ikvot 9 shirim shel Biyalik* [Ronny Someck: Khawaja Bialik—ten sketches and a poem following nine poems of Bialik]. Edited by Nitza Ḥozez. Exhibition catalog for "Khawaja Bialik," curated by Meir Ahronson. Ramat Gan: Museum of Israel Art, 2004.

Somekh, Sasson. "Anton Shamas: ha-targum ke-etgar—'al targum yetsirot Imil Habibi le-'ivrit." [Anton Shammas: Translation as a challenge—on the translation of Emile Habiby's works into Hebrew]. In *Targum be-tsidey ha-derekh: 'iyunim be-targumim min ha-sifrut ha-'arvit le-'ivrit be-yameynu* [Translation as a challenge: Papers on translation of Arabic literature into Hebrew], edited by Sasson Somekh, 41–51. Tel Aviv: Universitat Tel Aviv, 1993.

——. *Baghdad, Yesterday: The Making of an Arab Jew*. Jerusalem: Ibis Editions, 2007.

——. "Lost Voices: Jewish Authors in Modern Arabic Literature." In *Jews among Arabs: Contacts and Boundaries*, edited by Mark Cohen and Abraham Udovitch, 9–19. Princeton, NJ: Darwin Press, 1989.

——. "Lost Voices: Jewish Authors in Modern Arabic Literature." In *What Is Jewish Literature?*, edited by Hana Wirth-Nesher, 188–198. Philadelphia: Jewish Publication Society, 1994.

——. "Ha-opsimist ve-ha-pesimist" [The pessoptimist and the pessimist]. *Erets aḥeret* 13 (May–June 2003): 64–67.

——. "Reconciling Two Great Loves: The First Arab-Jewish Literary Encounter in Israel." *Israel Studies* 4.1 (1999): 1–21.

——, ed. *Targum be-tsidey ha-derekh: 'iyunim be-targumim min ha-sifrut ha-'arvit le-'ivrit be-yameynu* [Translation as a challenge: Papers on translation of Arabic literature into Hebrew]. Tel Aviv: Universitat Tel Aviv, 1993.

Sommer, Dorris. *Bilingual Aesthetics: A New Sentimental Education*. Durham, NC: Duke University Press, 2004.

——, ed. *Bilingual Games: Some Literary Investigations*. New York: Palgrave Macmillan, 2003.

——. "A Rhetoric of Particularism." In *Proceed with Caution, When Engaged by Minority Writing in the Americas*, 1–31. Cambridge, MA: Harvard University Press, 1999.

Spolsky, Bernard. "Hebrew and Israeli Identity." In *Language and Identity in the Middle East and North Africa*, edited by Yasir Suleiman, 181–192. Richmond, UK: Curzon Press, 1996.

———. "The Situation of Arabic in Israel." In *Arabic Sociolinguistics: Issues and Perspectives*, edited by Yasir Suleiman, 227–234. Richmond, UK: Curzon Press, 1994.

Spolsky, Bernard, Muhammad Amara, Hanna Tushyeh, and Kees de Bot. "Language, Education, and Identity in a Palestinian Town: The Case of Bethlehem." Unpublished manuscript, n.d.

Spolsky, Bernard, and Elana Goldberg Shohamy. "Language in Israeli Society and Education." *International Journal of the Sociology of Language* 137 (1999): 93–114.

———. *The Languages of Israel: Policy, Ideology, and Practice*. Clevedon, UK: Multilingual Matters, 1999.

Starr, Deborah. *Remembering Cosmopolitan Egypt: Literature, Culture, and Empire*. New York: Routledge, 2009.

———. "Reterritorializing the Dream: Orly Castel-Bloom's Remapping of Israeli Identity." In *Mapping Jewish Identities*, edited by Laurence J. Silberstein, 220–249. New York: New York University Press, 2000.

Starr, Deborah A., and Sasson Somekh, eds. *Mongrels or Marvels: The Levantine Writings of Jacqueline Shohet Kahanoff*. Stanford, CA: Stanford University Press, 2011.

Stavans, Ilan, ed. *Border Culture*. Santa Barbara, CA: Greenwood, 2010.

———. *Resurrecting Hebrew*. New York: Nextbook/Schocken, 2008.

Stern, Ramon. "Aqud: A Reading with Author Albert Swissa." Text for event at the University of Michigan, Ann Arbor, March 29, 2012. Accessed August 30, 2013. http://www.lsa.umich.edu/vgn-ext-templating/v/index.jsp?vgnextoid=881cf16e8a3e5310VgnVCM100000c2b1d38dRCRD&vgnextchannel=73984bb4e7adf210VgnVCM10000055b1d38dRCRD&vgnextfmt=detail.

Sucary, Yossi. *Emilya u-melaḥ ha-arets: vidui* [Emilia and the salt of the earth: A confession]. Tel Aviv: Bavel, 2002.

Suchoff, David. "Kafka's Canon: Hebrew and Yiddish in the Trial and Amerika." In *Bilingual Games: Some Literary Investigations*, edited by Doris Sommer, 251–274. New York: Palgrave Macmillan, 2003.

Suleiman, Yasir. *A War of Words: Language and Conflict in the Middle East*. Cambridge: Cambridge University Press, 2004

Swissa, Albert. *'Akud* [Bound]. Tel Aviv: Ha-kibuts ha-me'uḥad, 1990.

Tamari, Salim. "Ishaq Shami and the Predicament of the Arab Jew in Palestine." In *Mountain against the Sea: Essays on Palestinian Society and Culture*, 150–166. Berkeley: University of California Press, 2009.

———. *Mountain against the Sea: Essays on Palestinian Society and Culture*. Berkeley: University of California Press, 2009.

Tanakh: The Holy Scriptures. Philadelphia: Jewish Publication Society, 1985.

Tchernichowsky, Saul. *Kol kitvey Sha'ul Tsherniḥovski, kerekh alef (shirim u-valadot)* [Collected writings of Tchernichowsky, vol. 1 (poems and ballads)]. Tel Aviv: 'Am 'oved, 1990.

——. *Tsherniḥovski, Sha'ul: meḥkarim u-te'udot* [Saul Tchernichowsky: Studies and documents]. Edited by Boaz Arpaly. Jerusalem: Mosad Biyalik, 1994.

Thiong'o, Ngũgĩ wa. "The Language of African Literature." In *Postcolonialisms: An Anthology of Cultural Theory and Criticism*, edited by Gaurav Desai and Supriya Nair, 143–168. New Brunswick, NJ: Rutgers University Press, 2005.

"Toldot ha-sifrut ha-'ivrit: tkufat yamey ha-benayim, reshimot 'al-pi shi'urav shel Ḥ. N. Biyalik" [History of Hebrew literature: Medieval period, notes on Ḥ. N. Bialik's lectures]. Odessa, 1918.

Traum, Riki. "From the Wildness We Feared, from the Paleness We Are Dreaded—An Examination of Space, Place, and Memory in Ronit Matalon's *The Sound of Our Steps* [2008]." Paper presented at the Association for Jewish Studies, Los Angeles, 2009.

Tripp, Charles. *A History of Iraq*. Cambridge: Cambridge University Press, 2000.

Tsal, Na'ama. "He Is Missing. You Were Missing. Home Is Missing: Formation, Collapse, and the Idea of Home in the Later Poetics of Ronit Matalon." *Prooftexts* 30.3 (2010): 303–320.

Twersky, David. "An Interview with Amos Oz." *Tikkun* 1.2 (1986): 23–27.

Ungerfeld, Moshe, ed. *Biyalik ve-sofrey doro: dvarim beyn Biyalik le-sofrey doro le-tsiyun yovel ha-me'a le-holadato ve-arba'im shana le-ftirato* [Bialik and his contemporaries: Letters between Bialik and his contemporaries to mark the centennial of his birth and forty years since his death]. Tel Aviv: 'Am ha-sefer, 1974.

——, ed. *Shir ha-sharim le-Ḥ. N. Biyalik: mivḥar shirim be-khama safot 'al Ḥ. N. Biyalik vi-yetsirato she-nilketu mi-tokh sfarim u-khitvey 'et, bi-melot 'esrim ve-ḥamesh shana li-ftirato* [Poems written for Ḥ. N. Bialik: A multilingual collection of poems about Ḥ. N. Bialik and his works compiled from books and journals to mark twenty-five years since his passing]. Tel Aviv: Hotsa'at ma'aritsey Biyalik, 1959.

Venuti, Lawrence. *The Scandals of Translation: Towards an Ethics of Difference*. London: Routledge, 1998.

Waugh, Patricia. *Metafiction: The Theory and Practice of Self-Conscious Fiction.* London: Routledge, 1984.

Wehr, Hans. *A Dictionary of Modern Arabic*. 3rd ed. Edited by J Milton Cowan. Ithaca, NY: Spoken Language Services, 1976.

Weissbrod, Rachel. "Implications of Israeli Mutilingualism and Multiculturalism for Translation Research." In *Beyond Descriptive Translation Studies: Investigations in Homage to Gideon Toury*, edited by Anthony Pym, Miriam Shlesinger, and Daniel Simeoni, 51–66. Amsterdam: John Benjamins, 2008.

Weymouth, Lally. "An Interview with Avigdor Lieberman." *Washington Post*, March 1, 2009.

Wolf, Michaela. "The *Third Space* in Postcolonial Representation." In *Changing the Terms: Translating in the Postcolonial Era*, edited by Sherry Simon and Paul St. Pierre, 127–145. Ottawa: University of Ottawa Press, 2000.

Yacoby, Haim, and Erez Tzfadia. "Multiculturalism, Nationalism, and the Politics of the Israeli City." *International Journal of Middle Eastern Studies* 41 (2009): 289–307.

Ya'oz, Hannah, Ya'akov Beser, and Itamar Ya'oz-Kest, eds. *Shira tse'ira: antologya murḥevet* [Young poetry: An expanded anthology]. Tel Aviv: 'Eked, 1980.

Yehoshua, A. B. *A Journey to the End of the Millennium*. Translated by Nicholas de Lange. New York: Doubleday, 1999.

———. *Ha-kala ha-meshaḥreret* [The liberating bride]. Tel Aviv: Ha-kibuts ha-me'uḥad, 2001.

———. *Ha-kir ve-ha-har* [The wall and the mountain]. Tel Aviv: Zmora-Bitan, 1989.

———. *The Liberated Bride*. Translated by Hillel Halkin. San Diego: Harcourt, 2003.

———. *The Lover*. Translated by Philip Simpson. New York: Doubleday, 1978.

———. *Ha-me'ahev*. [The lover]. Jerusalem: Schocken, 1977.

———. "Mul ha-ye'arot" [Facing the forests]. In *Kol ha-sipurim* [Collected stories], 99–127. Tel Aviv: Ha-kibuts ha-me'uḥad, 1993.

Yildiz, Yasemin. *Beyond the Mother Tongue: The Postmonolingual Condition*. New York: Fordham University Press, 2012.

Zabus, Chantal. *The African Palimpsest: Indigenization of Language in the West African Europhone Novel*. Amsterdam: Rodopi, 2007.

Zerubavel, Yael. "Memory, the Rebirth of the Native, and the 'Hebrew Bedouin' Identity." *Social Research* 75.1 (Spring 2008): 315–351.

Zohar, Zvi. "A 'Maskil' in Aleppo: 'The Torah of Israel and the People of Israel' by Rabbi Yitzhak Dayyan (Aleppo, 5683/1923)." In *New Horizons in Sephardic Studies*, edited by Yedida K. Stillman and George K. Zucker, translated by Sandra Becker, 93–107. Albany: State University of New York Press, 1993.

Zonshteyn, David. "Biyalik ve-Darwish mazhirim: ha-shir hu tehom" [Bialik and Darwish warn: Poetry is an abyss]. *Haaretz*, October 18, 2007. Accessed August 28, 2013. www.haaretz.co.il/literature/1.1450959.

Index

Page numbers in italics refer to figures

CPSIA information can be obtained
at www.ICGtesting.com
Printed in the USA
BVOW08s0500131017
497568BV00002B/33/P

9 780691 176093